English G 2000

A3

für Gymnasien

Cornelsen

English G 2000
Band A3

Im Auftrag des Verlages herausgegeben von
Prof. Hellmut Schwarz, Mannheim

Erarbeitet von
Barbara Derkow Disselbeck,
Laurence Harger, Michael Macfarlane,
Allen J. Woppert

unter Mitarbeit von
Wolfgang Biederstädt, Köln; Joachim Blombach, Herford; Helga Estor, Darmstadt; Dr. Jens-Peter Green, Oldenburg; Martina Kretschko, Dresden; Mervyn Whittaker, Bad Dürkheim; Herbert Willms, Herford *sowie* Erich Fleischhack, Ebern

in Zusammenarbeit mit der Englischredaktion
Cedric J. Sherratt (Projektleitung), Hartmut Tschepe (verantwortlicher Redakteur), Kirsten Bleck, Susanne Döpper, Gareth Evans, Uwe Tröger, Dr. Gunther Weimann; John Stevens (Redaktionsdienst Context, Bad Münstereifel) *sowie* Jenny Dames, Claudia Rothe (Assistenz)

Beratende Mitwirkung
Prof. Dr. Peter Bruck, Werne; Angelika Hauß, Weinheim; Prof. Dr. Liesel Hermes, Karlsruhe; Wolfgang Neudecker, Mannheim; Albert Rau, Brühl; Wolfram Schnaidt, Schwäbisch Hall; Dr. Jana Schubert, Leipzig; Markus Vetter, Mühlacker; Harald Weißling, Mannheim; Manfred Wildhage, Braunschweig *sowie* John Eastwood, Street

Illustration
David Barnett, Oadby, Leicester *sowie* Linda Rogers Associates, London: Roger Fereday, Martin Orme; Gabriele Heinisch, Berlin; Skip G. Langkafel, Berlin; Constanze Schargan, Berlin; Katharina Wieker, Berlin

Gestaltung und technische Umsetzung
Gisela Hoffmann, Susanne Meyer

Zusatzmaterialien zum vorliegenden Schülerbuch

Workbook
ISBN 978-3-464-35061-4
2 Kassetten zum Schülerbuch (Lehrerfassung)
ISBN 978-3-464-35131-4
2 CDs zum Schülerbuch (Lehrerfassung)
ISBN 978-3-464-35111-6
Auf weitere Bestandteile wird im Handbuch für den Unterricht verwiesen.
ISBN 978-3-464-35072-0

www.cornelsen.de

1. Auflage €
11. Druck 2007 / 06

Alle Drucke dieser Auflage sind inhaltlich unverändert und können im Unterricht nebeneinander verwendet werden.

Druck: CS-Druck CornelsenStürtz, Berlin

ISBN 978-3-464-35045-4 – broschiert

ISBN 978-3-464-35046-1 – gebunden

Inhalt gedruckt auf säurefreiem Papier aus nachhaltiger Forstwirtschaft.

Contents

∘ fakultativ * in einigen Bundesländern „*Revision*“

◦ fakultativ * in einigen Bundesländern „*Revision*“ [ ] nicht in allen Bundesländern obligatorisch

Dein Englischbuch enthält folgende Teile:

UNITS	die sieben Kapitel („Einheiten") des Buches
REVISION	zwei Seiten Wiederholungsübungen (zum Selbermachen)
TRANSLATION	Übungen und Tipps zum Übersetzen (Englisch-Deutsch)
INTERPRETING	Dolmetschübungen
UK MAG	eine englische Jugendzeitschrift mit Geschichten, Berichten, Liedern usw.
LANGUAGE SUMMARY (S)	eine Zusammenfassung der Grammatik jeder Unit
VOCABULARY (V)	das Wörterverzeichnis zum Lernen der neuen Wörter
DICTIONARY (D)	das alphabetische Wörterverzeichnis zum Nachschlagen
LISTS	Listen: *Names, Countries and Continents, Grammatical Terms, Irregular Verbs, Classroom Phrases*

Die Units bestehen aus diesen Teilen:

'LEAD-IN'	die erste (Doppel-)Seite einer Unit; Einstieg in das neue Thema
▶ A: A-SECTION	der neue Lernstoff mit ersten Übungen
▶ P: PRACTICE	Übungen, Sprachspiele und Aktivitäten
▶ T: TEXT	z. B. eine Kurzgeschichte, ein Zeitungsartikel, ein Interview
▶ H: HOW TO ...	Übungen und Tipps zum Training der Fertigkeiten *reading, writing, listening* und *speaking*

In den Units findest du diese Überschriften und Symbole:

▶▶▶ NOW YOU	Hier kannst du über dich selbst sprechen oder schreiben.
ACTIVITY	Aufgaben, bei denen du etwas tust – z.B. eine Collage gestalten
GAME	Spiele für zwei, für eine Gruppe oder für die ganze Klasse – natürlich auf Englisch
ROLE-PLAY	Vorschlag für das Spielen einer Szene mit verteilten Rollen
PROJECT	Hier kannst du allein, zu zweit oder in der Gruppe Informationen sammeln und dann anderen vorstellen.
FOCUS ON GRAMMAR	Hier lernst du neue Grammatikstrukturen kennen.
FOCUS ON WORDS	Hier sammelst, ordnest und verwendest du neue Wörter und Ausdrücke.
WORD WATCH	Unter dieser Überschrift geht es immer um Übungen zum Wortschatz.
LISTENING	Hier gibt es Hörtexte auf Kassette/CD und dazu Aufgaben im Buch.
REVISION	Hier wird wiederholt – damit du nichts vergisst.
WORKING WITH THE TEXT	Unter dieser Überschrift stehen Aufgaben zum vorangehenden Text.
◆◆	Partnerarbeit
❖	Gruppenarbeit

OUR HEROES

We're looking for everyday heroes. Has someone from your town, your street, your school or your family done something special – something brave, kind or thoughtful? Do you have an everyday hero? Write to us and tell us about him or her. Perhaps we'll invite you and your hero to the BBC's 'Our Heroes Special'. Send your story now. All letters must be with us by 31st May.

Or come and see us – there's a BBC office near you.

BBC SPECIAL BBC SPECIAL BBC SPECIA

ACTIVITY

Start an English album. Bring a photo of one of your heroes to school and stick it in your album. Under the photo write about your hero. Explain what makes him or her special.

How many times can you find the OUR HEROES poster – or part of it – in this book?

This album belongs to *Petra Schulz.*
My address is *Schmiedtorstraße 15,*
72070 Tübingen.
My phone number is *(07071) 36 513.*
I go to *Ludwig-Uhland-Gymnasium.*
I am in Form *7B.*
My favourite subjects are *English and Music.*
My hero is/My heroes are
because

Bangor
WALES
Camden Town bus timetable
Camden Town Kentish Town Hampstead
London Transport Buses
Jack Straw's Castle
CD 7111
Child
Child Rate

Find out as much as you can about Megan Owen from these two pages. Make notes like this:

old country: Wales	–	*new country: ...*
old town: Bangor	–	*new town: ...*
school: ...	–	*school journey: ...*
family: ...		
hobbies: ...		

Compare your notes with your partner's notes.
Megan's old country was Wales. I think her new country is ...
Now tell your class about Megan.

▶▶▶ **NOW YOU** and a partner

a *Is there a new pupil in your class? Talk to him/her and take notes about his/her home, old school, family and hobbies. Then tell the class about him/her – in English.*

b *Or imagine a famous person is a pupil in your class. Who could it be? Make notes and tell the class about him/her.*

1 A

▶ 1

Until she was thirteen, Megan Owen lived in a village near Bangor, a town in North Wales. Two years ago – when she was eleven years old – her mother died. Even months later Megan still felt very miserable. After a year and a half her father found a new job in London. In July he sold the house in Wales and moved with Megan to a small flat in the big city.

▶ 2

On the morning of her first day at her new school, Megan was writing a letter when her dad came into the kitchen.
'Dad, I'm really scared about the new school,' she said.
'Poor Meg! Oh, have I given you your lunch money yet?' her dad asked.
'Yes, you have,' Megan laughed. 'You gave it to me half an hour ago. You've never been so nervous before, Dad.'
'Oh, well. Look, I have to go now,' he said. 'Good luck, Megan! And this evening … er, for dinner … I …'
'Yes, Dad? Shall I cook?'
'No, no. Let's go out for a pizza. OK?'
'Great, Dad! Thanks.'

→ P 1, 2, 3

▶ 3

'New places, new faces! It's better this way,' my dad said. But I'm not so sure. I still hate the traffic noise here in London. I miss the country and I feel so lonely. I haven't spoken to another teenager since July! (That's when I left Wales, remember?) It's the first day of term today and I don't know anyone at Tufnell Park. I miss you and all my other friends in Wales. I haven't heard anything from you since 1st August. Please write soon! I must stop and get dressed for school now or I'll be late.

? *Why do you think Megan wrote a letter before school? How did she feel? Why?*

TPS **Tufnell Park School, Burghley Road, London NW5 1UJ**
Headteacher: Philip O'Hear, Telephone: 0171/4858515 Fax: 0171/2843462

Dear parent,

MIDDAY MEALS

Please complete the bottom part of this form about your child's lunch. Sign one line and cross out the others.

✂ -

Pupil's name MEGAN OWEN Form 9

1. My child will have school lunch. D. Owen
2. ~~My child will bring sandwiches to school.~~
3. ~~My child will have lunch at home.~~

(Lunch begins at 1.05 pm. All pupils should return to school at 2.00 pm. School starts at 2.05 pm.)

Address 93 ANSON ROAD
LONDON NW5 2QU

▶ 4

SECRETARY Oh, sorry, I didn't see you.

MEGAN It's OK. I've only been here for a few seconds. I'm Megan Owen.

SECRETARY Ah, yes, Megan. Welcome to Tufnell Park. You haven't lived in London for very long, am I right?

MEGAN Yes, we've only been here for six weeks.

SECRETARY I'm sure it's all still very strange for you then. Now, I've got your midday meal form. So that's everything. Listen, dear, I usually take new pupils to their classroom, but I'm alone today. So you'll have to find it on your own. Is that all right? It's room 105. Good luck. And don't be scared, dear. We're really very friendly here at TPS.

▶ **5**

MEGAN Excuse me, please, where's room 105?

TEACHER You don't know where room 105 is? Are you new?

MEGAN Yes, I've only been here since this morning.

TEACHER Oh well, go down this corridor – and then up the stairs.

MEGAN Yes.

TEACHER Turn right, go to the end of the corridor and room 105 is on the left, opposite the library.

MEGAN Thank you.

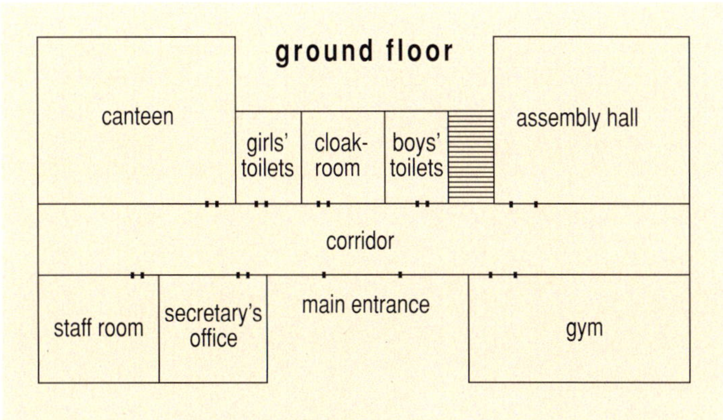

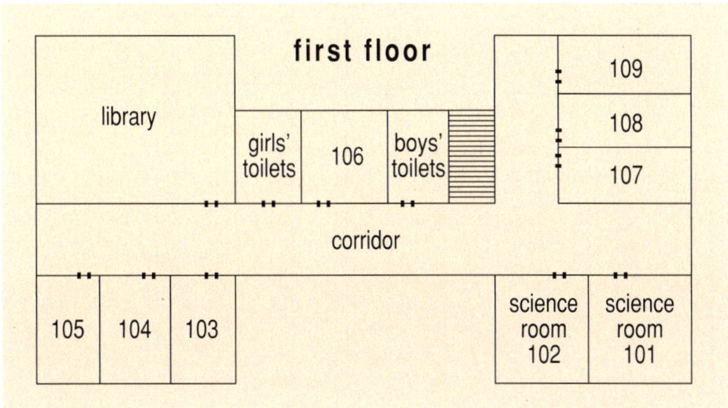

GAME Guess the room

One of you explains the way from your classroom to another room in your school. But don't say the name of the room. The others have to guess. Example:

Go out of the classroom, turn right/left. Go straight down the corridor and then up/down the stairs. The room is next to/ opposite/...

The others must guess the room.

I think the room is the gym/the ...

▶ **6**

There were lots of kids in room 105 and Megan felt very nervous. One girl came to talk to her.
'Hi!' she said. 'Are you new?'
'Yes, I'm Megan Owen. Hello.'
'I'm Hannah Grant. Where are you from, Megan?'
'Wales,' answered Megan. 'How long have you lived in London?'
'Only for a few weeks,' Megan said.
'Is that right?'
'Yes, we've only been in London since last month.'

FOCUS ON GRAMMAR

1 *Look at A3 – A6 and find all the sentences with* since *and* for. *Make a table like this:*

Sentences with 'since'	*Sentences with 'for'*
...	...

2 *What German words do you use for* since *and* for?

3 *When do you use* since, *when do you use* for?

4 *Look at the sentences with* since *and* for *again. What tenses are they in? What tenses can you use in German?*

▶▶▶ **NOW YOU** and a partner

a *Ask your partner*
– who his/her best friend is and how long he/she has known him/her,
– who his/her favourite singer is and how long he/she has been his/her fan.

A Who's your best friend?
B Florian.
A How long have you known him?
B For two years.
A And who's your ...?

b *Tell the class about your partner.* → S 1: 2 (p. 122)
→ P 4, 5, 6

▶ 7

'We live in a flat quite near the school, in Anson Road,' Megan told Hannah. 'It's very different from our house in Wales.'
'I've been to Wales,' said Hannah. 'I was there one day last year. It was when I stayed with my cousins Nick and Debbie in Chester. Have you ever been to Chester?'
'No, I've never been there.'

Suddenly the room was quiet. Megan looked up and saw a teacher.
'That's Herby,' whispered Hannah, 'Miss Herbert – our form teacher. She has brought the timetables.'

▶ 8

TIMETABLE – YEAR 9

	Monday	Tuesday	Wednesday	Thursday	Friday
9.10	Maths	French	RE	Geography	Spanish
9.55	Science	Design & Technology	History	Maths	Science
10.35	Science		English	PE	Science
Break 11.20 – 11.40					
11.40	Art	Geography	Maths	English	RE
12.20	Art	English	French	Spanish	English
Lunch 13.05 – 14.05 and Assembly 14.05 – 14.15					
14.15	History	PE	Science	Design & Technology	Maths
14.55	English	Drama	Dance		Music

HANNAH Yuck! Maths first lesson on Monday. I hate Maths!
MEGAN Oh, I like Maths – I'm good at it. But my favourite subject is Music. What's yours?
HANNAH Mine is English.

FOCUS ON WORDS

Collect 'school' words and phrases (e.g. at school, good at Science, …) and make a network. Then talk about your subjects. Say why you like or don't like them.

I enjoy English because the stories are interesting.
I'm good at Science because my teacher is so good.
We have two Geography lessons every week but we haven't studied any interesting countries yet.
I hate German because I often get bad marks.

▶▶▶ **NOW YOU** and a partner

Write your own timetable in English. Compare your timetable with Megan's. What is different? What is the same? What do you think is better or worse?

A In Germany we usually start school at … . But in England they … . I think that's better because …
B We've got four periods of English. Have they …, too?
A Yes,/No, … . They …
B Our lessons are … minutes long.
A …

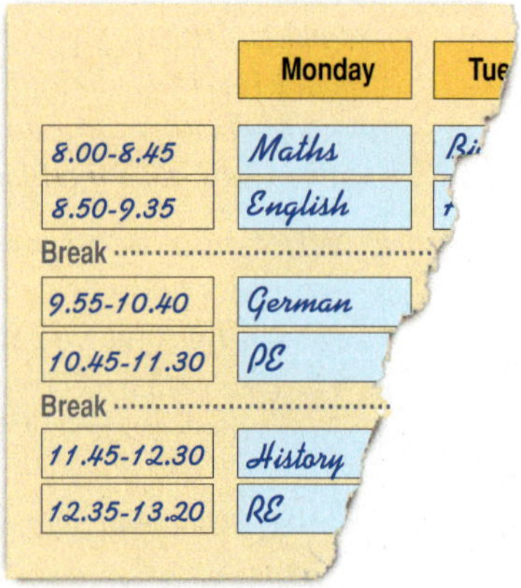

▶ 9

After lunch Megan waited for Hannah. At last she arrived and said, 'Sorry, Megan. I've been looking for my friends. And they've been sitting here all the time. Come and meet them.'
She pointed at a canteen table. There were four pupils there. 'How long have you been sitting here?' she asked them. 'I've been trying to find you everywhere.' Then she introduced Megan to Tony, Marie, Ali and Winston.
They talked about school clubs. Marie and Winston were music fans and told Megan all about the choir, the jazz club and the school bands. For the first time, Megan began to feel happy in London.

▶ 10

After school that day Megan came home and waited for her father. At 5.30 the phone rang.

MR OWEN Sorry I'm late, Meg. It's the buses.
MEGAN Have you been waiting long, Dad?
MR OWEN Yes, for half an hour. Are you very hungry?
MEGAN No, it's OK, Dad. I didn't get home till 4.30. And I've been writing my diary since then.
MR OWEN Oh, I can see the bus now, Meg. So I'll be home soon.
MEGAN OK, Dad, bye!

▶ 11

clubs. I began to feel happy here for the first time. Then Hannah left the table. Tony looked at me and said, 'There's a rule here, you know. All new kids have to write their names on the cloakroom wall.' Winston gave me his felt-tips.
So I went to the cloakroom and started to write my name. Suddenly a teacher came in and shouted at me angrily. 'That's vandalism,' she said and asked for my name. I was terribly frightened. I couldn't answer. Then Hannah arrived. 'It isn't her fault, Miss Picken,' she said quickly. 'She's new and some kids have played a trick on her.' Then the teacher smiled. She said, 'New Kids' Trick Number 25' and told me that I should clean the wall. Hannah is great: she saved me from Miss Picken and she helped me to clean the wall. She's my hero! She has invited me to the market at Camden Lock on Saturday. I'm really excited!

*

It has been a great day. Dad and I found a really good pizza place and I told him all about my first day at TPS. I've been thinking about Camden Lock since we got home. It's quite famous but I don't know anything about it. What will it be like? Well, I'll know soon!

? *Why do you think Hannah helped Megan?*
What tricks do people play at your school?

→ P 7

FOCUS ON GRAMMAR

1 *Look for examples of* I've/you've/… been *in A9–A11. What kind of words come after* been?
I've been looking … / How long have you been sitting … ?

2 *This is a new tense. How do you form it? Can you imagine what it is called?*

3 *What can you say about actions in this tense? When did they begin? Are they still going on?*

→ S 1: 3, 4 (p. 123)
→ P 8, 9

FOCUS ON WORDS

Lots of words and phrases in this unit tell you how people feel. Collect them and arrange them in two groups (good feelings and bad feelings). Can you remember any others? Add them, too.

+	–
feel happy	*feel very miserable*
be really excited	*be scared*
…	…

▶▶▶ NOW YOU

Look at the poem on the right. Then use one of these adjectives – happy, fine, angry, miserable, sad *– and try to write a poem about your feelings.*
You can put your poem in your album.

Long, long afternoons
Only me and my music.
No friends!
Evening comes. I'm
Looking for
You.

Hours of good feelings
A good …
P …
P
Y

→ P 10, 11, 12
→ UK Mag, pp. 98–100

1 REVISION Where did they go and what did they do? → S 1: 1d (p. 121)

1
Liz
Italy / last summer – stay / hotel

2
Eddie
Scotland / a week ago – visit / Highlands

3
Tom
Germany / when he was in Year 10 – go / Dresden

4
Diana
the USA / three years ago – fly / Chicago

5
Sue
New York / last May – see / Statue of Liberty

6
Andy
Cardiff / for a week last year – learn some Welsh

1 *Liz went to Italy last summer. She stayed at a hotel.* 2 *Eddie went ...*

2 REVISION A letter to an old friend → S 1: 1c (p. 121)

Write Megan's letter again. Put the verbs in brackets in the present perfect.

> Dear Ruth,
> Thanks for your letter. I (be) so happy all day because you (not forget) me! And you see, I (not forget) my old friends yet either! We only moved to London five weeks ago but a lot (change). Dad (buy) so many new things for the flat. But he (not open) a lot of our boxes from Wales yet! I think he wants to start a new life. And my life will change soon, too. I (not start) at my new school yet and I'm very nervous about it. But the school (send) us a lot of information. Dad (just come) home with more boxes. So I must stop now and help him.
> Love, Megan

3 REVISION They are playing ... → S 1: 1b, c, d (p. 121)

a *What are they doing? Choose phrases from the box and make sentences.*

cook a meal • eat Indian food play beach volleyball • sing in a choir watch a play

1 *They are playing ...* 2 ...

1

2

◆◆ **b** *Has your partner ever done these things? Did he/she like them? Ask questions.*

A Have you ever played beach volleyball?
B Yes, I have.
A When did you play it last?
B When I was in Spain. / In the summer.

3

4

5

c *Think of more questions.*

4 ▶ More about TPS

In these sentences about Tufnell Park School, a computer virus has put ΔΔΔΔΔ where the words since *and* for *should go. Write the sentences again with the right words.*

1 TPS has had a drama teacher ΔΔΔΔΔ 15 years.

2 Mr O'Hear has been headteacher ΔΔΔΔΔ 1993.

3 Mrs Johnson has been a PE teacher ΔΔΔΔΔ last year.

4 Mr Addison has known Miss Berwick ΔΔΔΔΔ half a year.

5 PUPILS HAVE BEEN ABLE TO USE THE SCHOOL'S COMPUTERS ΔΔΔΔΔ A LONG TIME.

6 The school has had a chess computer ΔΔΔΔΔ six months.

7 THERE HAS BEEN A COFFEE MACHINE IN THE STAFF ROOM ΔΔΔΔΔ LAST CHRISTMAS.

8 Megan Owen has only been a TPS pupil ΔΔΔΔΔ this morning.

9 Rooms 101 and 102 have been science rooms ΔΔΔΔΔ January.

1 *TPS has had a drama teacher for 15 years.*
2 *Mr O'Hear ...*

❖ 5 ▶ Who is it?

a *Everyone in the group uses some of the verbs below and completes the sentences on a piece of paper.*

be • have • know • like • live • see

1 I've ... for ... years.
2 I haven't ... since ...
3 I've ... for ...
4 My favourite star has ... since ...

b *Now work with another group. Someone reads the sentences on one piece of paper (not their own) to the other group. Can that group guess who wrote them?*

◆◆ 6 ▶ They aren't Londoners

a *Partner B: Look at page 116.*
Partner A: Look at the chart. Some of Megan's classmates are from other places, too. Some information about Mark, Sandra, Thomas and Moira is missing. Ask your partner 'How long ...?' and answer his/her questions.

A How long has Mark lived in London?
B For ... .
How long has ...?
A ...

	Mark	Sandra	Thomas	Moira
live in London	?	last summer	3 years	?
be at TPS	this morning	?	?	March
know his/her best friend	6 months	?	2 years	?
have Miss Herbert as a form teacher	this morning	1 day	?	?

b *Now write about two of Megan's classmates. Example:*

Mark has lived in London for three weeks. He has been at Tufnell Park School since ...

❖ 7 **LISTENING** On Megan's first day

a *Listen to the cassette/CD in groups of three or four. Talk about each scene and decide where it is happening and who is there.*
Say how you know this. What words, phrases or sounds helped you to guess?

b *Listen to the cassette/CD again. Find out …*
- *what time Mr Owen gave Megan her lunch money and what he did then,*
- *which room Mrs Coakley is in,*
- *what the secretary is doing before she sees Megan,*
- *what years and which country Megan's class is going to study,*
- *what music Megan doesn't know much about,*
- *who is in the TPS choir.*

c *Can you remember your first English lesson of the year? What happened? What did you do? What did your teacher do? In your group write a short dialogue of one scene from that lesson and act it for the class.*

8 ▶ **How long?**
How long have they been doing these things?

1 *She has been walking through walls since 1800.*
2 *The earth has been … for …*
3 …

1 1800

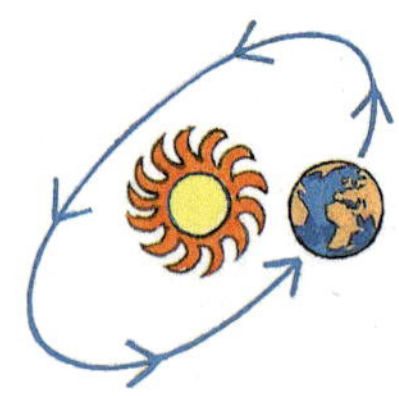
2 4 billion years

3 four o'clock

4 breakfast

5 ten months

6 four hours

7 8.00

8 half an hour

9 ▶ **Why do they feel this way?**

a *Why do the people in the pictures feel angry/…? What have they been doing? Write sentences.*

1 angry

2 hot

3 thirsty

4 happy

1 *The woman feels angry because she has been waiting for the bus.*
2 *The boy feels … because he has been …*

5 cold

6 tired

◆◆ **b** *Now draw a picture of yourself and give it to your partner. (You look angry/tired/…) Your partner must say what you have been doing so that you feel this way.*

WORD WATCH

10 ▶ A funny person, a stupid animal, an exciting book

a *Which adjectives in the box go with:*

a person	an animal	a thing

beautiful • big • black • blue
boring • brave • brown • busy
cheap • clean • dangerous • dirty
divorced • excited • exciting
expensive • fast • friendly • funny
great • green • grey • long • loud
lucky • married • nervous • new
old • quiet • red • sad • scared
silly • slow • small • stupid • tall
white • wild • yellow • young

b *Now write a few sentences about a person in your family, about your pet (or a friend's pet) and about something in your room at home.*

1 *My mum is the funniest person. She always tells silly jokes.*
2 *My friend's dog is a stupid animal. It's scared of cats.*
3 *I've got a new poster of my favourite group in my room.*

11 ▶ A person can have ...

a *Draw a famous person – the drawing doesn't have to be very good.*
Now write about him/her and describe at least three of the things in the box on the right. Use some of the adjectives from P10 (or other adjectives). You can put your picture and your text in your album.

clothes • eyes • face • hair • hands
legs • mouth • nose • teeth

◆◆ **b** *Now describe your person to your partner. Your partner should draw your person from your description. Does his/her drawing look like yours? Can he/she guess who your person is?*

12 ACTIVITY

1 *Which film, sports or music stars don't you like? Bring a picture of one of them to your next lesson. Write a few sentences about the person in your picture. Use words from P10 and P11. Example:*
Lots of people think this person is funny but I think he is boring and looks stupid.

2 *Make a wall display of all the pictures. Leave room for your texts under the pictures.*

3 *Collect all the texts in a box. Each pupil has to take one text out of the box and match it to the right picture on the wall display.*

The Boy with Green Hair

Look at the title and the pictures. What do you think the story is about?

Breakfasts at the weekend were always special for Megan and her dad – no work, no school. Mr Owen made bacon and eggs, Megan made lots of toast and then they sat and talked – sometimes until 11.00 or 11.30. This Saturday Megan talked a lot about her new school and about Hannah.
'She sounds really friendly. I need a hero like Hannah at my new office!' laughed her dad. 'Oh, there's someone at the door.'
'That will be Hannah,' said Megan.
'Meg, what is the market at Camden Lock like?'
'I don't really know, Dad.'
'Well, be careful! And don't talk to strangers ... '

When Hannah and Megan got to the market, it was already very noisy and full.
'People come here from all over London,' Hannah told Megan.
Just then they heard two kids: 'Das ist ja total billig!' – 'Ja, irre!'
'And from all over the world!' laughed Megan.
They met Hannah's friends at a clothes stall.
'Hi, everyone!' said Hannah.
'Oh, I haven't seen blouses like these for years. They're beautiful! My mum made blouses like these,' Megan said sadly.
'Well, meet Sue. She made these.'
'Hi!' said the girl behind the stall.
The group walked to the next stall. Then Marie said: 'Let's go to *Scoobidoo*.'
'Good idea!' said Hannah. 'Megan, you wanted to ... Oh no! Where's Megan?!'

Just a minute away from the noise of the market, Megan sat on a bench by the canal. She looked sadly into the dark water. Then she saw a little bird on the path. It looked up at Megan. She smiled. The bird found a piece of bread and flew away.

Then Megan heard music. She looked around. The music came nearer ... *call – and I'll be there, – you've got a friend ...*
Suddenly a busker stood in front of her.
He looked a bit scary – he was very tall and he had green hair, black clothes and big black shoes.
Megan looked away again. 'I've been here too long,' she thought. 'I should go back and look for the others.'

Back at the market Hannah was frantic! '"Don't worry!" I said to her dad. "I know Megan is from the country, but I'm a real Londoner: I'll look after her." What will he say? I'll never be able to look at him again!'
'Megan comes from the country but she isn't stupid!' said Tony. 'We talked about our favourite café at school. She won't forget a name like *Scoobidoo* – she'll meet us there, you'll see!'
But Hannah was still very worried so she told Sue, 'We can't find Megan anywhere.'
'Well, I haven't seen her since she went down to the canal – about five minutes ago. I thought she looked a bit sad.'
'Thanks, Sue,' said Hannah. 'Quick, Tony, let's go!'
The two of them ran through the market. Soon they came to the footpath by the canal. They looked left, they looked right: no Megan.
'Come on, this way!' Hannah said.
'Oh Hannah, must we?'
'Yes, Tony, we must,' said Hannah. 'Maybe Megan needs our help.'
About half a mile along the canal, the footpath went through London Zoo. On the other side of the canal you could see the giraffes, and on this side you could see the aviary.

'They're beautiful, Bert!' said Megan as she stood and watched the birds with the busker. 'I can't believe it: you love music *and* birds – like me!' She looked at her watch. 'Oh no! We've been watching the birds for ages. I really must go and meet my friends now ... maybe you would like to come, too.'
'Thank you, Megan ...'
'Megan! Megan!'
They turned around. It was Hannah.
'Megan, we've been looking for you. Is everything all right?' She looked nervously at the boy with green hair.
'Oh, yes!' said Megan. 'I thought London was a terrible, dirty, noisy place. But now I've found this lovely path and the birds in the aviary and ...'
'Well, panic over!' said Tony. 'Come on, everyone, let's go to *Scoobidoo.*'
'I have to go and sing,' said Bert. 'No songs, no money! But I'm down here every Saturday. Maybe I'll see you next week?'
'Maybe,' said Hannah. 'Come on, Megan!'
'Goodbye, Bert!' said Megan.
'Goodbye, Megan. And remember ... *You've got a friend!*'

WORKING WITH THE TEXT

1 ▶ Right or wrong?

a *Are these statements right or wrong?*

1 Megan's father was very happy when she left after breakfast.
2 Sue said, 'Megan went to the bus stop.'

◆◆ **b** *Make two or three more statements like these. Your partner must decide: are they right or wrong? Then it's your partner's turn.*

◆◆ 2 ▶ New words

Remember: you can understand many new words from the context or from the pictures. And some new words are like German words. Explain to your partner how you can understand these new words: strangers (p.18, l. 18), clothes stall (l. 27), canal (l. 40), frantic (p. 19, l. 1), footpath (l. 19), ages (l. 35).

3 ▶ What about Megan?

Megan left the others and went down to the canal alone. What do you think of that? Was it a good or a bad idea? Say why you think so.

4 ▶ Megan's diary

Imagine what Megan was thinking when she was sitting on the bench by the canal. Make notes. Then use your notes and write Megan's diary. You can begin like this:
The market was full of people so I went down to the canal. It was quieter there ...

HOW TO ... describe people

1 READING Megan's new friend

a *People love to talk about others. Read what Megan wrote about her new friend, Hannah, in a letter to an old friend.*

There are quite a lot of black kids in my class and one of them is my new friend, Hannah. You can't tell from the photo but she's tall and, as you can see, she has got black hair, brown eyes and a friendly face. That's because she laughs all the time. She knows some great jokes and she isn't scared of any of the teachers — well, only of 'Herby', our form teacher: everyone is scared of her!

Hannah has always lived in London. She has got one brother, Zack. She has got a black dad and a white mum. He has got a business and she's in the police. Imagine that — a police officer as a mum!

Last week I visited her at home and we listened to music. She has got some great CDs. Most of them are black music. But she can't sing so she isn't in the choir at school. I joined the choir last week. But I don't think Hannah likes choir music.

I met Hannah on my first day at TPS. She came and talked to me when she saw that I was new. But she talks to everyone — even to the horrible kids in our class. Sometimes I don't understand why she has to be friends with them, too. But she has been so kind and has helped me a lot. She took me to Camden Market last weekend and we had a great time. It's never boring when Hannah is around. She's really fun and I'm very happy that I met her.

b *Copy the chart below. Then look at Megan's letter again and take notes on Hannah. Compare your chart with a partner's.*

Describing people	*Notes on Hannah*
what the person looks like	*tall, black hair, ...*
his/her character	
his/her family	
he/she likes/doesn't like	
his/her past	
a special incident	
your opinion of him/her	

2 WRITING The nicest person

a *A magazine has a competition 'Who's the nicest person – apart from you?'. Who could you write about? It could be a friend, a relative or someone famous. Copy the chart from* **1b** *and make notes on your 'nicest person'. Look back at P10 – P12 for help with your English.*

b *Decide how you can write an interesting entry for the competition:*

- *What order are you going to put your information in? The order in the chart?*
- *What will make an interesting beginning or end? Should you start or finish with your opinion?*
- *Should you describe how you first met/found out about this person? Or should you tell a funny story about him/her?*
- *Which information should go into which paragraph?*

REMEMBER

1. When you write about a person, think about what information will be interesting for the reader: character, what he/she looks like, family, etc.
2. Make notes first. Read your notes and decide on an order for them.
3. Think of an interesting beginning and end.
4. Write your text. Put different information in different paragraphs.
5. Read your text and then correct it.

◦ English Songs

You can hear English songs everywhere. But how can you understand them better and talk about them? Here are some ideas.

1 *You all know some English songs. What is your favourite one at the moment? How could you describe it? Think about:*
- *the sort of music it is,*
- *how slow/fast it is,*
- *who the singer/group is,*
- *where the singer/group is from,*
- *what the song is about,*
- *why you like it.*

You can use these expressions:
It's a pop/rock/folk/rap/jazz/… song.
It's fast, very slow, … / It changes a lot.
It's by a singer/group/band called …
He's/She's/They're from …
It's a love song. / It's about life in … / …
I like this song because …
it's beautiful.
the singer has got a great voice.
it makes me feel sad/happy/…
it's great for dancing.

2 *In 'The Boy with Green Hair' Bert, the busker, sang the song 'You've got a friend'. Look at the parts of the song below – they are in the wrong order. Try and write the letters (A–F) in the correct order in your exercise book. Now listen to the song. Did you get it right?*

A You just call out my name,
and you know wherever[1] I am,
I'll come running to see you again.

B When you're down and troubled
and you need some loving care[2],
and nothing, nothing is going right,

C Keep your head together[3],
and call my name out loud.
Soon you'll hear me
knocking at your door.

D Close your eyes and think of me
and soon I will be there
to brighten up[4] even your darkest
night.

E If the sky above[5] you
grows[6] dark and full of clouds
and that old north wind begins to
blow,

F Winter, spring[7], summer or fall[8],
all you have to do is call,
and I'll be there.
You've got a friend.

❖ **3** *Here is part of another song. The last word of every line is missing. Try and complete the lines. Check with your group and with other groups. What do they think? Now give the song a title. Then listen to the song and check. Did you get any words right? Is 'your' song or the real song better?*

I miss ☆
but I haven't met you ☆ .
So ☆ –
but it hasn't happened ☆ .
You are ☆
but I haven't met you ☆ .
I ☆
but it hasn't happened ☆ .

And if you believe in ☆
or, what is more ☆ ,
that a dream can come ☆ ,
I will meet ☆ .

4 *Bring some English songs to school and listen to them. How can you describe the songs? (Look at* **1** *for help.) What are the songs about? How do you know?*
How does each song make you feel? Why does it make you feel like that?
Say why you like or don't like the song.

[1] wherever [weər'evə] *wo auch immer* [2] loving care etwa: *liebevolle Zuwendung* [3] Keep your head together. *Versuche, ruhig zu bleiben.* [4] (to) brighten up [ˌbraɪtn_'ʌp] *erhellen* [5] above [ə'bʌv] *über* [6] (to) grow [grəʊ] *werden* [7] spring ['sprɪŋ] *Frühling* [8] fall [fɔːl] *(American English) Herbst*

Sports Freak or Couch Potato –

WHICH ARE YOU?

Write down your answers to the following questions. You can check your score on page 116.

1 How many hours of sport do you do in a week?

A Only the PE lessons at school.
B 1 to 3 hours after school.
C More than 3 hours after school.

2 How many different sports do you do?

A None.
B 1 sport.
C 2 or more sports.

3 What would you most like to do on a sunny winter day?

A Go ice skating or skiing.
B Go ice skating *and* skiing.
C Drink a cup of hot chocolate and watch TV.

4 What do you most agree with?

A Sport is only important for boys.
B Sport is important for everyone.
C Too much sport is bad for you.

5 Imagine you're going to school and the bus is coming. You're 100 metres away from the bus stop. What do you do?

A Run to the bus stop and take the bus to school.
B Walk to the bus stop and wait for the next bus. It'll come in 15 minutes.
C Go back home and go to bed.

6 What sport are these Welsh teams playing in the photo?

A Baseball.
B Rugby.
C Who cares?

7 At what sport have women called Graf, Hingis, Navratilova and Seles all been the best in the world?

A Chess.
B Skiing.
C Tennis.

8 Which sports can you match to A–D?

A Air Jordan.
B Kaiser Franz.
C The All Blacks.
D Quarterback.

TOPS 17

ACTIVITY Fitness for couch potatoes
Listen and move to the music.

▶ 1

'Rubbish!' said David as he threw the magazine away. 'I like sport, but I'm not a freak!'
'Maybe not, but everyone knows you're only interested in bike racing and rugby,' said his friend Colin.
The Aberaeron[1] school rugby team was getting ready for training. There were two really good school rugby teams in the county of Dyfed[2] in Wales – the one from Aberaeron and the one from Llandysul[3]. The big question at both schools was: 'Who will play for Dyfed in the Welsh schools championships?'
After training that evening Colin asked, 'Are you going to come to Cardigan with me on the Sunday after the match?'
'No, I can't,' David answered. 'I've got a bike race. An important one, remember?'
'See, you *are* a sports freak,' laughed Colin.

→ P 1, 2

[1] Aberaeron [ˌæbər'aɪrən] [2] Dyfed ['dʌvɪd] [3] Llandysul [læn'dɪsɪl]

▶ 2

SOME OF THE RULES OF RUGBY

- The rugby ball is oval, not round.
- There are 15 players in a team.
- A game lasts 80 minutes.
- Players can kick, carry or throw the ball (but they mustn't throw the ball forward).
- Players can tackle the player with the ball and bring him down. That player must then give up the ball. Another player can then take it.

The man in white has tackled the one in black, so that player must give up the ball.

- A player can put the ball on the ground behind the other team's goal-line. This is a 'try' (5 points).
- There are three types of goal:
  1) After a team gets a try, a player from that team can kick the ball over the other team's goalposts for a 'conversion' (2 points).
  2) A player can also drop-kick the ball over the crossbar of the other team's goalposts when he is running with it. This is a drop goal (3 points).
  3) A penalty goal after a foul also gets 3 points.

? *Look again at the rules of rugby. How many points will the man in white above get?*

▶▶▶ **NOW YOU** and a group
Look at the rules of rugby again. What is different from football or other ball games? Find three things.

Example: In rugby the ball is oval. In football/basketball/...

Now try and write some rules for your favourite game or sport. Read the rules to the class. Can anyone guess the game?

→ P 3, 12

▶ 3

1ST MAN So, Tim, do you think our boys will beat Llandysul when they play them on Saturday?

2ND MAN Well, they're the better team. If they play well, they'll win.

3RD MAN And is your David in good form?

2ND MAN He's in top form, but he's got a bike race the next day. He'll be tired on Sunday if it's a hard match.

1ST MAN Yes, David may be the best athlete in the area, but will he win the race if he's tired? Isn't that too much sport for one weekend?

2ND MAN I don't know … You might be right.

? *What town are the men from?*
Who is the 'second man'?

▶ 4

Three days before the big match against Llandysul, the Aberaeron boys weren't in very good form. Their coach was very angry.

'You won't win on Saturday if you play like this,' he shouted.

'We'll be better on Saturday,' said David.

'Oh, will you? Well, you've been playing badly today. What have you been thinking about? Your bike race?'

David looked at the ground and said nothing. 'Forget about everything else if you want to win,' the coach shouted. 'If you want to win, you must work hard. And if you work hard, you *can* win! All right?'

The boys had to stay till 7.00 pm. After training, David got dressed quickly and rode home on his bike. 'If I get home by 7.30, I can watch *Champions' League*,' he thought.

▶ 5

If David turns on BBC 1 at 7.30, he can watch … .
If he turns on … at …, he can … . …

BBC 1 Wales		**HTV Wales**		**S4C**	
6.00	Six O'Clock News	**6.00**	Home and Away	**6.00**	Newyddion
6.30	Wales Today	**6.25**	Wales Tonight	**6.15**	Heno
7.00	Small Talk	**6.50**	Coronation Street	**7.00**	Pobol y Cwm
7.30	Wednesday Night Football: Manchester United v Parma	**7.20**	Champions' League	**7.25**	Eisteddfod Yr Urdd Bro Maelor
		10.00	News at Ten	**8.00**	American Football: London Monarchs v Amsterdam Admirals
9.00	Nine O'Clock News	**10.30**	Local News, Weather		
9.30	Formula One Racing	**10.40**	Football Weekend Countdown		
11.45	Bad Boys	**11.10**	Something Strange	**10.15**	NBA Basketball

FOCUS ON GRAMMAR Revision

1 *Find all the sentences with* if *in A3 and A4. Write them down in a table like this:*

If-clause	*Main clause*
If they play well,	*they'll win.*

2 *What verb forms appear in the two clauses?*

3 *Look at A3 again. What do you think is the difference between* <u>when</u> they play them on Saturday *and* <u>if</u> they play well?

▶▶▶ NOW YOU and a group

a *Tell your group what you'll do on Saturday afternoon:*
If it rains on Saturday afternoon, I'll …
If the weather is fine, I'll …

b *One person in the group begins a sentence. Everyone in the group must finish it differently! For example:*
If my parents are away next weekend, I'll …

Then it's the next person's turn to begin. And so on.

→ S 2: 2a (p. 125)
→ P 4, 5, 6

▶ 6

Chwaraeon mwyaf poblogaidd yngh Nghymru

Merched	Bechgyn
1 nofio	pêl droed
2 aerob	rygbi
	beicio
	nofio
	loncian
	golff
	tenis
	pêl fasged

Most popular sports in Wales

Girls	Boys
1 swimming	football
2 aerobics	rugby
3 jogging	cycling
4 cycling	swimming
5 badminton	jogging
6 tennis	golf
7 athletics	tennis
8 riding	basketball

? *Are you a good language detective?*
In Wales lots of people speak two languages, Welsh and English. Compare the two tables. Can you find the Welsh words for 'girls' and 'boys'? And the word for 'ball'?

FOCUS ON WORDS

Different sports have different verbs. For example:

Let's go ...	*Let's do ...*	*Let's play ...*
swimming	*aerobics*	*badminton*
jogging	*...*	*...*

Copy the chart into your exercise book and add the names of the sports from A6.

→ P 7, 13, 14

❖ PROJECT 1 Sport and you

When you are working on this unit, you could prepare and make a presentation on sport. It could be about your favourite sport, your favourite sports star, your favourite sports team, your sporting week/year, …

(If you are not very interested in sport, your project could be about Wales. There are ideas for a Wales project on page 27.)
Do your project with a partner or in a group. Make a presentation for the class.

1 *First you must decide: have you got enough information for your project? If not, where could you get more? Collect ideas.*

You can talk about it like this:
We could go to the library/a sports club/…
Why don't we look for information on the Internet/in an encyclopedia/…?

2 *Take notes on the most important information. (Page 33 shows you how you can do this.) You could write your notes on cards.*

born in ... in 19...
has lived in Chicago since ...
has played ... for ...

favourite food: pizza
car: Ferrari
holidays in: Hawaii, Australia

3 *How do you want to make your presentation? Discuss your ideas.*

You could use these expressions:
Let's make a poster/transparency/…
Why don't we make a map/draw …/…?
I think we should … / I'd like to …

4 *Practise your presentation. Don't forget: check your English. You can use the dictionary and the language summary at the back of this book.*

Think about:
- Who is going to present which part?
- How can you make the presentation more interesting?
- What will you need?
- How long can your presentation be?

Remember: speak loudly, clearly and slowly.
Ask for questions from the class.

▶ 7

The evening before the big match David was at his girl-friend's house. He and Emma wanted to plan their holiday.

DAVID If I won £100,000, I'd fly to Florida.

EMMA Yes, and if I had a wish, I'd buy a ship and sail around the world on it. Be sensible, Dave. Look, I found this guidebook at the library. It's about bike tours.

DAVID Bike tours? Now that's a good idea!

▶▶▶ NOW YOU

What would you do if you had three wishes? Tell the class.

If I had three wishes,
– I'd travel to another country,
– I'd have a big party and
– I'd live in a house on the beach.

▶ 8

A word to tourists

About 550,000 of the 3 million Welsh people speak Welsh. Most Welsh speakers live in the north and west of the country (Tours 1–4 and 6).

But don't worry! Most signs are in English – or in both languages. And everyone speaks English, too. But why not try and learn a little Welsh? Croeso i Gymru! – Welcome to Wales!

▶ 9

If we did Tour 4, we could visit your sister in Chester. Doesn't she live there?

Tour 3

This tour starts near famous Caernarfon Castle. It is on the road and on cycle tracks. Some hills. Look east and you'll see the mountains of Snowdonia. Look west and you'll see the coast and the sea.

Yes, she has lived in England since she finished school. But what else would we do if we visited her? We wouldn't have much time for the rest of the tour.

Tour 4

On this tour you'll ride through one of the most beautiful valleys in North Wales. Lots of hills. You'll visit Denbigh with its famous castle and town walls and the small cathedral town of St Asaph.

▶ 10

Tour 11
A tour of South Wales. All cycle tracks, not hilly. You can visit the beautiful countryside of Brecon Beacons National Park, ride its Mountain Railway and spend a day in Cardiff, the exciting Welsh capital.

? *What have you learned about Wales? Look again at pages 24–27 and find five facts. Make questions and test your partner.*

FOCUS ON GRAMMAR

1 *Find all the sentences with* if *in A7 and A9 and make a table like this:*

If-clause	*Main clause*
If I won £100,000,	*I'd fly to Florida.*
...	...

2 *What verb forms appear in the two clauses? What time does the* if*-clause refer to – past, present or future? What verb forms do you use in this sort of sentence in German?*

3 *Compare these two sentences:*
A If I win £100,000, I'll fly to Florida.
B If I won £100,000, I'd fly to Florida.

Who is more of an optimist, who is more of a pessimist?

▶▶▶ NOW YOU

Read the poem. What would you do if you were a teacher/ a pop star/ an animal? Write a short poem (2–4 lines). Read all the poems in your class.

If I was an apple
And grew on a tree,
I think I'd fall down
On a nice girl like me.

→ S 2: 2b (p. 126)
→ P 8, 9, 10, 11, 15
→ UK Mag, pp. 101/102

❖ PROJECT 2 Wales

Now that you have found out a bit about Wales, perhaps you would like to do your project on that country. You could plan a holiday in Wales with a group of friends, find out more about the Welsh language, ...
Look at the section on how to do a project on page 25 again. You could also find information at a travel agent's. Or you could write a letter to the Wales Tourist Board.

Perhaps you want to know:
- *how you can get to Wales/Cardiff from Germany*
- *where you can find cheap places to stay in Cardiff and other parts of Wales*
- *what you can do/see in Cardiff/Wales*
- *where you can learn some Welsh*
- ...

→ How to take notes, p. 33

<your address>
<the date>

<address of the Wales Tourist Board>

Dear Sir or Madam,

...

Thank you for your help. We look forward to hearing from you soon.

Yours faithfully,
<Your names>

◆◆ 1 REVISION That one is mine!

Everyone in the class puts something (school bag, pen, key, ...) on a desk. One person works in the lost-property office. Tell him/her what you have lost.

A Excuse me. I've lost my ...
B Can you see it/them here?
A Yes, the white/... one is/ones are mine.

Now you work in the lost-property office and the next pupil tells you what he/she has lost.

◆◆ 2 REVISION The weekend → S 1: 1f, g (p. 121)

a *Write down your plans for the weekend on a piece of paper like this:*

On Friday I'm going to see a new film/...
On Saturday I'm ...
And on Sunday ...

Give the piece of paper to your partner.

b *Look at your partner's plans for the weekend. What do you think will (or won't) happen? Write it down and then tell the class.*

Nadja is going to see a new film on Friday. I think she'll go to the Roxy.
On Saturday she's ...
...

3 REVISION Signs → S 2: 1 (p. 124)

a *An English friend wants to know what the signs below mean. Can you tell him? Use* can, can't, must, mustn't *or* needn't.

1 You ... close this door.
2 You ... play ball here.
3 You ... wait for the bus here.
4 You ... get a ticket here.

◆◆ b *Draw two or three more signs and put them in your English album. They can be funny, too. Can your partner say what your signs mean?*

◆◆ 4 ▶ What if ...?

Partner A: Tell your partner what you want to do and when. (Use the information below.) Then answer his or her questions.
Partner B: Ask questions about your partner's plans.

1 A play tennis – next Saturday
B it – rain?
A do – homework

Example:
A I want to play tennis next Saturday.
B But what will you do if it rains?
A Then I'll do my homework.

2 A go sailing – at the weekend
B there – be – no wind?
A visit – friends

3 A go on a bike tour – with my friends – in the holidays
B they – not want to come?
A go – alone

4 A visit – my friend David – tonight
B ...
A ...

5 A go to a pop concert – on Saturday
B ...
A ...

❖ 5 **GAME** If …

In your group, make a chain like this one. Which group can make the longest chain?

❖❖ 6 ▶ **A trip around Nameshire**

Partner B: Look at page 117.

Partner A: Here is a map for a trip around the county of Nameshire. Some of the information about activities in Nameshire is missing. Ask your partner.

A What can I do if I go to Peterpool?
B If you go to Peterpool, you can … .
What can I do if …?

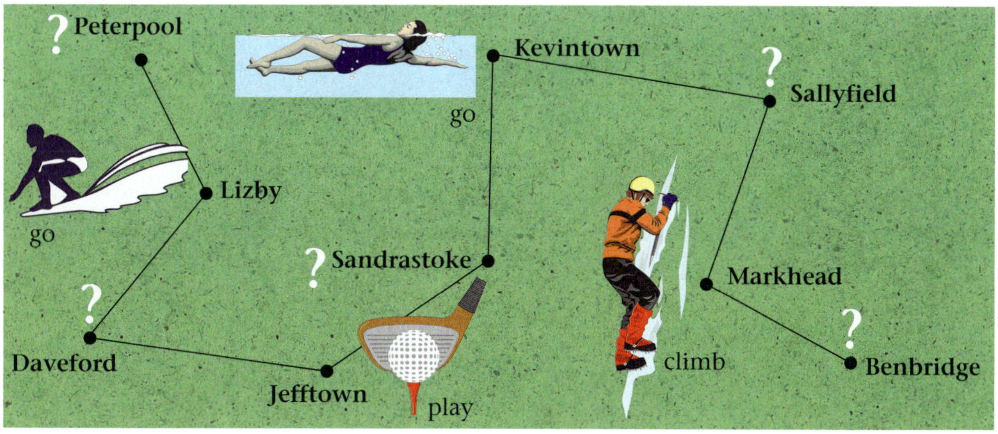

7 **LISTENING** Radio commentaries

a *Have you ever listened to sports on the radio? Listen to these sports reporters and try to guess what sports they are talking about. Choose from:*

athletics (running) • basketball
cricket • football • ice-hockey
riding • tennis • volleyball

❖ b *Now listen to the commentaries again. You want to tell your friends as much as you can about what is happening. Take notes and then check with your group. How much did you find out?*

c *The words of the song are on the right. When and where do people usually sing it? Have you ever sung it? When?*

We are the Champions Words and music by Queen

We are the champions, my friend.
And we'll keep on fighting[1] till the end.
We are the champions. We are the champions.
No time for losers 'cause we are the champions of the world.

[1] (to) keep on fighting ['faɪtɪŋ] *weiterkämpfen*

8 ▶ Bike Tour 11

David and Emma talked some more about Bike Tour 11 in the brochure. What did they say?

1 EMMA do Tour 11 – stay in Cardiff for a few days

If we did Tour 11, we could stay in Cardiff for a few days.

2 DAVID spend a few days in Cardiff – have to stay at the Youth Hostel

3 EMMA be in Cardiff – not want to miss the 'Techniquest' museum

4 DAVID you go to Techniquest – I visit Cardiff Arms Park

5 EMMA we go on this tour – also like to walk in Brecon Beacons National Park

6 DAVID be there at the right time – go to the Brecon Jazz Festival

◆◆ 9 ▶ Just imagine!

a *Partner B: Look at page 117. Partner A: Ask your partner these questions and write down what he/she answers. Answer your partner's questions and give reasons for your answers.*

1 If you could meet anyone in the world, who would you like to meet?
2 If you could buy just one thing, what would you buy?
3 If you could have any job in the world, which job would you like to have?

b *Now think of one more question for your partner.*

❖ 10 ▶ The beginning and the end

a *Think of the beginning of a sentence with an if-clause and write it down on a piece of paper. You can make it funny or interesting. Examples:*

If I found a lot of money in the street, ...
If a tiger came into the room, ...
If I had just one wish, ...
...

b *Now swap your sentence beginning with your partner's. On a different piece of paper, finish his/her sentence.*

c *Put all the sentence beginnings in one box and all the sentence ends in another. Each pupil then takes one piece of paper from each box and reads the sentence to the class.*

❖ 11 ▶ Well, but if ...

*Work in groups of five or six. Partner **A** starts and asks a question like this:*
What would you do if ...
– you saw a house on fire?
– you lost your English book?
– ...

***B** answers the question.*
I'd call the fire brigade. / ...

***C** thinks of a 'Well, but if ...' question.*
Well, but if you couldn't find a phone, what would you do then? / ...

***D** answers this question.*
I'd run ...

***E** thinks of the next 'Well, but if ...' question and **F** answers it and so on. Then **B** starts.*

WORD WATCH

12 WORD BUILDING The suffix *-er*

You can sometimes add suffixes like -er *to the ends of words and make new words. In the 'WORD BUILDING' exercises in this book, you'll learn some of the most important suffixes. Then you'll understand lots of new words when you hear or read them.*

a *You know some nouns with the suffix* -er. *Make nouns with an* -er *ending from these verbs and use them in the sentences below.*

listen • lose • run • sing • write

1 Radio Chester is giving away prizes. ...s can win £1000.
2 Stephen King is a great ...
3 Last year 500 ...s ran in this race.
4 What a voice! She's a great ...
5 Paul was angry when the other team won the match. He's a very bad ...

◆◆ **b** *Choose two verbs and make nouns with an* -er *ending. Write sentences for the new nouns. Can your partner guess your words?*

dance • kill • plan • rescue
ride • speak • spell • use • work

A I don't go to discos because I'm not a good ...
B Oh, I know. Your word is 'dancer'.

13 WORD LINK

Look at the verbs in the box and say which ones fit in the sentences below.

break • carry • change
cheer • drop • explain • hit
know • listen • lose • make • play
practise • scream • shout • sing
throw • watch • win

1 You can *carry, drop,* ... a ball.
2 You can *break,* ... a rule.
3 A team can ...
4 Fans at a match can ...

14 TROUBLE SPOT Which word is right?

1 I want to make a (lettuce/salad), so I need some (lettuce/salad).
2 The film was very (scared/scary). I was really (scared/scary).
3 It's warm, so I'm not going to (carry/wear) a jacket. But it might be cold later, so I'm going to (carry/wear) a pullover over my arm.
4 Kim has always been (interested/interesting) in sport, so I'm sure she'll find this book (interested/interesting).
5 I don't know Paris very well, so let's take a (card/map). Don't forget the concert (cards/tickets)! And we mustn't forget to send a (card/map) home!

15 ▶ In the open air

a *Copy this 'open air' network into your exercise book. Write the correct words under the pictures. Then think of more words and pictures for the network.*

b *Imagine you are on holiday. Write a card to a friend and tell him/her what the countryside is like and what you are doing.*

The Race

Answer these questions about the two newspaper articles as quickly as you can:

- What part of the newspaper are they from?
- What is the first article about? And the second one?
- What do the two have in common?

Aberaeron will go to championships!

Aberaeron 24 : Llandysul 17

by Barry Masters

After their big win against Llandysul at Aberaeron stadium on Saturday, our boys are on their way to the Welsh Schools Rugby Championships. If they play well again, they could even win. Aberaeron's team captain

Steve Phillips scored the first try after only 17 minutes of play. It came after a great pass by team-mate David Evans. 'It was brilliant,' said Phillips. 'The players from the other team were really surprised. David usually goes for the try. But today he threw the ball to me, and I just ran with it.'

Local boy 3rd in cycle race

by Will Roberts

Aberaeron's own David Evans, 16, took third place in the Junior Welsh Cycling Championships over 60 kilometres yesterday. He came in after Tom Porter, 18, from Cilcain, and Nathan Rosser, 17, from Cardiff.

The favourites in the race were Evans and 16-year-old Aled Jones, from Bangor. For a long time the two boys were ahead of the others. They were together at the 55-kilometre checkpoint, but Jones fell only three kilometres before the finish. An ambulance took him to hospital with a broken leg.

No one knows why Evans did not win after his rival fell. We have been trying to reach him all weekend for an interview but have not been able to do so.

WORKING WITH THE TEXT

1 ▶ Heads and tails

a
1 Aberaeron scored the first try …
2 After a pass from David …

… Steve was able to run for the try.
… after 17 minutes of play.

b *Now make two or three sentences like the ones in* **1a**. *Your partner must match them correctly.*

2 ▶ What happened?

a *Why didn't David win after Aled fell? Here is an idea:*

David didn't win because he was tired after his rugby match on Saturday.

Is this a good explanation? Can you think of a better one?

b *Imagine you are David. Use your favourite idea from* **2a** *and tell someone why you didn't win the race. Perhaps make notes first.*

3 LISTENING A radio interview with Aled Jones

Now listen to the radio interview with Aled and find out what really happened.

HOW TO ... take notes

1 READING Notes on Wales

a *If you just read or listen to something, you often can't remember it very well. It is easier if you take notes.*
Look at these notes on Wales (from pages 23–27). How does the writer make them clear and easy to read? What type of words (nouns, verbs, pronouns, adjectives, prepositions, conjunctions, articles) does he/she mostly use? What type of words doesn't he/she use much?

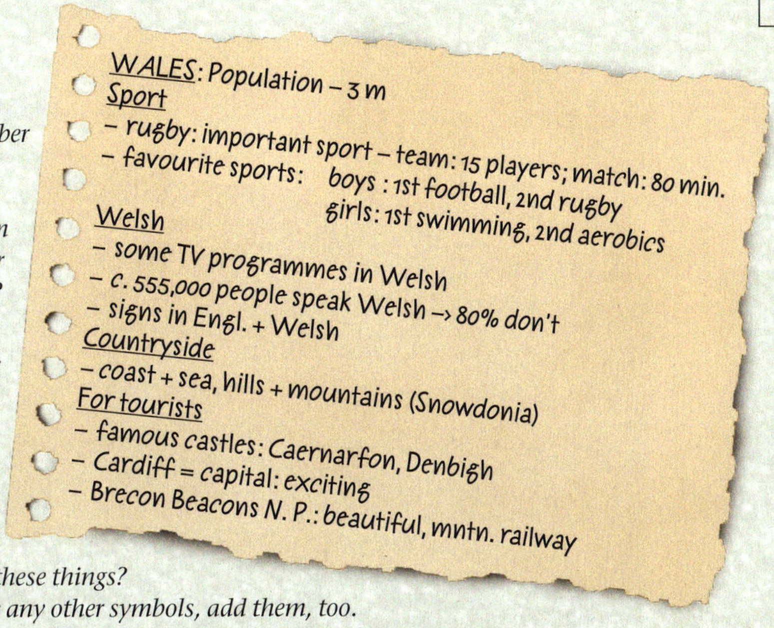

WALES: Population – 3 m
Sport
– rugby: important sport – team: 15 players; match: 80 min.
– favourite sports: boys : 1st football, 2nd rugby
girls: 1st swimming, 2nd aerobics
Welsh
– some TV programmes in Welsh
– c. 555,000 people speak Welsh –> 80% don't
– signs in Engl. + Welsh
Countryside
– coast + sea, hills + mountains (Snowdonia)
For tourists
– famous castles: Caernarfon, Denbigh
– Cardiff = capital: exciting
– Brecon Beacons N. P.: beautiful, mntn. railway

b *What do the symbols in the notes mean? Make a list.*
What symbols would you use for these things?
Add them to your list. If you know any other symbols, add them, too.
– pound(s) – dollar(s) – is more than – is not the same as – positive – negative

c *What do the abbreviations in the notes mean? Make a list.*
What are the abbreviations for these words? Add them to your list.
– and so on – disc jockey – electronic mail
– somebody – page – pence
What other abbreviations do you know? Add them to your list, too.

d *Some words in the notes are underlined. Why? Can you say how this helps?*

◆◆ **2 SPEAKING AND WRITING** All about Wales

a *Use the notes from* **1** *and tell your partner about Wales. Don't look at pages 23–27!*

b *When you take notes on a text, you want to get all the important information out of it.*
Now look at pages 23–27. Is any important information missing in the notes? Add notes on this information.

◆◆ **3 YOUR OWN NOTES** Practise what you have learned

a *Partner A: Look at the UK Mag (page 101) and take notes on the Welsh language.*
Partner B: Look at the text 'Who was the first European in America?' in the UK Mag (page 102) and take notes on 'Madog'.
(Don't be scared of the new words. Remember how you can understand them. You can also use the dictionary on pages 171–194 or an English-German dictionary.)

b *Now use your notes and tell your partner what you have found out. Listen to what he/she has to say, too. Then check his/her notes and see if he/she has got the most important information.*

REMEMBER

1. Notes help you to remember what you have read or heard.
2. Only write down words and phrases with important information.
3. Give each topic a heading.
4. They are *your* notes, so you must decide which symbols, abbreviations, etc. you want to use.
5. Your notes should be clear and easy to read.
6. Your notes can help you to tell others what you know.

? 1 *How does the machine work? Use these verbs to explain:* climb, fall, go, hit, put, turn.

When a burglar *climbs* through ..., he ... his foot on A, and it ... down. This ... B, and B ... C, and the boxing glove ... the burglar on the head, and he ... through ...

2 *Look at the machine again. What else happens? You can use these verbs:* pull, push, ring, turn.

▶▶▶ NOW YOU

Imagine Professor Branestawm has given you a robot. Choose a job for it, and explain why you want to give it this job:

When I get my robot, it will wash the dishes. So I won't have to wash them when my favourite TV show is on. When I get ..., it will ...

THEY ALL COME FROM SCOTLAND!

Scotland is a small country, but a lot of important inventions and discoveries have come from there. Here are just a few.

Do you want a cold drink? The FRIDGE keeps food and drinks cold. A great Scottish invention by James Thomson.

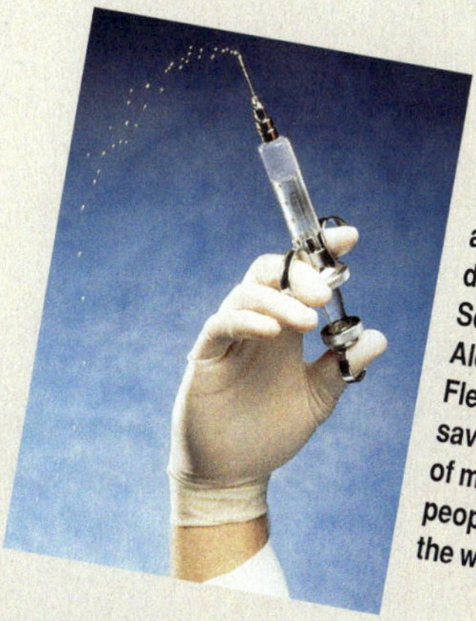

PENICILLIN – a fantastic discovery by Scotsman Alexander Fleming. It has saved the lives of millions of people all over the world.

Think of life without your favourite programmes! Difficult? Well, say 'thank you' to Scotsman John Logie Baird for TELEVISION!

Have you ever been on holiday by plane? RADAR got you there safely. Scottish inventor: Robert Watson-Watt.

→ P 1

? Do you know any inventors from *your* country? What did they invent?

FOCUS ON WORDS

Collect words for machines and gadgets in your home. Make a table like this.

in the kitchen	*in my room*	*in other rooms*
cooker	*CD player*	*TV (living-room)*
...	...	...

answering machine • cassette recorder • CD player • clock
computer • cooker • fax machine • fridge • microwave • radio
stereo • telephone • TV • video recorder • washing-machine

▶▶▶ NOW YOU and a partner

Choose three machines. Explain how your life would be different without them.

If we didn't have a TV, we would have a lot more time for our families/ ... If we didn't ...

→ P 12

▶ 1

Sheena Stewart looked up from her homework. 'All these fantastic inventions – they aren't giving me any ideas for my project!' she complained. '*What* am I going to do?' She looked again at her project instructions.

INVERNESS HIGH SCHOOL – YEAR 9
DESIGN & TECHNOLOGY PROJECT

Instructions

1. This project will be all your own work – your ideas and your designs.
2. Your project must be the answer to a real problem. So first find an interesting problem.
3. What's the best answer to the problem? Why? Make notes.
4. Your project report is very important. So think. How can you explain your ideas best? Don't just write about them. Pictures and photos will help you to get better marks.

▶ 2

All Their Own Work

by Jason Barnes and Lucy Rice

This week we're looking at 'Design and Technology'. It isn't an easy subject, and not everyone chooses it. The pupils who do it have to work very hard. They have to make a machine or gadget which they invented on their own. First of all, they study design. They learn a lot of things that will help them with their project.

Next they find out about the most useful materials and technology. Then they design and make their own machines and gadgets.

We talked to lots of young people that are all working on interesting projects. Here are just some of their many ideas.

Jenny Alsford
Chiltern Edge School

My family never has time to sit together and talk. We're always busy. So I'm designing a sort of message box. It's a gadget which will help us all. We can leave messages on a cassette in the box. When someone opens the box door, the cassette starts automatically.

22

Lisa McKenna
Bass Rock High School

You don't just make things. You invent things. That means you have to think and plan really carefully before you start. I'm designing an automatic cat feeder. It's a gadget which will feed the cat automatically every day. I'm going to use it when we go away and have to leave the cat at home.

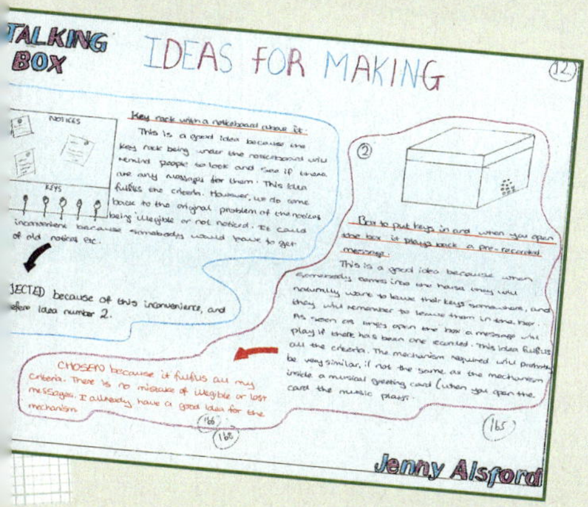

Andrew Mitchell
Portsmouth High School

I've got no left hand, but I love windsurfing. So I've made a gadget that helps me to hold on to my board. I've tried it and it works. It's a great feeling. Maybe I'll be an engineer when I leave school.

? *Why do you think Jenny's family is so busy that they need a message box? Would it be useful in your family? Have you heard of the 'Jugend forscht' programme in Germany? What sort of things do people do for it?*

FOCUS ON GRAMMAR

1 *Look at A2 again and find sentences like the ones below. Write them in your exercise book. Underline the clauses with* who, which *and* that.

The pupils who do it have to work very hard.
They have to make a machine which they invented on their own.
They learn a lot of things that will help them with their project.

2 *What words do* who, which *and* that *refer to? Show this with arrows (↵), as in the examples.*

3 Who, which *and* that *are relative pronouns and they are in relative clauses. Which relative pronouns can you use for people, which ones for things?*

4 *Copy the first six sentences of A2 without the relative clauses. Compare your text to the one in the book. Why are these relative clauses important?*

▶▶▶ NOW YOU

Read this poem.

MESSAGE BOXES
I like families that sit together and talk.
I love dads who play football with their daughters.
I like mums who listen to their kids.
But I hate message boxes that are voices without bodies.

Now write your own poem. What kinds of people, inventions, etc. do you like/love/hate? Put your poem in your English album.

→ S 3: a, b (p. 127)
→ P 2, 3

▶ 3

Sheena looked up again. She still had no ideas for her project. Then she noticed some old postcards on the wall. They were from different parts of Scotland, and they were all from her grandad. Before his accident on an oil rig, he was an engineer whose work took him all over Scotland. 'Hey!' she thought. 'Grandad knows *everything* about technology. Maybe he can help!'

→ S 3: c (p. 127)
→ P 4, 13

2

3

1

4

1. *Look at Grandad's postcards (1–4). Then match them to what he wrote (A–D).*
2. *Read them and answer these questions:*
   - *How does Grandad feel about London?*
   - *What is 'black gold'?*
   - *Why does he like Arran?*
   - *He saw sports at Braemar. What else did he see?*

A

Hi Sheena,
I'm now part of the great Scottish oil industry! This is a picture of the place which I now call home – an oil rig. It's an hour by helicopter across the North Sea from Aberdeen. And a kilometre under my feet is the 'black gold'. We work very hard when we're on the rig, so I look forward to the long holidays that we get, too.
Love, Grandad

B

Dear Sheena,
See the castle in the picture? Well, this time I'm working there – it's the type of big job that I like. I'm on the island of Arran, on the way from Glasgow to Ireland. It's lovely here, with the sea all around and friendly people who I've really learned to love.
Love, Grandad

C

Dear Sheena,
It's great to be back in good old Scotland after that job down south. The country is all right, but I don't really like London! Edinburgh is a much better capital. It's not too big, and it's much friendlier and we've got our own parliament now, too. And there's the wonderful castle you can visit on the hill. This is the city I love!
Love, Grandad

D

Dear Sheena,
Here's a card from the Highland Games at Braemar. The new hydroelectric power station I'm working on is in the mountains quite near Braemar, so I went to the Games last Saturday. They were fun, and the music and dancing they had were great, too. You must go next year!
Love, Grandad

ACTIVITY

Find a map of Scotland. Copy it and label it with the names of the places in Grandad's cards. Can you add any other place names? What other information can you put on your map?

▶ 5

It was raining when Sheena got to Grandad's house. She rang the doorbell, but nobody came. 'He isn't here!' she thought. She was cold and her coat was wet. But then the door opened. 'Ah, Sheena!' Grandad said. 'You're all wet.'

'Don't worry, Grandad. Look, here's all the post I found in your postbox.'

'Oh, thank you!' There were some letters he was really pleased about. 'I can't get down to the postbox very easily in bad weather. It's these thin old legs. They're useless!'

For three hours Sheena and her grandad talked about her project. He had some great ideas that she wrote down. Then he said, 'If I were you, I'd go down to the bus stop now, Sheena. Or you won't get home tonight. Oh, and take this umbrella, too.'

Together they went slowly to the door. 'Grandad,' Sheena asked, 'what were you doing when you had your accident on that oil rig?'

'Oh, I was pulling a man out of a fire. It started in a storeroom he was working in. Something heavy fell on me.'

On the bus home Sheena thought about Grandad and his bad legs. She really wanted to help him. But how? *How?*

Then the bus passed the ski-lifts of Aviemore – and they gave her a fantastic idea …

→ How to tell a story, p. 47

FOCUS ON GRAMMAR

1 *Look at postcards A and B in A4. Write down the sentences with relative clauses.*

This is a picture of the place which I now call home.

…

Are the relative pronouns the subject or the object of the relative clauses?

2 *Now look at postcards C and D in A4 and at A5. There are relative clauses without relative pronouns here. Try and find these 'contact clauses'.*

3 *When can you leave the relative pronoun out?*

▶▶▶ NOW YOU and a partner

Imagine you aren't happy with some things you've got at home. Talk to your partner and complain about them like this:

- fridge – buy last week – doesn't work

  The fridge we bought last week doesn't work.
- stereo – have got in my room – not loud enough

Now think of two or three more ideas.

→ S 3: d, e (p. 128)
→ P 5, 6, 7, 8, 9

▶ 6

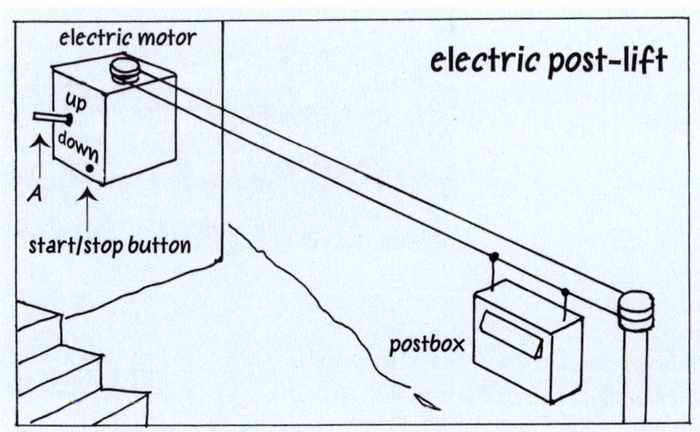

? *How does Sheena's electric post-lift work?*

Grandad pushes the button. This starts … . Then he moves A to 'up', and … moves up from the garden gate to … . Then he pushes … and takes out his letters. He pushes … again, moves A to … and sends … back …

→ P 10, 11, 14, 15
→ UK Mag, pp. 103–105

1 **REVISION** Television – past and present → S 1: 1a, c, d (p. 121)

Put the verbs in the correct forms. Choose the simple present, simple past or present perfect.

1 How much TV (you / watch) every day?
How much TV do you watch every day?
2 My sister often (watch) about six hours!
3 What programmes (Tony / like)?
4 John Logie Baird (invent) television in 1923.
5 How (people / live) without television before 1923?
6 (Claire / find) the video yet? I (need) it.
7 I (just buy) a fantastic new TV. I (get) it yesterday. (you / want) to see it?
8 (you / record) that film on Sunday?
– No, I (do). I (forget). I (be) sorry.

◆◆ 2 ▶ **What are their names?**

Partner B: Look at page 118.
Partner A: Look at pictures 1–3. Find out from your partner the names of the people and pets in the pictures. Ask like this: What's the name of the boy who is/has got …?
Then answer your partner's questions about pictures 4–6.

1

– dancing with the girl
– wearing a big hat

2

– using the computer
– pointing at the picture

3

– has got big ears
– has got sad eyes

4

Robot A Robot Z

5

Tiddles Tomboy

6

Kim Jane

3 ▶ **What are they?**

Use relative clauses and describe these people and things. Make a graffiti poster for the classroom.

Parents are people who/that …
Computers are machines …
A teacher is someone …
A car is a thing …
…

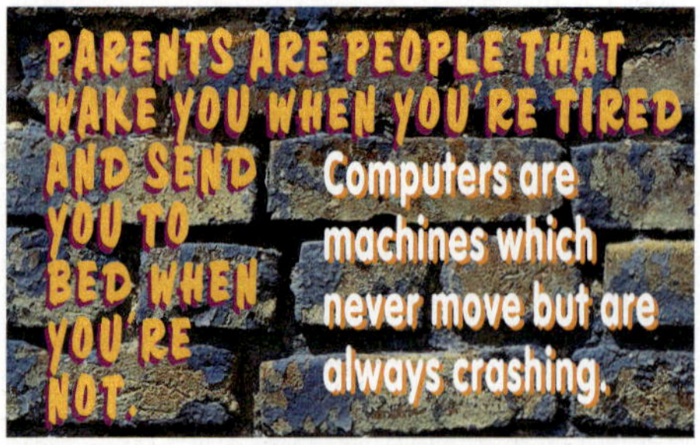

❖ 4 **GAME** Who am I thinking of?

Think of a famous person and important facts about him/her. Tell the others about him/her. They have to say who it is.

She's the woman who won at Wimbledon last year.

He was the singer whose house was called *Graceland*.

5 ▶ Sheena's grandad

Join the sentences together. Use contact clauses.

1 Look at that beautiful castle. Sheena's grandad visited it on Arran.
Look at that beautiful castle Sheena's grandad visited on Arran.

2 Sheena has got a photo of an oil rig. Her grandad sent it to her.

3 'Black gold' is a name for oil. Workers on the oil rigs often use it.

4 Edinburgh is a city. Sheena's grandad really loves it.

5 He went to the Highland Games. They held them in Braemar.

6 He really loved the dances. He saw them at the Highland Games.

7 Rob is the thin man. Sheena's grandad pulled him out of the fire.

8 The reporters took photos of the two men. The helicopter took them to hospital.

9 Sheena's grandad has still got the story. The newspaper wrote it about him.

10 Sheena still keeps the copy of the story. She made it at the library.

6 ▶ Project reports

When Lisa McKenna and Jenny Alsford wrote their project reports, they were too long. Make the reports shorter. Take some of the relative pronouns out.

Here are the things that I needed for the automatic cat feeder:
– a box which I could use for the cat food
– an electric clock which I could use as a timer
– a cup that was the right size for the cat's food for one day
– a motor that opens the door in the box

I had to make a box which had two parts: one that I could use for the messages that we write and one that I could put the cassette recorder in. There was a problem which I found very difficult. How could I make a cassette recorder that starts when someone opens the box? I found an answer in an Internet technology group that I contacted. Someone wrote that I

7 ▶ Scottish people and places

Match each picture to a phrase from A and a phrase from B and make sentences with relative clauses. Use a relative pronoun only where you need one.

A a ski area • the island
an invention
the great discovery
the boy
the Scottish inventor

B Alexander Fleming made it
he has only got one hand
he invented the telephone
it gave Sheena a great idea
it makes airports safe
Sheena's grandad liked it a lot

1 *Andrew Mitchell is the boy who has only got one hand.*
2 *Penicillin was ...*

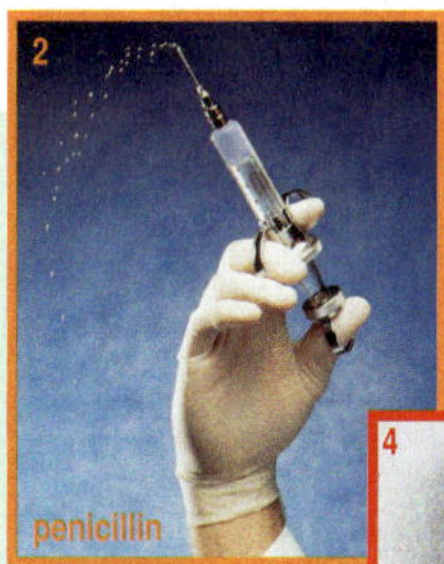

8 ▶ Lorna's story

a *Match the parts of the sentences and write the beginning of Lorna's story.*

1 Lorna was a young girl	– she dreamed about.
2 But it was a life in Edinburgh	– she talked to.
3 In her village she told this to everyone	– that everyone laughed at.
4 But she didn't find many	– that was long and difficult.
5 Lorna was just the silly girl	– the long journey didn't frighten.
6 But she never listened to the people	– the people in the village knew little about.
7 Edinburgh was a big city	– who laughed at her.
8 You could only get there after a journey	– who lived in the Highlands a long time ago.
9 There was only one person in the village	– who listened to her.

b *Now write two or three more sentences and finish Lorna's story. Use relative clauses.*

9 REVISION That cat again! → S 1: 1d, e (p. 121)

What were these people doing when the accident happened? Use the simple past and the past progressive.

1 BOY my dog (run) after a cat – I (stop) him
My dog was running after a cat when I stopped him.

2 GIRL I (walk) home – I (see) a cat in the road

3 WOMAN I (stand) at the bus stop – a cat (jump) in front of a car

4 1ST DRIVER I (drive) along the road – that stupid cat (run) in front of me

5 2ND DRIVER I (go) along behind the blue car – it suddenly (stop) and I ...

10 LISTENING How things work

a *Listen to the cassette/CD. What sort of place can you hear on it? What do people do there?*

b *Now listen again. People are explaining how different things work. What are they talking about? Choose from:*

bike • CD player • computer
cooker • fitness machine • fridge
microwave • radio • stereo • TV

What words or phrases helped you to guess?

❖ **c** *Listen again and take notes. Compare the information you got in your group. Choose one conversation and tell the class what it was about.*

○ 11 ▶ Flat swapping

a *The Meyers are going to swap their flat for the holidays with an English family. They want to leave some notes for the family in their flat – but Herr and Frau Meyer don't speak English. Their children have to translate the notes for them. Can you help?*

◆◆ **b** *Write a note in German about a machine in your flat or house. Give it to your partner. He/She has to translate it into English.*

1 Wir haben zwei Faxgeräte. Das Faxgerät, das Sie verwenden können, ist auf dem Schreibtisch im Schlafzimmer. Legen Sie Ihre Briefe darauf, tippen[1] Sie die Faxnummer ein und drücken Sie den grünen Knopf.

2 Die Waschmaschine darf nicht zu voll sein. Wählen Sie zuerst die Temperatur[2], die für Ihre Kleidung richtig ist. Drehen Sie dann den linken Knopf auf 2 und drücken Sie den rechten Knopf.

3 Unsere Fahrräder sind in der Garage. Der Schlüssel für die Garage ist in der Küche auf dem kleinen Schrank. Den Schlüssel nach rechts drehen und die Tür geht automatisch[3] auf.

[1] (to) type [taɪp] [2] temperature ['temprətʃə] [3] automatically [,ɔːtə'mætɪkli]

WORD WATCH

12 ▶ How do you use them?

a *Look at your table from 'Focus on Words' on page 35. How do you use those machines and gadgets? Write ten sentences like this:*

1 *I cook eggs for breakfast on the cooker.*
2 *I play all the new hits on my CD player.*
3 *I often watch football on TV.*
4 ...

b *Now use one of your sentences and write a short story (not more than ten lines) that starts like this:*
I was (cooking eggs for breakfast on the cooker/playing with .../...) when ...

It can end like this:
So I went back home and (talked to my friend X on the telephone/watched TV/...).

◆◆ 13 ▶ What is it?

Partner B: Look at page 118.
Partner A: Explain the pictures to your partner. Use the phrases in the box on the right. Can your partner guess who or what it is?

A This is a thing which ... / a person who ...
B Is it a/an ...? / It must be ...
A That's right. / No, sorry. Try again.

carries people from station to station
designs roads and bridges
helps in a shop
takes other people's things
takes photos
shows you your lesson times

14 WORD BUILDING *-ion/-tion/-ation*

a *Copy and complete the table.*

Verbs	Nouns
invent	?
suggest	?
?	description
?	collection
imagine	?
?	invitation
pollute	?
?	explanation

b *Complete the sentences with words from the table.*

1 The man gave the police a ... of the thieves.
2 I've got a ... for the weekend. Why don't we go to the cinema?
3 Did Gloria ... you to her birthday party?
4 I can't write good stories. My ... isn't very good!

c *Now write four more sentences with words from the table.*

15 TROUBLE SPOT Which word is right?

Complete the sentences. Choose the right word from the brackets. Use the correct form.

1 Sheena (life/live) in Scotland, and she loves (life/live) there.
2 Every afternoon she (make/do) her homework.
3 She wants to get good (marks/notes) for her school project.
4 She was happy when she found her project (marks/notes) again.
5 She wants to (make/do) a sort of ski-lift for letters.
6 'Are you (sure/safe) your idea will work?'
7 'Don't worry, Mum. It'll be (sure/safe) and Grandad will love it.'
8 Sheena's mother's (sister/nurse) is a (sister/nurse) at a hospital in Edinburgh.

Dr Joe's Antiseptic

Look at the picture below. Where are the people? What do you think is happening? How long ago? Give reasons for what you think.

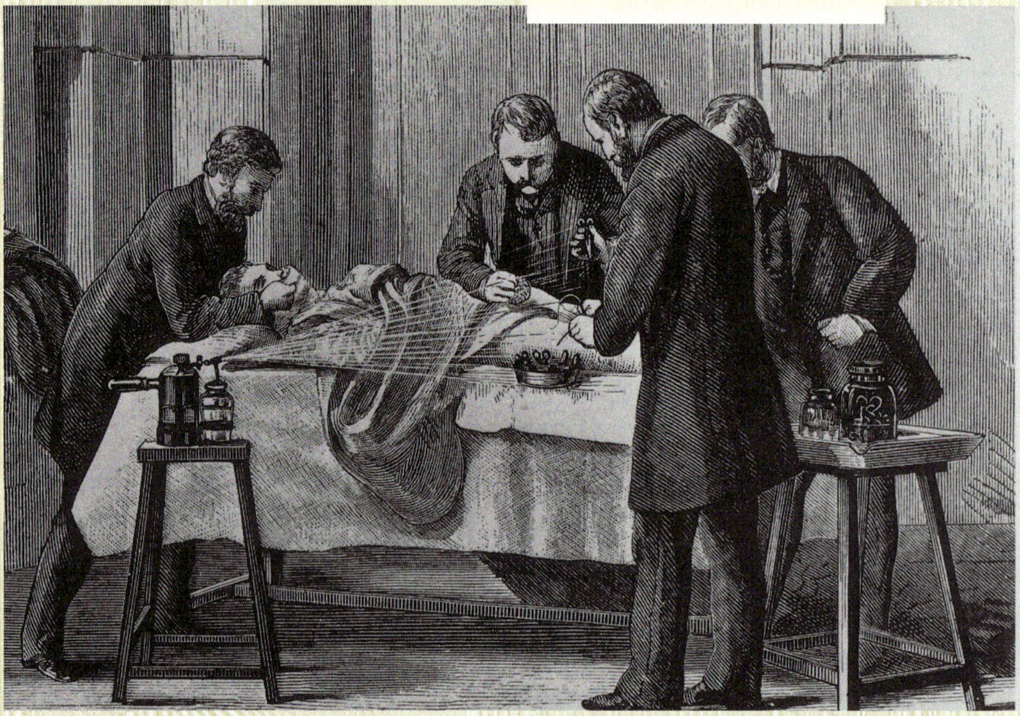

The 11-year-old boy was crossing a Glasgow street when a cart hit him and he flew through the air. Crack!! Everyone heard the horrible sound. Seconds later the boy was in the road with a crowd of people around him. They could see his bone in the open wound on his thin little leg. A broken leg like that needed an operation – so the boy was going to die. That's what many in the crowd thought as they watched him there on the road. But things happened differently for James Greenlee.

Joseph Lister

It was 1865 and very often patients died even after easy operations. This was because their wounds almost always became infected.

They took James Greenlee to a Glasgow hospital after his accident. The doctor there, a man called Joseph Lister, did an operation on the boy's broken leg and then put bandages around the wound. Then he waited and hoped. When Lister took the bandages off four days later, the wound was clean and was not infected. James Greenlee was going to live. But who was this man who saved the boy's life and how did he do it?

After young Joseph Lister became a doctor in 1852, he left London and went to Scotland to work with the most famous surgeon of the time, James Syme. In 1856, Lister married Syme's daughter, Agnes, and got a job as a surgeon at an Edinburgh hospital. Three years later he moved to Glasgow when he became a professor there. Why did so many people die after operations? This was the problem he wanted to work on. Other doctors thought he was mad . 'If you cut off an arm or a leg,' they said, 'it will soon become infected. It follows as night follows day.' But Joseph Lister did not think so. He tried to keep everything clean in his part of the hospital but still the wounds became infected. Lister read everything he could find on the subject. Some people believed that wounds became infected because of bacteria – things that were so small you could not see them. Some doctors believed that bacteria came from inside the body but Lister believed they came from the air around it.

At that time hospitals made bandages from old clothes that people gave them. They did not wash the bandages. They just cut them up and used them on patients' wounds. Surgeons wore ordinary clothes when they did operations, clothes which were often dirty from earlier operations. No one cleaned the operating rooms. Most patients felt they were already dead when they went into hospital for an operation.

Then one day Lister heard about something called carbolic acid. In the town of Carlisle people discovered that when they put carbolic acid down the drains, the drains smelled better. Lister asked for some carbolic acid. If it keeps drains clean, he thought, it might do the same for wounds. But when he tried it, it burned his hand, so he added water. Now it wouldn't burn the patient but perhaps it would kill the bacteria.

This was when James Greenlee, the boy with the broken leg, arrived at Lister's hospital. After he saved James Greenlee, Lister tried the method on other patients. And in the next two years 9 out of 11 lived. The two who did not live died for other reasons. In Lister's part of the hospital wounds did not become infected because he used carbolic acid on the bandages. In other parts of the same hospital, patients were dying as before. In Glasgow an operation was like a death sentence, unless 'Dr Joe' did it.

Lister wrote about his ideas but many surgeons just laughed at him. Others, especially in Germany, followed his methods and got the same good results.

Lister believed that bacteria were in the air, so he cleaned everything in his operating room with carbolic acid. He even cleaned the air with a carbolic spray which filled the operating room with 'antiseptic', as he called it. The antiseptic fell on the doctor's hands and on the patient's wound.

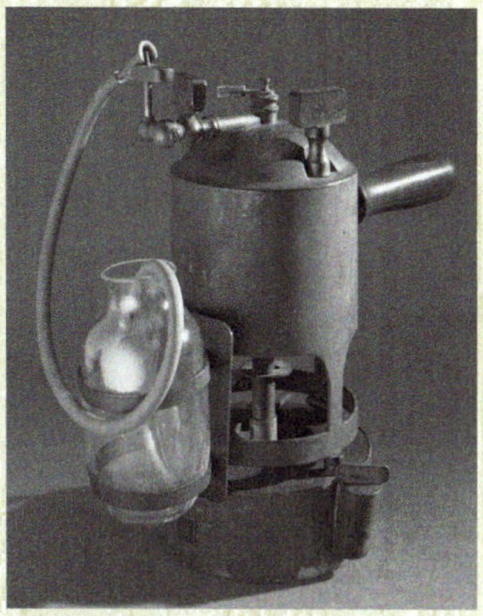
Carbolic spray

Although other doctors didn't believe in his ideas, Dr Joe's patients lived and became well again. Slowly doctors everywhere began to agree with his ideas and Lister became the most famous surgeon in the world.

Based on *Two Great Discoveries* by B. MacLaverty

WORKING WITH THE TEXT

1 ▶ Newspaper interview

a *Imagine you are a reporter for a newspaper in Glasgow in 1865. You ask Dr Lister these questions. How will he answer?*

1 Dr Lister, why do you think wounds become infected after operations?
2 What do you use to stop this?
3 How did you find out about this 'antiseptic', as you call it?

◆◆ **b** *Think of four or five more questions for Dr Lister. Then, act out the interview for the class. Listen to the other interviews and compare yours with theirs.*

2 ▶ Newspaper report

Write a short report on Dr Lister's work for your newspaper. Don't write more than ten lines.

3 ▶ By accident

An accident helped another great scientist in Scotland to make a discovery. His name was Alexander Fleming. You read about him on page 35. Find out something about him and report back to the class.

4 ▶ Your own story

Write a story about something good that happens by accident. Before you start, make notes under the headings who, what, where, when, how *and* why.

❖ 5 **ROLE-PLAY** I don't believe it, Dr Lister

A week after James Greenlee's operation, Dr Lister visits the boy with his wife and another surgeon from the hospital.

Do the role-play in groups of four.

a *Before you start, read your role card carefully and try to imagine the situation. Make sure you 'know' your character well. Think of a favourite phrase that makes him/her real. Write down some of the things that your character might say. Try and use the expressions on your role card.*

b *Now do the role-play in your group. Perhaps you can act it out for the class later.*

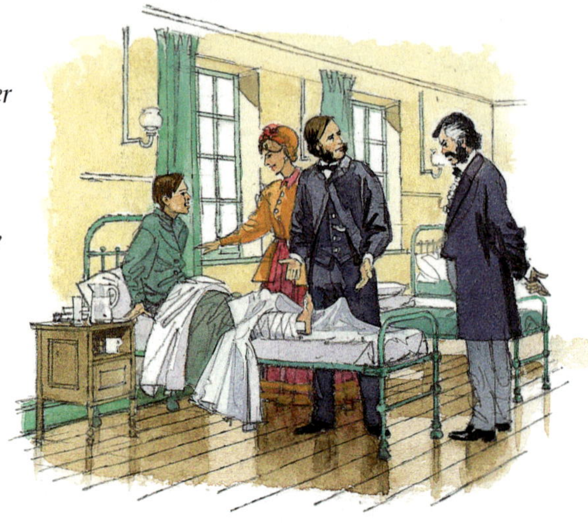

ROLE CARD 1

It is 1865. You are **Dr Joseph Lister**, a surgeon in Glasgow. You are trying to persuade another surgeon, Dr Alan Lee, that your new operation methods will save lives. You show him James Greenlee's leg and tell him about the operation and your ideas on how wounds become infected.

Useful expressions:

Let me explain how …
Now just look at …
What I'm trying to say is …
I see what you mean, but …
…

ROLE CARD 2

It is 1865. You are **Dr Alan Lee**, a surgeon in Glasgow, where you work with Dr Lister. He is showing you James Greenlee's leg. You have been a doctor for many years but don't understand Dr Lister's new methods. You can't believe that wounds become infected because of bacteria in the air. So you think Dr Lister's ideas are silly. You make your opinion clear but still try to be polite.

Useful expressions:

What do you mean by …?
I just can't believe …
How can something no one can see …?
If you're right, …
…

ROLE CARD 3

It is 1865. You are **Agnes Syme Lister**, Dr Lister's wife. You are in a hospital in Glasgow where your husband works. You talk to James Greenlee and find out how he feels today. Then you listen to the discussion between your husband and another surgeon at the hospital, Dr Alan Lee. You know all about your husband's ideas because you work very closely with him. You think he has made a great discovery and support him when Dr Lee disagrees.

Useful expressions:

How are you feeling …?
I hope you'll …
You must agree that …
Don't you see that …?
…

ROLE CARD 4

It is 1865. You are **James Greenlee**, an 11-year-old boy in a hospital in Glasgow. You broke your leg in an accident about a week ago. It hurt a lot at first but after the operation you soon began to feel better. You are very grateful to Dr Lister but are a bit scared of him, too. You like his wife because she is very nice to you. You hope you can go home soon.

Useful expressions:

I'm fine/much better/…
First I thought I was going to …, but now …
You've been so good to me, …
I hope I'll …
…

HOW TO ... tell a story

1 READING What happened on the oil rig?

People often tell stories about something that has happened to them or to someone else. Look at how Sheena's grandad told her about the day that changed his life. This will help you when you want to tell stories about other exciting situations.

1 *'I'll never forget that day – September 1st, 1993. It was about five o'clock. I was working in the control room when suddenly the emergency phone rang.'*

2 *'It was Rob McGregor. He called for help because there was a fire in the store he was working in. So I ran to the store and opened the door.'*

3 *'There was thick black smoke everywhere and I couldn't see much at first. Then I saw Rob. He was lying on the floor. I shouted to him but he didn't answer, so I put my coat over my head and went in. I was trying to pull him out when something heavy fell on me and I couldn't move.'*

4 *'But I was lucky. Some other men saw the fire. They came and saved me and Rob just in time. Then a helicopter arrived and flew me and Rob to Aberdeen.'*

5 *'My legs were broken and I had to stay in hospital for five weeks. I've never worked on an oil rig again since I had that accident.'*

a *When you tell a story, you usually answer the following questions:* Who? What? Where? When? How? Why? *Find this information in Grandad's story.*

b *How does Grandad start and finish the story?*

c *Find all the time expressions in the story, like* September 1st, suddenly, *etc.*

d *Which linking words like* and, when, *etc. can you find?*

2 SPEAKING Rob McGregor's story

Rob McGregor's grandchildren often ask him about the fire on the oil rig. How does Rob tell his story? Make notes first. You can look at the REMEMBER box for help.

3 WRITING Can you tell this story?

a *Look at the pictures and write the story. Use the REMEMBER box for help.*

b *Write your own story about an exciting situation where someone helps someone else. Make notes first and look at the REMEMBER box for help.*

REMEMBER

1. In your story, answer the questions *Who? What? Where? When? How? Why?*.
2. Think about how you can start and finish the story.
3. Use time expressions like *now, suddenly, then, at first, after that, later, the next moment*, etc.
4. Don't forget linking words like *after, and, because, before, but, or, so, when*, etc.
5. Check your story (or let your partner check it). Are the grammar, spelling, vocabulary correct?

4 UNIT 4 London

Thames River Tours

★ See the sights from the river!
★ Tours start at Westminster Pier, only two minutes from the Houses of Parliament.

Summer season
(27 May to 1 September)

1100	1130	1200	1225
1300	1325	1400	1430
1455	1530	1600	1630
1700	1730	[illegible]	1830

Prices
Adult
Students/
Senior Citizens
Child 2–15 yrs
Family
(Two adults an[d]
two children)

What do you know about London? Work in groups and write down in a network what you know. Then talk about the city.
Next look at the brochure on the left and the map. Where do the Thames River Tours start?

Sir Christopher Wren's most famous building

An important building for Britain's kings and queens

You can be Superman or Superwoman for a day

The Crown Jewels

Learn about London's violent history

LISTENING

1 *Listen to the guide on a Thames River Tour boat. You can follow the tour on the map. What sights does the guide mention? Which photos show them? (You can find a list of all these sights in the vocabulary on page 155.)*

Photo 1 shows ...
I think photo ... shows something in/from ...

2 *Write down the names of two interesting places on the tour. Now listen to the guide again. Write down what you learn about those places. Then compare your information with your partner's.*

3 *Which places would you like to visit? Tell your partner why.*

... sounds interesting. I'd like to go there because you can ... there.

▶ 1

Some children and teachers from Kingsway High School in Chester have just arrived at Euston Station in London. They are on a school trip.

MRS MARTIN OK, everyone. Please stay together. We're going to take the underground to our hotel.

MR MARTIN Yes, it's in Bayswater, near Queensway Station.

DEBBIE Can I go and fetch tube maps for everyone, Mrs Martin?

MRS MARTIN Not yet, Debbie. Please stay with the group. Mr Martin will fetch the maps. – Jeff?

MR MARTIN I'm on my way, Christine. Now where's a ticket office? That's where they have underground maps.

BEN Over there, Mr Martin, next to the pizza place.

▶ 2

LRT Registered User No 98/2807

? *Where is Euston Station on the underground map?*

It's on the ... Line and the ... Line.

Now find Queensway. What is the Kingsway group's best route from Euston to Queensway?

They should take the ... Line southbound to ... . There they should change to the ... Line and take a westbound train and get off at Queensway.

GAME What's the best route?

Ask your partner for the best route from one station to another. Don't make it too easy! Then swap.

A What's the best route from ... to ...?

B Well, you should take the ... Line (eastbound) to ... .
Change to the ... and get off at ... .
Now, what's the best route ...?

▶ 3

On their first afternoon in London some of the Kingsway group went with Mrs Martin to Madame Tussaud's wax museum.

Marie Tussaud

Marie Tussaud (1761–1850) made wax figures at a show in Paris for more than 20 years before she became its owner in 1794. She was famous for the masks she made of dead people's heads in the French Revolution.
In 1802 she left France with her two sons and took the wax show to Britain. She became very successful there but never saw France or her husband again.

Madame Tussaud's

The famous wax show was taken to Britain in 1802. For the next 30 years the wax figures were shown all around the country. Then, in 1835, they were moved to London. A museum was opened not far from the one you can still visit today.
Most of the figures in today's museum (known as 'Madame Tussaud's') are new but there are still some of the old ones that were made last century.
About two million people visit Madame Tussaud's every year.

Henry VIII, king of England (1509–1547), and his six wives as wax figures. Two of Henry's wives were executed.

▶ 4

Mr Martin took the other pupils to MOMI – the Museum of the Moving Image.

Enjoy the **Museum of the Moving Image** where visitors are taken on a journey from old Chinese shadow plays through the early years of cinema to a modern TV studio. The 3000-year-old story of moving pictures is presented in an intelligent, interactive way. With its teams of actors and new technology, MOMI is a fun place for all the family. Enjoy Charlie Chaplin's famous little tramp, fly like Superman, be a TV newsreader, win a role in a Hollywood film. See and feel the story of cinema as it is brought to life in front of your eyes.

▶▶▶ NOW YOU and a partner

Complete the four sentences below. Three must be right and one must be wrong. Then give your sentences to your partner. He/She has to decide which is wrong. If he/she doesn't get it right, ask someone else.

1 … was born in …
My mother was born in Ankara.
2 … was built in …
3 … is spoken in …
4 … is made of/in …

FOCUS ON GRAMMAR

1 *Look at the verb form in this sentence.*
The wax show was taken to Britain.
We call this form the passive.
Find more passive forms in A3 and A4 and write them down.
was taken, were …, are …, …

2 *What tenses are the passive forms in?*

3 *How do you form the passive?*

→ S 4: 1a, b (p. 129)
→ P 1, 2

▶ 5

The next morning the Kingsway group was picked up by a tourist guide in front of their hotel. They were taken to all the important sights. In the coach the guide told them everything they wanted to know.

Buckingham Palace is where the king or queen lives. In the summer tourists can visit some of the rooms. The Changing of the Guard ceremony is watched by hundreds of tourists. But it isn't held every day, so phone for information.

Trafalgar Square is used by Londoners, tourists *and* pigeons. That's the famous Nelson's Column with Admiral Lord Nelson on top. It was built in 1842.

There are a lot of homeless people on the streets of London. That young woman stands there every day and sells *The Big Issue*, a magazine which is written by homeless people. She gets 60p for each paper she sells.

FOCUS ON GRAMMAR

1 *Compare these two sentences:*
Homeless people sell The Big Issue.
The Big Issue is sold by homeless people.
In which sentence does the subject do something?
What is different in the other sentence?

2 *What do you add to a passive sentence when you want to say who does the action? Look for more examples on this page.*

→ S 4: 1d (p. 130)
→ P 3, 4

▶ 6

THE BIG ISSUE

How much do you know about homelessness? Not many people know about it, but we at *The Big Issue* have all been homeless. We know. *The Big Issue* is only sold by homeless people. They buy the magazine for 40p and sell it for £1. For a few pence you can help someone to get off the streets. A little money can go a long way. Please take a little time and talk to us. It's only a few minutes for you, but it means a lot to us. Thank you.

▶▶▶ **NOW YOU** and a partner

Why do you think people become homeless? Think of questions you would like to ask one of the homeless people in the photos on page 52. Talk about your ideas. Now imagine how the homeless person might answer your questions and write an interview with him/her. → P 5, 8

LISTENING Another Day in Paradise

1 *Listen to the first verse of the song. Is the homeless person a man or woman? Who does he/she speak to?*

2 *Now listen to the rest of the song.*

FOCUS ON WORDS

Look at pages 48–53 and collect the 'city' words and phrases. Add other words you know and put them in groups (e.g. **transport:** take the underground, get off the tram, ...; **buildings:** visit a cathedral, go to the town hall, ...; **events:** watch a ceremony, ...; **sights:** ...). *How can you arrange them? Continue to collect these words and phrases for the rest of the unit.*

▶ 7

Dear Mum and Dad,

London is great! We spent our last afternoon at Covent Garden. There were lots of people from all over the world there and something really exciting happened!

We were watching a fantastic mime group when suddenly one of the boys in the group jumped up and ran to Mrs Martin. A pickpocket was trying to rob her. But Winston – that was the boy's name – chased him away. He was a real hero so I took a photo of him!

Love,
Debbie

We saw about six different street entertainers at Covent Garden and they were all great.
See you tomorrow!
Nick

Winston, the boy who saved Mrs Martin's handbag – and everyone's day

▶▶▶ **NOW YOU**

Think of a city you have visited or a city you would like to visit. Imagine you are there. Write a postcard for your English album. Here is some help:

Dear ...,
... is great/fun/interesting/boring/... . The weather ... . We've just ...

▶ 8

It was Chinese New Year on Sunday and the Kingsway group wanted to go to Chinatown and see the parade. When they got off the bus at Piccadilly Circus, Sita and Jenny saw a warning about pickpockets. A young, homeless person spoke to them.

PAUL Be careful now. I've been robbed three times this year.
SITA Three times? That's terrible! Have the police caught anyone?
PAUL The police! No, they haven't.
JENNY You've been robbed three times and no one has been caught?
PAUL No, and no one will be caught. The police don't care about homeless people. – I'm Paul, by the way.
SITA I'm Sita and this is Jenny. Look, we have to go now, Paul. We're going to the Chinese New Year parade.
PAUL Just follow the crowd then. The parade is in Gerrard Street. You can't miss it.

▶ 9

Watch out – there's a thief about!

Going to the Chinese New Year parade?
The pickpockets are, too!
If you are not careful, you will be robbed.
Remember, purses can be stolen very easily from jacket pockets. Bags should be kept closed at all times.

More information on pickpockets in London can be found at any police station.

FOCUS ON GRAMMAR

1 *Find all the passive forms in A8. What tenses are they in?*

2 *Find the examples of the passive with modal auxiliaries in A9. What form of the verb is used after* can, should, *etc.?*

3 *Paul says* 'I've been robbed'. *Could he say the same with an active form?*

→ S 4: 1b, c (pp. 129/130)
→ P 6, 7, 9, 10

❖ ACTIVITY A tour of London

Imagine your class is on a tour of London. Five or six of you are guides – each for one of the famous sights (e.g. Buckingham Palace). When your class arrives at one of the sights, the guide tells you all about it. The tourists can ask questions.

▶ 10

On the train back to Chester Debbie was talking to Mr Martin. 'There's one thing I don't understand,' she said. 'I was talking to an old Chinese man at the parade. He's a Londoner, he says, because he lives there. But he wasn't born there. *You* say you're a Londoner because you were born there. But you don't live there. What exactly *is* a Londoner?'
Mr Martin looked pleased, but Mrs Martin didn't. 'Oh no,' she said. 'He's going to sing now, and it's all your fault ...'

→ UK Mag, pp. 106/107

❖ 1 ▶ Places in town

a *Think about three places in town. What things are usually done there? Write down in a list four sentences for each place.*

- a railway station
- a theatre
- a school
- a hotel
- a sports centre
- a(n) ...

railway station
Tickets are sold.
Information is given.
Trains are cleaned.
Newspapers are bought.

b *Swap your lists with another group. Try and add sentences to their lists. The group that can add most sentences is the winner.*

2 ▶ Yesterday's news photos

a *Look at the news photos and say what happened yesterday. Use the simple past passive.*

hurt • kill • open • steal

1 *A new bridge was ...*

b *Look at yesterday's newspaper. Find three or four things that happened to someone or something. Tell the class about them in English. Use the simple past passive.*

3 ▶ The Prince's school friend

Choose the right verb forms for this article.

Last week Prince Charles (visited / was visited) the offices of *The Big Issue*, a magazine that (writes and sells / is written and sold) by homeless people, – and there he (met / was met) an old friend. Charles (surprised / was surprised) by one of the magazine's reporters who said, 'I remember you from school.'

The reporter was Clive Harold – a man who was born rich and went to the same school as Prince Charles 40 years ago.

Later he (made / was made) homeless by alcohol problems. At first Prince Charles (didn't remember / wasn't remembered) him, but later the two (spoke / were spoken) happily together about old teachers and football games. Harold (told / was told) his future king, 'We've both had good and bad times. But you were the only one in the school who had bigger ears than I had.'

4 ▶ **London sights**

Complete the following information about some of London's sights. Use the notes in brackets and the passive of the simple past or simple present.

1 William I decided to build a castle soon after he became king of England.
(So – Tower of London – begin – 1066)
So the Tower of London was begun in 1066.

2 Christopher Wren designed St Paul's Cathedral in 1675.
(building – finish – 1710)

3 Big Ben is the most famous bell in the world.
(hear – by millions – BBC radio – every day)

4 Tower Bridge is more than 100 years old.
(open – 1894)

5 London has had an underground railway for a very long time.
(first tube line – open – 1863)

6 Why is Westminster Abbey important?
(Because – kings and queens of Britain – crown – there)

7 The Houses of Parliament were built in the 19th century.
(old building – destroy – by fire – 1834)

◆◆ 5 **REVISION** At a party → S 4: 2 (p. 130)

Partner B: Look at page 119.
Partner A: Look at the picture with food and drinks at a party. (Your partner has got a different picture.) Ask about the things in the list below.
Then answer your partner's questions. Use a little / a few / a lot / not … any.

A Have you got any apples?
B Yes, … / No, …

B Have you got any sandwiches?
A Yes, I've got a few / a lot. *or:* No, I haven't got any.

6 **LISTENING** Conversations on a London bus

a *The Kingsway kids loved the buses in London and all the conversations people had on them. Listen to these three conversations. What do they tell you about the people who are talking? What do you understand? Copy the chart and fill it in when you listen the second or third time.*

Speakers	*Londoner or visitor?*	*Where are they going?*	*What do they discuss?*
1 girl	*Londoner*	*music shop*	*Where can the girl buy a cheap*
boy	*Londoner*	*Don't know.*	*CD for her …?*
2 …			

◆◆ **b** *Choose one of the conversations you have heard. Imagine what the people will say when they meet again or get off the bus. Write a short conversation and act it out for the class.*

7 ▶ Changes

a *Compare the two maps. Write down what has been changed. Use these verbs:*

add • build
make bigger • put in

A garden has been added to ...

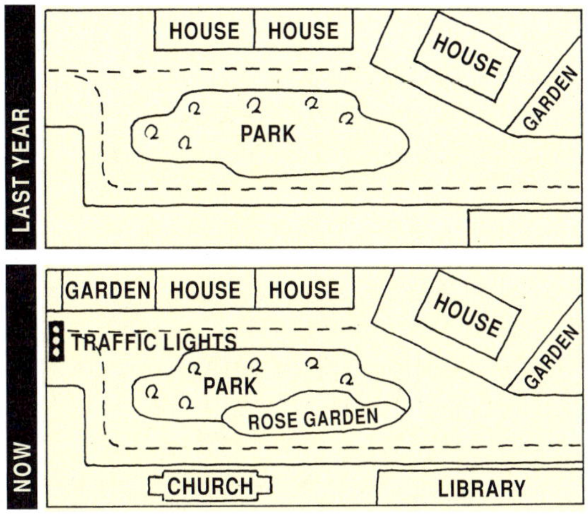

b *What has been changed in your area this year? Collect ideas and make a list in class.*

c *How can your area be made a better place for young people? Make suggestions. Use* could/should/must be + *past participle.*
A new swimming-pool should be built.

WORD WATCH

8 WORD BUILDING The suffix *-ness*

a *You already know the noun* homelessness. *What adjective does it come from?*

b *Now make new nouns with a* -ness *ending from these adjectives. Mind the spelling. For example:*
silly + -ness = silliness

bright • clever • dark • friendly
happy • ill • lonely • sad • silly

c *Use the nouns from* **8b** *in the following sentences.*

1 Nick likes to play the clown at school. His *silliness* often gets him into trouble with his teachers.
2 The sun on this white paper is terrible. The ... makes it really hard to read.
3 The doctors don't know what's wrong with Sandra. She has got a mystery ...
4 Everyone loved the king, so there was great ... in the country after he died. The queen died a few months later. People say she died of ...
5 I don't want to be an underground train driver. Just imagine: eight hours of ... every day!
6 People called him 'clever Dick' because of his ...
7 Money is nice, but it can't buy you ...
8 When I go to Britain, I always like the ... of the people.

9 WORD LINK

a *Find verbs from the box for the groups of words below.*

get • have • take • visit

... a bath, breakfast, fun, lunch, a party, a shower, time
... friends, a museum, the sights
... dressed, off a train, on a bus, pocket money, ready, to Trafalgar Square
... notes, a photo, a train, the underground

b *Now use one phrase from each group and write a short story.*

10 TROUBLE SPOT *the* or not?

Do we use the *with these expressions? (If you aren't sure, look back at the unit.)*

near ... Queensway Station (p. 50)
go to ... Museum of the Moving Image (p. 51)
not far from ... Trafalgar Square (p. 52)
spend some time at ... Covent Garden (p. 53)
walk through ... Chinatown (p. 54)
get off at ... Piccadilly Circus (p. 54)
in ... Gerrard Street (p. 54)
close to ... Houses of ... Parliament (p. 56)
visit ... St Paul's Cathedral (p. 56)

Save the Crown Jewels

The following text is a maze. Don't try to read it like other texts! Just go where the text tells you. You are in the story: you are Agent 101, and you must save the Crown Jewels. At each step you and your partner have to agree what you want to do next. Copy the table and write in the numbers of the steps you choose and how long they take. You mustn't go over 300 minutes, or ... BOOM!

These phrases and the table will help you:
I think the clue means we should ... / Why don't we try ...?
That will take too long. / That's too easy. / That isn't hard enough. / I don't think that's the right decision. / No, let's go to ...

Step	Time	Total
1	20 mins	20 mins
2	30 mins	50 mins
	+ ?	?
?	?	?

1 You are Agent 101 from the British Secret Service. Your phone rings at 6 o'clock in the morning. It's your boss. 'Come to the office at once.'
Half an hour later you're there. '101,' your boss says, 'Max Gladstone has put a bomb in the Tower of London. He says the Crown Jewels will be destroyed at 12 o'clock.'
'Our people can't defuse his bombs – not without the code,' you say. 'What's the game this time?'
'Here, he left this note for you.'

To my old friend, 101
I've got another little game for you, 101. If you can find five clues – and the answers – by 12 o'clock, you'll find the code for the bomb. If not: BOOM! Here's your first clue:
When he was alive, he wasn't a tall man. Now he's dead, and he's the tallest man in London. Visit him, and he'll give you your next clue.
Yours,
Max G.

'What does it mean?' your boss asks.
'Nelson,' you tell her. 'Admiral Lord Nelson was a small man, but his statue was put on top of the column in Trafalgar Square. So now he's the tallest man in London.'
'Brilliant, 101!'
'Yes, I am. ... Now, I must get to Trafalgar Square at once.'
'A car and driver are waiting for you, 101. You have five hours – 300 minutes.'
Go to 2, Trafalgar Square. This takes **20 minutes**.
Remember: you must add your time at each step!

2 You're at Trafalgar Square. But where's the clue? Then you remember: 'The clue is about Nelson, not Trafalgar Square!'
'Get me a rope,' you say to your driver, and you climb the 44 metres up to the statue. Nelson is holding the next note from Gladstone in his hand: 'That was too easy, 101. Try this one: Everyone knows, "To be or not to be." But do you? Put that in your pipe and smoke it.'
30 minutes have passed. What's next?
a You know that 'To be or not to be' is from a play by William Shakespeare, so you drive to Shakespeare's Globe Theatre on the Thames. **40 minutes**. *Go to 7*.
b Suddenly you see something in the note: 'Everyone knows, "To be or not to be."'
'One' = 1; 'to' = 2; 'be' = B; 'to' = 2; 'be' = B. 12B2B. 'Of course! The numbers and letters are in the wrong order!' you shout. '2 2 1 B Baker Street! Sherlock Holmes's address.' You drive to Baker Street. **20 minutes**. *Go to 6*.

3 Why are you reading this? *Go back to 2* and follow the directions. Add 10 minutes to your time.

4 You get off the train in Oxford and walk to the taxis outside. Before you get there, you hear your name. At the information desk a message has been left for you: 'A clown like you should be in a circus. Max G.'
55 minutes have passed. What's next?
a You decide that Oxford was a mistake, so you catch the next train back to London. When you arrive at Paddington Station, you take the tube to Oxford Circus. This takes **150 minutes**. *Go to 13*.
b You decide that you must be in the right place because Max has left a message for you. You take a taxi around the university. *Go to 16*.

5

The man at the London Dungeon tells you that they *have* got figures of Henry and his wives, that the figures *are* having dinner and that one of them *is* a ghost.

You say you're going to drive there and look at it, but he says you needn't come because they've turned off the power. 'The ghost of Anne Boleyn is a hologram,' he explains. 'She doesn't usually talk. But today she was talking.'

'What was she saying? Can you remember?'

'Yes, of course. She said: "Where did you go to university, you clown?"'

This has taken **10 minutes**. What now?

a You went to university in Oxford, so you take the tube to Paddington Station. The trains to Oxford leave from there. *Go to 8.*

b 'Oxford, you clown!' you think. Then: 'Clown – circus – Oxford Circus!' You take the underground to Oxford Circus. This takes **6 minutes**. *Go to 13.*

6

You're at the Sherlock Holmes Museum, but where's the clue? Then you remember: 'Put that in your pipe and smoke it.' Of course, Holmes's famous pipe! Max's note has been hidden inside the pipe: 'He was married to three Catherines, two Annes and a Jane. Two lost their heads – poor things! Now they're all together for dinner, but one of them is a ghost.'

'He means Henry VIII and his wives,' says your driver.

'But where are they together for dinner?' you ask.

This has taken **10 minutes**. What now?

a You remember that Madame Tussaud's has figures of Henry VIII and his wives. You're very near there, so you decide to send your driver away and walk. This takes **15 minutes**. *Go to 17.*

b You think there are figures of Henry VIII and his wives in the London Dungeon, but you aren't sure. You decide to phone there. *Go to 5.*

7

You don't find anything at the Globe. Then you think, 'That was too easy! Max isn't going to make things easy for me.'

45 minutes have passed. What now?

a You remember your other choice and go there. The journey takes **60 minutes**.

b You can't remember your other choice and must *go back to 2* and look again. This takes **50 minutes**.

8

You arrive at Paddington Station by tube and buy a train ticket. You're waiting on the platform for the train to Oxford when you suddenly hear: 'The next train to Oxford will be 45 minutes late. We are very sorry ... '

35 minutes have passed. Now what?

a You wait for the next train to Oxford. This takes **45 minutes**. *Go to 4.*

b You decide that Oxford Circus wasn't a bad idea and go there. This takes **17 minutes**. *Go to 13.*

9

You run from Tower Hill underground station to the Tower of London, then to the Jewel House. This has taken **10 minutes**. *Go to 10.*

10

The microchip fits into a hole in the bomb. You put it in, a small door opens and a figure jumps up. It looks like Max Gladstone. Then you hear Max's voice: 'Very good, 101. You're better than I thought. You've saved the Crown Jewels.'

'Yes, I have! That's enough games, Max!'

'Maybe ... but you'll hear from me again, 101. Our little games are really fun!'

11

You take a Central Line train to Liverpool Street, change there to a southbound Circle Line train and get off at Tower Hill.

This takes **29 minutes**. *Go to 9.*

12

You quickly find the figures of Henry VIII and his wives and know you've made a mistake. (Look at the picture on page 51.)

This has taken **25 minutes**. If you still have time, you can phone the London Dungeon. *Go to 5.*

13

You're at the tube station at Oxford Circus, but you can't find the clue. Then you see the sign which usually tells you when the next train will be there. But today it says 'Fish and chips – that great British invention.' This means nothing to you. But then you see a poster for the London Aquarium with a big picture of a fish. You look at it carefully and see that something has been stuck onto the eye of the fish. It's a microchip – fish and chips! You take the microchip and decide that you have to get to the Tower of London at once.

This has taken **15 minutes**. *Go to 11.*

14 You're looking around Madame Tussaud's when the police come. They take you to the police station and keep you there until your boss phones. The Crown Jewels have been destroyed. You can look for a new job.
This is the end of the story for you.

15 You get into Madame Tussaud's and find the figures of King Henry VIII and his wives. They aren't having dinner. (Look at the picture on page 51.)
This has taken **115 minutes**. If you still have time, you can phone the London Dungeon. *Go to 5.*

16 You drive around the university but find nothing. Oxford was a mistake, so you drive to Oxford Circus in London.
This has taken **60 minutes**, and the drive into London takes **90 minutes**.
Go to 13.

17 About 500 people are waiting in front of Madame Tussaud's, so you go to the door and tell them you're from the Secret Service. They say you have to wait like everyone else. What do you do now?

a You show them your gun and tell them that you can't wait. You have to see Henry VIII and his wives now. They open the door for you. *Go to 14.*
b You wait like everyone else. *Go to 15.*
c You ask the people at the door to phone their boss. You explain everything; then you can go inside. *Go to 12.*

WORKING WITH THE TEXT

❖ **ROLE-PLAY** At Madame Tussaud's
In groups of three, act out the scene at Madame Tussaud's (Step 17). One of you plays Agent 101, another plays the person at the ticket office, a third plays the manager of Madame Tussaud's.
You can use role cards for this activity.

HOW TO ... scan a text (a reading technique)

1 ▶ **Before you scan a text**
Sometimes you want to find some specific words or information in a text quickly. How do you do it? Close your eyes and try to see the words as a picture in your head.

2 ▶ **Find the information**

a *Try to find the words 'Trafalgar Square' in the text on page 58. Just move your eyes very quickly along the text. You should still have a picture of the two words in your head. When you move your eyes past the words, they will suddenly be clear. Try it now. Find the steps the two words are in and take notes on what you find out about Trafalgar Square.*
Now use the same technique and scan pages 58–60 quickly for these: Sherlock Holmes, Madame Tussaud's. *Note down all the information about them.*

b *Now try different ways to scan: move your finger in wavy lines or move your finger along the edge of the text. Scan for and take notes on:*
Henry VIII, Max (Gladstone).

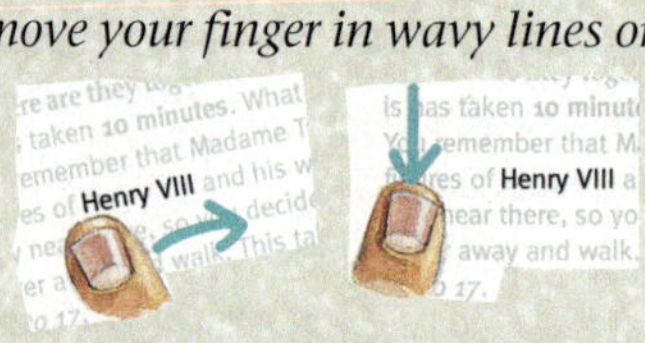

REMEMBER

1 **Before you scan for information,** imagine the word or words you are looking for.
2 **When you scan,** move your eyes quickly down the text. The word or words will 'jump out at you'. Then you can take notes on the information you need.

BRADFORD FESTIVAL

The Mela

Lister Park

Saturday & Sunday 6th & 7th July

Europe's biggest Asian festival – over 100,000 people come every year!
'Mela' means 'bazaar' in India and Pakistan –
so come and enjoy yourself at the most exciting bazaar in the country!
Everyone is welcome!

LISTENING

1 *On the cassette/CD there is a radio interview about the Mela and ethnic minorities in Britain. Before you listen, copy the table on the right into your exercise book.*

2 *Listen and fill in the correct minority names from this list: Indian, Pakistani, Bangladeshi, Afro-Caribbean. (Why aren't these people called foreigners in Britain?) Which minorities are mainly Christian, which Muslim, which Hindu?*

Minority	Main religion	Numbers in Britain	Where from?
?	?	895,000	?
?	?	582,000	?
?	?	198,000	?
?	?	500,000	?

3 *Finish the table. (You may have to listen again.) Then find the places on a world map.*

▶ 1

'I'm sorry, Yasmin,' said Mrs Patel, 'but I have to go and see Aunt Nazreen. I'm afraid she's not well.'
'But, Mum, she lives in Manchester!' Yasmin said. 'What about the English class you teach on Tuesdays?'
'I know. I tried to phone the Centre but I couldn't get through. Would you be a kind girl and go to my class for me? Tell them I'm very sorry, but I can't teach them today. OK?'

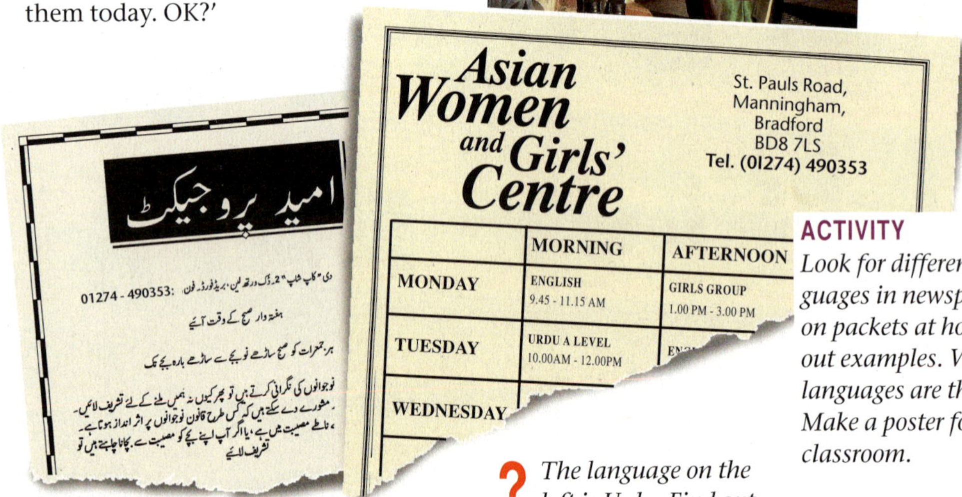

امید پروجیکٹ

01274 - 490353

Asian Women and Girls' Centre

St. Pauls Road,
Manningham,
Bradford
BD8 7LS
Tel. (01274) 490353

	MORNING	AFTERNOON
MONDAY	ENGLISH 9.45 - 11.15 AM	GIRLS GROUP 1.00 PM - 3.00 PM
TUESDAY	URDU A LEVEL 10.00AM - 12.00PM	EN…
WEDNESDAY		

ACTIVITY
Look for different languages in newspapers or on packets at home. Cut out examples. What languages are they? Make a poster for the classroom.

? *The language on the left is Urdu. Find out where it is spoken.*

▶ 2

When Yasmin arrived at the Centre, a woman she knew came out of the office.
'Yasmin!' said Mrs Mir. 'Where's your mother, dear? Her class is waiting.'
'My aunt in Manchester has hurt herself. She fell on the stairs and can hardly move, so Mum had to go and see her.'
'Oh, that's bad news. Well, let's go and tell the class.'

Ten Asian women were sitting in room 3. Some were testing themselves on the new vocabulary. Others were talking in Urdu.
'Ladies,' Mrs Mir began, 'this is Mrs Patel's daughter. Mrs Patel can't come today …'
'Oh,' one of the women said. 'I was beginning to ask myself where she could be …'
'Will we have to look after ourselves then this evening?' another asked.
'Yes,' said Mrs Mir, 'I'm sorry. You'll have to try and teach yourselves this evening.'

FOCUS ON GRAMMAR
Look at A2 again and complete these sentences with the missing reflexive pronouns.

I was teaching …
You were teaching **yourself**.
He asked **himself**.
Aunt Nazreen/**She** has hurt …
The cat/**It** was cleaning **itself**.

We were correcting …
You'll all have to teach …
They were testing …

▶▶▶ NOW YOU
Have you ever taught yourself an instrument or a game? What about your family? Write a few sentences about yourself and some of your family.

I've never tried to teach myself a musical instrument, but I taught myself chess a few years ago.
My sister has …

→ S 5: 1a (pp. 131/132)
→ P 1, 2

▶ 3

TOPS SPECIAL – ALL BRITISH

? *Explain the chart below:*
In Bradford there are more Pakistanis/... than ...
The ... are the largest/smallest ethnic group.

Hi, I'm **Jenny Lim** from Liverpool. My mum and dad are from Hong Kong.
When they arrived in England, they taught themselves English. My mum's English still isn't very good and my Chinese is even worse. So now we're teaching each other: I'm helping her with English and she's helping me with Chinese.
There are a lot of people of Chinese origin in Liverpool, so there's always a big celebration at Chinese New Year. Relatives visit each other – grandparents, aunts, uncles, cousins – everyone.

TOPS MAGAZINE
looks at the minorities in some British cities

BRADFORD
Total population: 457,344
Minorities: 68,299

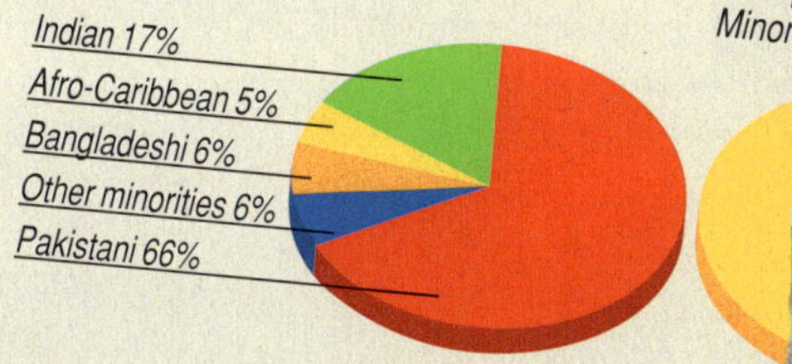

BRIST
Total p
Minorit

My name is **Leroy Bates** and I'm from Bristol. My grandparents came to England from Jamaica in 1946. Grandpa worked as a builder and Grandma made dresses which she designed herself. 'And they were very pretty dresses, too,' she always said. 'Even if I say so myself!'
My dad was born in Bristol. He couldn't get a job when he left school – because he's black, he says – but he's a taxi driver now.

FOCUS ON GRAMMAR

1 *Find the words* themselves *and* each other *in A3. Then match these sentences to the pictures below.*
Mrs Mir and Mrs Khan are testing themselves.
Mrs Mir and Mrs Khan are testing each other.

2 *How can you translate* themselves *and* each other *into German to show the difference?*

→ S 5: 1b, 2 (pp.132/133)
→ P 3, 4, 10

▶▶▶ NOW YOU

a *Are you or any of your friends (or anyone else you know) from a different country? What country do your/their parents come from? What cities or other places do you know in that country? What language(s) do you/they speak? Make notes.*

b *Look at a map and find the countries and cities that you have written down.*

c *Write a few sentences about one person you have made notes on.*

Ennis Gashi is from Albania. He is in my class. He speaks Albanian at home and German at school. He came here with his family two years ago.

▶ 4

UN says killings are racist

Überfall auf nigerianischen Asylbewerber

16-year-old beats up Indian shop assistant

Another black church burns

It's sad to see from the headlines above that there are racists everywhere. But there are also lots of people who are fighting hard against racism – as the brains in this famous anti-racist poster show.

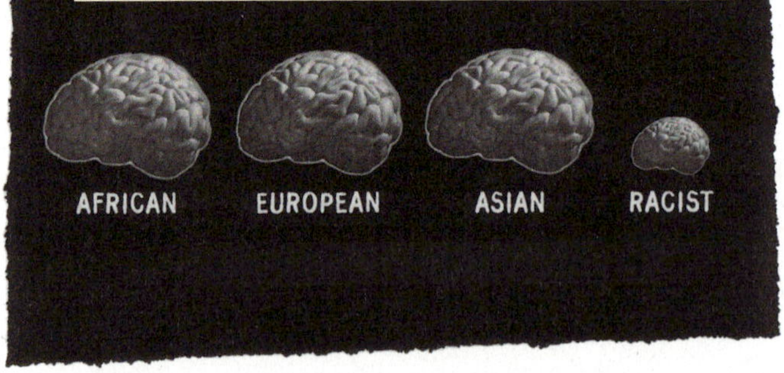

? *What do you think of the poster? Should there be posters like this in Germany? Why?/Why not?*

FOCUS ON WORDS

As you go through this unit, collect words and phrases under headings like **ethnic minorities** (Asian, ...), **language** (talk in Urdu, ...), **eating and drinking** (love Indian food, ...), **festivals** (Mela – the biggest Asian festival, ...). *You can also add words and phrases that you know from earlier units or books 1 and 2.*

→ P 5, 11

▶ 5

As she left the Centre, Yasmin met Tim, a boy from her class.
'Yasmin! Perfect! I was wondering who to ask and now you're here! I can ask you.'
'Hello, Tim. Ask me what?'
'It's the Mela on Saturday. I wanted to know where to go and what to do.'
'Easy: you go to Lister Park and you have fun!' laughed Yasmin.
They walked along together. When they got to Yasmin's street, she started to walk more slowly and became very nervous. 'I don't know how to say this, Tim,' she began, 'but my dad is so strict, he doesn't let me ...'
Tim understood. 'It's OK,' he smiled. 'See you on Saturday!' And he walked away quickly.

FOCUS ON GRAMMAR

1. 'I was wondering who to ask.'
   In this sentence who *is followed by a* to-*infinitive. Find more infinitives after question words in A5.*

   who to ask, ...

2. *Look at the infinitive constructions again. Do you use an infinitive if you want to say the same thing in German?*

→ S 5: 3 (p. 133)
→ P 6
→ How to interest people in something, p. 72

▶ 6

The day of the Mela came. The Patels arrived at Lister Park at about 11.30. They planned to meet some friends at one o'clock.
'Let's listen to one of the bands,' said Mrs Patel. 'It'll be harder to find a good place later.'
'Great idea, Mum,' said Yasmin.
'Well, my dear ladies,' said Mr Patel, 'I'm sorry, but I'm hungry...'
'As usual,' laughed his wife and daughter.
'... I think it would be best to eat first!'

▶ 7

'Hi, Yasmin!' Tim smiled at them. Yasmin blushed. 'Oh, Tim, hi!' she said shyly. 'Mum, Dad, this is Tim Hanson – he's in my class.'
'Hello, Tim,' said Mrs Patel.
Mr Patel turned to his wife: 'Come on, Zahida, Yasmin, we must go.'
'Can I get something for you?' asked Tim.
'No, thank you,' said Mr Patel.
'Don't be silly, dear,' said Mrs Patel. 'You're hungry. Here's some money, Yasmin. You and Tim can go and buy samosas for us all.'
'Tim won't like samosas,' said Mr Patel.
'But I love Indian food, Mr Patel,' said Tim.
Mrs Patel smiled. 'Yasmin, dear, we'll meet you over there in twenty minutes.'
'Thanks, Mum,' said Yasmin.

▶ 8

'Your mum is really nice!' said Tim.
'But my dad is so strict – and so rude! I can't believe how he spoke to you. Sorry, Tim.'
Yasmin was quite upset.
'That's OK. Dads often worry more about their daughters.'
'But Asian dads are the worst!' said Yasmin.
'I don't know. Look at my family,' Tim went on. 'I'm only fourteen and I can stay out till 9 o'clock. My sister is two years older than me. She's going to a party tonight but she still has to be back at 9.30!'
'Anyway, you're right about my mum,' said Yasmin, 'She's the greatest! She often helps me when there's a problem with Dad.'
Tim pointed to a BBC poster: 'A real hero!'
'Right,' Yasmin agreed. 'How long are you staying here, Tim? We're meeting some friends of my parents but they aren't arriving till about one. Shall we go and listen to the bands?'
'Great idea!' said Tim.

→ P 7, 12

▶▶▶ **NOW YOU**

The Patels have got a definite plan. They are meeting friends at the Mela at one o'clock. What plans have you made for tonight/ tomorrow/the weekend/...?

I'm playing football tonight.
I'm visiting my aunt and uncle ...

→ S 5: 5 (p. 134)
→ P 8, 9

❖ **ROLE-PLAY** What do Tim's friends think?

Tim likes Yasmin a lot. But will she go out with him if he asks her? Should he even ask? He isn't sure, so he talks to some friends about it.
Act out the scene. You can use role cards for this activity. Don't forget to write down some expressions that your character might use.

LISTENING Ebony and Ivory

Look at the pictures and listen to the song on the cassette/CD.
What do the singers say about ebony and ivory?
How should we live together?

→ UK Mag, pp. 108/109

1 ▶ Selima's trip to Bradford

Last weekend Yasmin's cousin Selima came to Bradford. Complete the sentences about her trip with reflexive pronouns.

1 'I can look after *myself*, Dad,' Selima said as the train left Birmingham station.
2 'Well, enjoy … and phone us when you arrive,' called Selima's mum.
3 At Bradford station Mr Patel said to …, 'Selima is so tall – she looks like a young lady.'
4 'Don't worry,' Mrs Patel said to her husband. 'The girls can look after …'
5 'I've taught … a song on the guitar,' said Selima at dinner.
6 'Great,' Yasmin said. 'I'll sing and we can record and listen to … later.'
7 But when Yasmin heard … on cassette, she said, 'Yuck, that can't be me!'

2 ▶ Look after yourself!

Mrs Patel is with her sister in Manchester. She is writing a card home. Complete the text. But be careful: sometimes you need reflexive pronouns with the verbs.

Dear Yasmin,

Good news: Aunt Nazreen (feel) a bit better now, but she still can't (move) very well and she can't (wash) yet. As you can (imagine), I haven't got time for a long letter. I'll have to stay till Monday. I can't (remember) when the trains back run, but I will phone you. And how are you, dear? Try to (enjoy). Why (you/not meet) those two nice girls from your class after school and (watch) one of our new videos? Be good and (look after), both of you!

Lots of love from Mum

◆◆ 3 ▶ Each other or themselves?

Partner B: Look at page 119.

Partner A: Look at these pictures. You and your partner have the same pictures, but in a different order. Tell your partner about your pictures and write down the order of your partner's pictures.

A In my picture 1, two kids are taking photos of each other.
B Oh, that's my picture 6. In *my* picture 1, a girl and a boy …

1

take photos of

2

think about

3

laugh at

4

think about

5

laugh at

6

take photos of

4 ▶ Yasmin and Sheila

Read about Yasmin and Sheila. Complete the sentences with each other, themselves *or* them.

1. Yasmin and Sheila are in the same class. They see … in school every day.
2. Sometimes they phone … in the evenings, too. They talk for hours!
3. Yasmin's parents speak Urdu, but Yasmin only speaks English with …
4. Yasmin and Sheila always speak English to …
5. Yasmin and Sheila are interested in Urdu, so they are teaching … the language in their free time.
6. Sometimes it's a bit difficult and Yasmin's mum has to help …
7. They bought … a new CD-ROM in Urdu last weekend.

5 REVISION Happy to hear you

Happy

I'm always happy to hear your voice.
I'm even happier to talk to you.
But I'm happiest to be with you.

a *Write a poem like 'HAPPY'. You can put it in your English album.*
Use one of the following beginnings:

GOOD	BORING	NICE
It's good to …	It must be boring to …	I think it's nice to …
It's even better to …	It must …	…
But it's best to …	…	…

b *Now choose a different adjective and write a poem you like.*
Read out your poems in class. Then collect them and make a poster for the classroom wall.

6 ▶ What should I do?

Yasmin and Tim are both worrying about the Mela on Saturday. Read what they are thinking and report. Then think of another question for each of them and report on those questions, too.

What can I wear to the Mela?
How can I get away from the family?
What should I say to Tim?
Who can I tell about my feelings?
…?

What should I wear?
Who can I ask about Yasmin?
Where can I go with Yasmin?
How much money should I take?
…?

Yasmin is thinking about what to wear to the Mela.
She isn't sure/doesn't know/ is wondering …

Tim … what to wear.
He …

7 **REVISION** Mrs Patel's English class → S 5: 4 (p. 133)

a *Look at the table and add the right names to the statements about the women in Mrs Patel's class.*

1 Mrs Anwar learns more quickly than Mrs … but not as quickly as Mrs …
2 Mrs … works hardest but Mrs … writes fastest.

	learns quickly	speaks clearly	reads well	works hard	writes fast
Mrs Khan	++++	++	+++	+	++++
Mrs Anwar	+++	+++	++	++++	+
Mrs Bhutto	++	++++	+	+++	++
Mrs Ahram	+	+	++++	++	+++

◆◆ **b** *Write five more statements (like the ones in* **a***) for your partner. Can he/she find the right name?*

◆◆ 8 ▶ **Can you play chess with me?**

Partner B: Look at page 120.
Partner A: You are Tim. It is Friday evening and your friend Layla phones you. She wants to play chess with you. Think of what you have planned already and try and arrange a time for a game with her.

LAYLA What are you doing on Saturday morning, Tim? Can you play chess with me?
TIM No, sorry, Layla, I'm meeting …
LAYLA What about the afternoon?
TIM … . But I'm not … in the evening.
LAYLA …
TIM …

❖ 9 **GAME** At the weekend

One pupil says what he/she is doing at the weekend. The next pupil repeats this and then adds what he/she is doing at the weekend. The next pupil repeats the first two, and so on.
When a pupil gets something wrong, he/she is out.

NIELS I'm cooking Sunday lunch this weekend.
NADJA Niels is cooking Sunday lunch this weekend. And I'm playing volleyball.
SAMUEL Niels is cooking Sunday lunch this weekend. Nadja is playing volleyball. And I'm going to the cinema.
GRIT Niels …

'Hi, it's me. Listen. It's David's birthday, so a few million of us are going out for a meal. Are you interested?'

WORD WATCH

10 ▶ One school – many nationalities!

a *The pupils at Eichendorff-Schule in Cologne are of many different origins. Look at the alphabetical list on the right and read the text.*

Report on different nationalities at the school:
The German group is the largest. The second biggest group is the Turkish group – with more than a hundred pupils. The next group – about twenty Italian pupils – is much smaller. There are also twelve Bosnian and eleven Croatian pupils. After that the numbers from other countries are very small. There are four Russian and four Polish children. The school has got three Austrian and three Dutch pupils. And there are two British and two Chinese children.

country	number
Austria	3
Bosnia	12
Britain	2
China	2
Croatia	11
Germany	479
Italy	19
Netherlands	3
Poland	4
Russia	4
Turkey	134

b *Copy the table on the right. Then complete it with the names of the countries from the list and with the adjectives from the report.*

country	adjectives		
	(-ish)	(-n/-an)	(others)
Austria	–	Austrian	–
Bosnia			

c *Now find out about the nationalities at your school. First make a list and then write a report.*

11 TROUBLE SPOT Singular or plural?

a *Put the verbs in brackets in the right form – singular or plural.*

1 When you phone 999, the police always (come) quickly.
2 Bright red clothes (be) very popular this summer.
3 But my red shorts (not fit) me now.
4 These jeans (not be) mine.
5 Good evening. Here (be) the news.
6 People of many different ethnic origins (live) in Britain.
7 Maths (be) my sister's favourite subject.

○ **b** *Translate these sentences into English. Be careful with your singulars and plurals.*

1 Die Treppe ist dort drüben.
2 Diese Hose sieht toll aus.
3 Informationen wie diese erscheinen normalerweise nicht in der Zeitung.
4 Gemüse ist gut für dich.
5 Warum gibt Herr Lange uns immer so viele Hausaufgaben?
6 Ich mag meine Haare, wenn sie kurz sind.
7 Die Polizei hat den Dieb gefasst.

12 ▶ Sounds great, sounds terrible

a *On page 65 Tim says 'I love Indian food' and later Yasmin says 'Asian dads are the worst'. What do you feel about the following?*

fishing • mornings in summer
November • parties
quiet evenings • soft sofas
sport • Sundays • tidy bedrooms
yellow

Put them in a table like this:

+	–
…	…

◆◆ **b** *Compare your own answers with your partner's. Try to explain the differences.*

A I really hate November because it's so dark and rainy.
B Well, I always feel good in November because my birthday is on the 24th.

Look at the title of the text. Then scan the interview on this page for the same words. Find out why Meera Syal felt that way.

'I Felt like a Monster'

Meera Syal is an actress and a writer. She was born and grew up in a village in the English Midlands. She went to the village school. In fact, Meera had an ordinary English childhood. There was only one thing that was special about the Syal family – they were the only Asian family in the village. Their faces were the only faces that weren't white.

Barbara Derkow Disselbeck interviewed Meera Syal for English G 2000.

ENGLISH G *When did your parents come to England, Meera?*

MEERA They came in 1960, from Delhi, the capital of India.

ENGLISH G *Did they speak English then?*

MEERA Oh, yes, they spoke English well. But their first language is Punjabi.

ENGLISH G What language did you speak at home?

MEERA English. My first language is English.

ENGLISH G *Do you speak Punjabi, too?*

MEERA Yes. I had to learn Punjabi when I was a bit older. All my family in India speak Punjabi.

ENGLISH G *Have you ever been to India?*

MEERA Yes, lots of times.

ENGLISH G *When was your first visit?*

MEERA When I was four years old. I remember the heat and the noise. And after cold, grey England it was so exciting to live outside almost all the time!

ENGLISH G *And the language?*

MEERA Punjabi! I couldn't speak a word at that time, but it was fine. My cousins spoke Punjabi, I only spoke English but … well, we understood each other – kids always do!

ENGLISH G *Back in England, you started school.*

MEERA Yes, and I loved it.

ENGLISH G *Lots of kids hate school! Why did you love it?*

MEERA Well, firstly my mum was a teacher. She really made it fun to learn. And secondly my parents, like all Asian parents, always said: 'Meera, education is a gift. Don't throw it away!' So I thought of school as a kind of present!

ENGLISH G *Were there any problems?*

MEERA Yes, sometimes, of course. I remember I cut myself on a bottle once and there was blood. The whole class came and looked. They couldn't believe my blood was red, just like theirs! I felt like a monster.

ENGLISH G *Now you're a famous actress and writer. How did that happen?*

MEERA I studied English and Drama at university. In my last year I did a one-woman show. Someone saw it and said, 'You're good: come and be an actress.' I was lucky.

ENGLISH G *And soon you were acting in London's West End theatres and on TV.*

MEERA Yes.

ENGLISH G *And then you started to write.*

MEERA Yes. I wrote a film script about Asian women in this country.

ENGLISH G *'Bhaji on the Beach'.*

MEERA That's right.

ENGLISH G *It was a wonderful film and it got lots of international prizes. And now you've written your first book, 'Anita and Me'.*

MEERA It's about Meena Kumar, an Indian girl who grows up in a village near Wolverhampton.

ENGLISH G *Is there a bit of Meera Syal in Meena Kumar?*

MEERA Oh, a lot!

ENGLISH G *Meera Syal, thank you for the interview.*

Here is an extract from the book Anita and Me. *Anita, a white girl, is Meena's friend. When Anita's mother runs away with another man, Meena's parents invite Anita and her sister, Tracey, to dinner.*

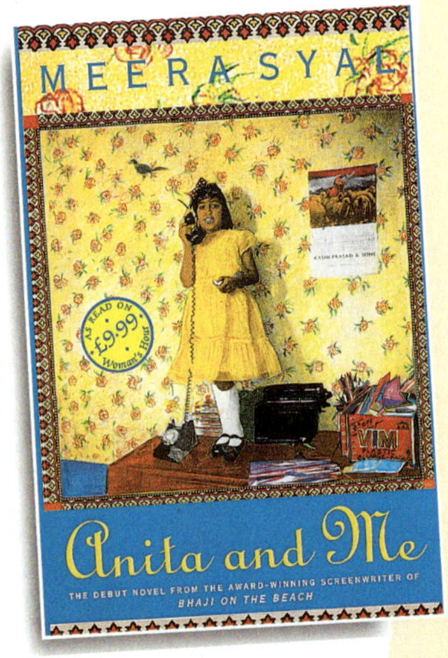

Anita arrived alone. 'Tracey didn't want to come,' was the first thing she said. 'Oh, that's OK, darling,' said mama. Papa took one of the place settings from the table. We never sat at the table with Indian guests. But tonight I told mama, 'Don't run to and from the kitchen like you usually do. Why don't we all sit and talk – like you're supposed to do at dinners?'

I knew Anita well enough but even I was surprised that she didn't show her feelings about her mother. She watched *Top of the Pops*. Papa tried to talk to her but didn't want to say anything about mothers. 'So, Anita ... um, how's school?' Anita turned up the volume of the TV. 'Your paren... your father, does he take you to school or do you go by bus?' Anita yawned and took another crisp.

Then she saw the dishes of food in front of her on the table. 'What's that?' she asked, as if there was a sheep's head on her plate. 'Oh that's mattar-paneer,' mama said proudly. 'A sort of Indian cheese, and those are peas ...'

'Cheese and peas?' said Anita. 'Together?'

'Well,' mama went on quickly. 'This is chicken curry. You have had chicken before, haven't you?'

'What's that stuff round it?'

'Um, just gravy, you know, tomatoes, onions, garlic ...'

'Chicken with tomatoes? What's garlic?'

'Don't you worry!' papa said quickly. 'We've also got fish fingers and chips. Is tomato ketchup too dangerous for you?'

Adapted from: *Anita and Me* by Meera Syal

WORKING WITH THE TEXT

1 ▶ Meera Syal

a *Read the interview again and fill in the missing information. Write notes only.*

Name: *Meera Syal*	Education: *?*
Place of birth: *?*	Languages: *?*
Information about parents: *?*	Work: *?*

◆◆ **b** *If you could interview Meera Syal, what other questions would you like to ask her? Here are some ideas.*

- plays/... she has been in?
- more Indian or more British?
- what work now?
- ...

2 ▶ 'Anita and Me'

1 *What things show you that Meena would be happier if her family was more like an ordinary English family?*
2 *How do you know that Anita doesn't want to talk to Meena's father?*
3 *Why do you think Anita asks questions about the food at Meena's house?*
4 *Is Meena's father angry or is he trying to be funny when he asks Anita if tomato ketchup is too dangerous for her? What do you think?*

3 ▶ Differences

What differences between people of Asian origin and other British people are mentioned in the interview and the book extract?

4 ▶ Beyond the text

1 *Do you think education is a gift? Say why or why not.*
2 *Collect names/examples of food from other countries that we can buy in Germany. What is your favourite?*

HOW TO ... interest people in something

1 READING 'You must come'

a *How can you make someone go to a great street festival, read a book you like or see a film you loved? Look again at the poster for the Mela on page 61 and read what the girl on the right says.*

Oh, you must come, Lucy. It's the best street festival ever! And there's a special costume event on Saturday, with fantastic prizes for the best costume. And they've got some really good live bands, too – *Red Hot* and some others. You'll love it, Lucy. Come on, please say you'll come!

b *What facts do the poster and the girl give about the festivals?*

c *What words and phrases do they use to make the festivals sound interesting?*

d *What do you notice about the adjectives?*

e *How do the poster and the girl persuade people to come to the festivals?*

2 LISTENING 'I couldn't put it down'

a *Listen to the cassette/CD. What are the people talking about?*
The first speaker is talking about ...

◆◆ **b** *Below are some phrases the boy on the cassette/CD uses. Work with a partner and put them in the right part of the table on the right.*

book of ghost stories
I couldn't put it down
the scariest story I've ever read
family gets lost in a snowstorm
you just have to read it

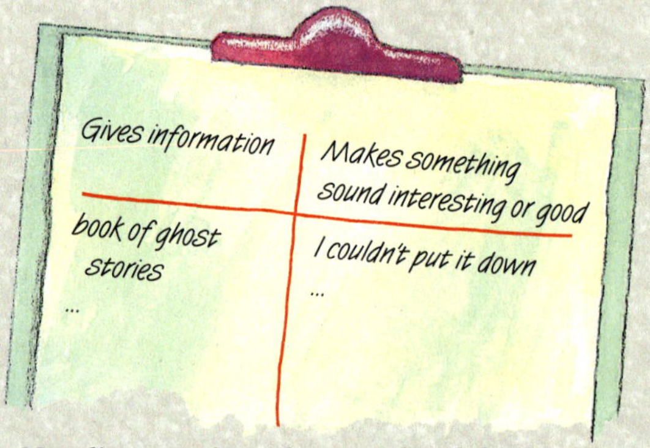

Now listen again to the second and third speakers and add more words and phrases to the table. (Finally, add phrases from **1***).*

3 WRITING AND SPEAKING Make it sound great!

a *Imagine you want to interest your class in a film you have seen, a CD you like, a new boutique, a holiday area, a great video game, etc.*
Make notes on the information you want to give.

b *Choose the right words and phrases that will make it sound great. (Look at your list from* **2b** *again.)*

c *Now write your text. Check it carefully. Is there enough information? Will people be interested?*

d *Record your text on cassette. Try and read it in different ways. Does it sound good?*

e *Learn your text by heart, then try it on the class.*

REMEMBER

1. If you want to interest people in something, say what is good about it. Use positive adjectives, superlatives and words like *so, really, ever,* etc.
2. Mention the things that will interest people.
3. Use phrases like *come and enjoy, don't miss, you'll love,* etc.
4. Show how much you like it when you speak.

UNIT 6 When the Romans Ruled Britannia

Archaeologists in the 'hot room' of some Roman baths in London. The baths were built about 70 AD. Remains like these can tell us a lot about everyday life in Roman Britain.

1 *Match these words to the photos of the objects.*

amphora • board-game • comb • hairpins
knives and spoons • oil-lamp • Roman coin

2 *Maybe you already know something about the Romans from your History lessons. Imagine that the objects on this page all belonged to a family in Roman Britain. What do the objects tell you about their lives? Try and describe some of them.*

The objects tell us that people in Roman Britain used/had/cut/played/liked/wore/looked/ ...

▶ 1

Time runs out for Roman site

TIME has run out for archaeologists at a Roman site on the new B2011 road near Dover. Work on the road starts again today.

'Unfortunately we didn't have much time. But we hope we got everything valuable,' said Dr Trisha Willis.

Work on the B2011 was stopped when the grave of a young girl from Roman Britain was dug up. In the three months

▶ 2

Melissa pointed at the B2011. 'Did your mum have to stop work on the Roman site?' she asked.

'Yes,' Mark answered. 'The bulldozers started and that was the end of it. They didn't find much anyway. Just an old grave.'

Melissa loved old things. 'I wish my mother had an exciting job like that!'

'Mum just looks through 1000-year-old rubbish dumps all day long,' said Mark. 'Do you call that exciting?'

They continued without a word until Melissa suddenly said, 'Maybe they didn't find everything.' Then, before Mark could stop her, she climbed over the fence.

→ P 1, 2, 3

▶ 3

Melissa came back with an old tile.

MELISSA I've found something.
MARK Oh, it's a tile, isn't it?
MELISSA Yes, and it looks really old, doesn't it? Look at the letters on it. Maybe it's valuable. You could ask your mum.
MARK It can't be very valuable, can it? If it was, it wouldn't still be there.
MELISSA Mark, please! You will show it to your mum, won't you? Promise!
MARK OK. Or, no, *you* show it to her. She'll be at the museum tomorrow.

▶ 4

The next morning, at the *White Cliffs Experience* museum in Dover, Melissa showed her tile to the woman at the desk.

WOMAN Well, it looks like a tile from the *Classis Britannica*.
MELISSA CLBR, of course! The Roman fleet in Britain. It was in Dover, wasn't it?
WOMAN Yes, it was. But I'm not an expert. I don't know if this tile is genuine.
MELISSA Dr Willis is here today, isn't she?
WOMAN Yes, she is. I can show it to her. Why don't you go and look at the *Roman Encounters* while you're waiting?

▶▶▶ NOW YOU

Write down four or five things you think are true about other pupils in your class. Then find out if you were right.

Jan, you hate cats, don't you? – Yes, I do. / No, I don't.
Silvia, your brother can't play the piano, can he?
– No, he can't. But he can play ... / Oh yes, he can.

→ P 4, 5

FOCUS ON GRAMMAR Revision

1 *Find the question tags ('Frageanhängsel') in A3 and A4. Then make a table like this.*

Main clause	*Question tag*
it's ...	*isn't it?*
it looks ...	...

2 *How do you form question tags? What are the differences between the main clause verb and the question tag verb?*

3 *Why do you think people use question tags in a conversation? How do we express the same thing in German?*

→ S 6: 1 (pp. 134/135)

▶ 5

Before she went into the museum, Melissa looked at some books about life in Roman Britain in the museum shop.

? *What are the modern names of the Roman towns on the map?*

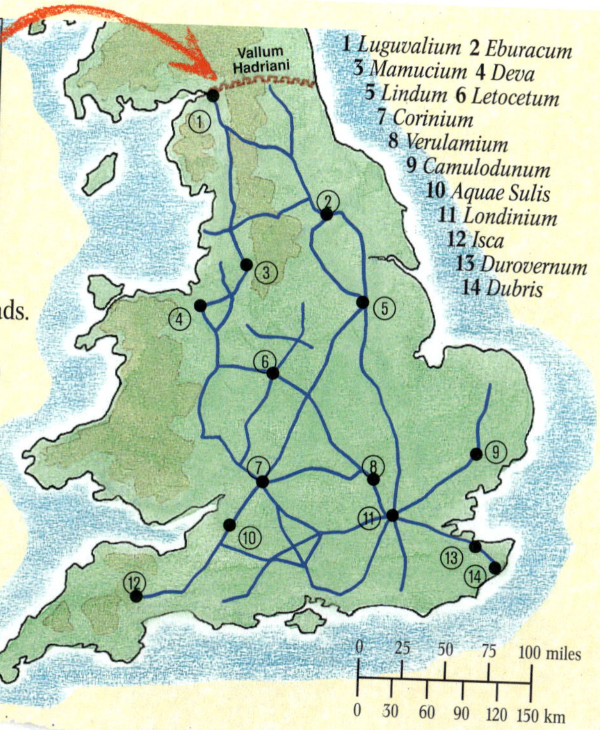

ROMAN ROADS

The Romans were famous for their roads. While they were in Britannia (from 43 AD to 410 AD), they built over 6000 miles of them from the south right up to Hadrian's Wall, where the Roman Empire ended. Soldiers could move quickly along these roads when there was trouble with the Celtic tribes. Roman roads were built so well that they lasted for a very long time. Many modern roads still follow the same routes today.

▶ 6

WHAT'S COOKING?

Roman Britons cooked food in pots over charcoal fires. Other food like bread was baked in charcoal ovens.
From the south of France and Spain, the Romans brought fish sauce and olive oil to Britain. These were used a lot and were kept in amphoras.

A Roman kitchen

AT THE BATHS

Visitors met friends and after exercise sat or took a bath in the 'warm room'. Next came the 'hot room' where they cleaned themselves and relaxed in the hot bath. After that they jumped into the cold bath. At the end of their visit oils and perfumes were rubbed into their skin.

The Roman Baths at Aquae Sulis (Bath)

→ How to listen for information, p. 85

▶ 7
From the shop Melissa went into the Roman street in *Roman Encounters*.

ROMAN ENCOUNTERS

The Roman street, with buildings on one side and a harbour on the other, is a fantastic interactive area that explains all about everyday life in Roman Dover (*Dubris*). Here you can:

- BUILD part of a Roman road or building.
- LOAD a ship in Dubris harbour.
- BECOME a slave on a Roman ship.
- TRY ON a Roman costume.
- DISCOVER what Romans used when they were ill.
- ENTER a Roman house and see how Romans lived and what they ate.
- SEE the real remains of the *Classis Britannica* fort.
- WATCH AND LISTEN TO some of the people at Dubris harbour.

→ P6

FOCUS ON WORDS

Collect words and phrases that can help you to talk about everyday life in Roman times and today. Put them in groups (*e.g.* **eating and drinking:** bake bread in charcoal ovens, …; **free time:** meet at the baths, …).
You can add more words and phrases later in the unit.

▶▶▶ NOW YOU

Do you wish you were a Roman Briton? Compare your everyday life to that of Roman Britons. Talk about what is the same/different and how their lives were better/worse/more exciting/less exciting/ … than yours.

▶ 8

Melissa enjoyed doing the activities in the Roman street. Then she continued walking around the museum. She imagined meeting some of the Roman Britons at Dover harbour. Suddenly a voice interrupted her dreams.

DR WILLIS Melissa! So *you* found this tile! Listen, it's genuine. Can you show me exactly where you found it?

MELISSA Yes, of course.

▶ 9

Four more weeks at Roman site

'**FINDING** an old Roman tile at the site of a new road was the start of an adventure,' said Melissa Wells. 'When I heard that the tile was genuine, I wanted to help. Organizing a demonstration was my friend Mark's idea.'
When road workers arrived at the site on Monday, a hundred children and their teachers were already there. The road workers were unhappy. But after they discussed things, building stopped and digging started again. The archaeologists have four weeks before the bulldozers return.

→ P 13

❖ **ROLE-PLAY** How did Melissa do it?

How do you think Melissa interested Mark, her classmates and teachers in her old tile? With your partner, act out their conversation. You can use role cards for this activity.

FOCUS ON GRAMMAR

1 *Write down each -ing form in A8 together with the word before it, e.g. enjoyed doing. What kind of word can come before an -ing form?*

2 *The -ing forms in A8 and A9 are called gerunds. A gerund can be the subject or the object of a sentence. Find examples in A8 and A9.* → P 7, 8, 9, 10

3 *When you have read A10, collect the gerunds and write down each of them with the word before it. What kind of word comes before the gerunds in A10?*

4 *Can you translate the sentences with gerunds from A8, A9 and A10 into German?*

→ S 6: 2 (pp. 136/137)

▶ 10

The next day Dr Willis thanked Melissa and Mark for organizing the demonstration.
'We've got a good chance of finding more important remains now,' she said. 'So here's a book about the Romans for you.'

▶▶▶ NOW YOU

Write about something you enjoyed doing in the past. Explain why you liked doing it. Try and use at least three verbs/phrases + gerund.

When I was ten, I really enjoyed fishing.
I liked going to the river in good or bad weather.
After a few months I was quite good at finding the right places for the best fish.

→ S 6: 2e (p. 137)
→ P 11, 12, 14, 15
→ UK Mag, pp. 110 – 115

GIRLS HAD IT HARDER!

A Roman girl was ready for marriage when she was 14. Who said so? Her father. What if she wasn't interested in getting married yet? Bad luck. A husband was chosen for her. Who by? Her father. What happened if she didn't like the idea of marrying this man? She had to marry him anyway.

ROMAN MATHS

The Romans didn't have the number 0. That made maths really difficult. If you aren't very good at doing sums, just look at this Roman sum:

LXXXVIII + XII = C.

Now do you see how lucky you are!?

1 **REVISION** Roman remains → S 1: 1 (p. 121); S 4: 1 (pp. 129/130)

Complete the sentences about the discovery of some Roman remains. The beginning of each sentence is given. Some sentences are active and some are passive. Be careful with the tenses.

1 discover – Roman remains – at – farm – near Cirencester
Roman remains have been discovered ...
2 farmer – take – archaeologists – to – site
Archaeologists were ...
3 farmer – take – some Roman coins – to – Corinium Museum – last week
The farmer ...

4 children – dig up – coins – in – potato field
The coins ...
5 archaeologists – work – in – field – all weekend
The archaeologists ...
6 find – 15 more objects
15 ...
7 put – objects – in – child's grave – in about 150 AD
The objects ...
8 archaeologists – now – believe – remains – part of – small Roman hotel
The archaeologists ...
9 build – hotel – in about 120 AD
The hotel ...

❖ 2 **REVISION** Quiz questions

a *Think of two questions with* do, does *or* did *and write them on yellow cards. Then write the answers on blue cards.*

b *Put all the yellow cards in one box and all the blue cards in another. Then each pupil in the class takes two yellow cards and two blue ones. Now ask your questions until you find the people who have the right answers.*

❖ 3 **REVISION** True or false?

a *On a piece of paper write five statements with* don't *or* didn't *about yourself. Four should be true and one should be false.*

I didn't grow up in Erfurt.
I don't eat meat.
I don't play football.
I didn't get a computer for Christmas.
I didn't get a 1 in the last English test.

b *Make groups and give your piece of paper to the others in your group. They must now talk to each other and decide which statement is false. Did they get it right?*

4 ▶ **At the Roman site**

Complete the conversation. Add the right question tags.

MELISSA Your mum is a real expert, ...?
MARK I suppose she is.
MELISSA She'll know how valuable the tile is, ...?
MARK Maybe.
MELISSA It could be *very* valuable, ...?
MARK Maybe.
MELISSA You aren't very interested in history, ...?
MARK You think you know a lot about me, ...?

5 ▶ That's right, isn't it?

a *In your exercise book complete the following sentences with statements you think are true.*

1 …, don't they?
2 …, weren't there?
3 …, haven't they?
4 …, can't you?
5 …, is it?
6 …, didn't we?
7 …, will she?
8 …, do you?

◆◆ **b** *Ask your partner if he/she agrees with what you have written.*

YOU Dolphins eat fish, don't they?
PARTNER Yes, of course they do. / I don't know.
YOU There were too many questions in the test last week, weren't there?
PARTNER Yes, there were. I agree.

6 LISTENING At Dubris harbour

a *In the* White Cliffs Experience *museum Melissa watched a video about some people at Dubris harbour in 150 AD.*
Listen to the cassette/CD and match the names to the jobs and problems.

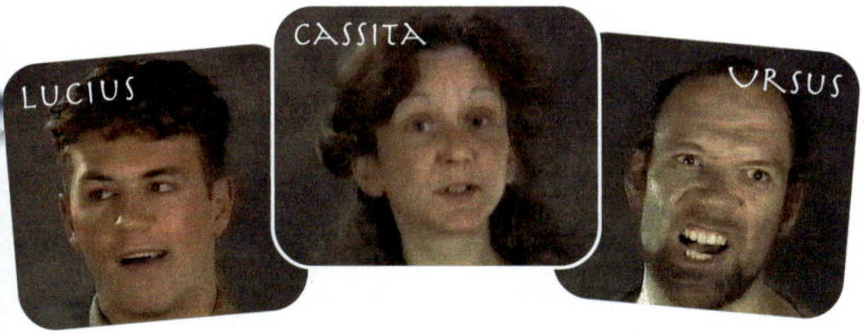

Jobs	Problems
soldier slave farmer	Life is hard. The old life is disappearing. Life is boring.

b *Listen again. What do Lucius, Cassita and Ursus think or feel about the following?*

Lucius	– the party tonight – Dubris – the game 'Soldiers' – the kid at the baths
Cassita	– the village – the future of Celtic life and the Celtic language – young people
Ursus	– the mines – his brother – his life now – his future

◆◆ 7 ▶ I know my partner

a *Ask your partner what he/she likes doing.*

YOU Do you like …ing?
PARTNER Yes, I do. / No, I don't.

cook • dance • do homework
go to museums • learn about history
travel by boat • get up early
watch films in English • … • …

b *Now make a window and fill it in.*

	My partner (=Lisa) likes	My partner (=Lisa) doesn't like
I like	Lisa and I like …	I like … but Lisa doesn't like …
I don't like	I don't like … but Lisa likes …	Lisa and I don't like …

❖ 8 ▶ How much can you remember?

How long can you make the sentences? Continue one sentence until a pupil gets something wrong. Then start again with the next sentence.

1 ANNA At the weekend I enjoy getting up late.
PAUL At the weekend Anna enjoys getting up late and I enjoy watching TV.
NORA At the weekend Anna enjoys getting up late, Paul enjoys watching TV and I enjoy …
KEREM At the weekend Anna …

2 In our English lessons I like …
3 In our English lessons I hate …
4 Sometimes I can't stop …
5 I never like …

◆◆ 9 ▶ What do YOU think?

Compare and discuss these things. Give reasons. Use the adjectives in brackets.

1 work in a group – work alone (good)
2 go on holiday with parents – go on holiday with friends (interesting)
3 use a fax machine – make a telephone call (easy)
4 send an e-mail – send a letter (cheap)
5 watch a film on TV – go to the cinema (nice)
6 eat salad – drink milk (healthy)

A I think working in a group is better than working alone. It's more fun. What do you think?
B Well, I don't agree. Working alone is better because no one interrupts you.

'He's not good at flying!'

10 ▶ A Briton in old York

Complete the text with the gerund or the to-infinitive of the verbs in brackets.

Usk didn't enjoy *going* to school in Eburacum. He tried hard (follow) the lessons but the teacher only spoke Latin, and Usk hated (learn) Latin. The other boys were Britons, too, and they never stopped (talk). Many of them didn't want (learn) anything. Usk sat in the classroom and imagined (ride) over the hills or (watch) the young girls at the market. 'Why do I have (come) here every day?' he thought. But he knew. 'You must promise (do) well at school,' his parents always said. 'That's your only chance of a better life if you're a Briton.'

11 ▶ About yourself

Finish the following sentences. Use gerunds.

1 I really love …
2 I'm very interested in …
3 I'm good at/not very good at …
4 I find … much easier than …
5 I often dream of …
6 I'm (sometimes) afraid of …

○ ❖ 12 PROJECT Signs of the past

Many remains from the past have been found in Britain. What remains have been found in your part of Germany? Find out who lived there, how they lived, etc. Look at page 25 (project 1) again and present information in English for visitors interested in the history of your area. Don't forget photos, pictures, maps, etc. Here are some ideas:

History

BC/AD	What happened ?
…	…
…	…

A museum
- where?
- opening times
- price
- what can you see?
- what can you do?
- …

An old site
- what?
- where?
- opening times
- how old?
- when discovered?
- …

Everyday life
- houses
- food and cooking
- farms
- festivals
- religion
- language
- …

Remains
- art
- graves
- personal objects
- walls and stones
- objects from houses

WORD WATCH

13 WORD BUILDING The prefix *un-*

a *You have already learned about some suffixes like* -er, -ness, -tion. *English also makes new words with prefixes like* un-, *e.g.* unhappy, unpack. *How does* un- *change the meaning of* happy *and* pack? *Now say what the following words mean (in English or German).*

unfriendly • unhealthy
unimportant • unload • unlucky
untidy • unusual

b *Complete the sentences with words from* **a**.

1 Slaves in Britain often had an … life, with bad food, too much work and cold rooms.
2 They had to … the ships at Dubris harbour.
3 Richborough was a big fort in Roman times but it's an … little place now.
4 The first Romans in Britain got an … welcome from the Celtic tribes.
5 The Britons found Roman towns very … at first.

14 ▶ Say it differently

Replace the underlined words with ones that mean the same.

1 When will the bulldozers <u>come back</u>?
2 At the *White Cliffs Experience* you can <u>go into</u> a Roman house.
3 Dr Willis <u>said 'thank you' to</u> Melissa.
4 Green Street? Just <u>drive on</u> along this road.
5 Before I could finish my question, Dennis <u>stopped me and said something</u>.
6 This amphora was <u>found in the ground</u> near Hadrian's Wall.

'Can't we do something other than Hadrian's Wall?'

15 ▶ Things from another world

a *You are an archaeologist in the future. You are digging things up from the time around 2000 AD. What do you find? Write down at least three objects under each of the following headings:* **eating and drinking, school, free time, home, communication.**

❖ **b** *Now work in groups. Imagine you are going to send a spaceship to another planet. Which seven objects will you put in the spaceship to tell aliens about the everyday life of young people today? Write the names of your objects on cards or draw them. Give the cards to another group.*

You can use these expressions when you talk to your group:
I think we should put a … in because …
… are very important to me, so let's …
Everyone uses … so we need …
No, a …/that won't tell the aliens much.
What about a …?

❖ **c** *Now you are the aliens. You have just found the spaceship. What do the objects on the cards tell you? Talk about them in your group and then write your ideas down.*

You can use these expressions when you talk to your group:
The … shows/tells us that they use/have …
They might … because …
If they have …, then they must/will …
Only people who can … could … a …
They may … if they …

How do you think this hairpin got to Hadrian's Wall?

The Golden Hairpin

One sunny morning Marcus Flavius rode past Nipius Ascanius's lead mine and into the forest along a path he did not know. He loved riding in the hills west of Deva. The countryside was always so quiet and beautiful. But this morning Marcus soon felt cold in the dark forest. He thought of the warm baths in Deva and decided to go back.

Suddenly he noticed something behind the trees. It was another mine. 'Why is it so carefully hidden?' he thought to himself, and then he heard a noise. Two men, one fat and one thin, were driving a cart full of stones out of the mine. Marcus couldn't see very well but he was sure that the fat one was Nipius Ascanius, the richest man in Deva and – it was said – the most dangerous. 'I should leave before they see me,' Marcus thought. But as he was riding away, his horse kicked a stone. The two men looked up, and then Nipius Ascanius shouted his name: 'Marcus Flavius!' Marcus didn't stop but rode away as fast as he could.

Marcus had a rich uncle in Eburacum. And although he was only 20, he ran a farm in Deva for his uncle. Marcus enjoyed being a farmer. All the work was done by slaves so he had lots of time for riding and the baths. But today there was no chance of spending the afternoon there. Nipius Ascanius had a secret lead mine in the hills. Mines had to pay taxes to the Empire but this one did not, Marcus was sure. That was why it was hidden in the forest. 'Nipius Ascanius won't be pleased that I've discovered his secret,' Marcus thought. 'It might be a good idea to visit my uncle in Eburacum.'

At the farm his slaves packed a bag for him and he was soon ready to leave. He opened the door and was walking out just as two large men came into the garden from the road. They did not look very friendly.

'I'm Otho,' began the first. 'And I'm Rautio,' finished the second. 'Nipius wants to see you.'

'Nipius?' Marcus asked.

'Nipius Ascanius,' said Otho.

'Oh, Nipius Ascanius. Well, I'm sorry,' said Marcus, 'but tell him I'm terribly busy, so ...'

'Now,' interrupted Rautio. 'He wants to see you now.'

'And he hates waiting,' added Otho.

'You were in the wrong place at the wrong time, Marcus Flavius, weren't you?' Nipius Ascanius had a cold voice, as cold as ice.

'But I won't tell anyone about the mine. I really won't,' Marcus said.

'You won't get the chance of telling anyone, Marcus Flavius. You see, you're going on a journey – to Luguvalium. The Selgovae live near there, on the other side of Hadrian's Wall. That's why the wall was built. It's best to keep tribes like the Selgovae out of the Empire. You'll see that when you're a Selgovae slave. It's funny, but their slaves must like it there – they never come back.'

Serena was bored and she was missing Rome. Why did she have to spend three months in cold, wet Britannia? She still couldn't understand why her father loved this country. He was the commander of the VIth Legion at Eburacum and talked of building a villa in Britannia and staying there.

Serena was returning to Eburacum from Mamucium, where some friends of her father had a villa. With her were her slave,

Juvena, and six soldiers. She wasn't allowed to go anywhere in this country without six soldiers. She was too young, her father said. She hated having the soldiers with her all the time. She always felt that they were watching her.

They arrived at a small *mansio* where they were going to stay the night. In her room Serena pulled the golden hairpin out of her long, dark hair. It was a present from Gaius, the man she was getting married to next year. Her father's idea. Gaius was a senator's son – rich, handsome and … boring. Serena couldn't imagine living with him. It would be like living with a stone.

Outside the *mansio*, Marcus Flavius was cold and frightened. He was in a covered cart next to some lead ingots. His legs were tied to the cart. There was something in his mouth so he couldn't shout for help. His arms were tied too.

But he could just move his hands, and that gave him an idea. He looked at the ingots. Lead was very soft. Now, if he found something hard, perhaps he could write a message on one of the ingots and push it out of the cart.

Serena was up early and looked out of the window. A covered cart with NIP.ASC. on the side started moving onto the road. As it did, something dark fell out of the back. 'What's that?' thought Serena and went out into the cold morning air to see. Juvena and one of the soldiers began to follow her. She said, 'I'll only be out there for a second.' The slave and the soldier looked at each other but stayed inside.

Serena soon found the dark object. It was a lead ingot. 'Not very interesting,' she thought. But then she saw some writing on the side. She picked up the ingot and read the message again and again.

I have been kidnapped. They are taking me to Luguvalium at Hadrian's Wall.
Marcus Flavius

Could it be true or was it just a joke? 'Well,' she thought, 'joke or not, it's more exciting than going back to Eburacum.' 'We're going to Luguvalium,' she told Juvena and the soldiers. 'I want to see Hadrian's Wall.'

Two days later they arrived at the *mansio* in Luguvalium. When everyone was sleeping, Serena quietly left her room and went outside. She walked quickly through the night. She did not notice that someone was following her. Soon she found the cart with NIP.ASC. on the side and looked carefully inside. A handsome young man was sleeping next to some lead ingots. She climbed inside and touched his blond hair. He woke up. Marcus thought he was dreaming. A goddess with long black hair said, 'Ssshhh!' Then she whispered: 'Marcus Flavius.'

'It must be a goddess,' he thought. 'She knows my name.'

The goddess went on, 'I found the ingot with your message. I'll be back with help soon.' Then she put her soft white hand on the side of his face and climbed out of the cart.

Outside, Otho and Rautio were waiting. Otho carried Serena back into the cart. Rautio went to the horses at the front, and in a moment the cart was moving east along the wall. When it disappeared, the thin figure of Juvena came out from behind a tree.

Marcus could see now that the goddess was a girl of about 16. Otho held his big, fat hand across her mouth. There were tears in her dark eyes but a fire burned there too. The cart stopped and Rautio shouted, 'We're there! I'm going up on the wall. Our friends should be on the other side.'

'Right,' Otho said to Serena, and he started pulling her out of the cart. When they were standing outside, Serena's hand suddenly went up to her dark hair. She pulled out Gaius's golden hairpin and, before Otho could stop her, stabbed him in the arm. Otho screamed. A quarter of a mile away, Juvena and the soldiers heard the sound in the quiet night and started riding towards it. Rautio came down from the wall. 'What's all the noise?' he whispered.

'The Selgovae aren't here yet. We'll have to wait.' But before he could get back into the cart, they all heard the sound of horses.

Two soldiers drove the cart back to Luguvalium with Otho and Rautio in the back. Juvena and the others waited with the horses as Serena and Marcus walked under the full moon on Hadrian's Wall.

'Why did Otho suddenly scream like that?' asked Marcus.

Serena's eyes laughed. 'I stabbed him with my hairpin.'

'But you're not wearing a hairpin.'

'Otho threw it away after I stabbed him,' Serena explained.

'Shall I look for it?'

'No, don't worry about it,' she answered. 'It was a present from the man I'm going to ... – from a friend in Rome. But I never really liked it. And who knows when I'll go back to Rome? Britannia is so much more exciting. Come on, you can tell me all about yourself on the way back to Eburacum.'

Then she took Marcus by the hand. As they walked down the stairs, hand in hand, she noticed he was shaking.

WORKING WITH THE TEXT

1 ▶ Who was it?

Choose the right characters from the list.

Juvena • Marcus
Otho and Rautio • Serena

Who ...

1 ... found a secret lead mine?
2 ... kidnapped Marcus?
3 ... wrote a message on a lead ingot?
4 ... found the lead ingot and looked for Marcus?
5 ... found Marcus but was caught by Otho and Rautio?
6 ... saw what happened and went for help?
7 ... stabbed Otho in the arm?
8 ... heard Otho's cry and saved Marcus and Serena?

◆◆ 2 ▶ The characters and places

Someone has started a diagram of the characters and places in The Golden Hairpin. *Copy it and complete it, or draw your own diagram. Then show it to your partner and talk to him/her about the characters and places in the story.*

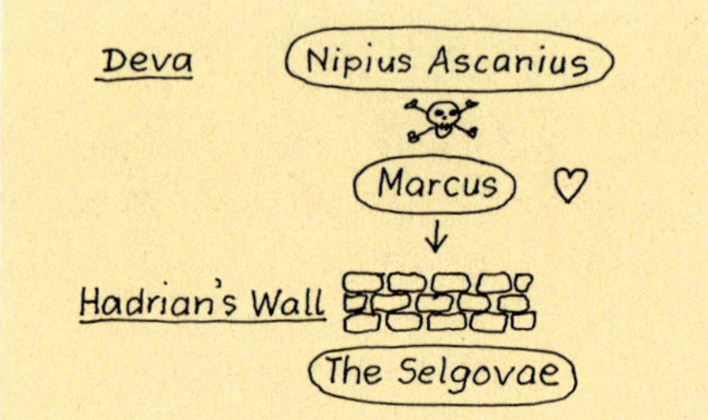

◆◆ 3 ▶ Now you write

Imagine what Marcus and Serena talked about on their journey back to Eburacum. Think about their characters first. Then write some of their conversation and act it for the class. Perhaps they talked about:

- where they live and what they think about their lives there
- their families/homes/friends
- how they spend their free time
- getting married
- ...

HOW TO ... listen for information

1 ▶ **Before you listen**
When you visit an old Roman site, you can often get audio tours about the place. You are going to listen to an audio tour of the Roman baths at **Wall**, *or* **Letocetum**, *as the Romans called it.*
You will find it easier to follow the tour if you prepare for listening. Look at the picture on the right. Remember what you already know about Roman baths. What do you think you will find out from the tour? Collect questions in class.

Inside the Letocetum bathhouse (in about 200 AD)

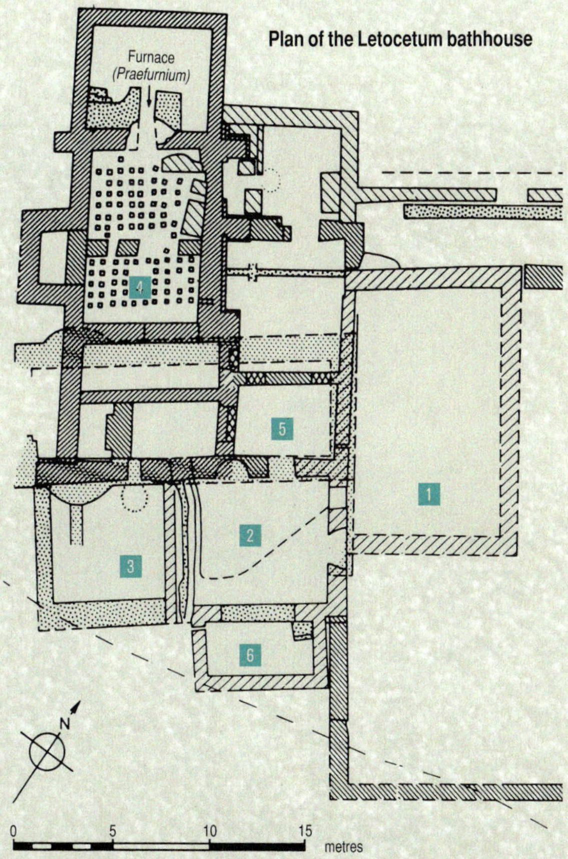

Plan of the Letocetum bathhouse

2 **LISTENING** An audio tour

a *Look at the plan of the bathhouse and follow the route of the audio tour. Try and 'see' the baths in your mind. What rooms do you hear about? Don't worry if you don't understand everything.*
Does the tour answer any of the questions you collected in **1**?

b *Listen again, for detail this time. What does the Roman soldier Gallus say about the different parts of the bathhouse? Take short notes.*

exercise room – ball games, ...
changing room – ...
furnaces – ...
...

3 **WRITING** A brochure about Wall Roman Site
Write part of a brochure (in easy English for foreign visitors) about the baths at Letocetum. Use your notes from **2b** *and write about two of the rooms. Copy or sketch the plan of the building and show where your rooms are.*

REMEMBER

1. Before you listen for information, prepare if you can.
2. Listen for the main information and don't panic if there are things you don't understand.
3. Listen again for details that you missed, if you can.
4. Short notes help you to remember what you heard and to tell others about it.

7 UNIT 7 A Very Special TV Special

Look at the picture. The people on the stage are the BBC's everyday heroes and the people who nominated them. You know them all.
Who do you think are the heroes?
Who do you think are the people who nominated them?
Make a list. Compare your list with your partner's. (You'll need your list again for page 91.)

A I think … is one of the heroes.
B I agree. / No, I don't think he/she is one of the heroes. I think …

LISTENING

a *Listen to the cassette/CD. You'll hear about different people and things. Look at the picture and try to find them.*

b *Now copy the two lists below into your exercise book. Listen again and match the names of the people to their jobs.*

Jack	carpenter
Maggie	electrician
Dave	presenter
Gerry	make-up person
Moira	floor manager
Eddie	director
Tina	assistant floor manager

▶▶▶ NOW YOU

Would you like to work in television? Why?/ Why not? Make some notes and then tell your class. These ideas may help you:

- TV: boring / fun / …
- I'm good at … at school.
- You can … famous people.
- hard work / good money / …
- I want to be famous / a star / …

You can start like this:
I would/wouldn't like to work in television because I think …

'OK,' called Jack. 'Get ready for a rehearsal ...'
Megan was very nervous. Hannah was, too. She checked her hair in the mirror for the tenth time.
Suddenly Mrs Patel shouted, 'Careful, everybody! That step – it's going to break ... it's very dangerous.'
Jack looked at the steps up onto the stage.
'Tina, get the carpenter – quickly,' he shouted.
'Oh no,' thought Tina as she left. 'I hope my last day isn't going to be too horrible!'
Jack spoke quietly into his walkie-talkie.
'Moira, sorry, we've got a problem ...'
'Young man,' called Mrs Patel. 'Excuse me, but I've seen two more dangerous things ...'

? *Can you find the other two dangerous things that Mrs Patel has seen? Look again at the picture on pages 86/87.*

→ S 7: 1 (p. 138)

'Funny,' said Tina.
'I checked the steps at ten o'clock. They were OK then.'
'Well,' said Dave, 'Maybe somebody ...'
'I don't really care how it happened, Dave,' Jack said. 'Fix it!'
'OK, OK.' Quietly Dave said to himself: 'Do this, do that! I'm glad I'm leaving tomorrow!'

Meanwhile Tina was talking to the electrician. 'Just look at this cable, Eddie. It's been cut, hasn't it? How could this happen?'
'Don't ask me. I checked everything before my coffee break at 10.15. And don't ask me how my tool box got up there. I left it on the floor by camera 1 when I went to the coffee shop.'

'Jack.' It was Moira on Jack's walkie-talkie. 'The show starts at six and the lunch break is in two hours. We must start!'

→ S 7: 2 (p. 138)

'Tina!' called Jack. 'I can't find my script. I haven't seen it since just after 10.30 ...'
'OK, I'll look for it,' said Tina. Suddenly she saw something on top of a bin.
It was Jack's script. She gave it to him and he opened it. 'Oh no!' he whispered.
'Look at this.'

Our heroes? Rubbish! There are no heroes in this world. I'm going to sabotage this stupid show. Don't try and stop me. Tomorrow I'll be far away...

? *What do you think the letter tells you about the person who wrote it? What are his or her feelings?*

I think the person is ... because ...

→ S 7: 3 (p. 139)

11:21 Jack and Moira were sitting in the gallery. They looked at the anonymous letter.
'The step, the cable, the tool box, and now this ...,' Jack said. 'I think someone really is trying to sabotage the show.'
'But who could it be?' asked Moira.
'Maybe Tina? She was here very early this morning ... and this is her last day. She has got a new job at BBC Belfast.'
'I can't believe it's Tina. Eddie maybe? He's leaving on a six-week trip to Australia tomorrow.'
'Eddie? Never!' said Jack. 'I've known Eddie for a long time. Dave maybe? He's in a bad mood ... and he's leaving tomorrow.'
'Well, whoever it is, I'm worried. I'll call the police ...'
'... and I'll go back to the guests,' said Jack as he ran back down to the set.
'Tina,' he said, 'get ready for a rehearsal.'

? *How many suspects do you have? Write down their names.*

11:29 Up in the gallery Moira put the phone down. 'Ready, sound? – OK, then good luck, everybody. Five, four, three, ...!'

We don't need another ...

All the guests looked very surprised. Tina smiled. Moira shouted, 'Stop!'
'Sorry, Moira.' It was the sound engineer. 'Five minutes ago I had the right tape. It's been swapped!'

LISTENING

Listen to the cassette/CD. Why isn't the first song right for the BBC special?
Why is the second one better?
The first song says .../ is about ... .
So I think ... .
The second one is better because ...

? *There have been five incidents now. Find them. Do you know when they happened? Make notes.*

1 *step – between 10.00 and 10.30*
2 ...

11:35 'Take a break, everyone,' shouted Jack.
David and Aled came down from the stage.
'Hi,' said Aled to Hannah. 'I'm Aled and this is David.'
'And my name is Hannah.'
'Where are you from?' asked Aled.
'I'm from London ... oh, and this is Megan – she's from your part of the country.'
'Hello, Megan,' said David. 'So, you're Welsh?'

12:09 'Get ready, everyone,' shouted Jack.
'See you in the lunch break?' Aled whispered.
'OK,' said Hannah. 'Oh, Aled, who's the hero – you or David?'
'Guess!' said Aled.
'Quiet, *please*! Ten, nine, eight ...'

'... three, two, one ...'
'Good evening and welcome to the BBC's "Our Heroes Special". My name is Gerry Logan, and I'm very happy to be with ...'
Suddenly all the lights went out. There were screams. 'Help! Help!'
'Don't move till the lights are on again,' called Jack. 'I don't want any accidents: cables are lying all over the floor.'
When the lights went on, all the clocks still showed 12.10.

Just then the police arrived. 'Don't move. We're here to find the saboteur. We have to interview everyone. You're all witnesses – and suspects.'

◆◆ ACTIVITY

Now six things have happened in the studio. Who is trying to sabotage the show? The police soon have three suspects – Tina, Dave and Eddie. All of them are leaving tomorrow.

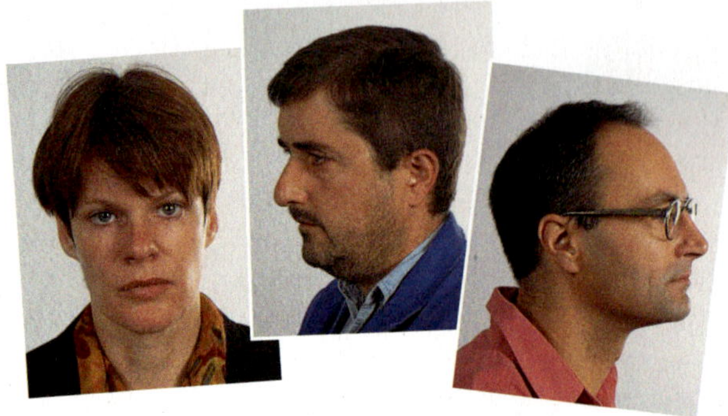

a *Copy the table below into your exercise book or ask your teacher for a copy. Work with a partner. Read pages 88/89 again. Where do Tina, Dave and Eddie say they were at the times in the left column? Did anybody (a witness) see them? Where? Fill in all the information you can find so far. You'll get more information as you go on. Under the table write down all the other things that you find important.*

time	**Tina**	witness	**Dave**	witness	**Eddie**	witness
10.00–10.30 *(step, cable, tool box)*	*studio at 10.30* ...	*Jack, Mrs Patel* ...	?	?	?	?
10.30–11.00 *(letter)*	*studio at 10.35*	?	?	?	?	?
11.00–11.30 *(tape)*	?	?	?	?	?	?

Other clues: 1. Jack says that Dave is in a bad mood. 2. Jack knows that Tina ...

b *Partner B: Look at page 120.*
Partner A: Read the police interview with Tina and add the new information to your table. Then tell your partner what you have found out about Tina. Your partner has the police interview with Dave. He/She will tell you what he/she has found out about Dave. Add this information, too.

POLICE When did you get here this morning, Miss McGough?

TINA Very early. I think I was the first person in the studio. I was busy with the guests till ten o'clock. I went to the coffee shop then. On my way I checked the steps onto the stage ...

POLICE And, were the steps OK?

TINA Yes, they were. Well, then I had my coffee. I saw Eddie in the coffee shop, too, but I was reading and I didn't want to talk. I was back in the studio at about 10.30. I don't know how that tool box got up onto the set wall – it's so heavy. I'm not strong enough to lift it.

POLICE When did you find the script with the letter in it?

TINA At eleven o'clock. It was on top of a bin, near the storeroom. After that I stayed in the studio and asked people questions. I wanted to know who was doing these terrible things.

POLICE Who did you talk to?

TINA Eddie, Da... no, Dave wasn't there.

POLICE And where were you at 11.30?

TINA I was here in the studio all the time. It was chaos! I'm glad I'm leaving tomorrow. Belfast can't be as bad as this!

c *Listen to the interview with Eddie on the cassette/CD together with your partner. Finish your tables. Who do you think is the saboteur? Why? Talk about your ideas with your partner.*

You can use these expressions:
It may/might/must be ...
It can't be him/her because ...
He says he was ... but she says ...
What he/she says isn't true because ...

14:36 After lunch everyone felt better. Everything was ready for a rehearsal. Gerry Logan stood nervously and waited.
'... five ... four ... three ...'
'Good evening and welcome to the BBC's "Our Heroes Special". My name is Gerry Logan and I'm ...'
Suddenly there was a loud noise as one of the big lights broke loose. Tina shouted: 'Gerry – move!' He turned and took a step towards her just as the light crashed onto the floor only centimetres away from him. Tina looked up into the lights. 'It's Dave! I can see him! It's Dave!' She ran towards the metal stairs that led up to the lights. The policewoman got there first. 'This is a job for the police.' She ran up the stairs as the second police officer climbed up on the other side of the studio. They could see Dave now. He was trying to get back to the wall.
'I'm going to fall!' he screamed.
'You'll be all right. Just look at me ...'

The police got Dave down safely.
'They threw me out,' he told them. 'I hated the job, but it was a job. After tonight – no work and no money! I had nothing to lose.'
Five minutes later Dave was taken away by the police.

That evening millions of people sat down and watched the BBC Special. And not one of them knew that this was the end of a difficult day at the studio. They just heard: 'And now the BBC proudly presents – the OUR HEROES SPECIAL!'

LISTENING Our Heroes Special

At last the 'Our Heroes Special' is on television. Listen to it on the cassette/CD.
On page 87 you made a list of heroes and the people who nominated them. Look at that list while you are listening. Were you right?

▶▶▶ NOW YOU

Which of the heroes and people who nominated them is your hero? Why?
On page 1 of your English album is a hero. Have your ideas about heroes changed? Why?/Why not?

◦ REVISION Do-it-yourself exercises

You don't know all the words on these two pages. But you'll find them in the dictionary on pages 171–194.

◆◆ *Do you have problems with English? Here is some help for you and your partner. Try and make your own do-it-yourself exercises.*

Partner A: What problems do you have? Make a list and show it to your partner. Partner B: Help your partner with his/her problems. Choose an exercise from below. Read the instructions, make the exercise and give it to your partner.

How to spell words
Vocabulary
Prepositions (*at*, *behind*, etc.)
Verb forms (*heard*, *saw*, etc.)
Word order (*to the big city in July*, etc.)

1 ▶ What are the words? Spelling

Find words that belong together, for example, school words. *Write them down with the letters in the wrong order. Can your partner put the letters in the right order?*

arribly, enacten, chearet, stoihry → *library, canteen, ...*

2 ▶ Dictations Spelling

Read a text of 50–60 words to your partner. Your partner has to write down the text. You can give punctuation in English like this:

.	=	full stop [ˌfʊl 'stɒp]	'	=	Open quotation marks. [kwəʊ'teɪʃn mɑːks]
,	=	comma ['kɒmə]	'	=	Close quotation marks.
?	=	question mark ['kwestʃn mɑːk]	:	=	colon ['kəʊlən]
			;	=	semicolon [ˌsemɪ'kəʊlən]
!	=	exclamation mark [ˌekskləˈmeɪʃn mɑːk]	–	=	dash [dæʃ]
			...	=	three dots *or:* dot–dot–dot [dɒt]

Read with pauses (//) after groups of words – like this:

Breakfasts at the weekend were always special for Megan and her dad – no work, no school. → *Breakfasts at the weekend // were always special // for Megan and her dad (dash) // no work (comma) // no school (full stop)*

Your partner checks his/her work. Then you read the text again: he/she checks again.

3 ▶ Find the words Vocabulary/Spelling

Find words that belong together, for example, places in town. *Write them down as on the right. Can your partner find all the words?*

B	R	H	O	U	S	E	B	U	S	M	A	R	K	E	T
A	C	A	T	H	E	D	R	A	L	H	O	T	E	L	E
N	S	A	P	O	I	W	E	L	Y	T	O	K	H	I	P
K	D	O	G	S	M	U	S	E	U	M	V	P	E	Y	B
F	A	R	M	P	O	P	C	I	T	Y	W	A	L	L	S

4 ▶ Odd word out Vocabulary

Find words that belong together. Add one word that doesn't belong. Can your partner find the odd word out? Maybe he/she can say why the word doesn't belong.

department store, bank, supermarket, newspaper shop
↓
The odd word out is 'bank' because you can't buy things there.

5 ▶ The fourth word Vocabulary/Grammar

Find and arrange pairs of words as in the examples below. Leave one word out. Can your partner find it? You can ask for words or for grammatical forms.

fast	slow
good	?

man	men
mouse	?

→

fast	slow
good	*bad*

man	men
mouse	*mice*

6 ▶ Fill in the right word Prepositions/Vocabulary/Grammar

a *Copy a short text from this book, but leave out some of the words, for example,* prepositions. *You can write these words next to the text – but in the wrong order. Can your partner put them in the right places?*

in • to
to • with

I've been ... Wales. I was there one day last year. It was when I stayed ... my cousins Nick and Debbie ... Chester. Have you ever been ... Chester?

→

I've been *to* Wales. I was there one day last year. It was when I stayed *with* my cousins Nick and Debbie *in* Chester. Have you ever been *to* Chester?

b *You can also take out every fifth word, for example. Can your partner fill in the missing words?*

I've been to Wales. ... was there one day ... year. It was when ... stayed with my cousins ... and Debbie in Chester.

→

I've been to Wales. *I* was there one day *last* year. It was when *I* stayed with my cousins *Nick* and Debbie in Chester.

7 ▶ Fill in the right form of the verbs Verb forms

Copy a short text from this book. For each verb, write the infinitive of that verb in brackets. Can your partner fill in the right verb forms? The list of irregular verbs on pages 199/200 will help you.

There (be) lots of kids in room 105 and Megan (feel) very nervous. One girl (come) to talk to her.
'Hi!' she (say). '(Be) you new?'

↓

There *were* lots of kids in room 105 and Megan *felt* very nervous. One girl *came* to talk to her.
'Hi!' she *said*. '*Are* you new?'

'Somewhere with no irregular verbs.'

8 ▶ Put the words in the right order Word order

Find sentences and write them with words and phrases in the wrong order. Can your partner write down the sentences correctly?

in a village / a small town / Megan Owen / near Bangor / lived / in Wales → *Megan Owen lived in a village near Bangor, a small town in Wales.*

for / in London / lived / very long / you haven't → *You haven't lived in London for very long.*

even months later / felt / Megan / still / very miserable → *Even months later Megan still felt very miserable. / Megan still felt very miserable even months later.*

◦ TRANSLATION[1] English-German

Beim Übersetzen kommt es darauf an, einen Text möglichst genau in einer anderen Sprache wiederzugeben. Dabei sind Wort-für-Wort-Übersetzungen meist nicht möglich, wie der Briefanfang rechts zeigt. Wenn du einen englischen Text übersetzen willst, lies ihn dir zuerst vollständig durch. Dann fertige eine Rohübersetzung an – wenn nötig mithilfe eines Wörterbuches oder des DICTIONARY *auf S. 171–194. Überarbeite sie, bis sie sich wirklich deutsch anhört. Achte dabei auf Folgendes:*

- *Die Wortstellung ist im Englischen und im Deutschen oft unterschiedlich.*
  Yesterday she went home at 7.
  (Gestern ging sie um 7 nach Hause.)
- *Manche englischen Wörter kann man verschieden wiedergeben.*
  go home (nach Hause gehen *oder* fahren)
  I think … (Ich denke/glaube/finde/…)
- *Manchmal muss man die Wortart ändern.*
  She likes dancing. (Sie tanzt gern.)
- *Die Wortverbindungen (Kollokationen) können unterschiedlich sein.*
  take a photo (ein Foto machen)
- *Wendungen muss man als Ganzes übersetzen.*
  How are you? (Wie geht es dir?)
- *Manchmal verwendet man im Deutschen eine andere Zeitform.*
  I'll come later. (Ich komme später.)
- *Ein ähnlich klingendes Wort ist nicht immer die richtige oder beste Übersetzung.*
  chips (Pommes frites, *nicht:* Chips)

AFTER UNIT 1

1 ▶ Camden Lock Market

A small hotel in London wants to translate this brochure into German for its German guests. Can you help? We have marked a few parts of the brochure. Be careful when you translate them.

Visit
Camden Lock
London's most popular market

Camden Lock Market has been the most popular of London's markets for many years. With its hundreds of stalls and shops next to the canal, the market is a magnet for Londoners and visitors. It is open all week but is busiest at weekends when more than 100,000 people come here for the sights, sounds and shopping. OPENING HOURS: 9.30 am – 6.00 pm. Most shops and some stalls are open SEVEN DAYS A WEEK.

Sollte man hier lock *übersetzen?*

„Ställe"?

Welche Zeitform verwendet man hier im Deutschen?

Welche Bedeutung von busy *passt hier?*

Ist die wörtliche Übersetzung die beste?

Sagt man das genauso auf Deutsch?

„Stunden"?

Wie gibt man diese Uhrzeiten im Deutschen an?

Wie übersetzt man die Wendung a week *hier?*

Hier muss man frei übersetzen, damit der Satz gut klingt. Verwende „wegen" oder „um … zu". Sights *sind hier ganz allgemein „Dinge, die es zu sehen gibt".*

[1] translation [trænsˈleɪʃn] *Übersetzung*

AFTER UNIT 4

2 ▶ Help the hotel again

You translated the Camden Lock brochure so well that the small London hotel wants your help again. Can you translate these notices from the hotel notice-board into German?

Welche Präposition verwendet man hier im Deutschen?

Soll die englische Bezeichnung auch im deutschen Text stehen?

Wie übersetzt man hier am besten das englische Passiv?

If you are in London for the first time, ask us for the brochure *10 London sights you mustn't miss*.

Travelcards can be bought at **Freeman's**, 287 London Road.
(2 mins. on foot)
The closest underground station to the hotel is **Chalk Farm** (Northern Line). Turn left out of the hotel. The station is 5 minutes' walk from here, at the end of Adelaide Road.

Are you looking for cheap theatre tickets? Get them half-price at the ticket office at Leicester Square (tube – Leicester Square, Charing Cross or Piccadilly).

Welche Übersetzung von get passt hier?

Kann man das auf Deutsch genauso kurz sagen?

Was kommt bei dem Relativsatz im Deutschen dazu? – Pass auf bei mustn't*!*

Braucht man diese Wörter in der deutschen Übersetzung?

Verwende einen Nebensatz mit „wenn".

Wie drückt man das auf Deutsch aus?

AFTER UNIT 6

3 ▶ Good book?

Your school has bought the English book Across the Roman Wall. *Now it wants a German description of the book for the library catalogue. Translate this text from the book cover.*

Geht es hier um Minuten oder was bedeutet das?

„hassen"?

Eine Fügung mit einem Gerundium wird oft durch einen Infinitiv übersetzt.

The minute that Marinetta and Lucius meet, they hate each other. Lucius is proud of being the nephew of a Roman senator. He thinks Marinetta is terribly provincial and she finds him very arrogant. But the year is 397 AD and life is getting dangerous – so Marinetta and Lucius are forced to act together.

An action-packed story from Roman Britain

„… das Jahr ist …" Fällt dir eine bessere Formulierung ein?

Du kennst action *und* pack. *Aber wie übersetzt du* action-packed story?

„das römische Britannien"? – Was ist damit gemeint?

◦ INTERPRETING[1]

AFTER UNIT 4

Situation 1

a *Look at the picture on the right:*

- What can you say about these people?
- Where are they?
- What is happening?

b *Read (or listen to) the following conversation. Then answer the questions in the box.*

BOY Kann ich Ihnen helfen?
MAN Ja, bitte. Ich spreche leider kein Englisch.
BOY Can I help?
TOURIST Oh, yes, please! I'm trying to get to the market, but I can't find it.
BOY Sie sagt, sie will zum Markt. Ich bin nicht von hier. Wissen Sie, wo der ist?
MAN Ja, meint sie den neuen oder den alten Markt?
BOY Do you mean the old market or the new one?
TOURIST I think it's the old market I want.
BOY Sie sucht den alten.
MAN Das ist ganz einfach. Sag ihr, sie soll die Straße hier geradeaus gehen und dann rechts in die Hansastraße einbiegen. Dort ist der Markt.
BOY OK, go along this street, then turn right into Hansastraße. That's where the old market is.
TOURIST Oh, thank you very much!

DOLMETSCHEN

Die kurze Szene macht deutlich, dass Dolmetschen etwas anderes ist als wörtliches Übersetzen (vgl. Translation *auf S. 94). Sprecht über folgende Fragen:*

1 *Was lässt der Junge beim Dolmetschen weg? Was behält er bei?*

2 *Welche Einleitung verwendet er, um deutlich zu machen, dass er wiedergibt, was eine andere Person gesagt hat?*

3 *Wie verändern sich die Pronomen beim Dolmetschen?*

I'm trying → sie will
meint sie ...? → ...
I want → ...

Situation 2

a *Now it's your turn to interpret like the boy in situation 1. What could you say in this situation?*

TOURIST Excuse me! I want to catch a bus to the castle. What time is the next one? Can anyone tell me?
YOU Sie will ...
WOMAN Das ist kein Problem. Der nächste kommt gleich. Alle Busse, die hier abfahren, halten am Schloss.
YOU ...
TOURIST Oh, thanks very much.

b *Listen to the cassette/CD and compare what the boy says with what you said.*

❖ **c** *Act the conversation (or a similar one) with two partners.*

[1] interpreting [ɪnˈtɜːprɪtɪŋ] *Dolmetschen*

AFTER UNIT 5

a *Look at the picture. Imagine you are Nina. Interpret for your grandma and your English pen-friend, Kate.*

OMA Kate, ich freue mich, dich kennenzulernen!
NINA My grandmother says …
KATE Nina has told me a lot about you, Mrs Berger. She always says that you tell great stories.
NINA …
OMA Das ist aber nett. – Wie gefällt es denn Kate hier in Düsseldorf?
NINA …
KATE It's great. But I'd like to speak German better. At the moment Nina has to interpret for me quite a lot.
NINA …
OMA Was habt ihr denn heute vor? Das Wetter ist so schön, da könntet ihr doch eine Bootstour machen.
NINA …

b *Listen to the cassette/CD and compare what Nina says with what you said.*

❖ **c** *Act the conversation (or a similar one) with two partners.*

AFTER UNIT 6

a *Look at the picture. Imagine you are Ute and interpret for Nils and Britta.*

b *Listen to the cassette/CD and compare what Ute says with what you said.*

❖ **c** *Act the conversation (or a similar one) with two partners. Then write and act a conversation between the three teenagers* after *their first surfing course.*

NILS Hi, Britta! I'm Nils. Er, Ute says you … er, you, er … Hilf mir doch mal, Ute. Du kannst doch so gut Englisch.
UTE Was willst du denn sagen?
NILS Was heißt „Schweden" auf Englisch?
UTE Sweden.
NILS Ja, klar, … er, you're from Sweden?
BRITTA Yes, have you ever been there?
NILS Wie bitte? Was hat sie gefragt?
UTE …
NILS Nee, … er, no, I have not. Er, … Ute, frag sie mal, ob sie gut surfen kann.
UTE …
BRITTA Well, I'm learning from my parents but I'm not very good yet. Are you good at surfing, Nils?
UTE …
NILS Oh, no. But I want to … er, … Sag ihr, ich will's lernen, Ute. Und hör mal: Es gibt hier jeden Tag Surfkurse. Was hält sie davon?
UTE …
BRITTA I think that's a great idea! We can all go together.
UTE …

UK MAG

Welcome to the UK Mag(azine). It's full of articles, stories and photos just like those in magazines for young people in Britain. You can read it on your own or with your class. You might not know every word in the magazine, but we're sure you'll understand most of it. The most important new words are in the dictionary on pages 171–194. Have fun with the UK Mag!

Great, no school tomorrow! Let's go and listen to CDs at that new shop.
I can't. I have to help Mum to tidy up the house.
9
Look, there's Kate. Do you want to go and talk to her?
No, Mum, I don't!
10
That afternoon ...
11
Hi, Kate! Would you like to come over and watch *Baywatch*?
12
Sorry! I'm helping Mum.
Later, Mandy went round to Kate's house ...
I thought: maybe I can help, too?
Mandy! ... Er, well, Diana has just come round, too, so, ... er, ...
13
14
I saw you with Diana this morning, too. I don't think you want to be my friend any more.
Well, Diana is more fun. But we can still meet sometimes, Mandy.
15
No, thank you, Kate. That's not what friends are about!
Next week at school ...
16
We've got another new pupil. This is Max.
Mmm, he looks nice!
After the first lesson ...
17
Of course you can, Max!
I know you. You're Mandy. You go to dance class with my sister. ... Can I walk to the gym with you?

In and out of School

Here in the UK kids have a long school day – from about 8.50 am to about 3.45 pm. After that they have school clubs and homework. Here's what one girl wrote. Next to her letter are some homework tips.

Debbie, 14, finds it a nightmare to study

'I've got a little sister and two little brothers so I can't do homework at home. I try to study in my bedroom but my sister, Angela, usually watches TV there or plays silly games with her friends. She says half of the room is hers, but I can't concentrate and we usually start to argue.'

FIND A SPACE

DO YOU HAVE A ROOM TOGETHER WITH A BROTHER OR SISTER? THEN TRY THIS: WHEN YOUR LITTLE SISTER IS WATCHING TV, DO SOMETHING ELSE. BUT SHE MUST AGREE TO LEAVE THE ROOM WHEN YOU WANT TO DO YOUR HOMEWORK. WITH A REGULAR 'HOMEWORK TIME' EVERY NIGHT YOU CAN CONCENTRATE MUCH BETTER, AND YOUR SISTER AND YOU WILL BOTH GET WHAT YOU WANT.

The BIG question this week: Should kids have to wear school uniform – yes or no?

School uniform

Your own clothes

	School uniform	Your own clothes
What teachers say	'Put on your tie, please.'	'Does your mother really let you wear that?'
What pupils say	'I hate the uniform, terrible colour, silly tie.'	'Do you like my new clothes?'
What parents say	'You are growing fast, dear.'	'Can't you wear nice clothes to school?'
Advantages	Doesn't cost as much. You don't have to worry about what you're going to wear every morning.	Cost more, but you don't have to wear anything stupid.
Disadvantages	Everyone looks the same. It never fits.	You think more about clothes than school. You have nothing new you can wear outside school.

And the winner is: school uniform.

You look terrible, but all the others look terrible too, and you don't have to find a new outfit every day.

A VISIT TO WALES

MAE'R GYMRAEG YMA O HYD

When Gwenllian Ellis tells her great-grandson stories of the fairies in the valleys near their home in the north of Wales, she tells her stories in Welsh – of course.

But, as Gwen told UK Mag, things weren't always like that. 'When I was a little girl in school, there was trouble if we spoke Welsh. "Speak English," the teachers always told us. And we tried. But sometimes, when we were excited, we forgot. Just one word of Welsh – the language we spoke at home – and we had to wear the Welsh Not. The teachers tied a piece of wood with the letters 'WN' round our necks, and we had to wear it all day. And everyone knew: that boy or girl spoke Welsh today. It was like something dirty. I only had to wear the Welsh Not once, but it was terrible.'

For a minute, Gwen didn't say anything. She looked out across the valley towards the sea. Slowly she started to smile. 'When I told my parents about the Not, they were angry. But they didn't go to the teachers and complain. We tried to speak English at home. Imagine, we stopped speaking our own language in our own home!

Gwenllian Ellis

Later I had children, too, and I never spoke Welsh to them. I remembered the Not, and I didn't want to see my children coming home with stories like mine.'

Of course things have changed since then. Gwen's great-grandson will speak Welsh and English at school. Some lessons will be in English, others in Welsh. He will listen not only to the best of English and American rock music, but also to Welsh pop and perhaps to traditional harp music, too.

'The Welsh language is very beautiful,' says Gwen. 'It's very good for poetry. The Welsh people have always been good at poetry and singing.'

Today people come from far away to Nant Gwrtheyrn (the National Welsh Language Centre) to learn Welsh. Many of the people who are learning the old language are Welsh. They don't have to worry about the Welsh Not any more.

Mae'r Gymraeg yma o hyd – Welsh lives on.

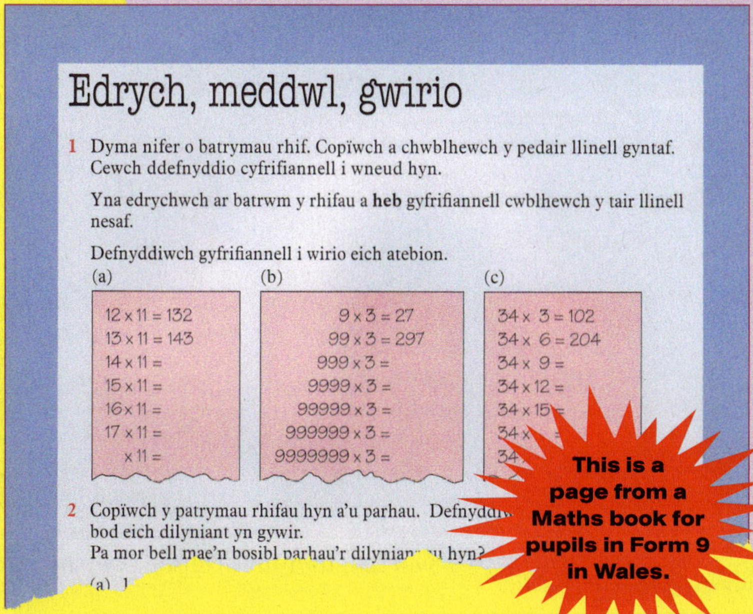

Edrych, meddwl, gwirio

1 Dyma nifer o batrymau rhif. Copïwch a chwblhewch y pedair llinell gyntaf. Cewch ddefnyddio cyfrifiannell i wneud hyn.

Yna edrychwch ar batrwm y rhifau a **heb** gyfrifiannell cwblhewch y tair llinell nesaf.

Defnyddiwch gyfrifiannell i wirio eich atebion.

(a)	(b)	(c)
12 x 11 = 132	9 x 3 = 27	34 x 3 = 102
13 x 11 = 143	99 x 3 = 297	34 x 6 = 204
14 x 11 =	999 x 3 =	34 x 9 =
15 x 11 =	9999 x 3 =	34 x 12 =
16x 11 =	99999 x 3 =	34 x 15 =
17 x 11 =	999999 x 3 =	34 x
x 11 =	9999999 x 3 =	34

2 Copïwch y patrymau rhifau hyn a'u parhau. Defnyddi... bod eich dilyniant yn gywir.
Pa mor bell mae'n bosibl parhau'r dilynian... hyn?

(a) 1

This is a page from a Maths book for pupils in Form 9 in Wales.

When people in other parts of Britain think of Wales, they think of music and of choirs, in particular. If a Welsh school wants to have a special evening for parents and friends, it will often be an evening of music. Here is part of the programme for one school's end-of-term celebration.

YSGOL GYFUN EMLYN

yn cyflwyno / presents

OCEAN WORLD

Woodwind Ensemble	WATER MUSIC SUITE (Handel)
Choir	BEATLES MEDLEY
3. Recorder Group	SEA MEDLEY
4. Brass Quintet	ACAPULCO BAY
5. Ensemble	OCEAN WAVES
6. Cor Ysgol y Ddwylan ac Ysgol Penboyr	A FUOCH CHI 'RIOE YN MORIO
7. Sing along	I DO LIKE TO BE BESIDE THE SEASIDE
8. Stephen Jackson	FFLAT HUW PUW
9. Triawd 'Arbennig'	AR LAN Y MÔR

Story-telling has a long tradition in Wales, and some 'English' legends really come from Wales – the story of King Arthur and the Round Table, for example. Read this story about the first European in America. Is it history or legend? What do you think?

WHO WAS THE FIRST EUROPEAN IN AMERICA?

'Christopher Columbus, of course!' will be the answer from an American or English schoolchild. But if you ask a Welsh boy or girl, he or she may give you a different answer: Madog.

Madog was a Welsh prince in the 12th century. When his father died, he and his brothers couldn't agree about what they should do with the king's money. Madog was angry, and he took his men and a ship and sailed west.

Over a year later, Madog came back to Wales and told people about a far-away land. A year after that, he took ten ships and sailed west again. No one ever saw Madog or the others after that.

300 years later, Columbus sailed to America. As more and more people from Europe came to America, there were reports of 'white Indians' around Louisville, Kentucky. And some of the first Europeans in America said that they met Welsh-speaking 'Indians'!

A Taste of Scotland

This week *UK Mag* goes north for a taste of life in Scotland. Your guide is our star reporter Fiona McPherson, from the West Highlands of Scotland. But first of all a word of warning for all visitors ...

Hi! Well, the first thing is this: Scotland is *not* a part of England – it's different. And the people are, too. You can call us Scots and you can call us British. But English? – Never!

If you don't believe me, go to a big Scotland – England rugby match and see for yourself!

Of course, the Scots and the English are friends most of the time. The crosses of their saints, St George (England) and St Andrew (Scotland), are in the British flag together with the cross of St Patrick (Ireland).

SCOTS HAMMER ENGLAND

Scotland was one big party last night after a great win against 'The Auld Enemy': 18–13 after 80 minutes of hard but brilliant play.

Cross of St George (England)

\+

Cross of St Andrew (Scotland)

\+

Cross of St Patrick (Ireland)

=

The British flag (since 1801)

Come with me to the Highlands where I grew up. It's a beautiful place, but you won't find many young people here because there aren't many jobs. People like me look for jobs elsewhere. But we all love to come home – for New Year or the summer festival, for example.

New Year – 'Hogmanay' we call it – is big in Scotland. When midnight comes, everyone holds hands and sings *Auld Lang Syne* together. Most people don't really understand the old Scots words, but they sing it all over the world these days.

Should auld acquaintance be forgot,
And never brought to mind?
Should auld acquaintance be forgot,
For the sake of auld lang syne?
Chorus: For auld lang syne, my dear.
For auld lang syne,
We'll take a cup of kindness yet
For the sake of auld lang syne.

For all you English speakers, the words of the song mean something like this: ***So we don't forget our old friends, let's drink together for the old times.***

After *Auld Lang Syne* people go 'first-footing' just after midnight: they visit friends and neighbours with a piece of coal. That's for a warm and lucky home all year. And you go in for a drink. And there's always something to eat – some traditional Scottish shortbread, maybe. My mum makes the best shortbread in the world. Here's her recipe. Why not try it?

Shortbread

1 Mix 150 g flour with a little salt. Then rub 100 g butter (in small pieces) into the flour.
2 Add 50 g sugar and make a ball.
3 Roll out the ball till it's about 1 cm thick.
4 Put it in the oven. Bake for 45 minutes at 150°C.
5 Take the shortbread out of the oven and cut it.

The summer festival is a great time, too. If you're not scared of water, there's a regatta with all kinds of boats. And there's a ceilidh – a party with music and dancing that goes on for three days! We like our parties in Scotland. And then at the end the piper plays from across the water and you look out to the mountains of the Isle of Skye. And you start to cry and you know you'll have to come back again next year!

Skye! It really must be the most beautiful of all the islands of Scotland. And there's a story about Skye, too – the story of Bonnie Prince Charlie and Flora Macdonald. It happened after the Highlanders fought their last battle against the English – the Battle of Culloden. That was a lot more than a rugby match. Thousands of Highlanders died for their prince that day in 1746.

After the battle Prince Charlie escaped to the islands, where he hid in lonely caves and huts. The English tried to find the prince and kill him. But a brave Highland woman, Flora Macdonald, saved the prince. She got him an Irish passport and some women's clothes. He then travelled with Flora as her servant, Betty Burke, over the sea to Skye. The English looked everywhere for him. They offered £30,000 to anyone who could give information about him. But not one Highlander said a word. Later, after many dangerous times, he escaped to France. He was never able to return to Scotland.
Many Scots remember the story sadly because Culloden meant the end of the old Highland way of life.

Netscape -

File Edit View Go Bookmarks Options Directory Window Help

Back Forward Home Reload Images Open Print Find Stop

Virtual London

You want to go to London, but you don't have the CASH?

You want to go to London NOW, but you have to be at school tomorrow morning?

You want to go to London, but your parents are AGAINST it?

NO MORE EXCUSES!

Through the magic of CYBERSPACE, you can visit Virtual London. Turn on your computer and warm up the modem for a WWW trip to the CAPITAL.

What's out there? – UK Mag shows you the BEST places in town.

Number 10 Downing Street
The home of the British Prime Minister!
http://www.number-10.gov.uk

The British Museum
One of the great museums of the world!
http://www.british-museum.ac.uk

The Natural History Museum
Find out about the awesome dinosaurs!
http://www.nhm.ac.uk

The British Monarchy Website
The Queen online!
http://www.royal.gov.uk

The Tower of London The virtual to
http://www.toweroflondontour.com/k

The London Aquarium
Meet the fish!
http://www.londonaquarium.co.uk

WHAT'S ON STAGE

UK Theatre Web What's on in the West End?
http://www.uktw.co.uk/index2.html

Document: Done

And what's behind the homepages?

Do the quiz on the kids' Tower of London Website!

Enjoy the underwater world at the London Aquarium!

The Reef & Living Corals

Be dazzled by the sheer brilliance and variety of exotic creatures such as sea-horses, clown fish, regal tang, dogface puffers, angel fish and invertebrates of the reef and tropical seas.

And the OTHERS?

You'll have to GO there yourself.

Enjoy your TRIP to Virtual London!

Coloured

What do kids think about colour? *UK Mag* is finding out.

POETRY COMPETITION
Are you black, brown, white or yellow? Write a poem about how you see the world. Send it to us, here at *UK Mag*. We'll print the ten best poems – and the winners each get a *UK Mag* T-shirt. Maybe you can write a poem like this one? Milly Maceba, 13, from Birmingham sent it to us:

BLACK
is beautiful,
black is strong.
Sometimes black is lonely
but never white, always black.
Black and white together
can be beautiful,
and strong –
FRIENDS

OUT OF THE MOUTHS OF BABES?

'Come and meet my friend on Sports Day, Mummy.'
Sports Day came.
'Where's your new friend, Paul?'
'He's sitting on the front bench.'
There were ten on the front bench.
'He's wearing red shorts.'
There were three boys with red shorts.
'His hair's curly.'
'Oh, the black one,'
said Mummy.

Kathryn Clarke, 15

COLOURED

An Australian Aboriginal wonders about the word 'coloured'.

Dear White Fella,
Couple things you should know:

When I born, I
When I grow up, I
When I go in sun, I
When I cold, I
When I scared, I
When I sick, I
And when I die – I still
black.

You White Fella,
When you born, you pink,
When you grow up, you white,
When you go in sun, you red,
When you cold, you blue,
When you scared, you yellow,
When you sick, you green,
And when you die, you grey.

And you have the cheek
To call me
coloured?

(Written by an unknown author in aboriginal idiom)

Meet the reggae band *UB40* from Birmingham. The group takes its name from the number of a form you have to fill in if you are out of work in Britain. *UB40* have had lots of number one hits. You can listen to *Guns in the Ghetto* on our special cassette/CD.

GUNS IN THE GHETTO

Daddy don't go out tonight
Just stay home till morning light
Me and momma don't feel right
Please hold us tight

Daddy why do you go to work
When you know just how much we
love you so?
Please come back tomorrow

Chorus
They're giving out guns in the ghetto
They're saying they will set you free
One day I'll have children of my own
But I'm afraid they won't have me

INVADERS

History without the boring bits

Britain was last invaded a long time ago – in 1066. But for 1000 years before 1066 the invaders never stopped coming ...

THE BRITONS

When the Romans invaded Britain in 43 AD, Celtic tribes were living peacefully all over the country. Peacefully? Well, maybe not quite ...
The tribes spent a lot of time fighting each other. That made things easy for the Roman invaders.

Life for the Britons wasn't exactly exciting. Most of them lived in round farmhouses, often in small forts at the top of hills. Like the Romans, they had many gods. Theirs were the gods of nature. These farmers didn't go on holiday very much, so they didn't have real roads – just tracks across the countryside.

THE ROMANS

Life in Britain changed when the Romans invaded. They ruled Britannia from 43 AD until 410 AD and loved building. They built good straight roads with forts and towns along them. So their soldiers were able to move about the country quickly when there was any trouble (and there was!). The Romans also built villas in the countryside and temples to their gods. And the Emperor Hadrian built Hadrian's Wall so that Celtic tribes from the north couldn't invade Roman Britain.

Hadrian as he was building his wall

THE ANGLO-SAXONS

The Angles and Saxons started invading Britain when it was still part of the Roman Empire. When the Romans left, more and more Angles and Saxons came. They went up and down the long, straight Roman roads and burned and pillaged. Then they went back home again. But after a while they thought, 'This place isn't so bad, is it? Let's stay.'

The Angles and Saxons pushed the Celtic Britons into Cornwall, Wales and Scotland. At first they lived just like the Britons before the Romans came – they were farmers, and the different tribes loved fighting each other. But after about 450 years there was only one tribe left and the country it ruled was called England, 'Land of the Angles'.

THE VIKINGS

The Vikings – or Danes or Norsemen, as some people called them – were even better at burning and pillaging than the Anglo-Saxons. They sailed across the North Sea to England and decided to stay, too. When there were more of them in the east of England than Anglo-Saxons, they called that part Danelaw (no, not Vikinglaw or Norsemanlaw).

THE NORMANS

The Normans were the last invaders and are famous for the most famous date in English history – 1066. They came from France under William the Conqueror and beat the English at the Battle of Hastings.

But who were the Normans? (This is where it gets hard!) Well, they were really Vikings who went to the north of France in about 900 AD and became French. 150 years later they decided to become English, too. So they got in their ships and invaded. The Normans liked building almost as much as the Romans and they built castles all over England, like the Tower of London. The castles were full of Norman soldiers so that the Anglo-Saxons would know whose country it was now.

What the invaders left:

PLACES TO VISIT

HADRIAN'S WALL, Cumbria and Northumberland:
The best part to see is the 12 miles (19 km) between Birdoswald Fort (Banina) and Housesteads Fort (Vergovicium). Walk along the wall and imagine being a Roman soldier at night who is hoping the Selgovae aren't going to attack.

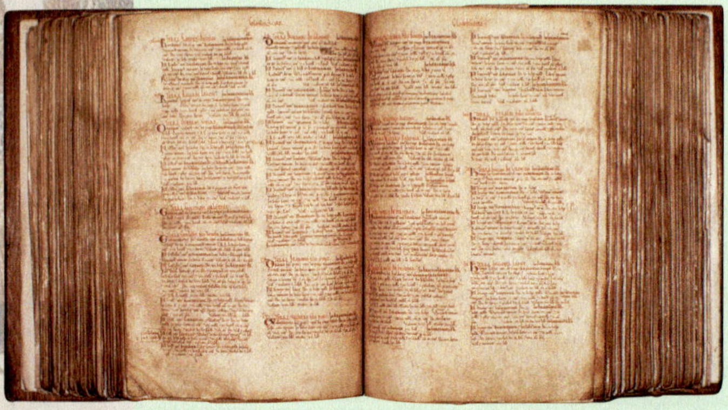

LONDON:
In 1086 King William I ordered a survey of the whole of Norman England. The **Domesday Book** gave details of the people, animals, buildings and land in every village in the country. You can see the original at the Public Record Office Museum in London.

DOVER, Kent:
See three periods of history at Dover Castle. The ruins of the pharos (a Roman lighthouse) and the Anglo-Saxon church, St Mary-in-Castro, are both inside the grounds of the Norman castle.
Then find out more about the history of Dover at Dover Museum and the White Cliffs Experience.

YORK, Yorkshire:
Go back in time to Roman York (Eburacum) or Viking York (Jorvik). At the Jorvik Viking Centre you can experience the sounds, sights and smells of life in Viking York in 948 AD.

ROMANS *Return*

A play to read, act and write

CHARACTERS

LAVINIA – a Roman girl from Aquae Sulis
QUINTUS – her father, a Roman businessman
OLIVER – a boy from modern Bath
CHRISSIE – Oliver's sister
WOMAN – sells fruit in the market
MOTHER – Oliver and Chrissie's mother
POLICEMAN

The Bath Chroni

Price: 60 pence — 1 April 199

BATHS SENSATION
– Two Romans asleep for 2000 years? –

BATH. Archaeologists were trying to find out yesterday if two people really 'slept' in the baths for 2000 years. A tourist who saw the man and girl in Roman clothes said, 'They were talking English but seemed very lost.'

Dr Sulis, the TV expert who worked on the 'Ötzi' mummy from the Alps, told our reporter: 'We know that the water here is very special. If it's true, maybe the water put them into a coma.'

Bath Museum guide Liz Croaker added, 'I suppose they heard us and the tourists while they were asleep and learned the language like that.' Others told our re-

LON and but whe did wea sun Prin Que we dea

Scene 1

In the market

(Lavinia and her father, Quintus Lavinius Timidus, are walking through the market in Bath.)

LAVINIA Pater, come along now. We must find the road to Londinium.

QUINTUS Oh, oh, poor me. Where is my villa? Where are my slaves? Lavinia, dear, run over to Maximus. I want to talk to him.

LAVINIA Pater, his house is gone.

QUINTUS Oh, what's wrong with this town? Lavinia, where is my TABERNA, ... er, shop? It can't be far.

LAVINIA Pater, we are out of our time. Everything has changed. And it's all because you slept too long again.

QUINTUS That's it! Perhaps we're still dreaming! I had such a funny dream. I dreamed of carts that moved without horses, imagine!

LAVINIA But that's real! That's now! All the Romans we knew have gone and we're alone.

QUINTUS Now, don't you worry, my dear. Remember you're the daughter of Quintus Lavinius Timidus, *Import and Export to all Four Corners of the Empire,* the richest man in Aquae Sulis. Remember that and hold your head high! – Oooh, ESURIO!

LAVINIA You're hungry? Here's some fruit.

(Not far away, Oliver and Chrissie are looking at the newspapers outside a shop.)

OLIVER See this, Chrissie? Two Romans woke up in the baths yesterday.

CHRISSIE What? You mean Romans from thousands of years ago?

OLIVER Yeah, here, look. There's a picture. The girl is nice.

CHRISSIE Stop it, Ollie. Let me see. – Oh I bet they feel stupid in those clothes ...

(Chrissie and Oliver are interrupted by Quintus' loud voice.)

QUINTUS And why can't I take the MALUM, I mean apple, my good woman? You should know that I am Quintus Lavinius Timidus, *Import and Export to all Four Corners of the Empire,* and I'm testing this apple.

WOMAN Well, you can buy it before you test it, Mr Caesar.

LAVINIA Pater, here's our last denarius, give her that.

QUINTUS Well, I'm not an unfair man. Here is a silver denarius. I'll have four pounds of apples for that, woman.

WOMAN You can keep your toy money, sir. And your silly Roman clothes. Some kind of show for the tourists again, is it?

QUINTUS By Jupiter!

WOMAN No bad language, here, thank you! In front of his daughter, too!

OLIVER Excuse me, er, can we help you? Are you in trouble?

QUINTUS My daughter is already married – go away!

LAVINIA Pater!

CHRISSIE Ollie, let me do this – ESURITISNE? MALUMNE EDERE VULTIS? ECCE 50 pence.

QUINTUS How can I thank you, my dear child? Two apples, please.

(The woman gives them the apples, Quintus eats.)

LAVINIA Kind people, we are lost. We can't find our villa or the temple. We want to go home to Rome. We've got nowhere to stay here.

OLIVER Look, why don't you come home with us? You can have some real food. Then we can help you.

LAVINIA Kind sir, I thank you.

CHRISSIE Mum won't like it ...

QUINTUS Did he say food?

(They leave the stage.) ➤

Scene 2

At Oliver and Chrissie's house in the dining-room

(Oliver, Chrissie, Quintus and Lavinia enter.)

CHRISSIE Now, this is the TRICLINIUM.

OLIVER No, it isn't. It's the dining-room.

CHRISSIE That is 'dining-room' in Latin, stupid!

OLIVER Well, please sit down, and we'll look for some lunch.

QUINTUS Food, eh? Well, I'm ready for it!
(climbs onto table and lies down on it)
Your sofas are very high.
(starts eating peanuts)

MOTHER *(enters)*
Oh my ... What's going on in here?

LAVINIA SALVE, lady of the house. Your kind children have invited us to lunch. We're Romans out of our time.

MOTHER Yes, er, hello, dear. Oliver, why is that old man lying on the table?

OLIVER Well, it's a long story, Mum. I'll tell you in the kitchen. – Er, so what would you like to eat? Oh I know: pizza. You're from Italy, aren't you? You'll love pizza.
(pushes his mother out of the room)

CHRISSIE I expect you want a drink. Is cola OK for you?

QUINTUS Is that your name for VINUM ... er, wine?

CHRISSIE Er, well, some people like it more than wine. Here, try it.
(gives him a glass of cola)

QUINTUS Bah!
(claps hands and calls out into kitchen)
Slave woman! Bring me some wine!

MOTHER *(in the kitchen)* Well, really! That's enough! I don't care if he's the Emperor himself. He's rude and macho and I want him out of my house!

OLIVER OK, OK.
(re-enters dining-room)
Here we are – Pizza Furiosa!

QUINTUS Where's the slave woman with my wine?

MOTHER *(in the kitchen)* Oooh!
(looks angry, makes a phone call)
Police? Two crazy people have come into my house ... I don't know. They're 2000 years old ... No, *I'm* not crazy, *they* are! ... Yes, but hurry! ... 23 Augustan Way.

(In the dining-room)

LAVINIA Oliver, you are so kind to us, ...

OLIVER Oh, that's all right, we ...

LAVINIA ... but we must get back to Rome. It's our real home.

OLIVER Well, Rome is different today, too.

LAVINIA We must start at once. It is many weeks' journey and we must be home before winter starts.

CHRISSIE Don't be silly – you can fly from London.

QUINTUS *(mouth full)* Haha, fly like Daedalus, you mean?

CHRISSIE No, you take a plane, well, a flying machine.

QUINTUS No! Not for me. I'm too, er, I don't like being higher than on a horse.

OLIVER Well, there are other ways to get to ...

(A policeman is pushed into the room.)

MOTHER They're in there. Be careful, the man is crazy.

POLICEMAN Oh, it's you again. I remember you. You called that Scotsman a barbarian in the pub last night, didn't you?

QUINTUS SALVE. You must be a soldier.

CHRISSIE *(whispers)* Lavinia, he's a policeman. This means trouble.

POLICEMAN Have you got a passport, sir? Or a driving-licence?

QUINTUS Sir, I am Quintus Lavinius Timidus, *Import and Export to all Four Corners of the Empire.* How can I help you?

POLICEMAN That's enough of that. Would you come along to the police station, sir?

OLIVER Officer, we were just having a snack. Would you like a piece of Pizza Furiosa with us?
(gives him a plate with pizza on it)

POLICEMAN Well, that's very kind, ...

LAVINIA *(whispers)* Pater, do you want to go to prison or to Rome? Then move fast, please!

CHRISSIE Quick, out of the back door. Here's £20 from Ollie and me. It's all we've got.
(The pizza is too spicy for the policeman. Oliver gives him a drink.)

POLICEMAN Thanks, I needed that.

LAVINIA Chrissie, give my love to Oliver ...

QUINTUS *(finishes his cola)* Hey, don't hurry me.

LAVINIA Out here. Chrissie, take this hairpin so that you remember me.
(Quintus and Lavinia leave the stage.)

What happens next?

UK Mag hasn't got room for more of Lavinia and Quintus' story.
So it's over to you!
We've put together some of our ideas in this picture.

Now you can decide:

What do Lavinia and Quintus do?

What do they see?

Where do they go?

Who do they meet?

What do they think?

How do they go?

Write scene 3 of the play and send it to *UK Mag*.
We'll publish the best ideas in the magazine and
you can win a prize, too.

And don't forget:

When you act the play, take a photo
and send it to us here,
at *UK Mag*.
We hope you'll have fun.

1 B

Unit 1

6 ▶ They aren't Londoners

a *Look at the chart. Some of Megan's classmates are from other places, too. Some information about Mark, Sandra, Thomas and Moira is missing. Answer your partner's questions and then ask him/her 'How long ...?'.*

	Mark	Sandra	Thomas	Moira
live in London	3 weeks	?	?	6 years
be at TPS	?	4 months	March	?
know his/her best friend	?	last year	?	5 weeks
have Miss Herbert as a form teacher	?	?	today	half a year

A How long has Mark lived in London?
B For three weeks.
How long has Sandra ...?
A ...

b *Now write about two of Megan's classmates. Example:*

Mark has lived in London for three weeks. He has been at Tufnell Park School since ...

2 B

Unit 2

Sports Freak or Couch Potato – Which Are You? (p. 22)

Your score

1	A = 1;	B = 3;	C = 5
2	A = 0;	B = 3;	C = 5
3	A = 3;	B = 5;	C = 0
4	A = 0;	B = 5;	C = 0
5	A = 5;	B = 3;	C = 0
6	A = 0;	B = 5;	C = 0
7	A = 0;	B = 0;	C = 5

8 1 point for each correct answer:
A = Basketball;
B = Football;
C = Rugby;
D = American football

10 points or less
You're a couch potato. You spend too much time at home in front of the TV. Go out and do some sport. It's healthy, and you'll feel better, too.

11 to 29 points
You have a healthy attitude towards sport and exercise.

30 points or more
You're a real sports freak. But too much sport isn't always good for you. You should relax sometimes, too – it's healthier!

6 ▶ **A trip around Nameshire**

Here is a map for a trip around the county of Nameshire. Some of the information about activities in Nameshire is missing. Answer your partner's questions and ask him/her about the missing information.

A What can I do if I go to Peterpool?
B If you go to Peterpool, you can spend the night in a castle.
What can I do if I go to Lizby?

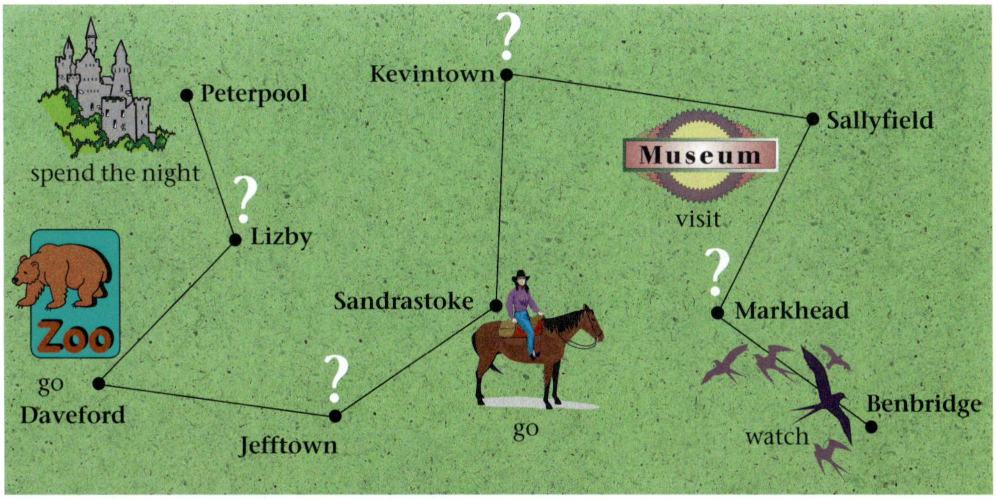

9 ▶ **Just imagine!**

a *Answer your partner's questions and give reasons for your answers. Then ask your partner these questions and write down what he/she answers.*

1 If you could be anywhere in the world tomorrow, where would you like to be?
2 If you could be a famous person for a day, who would you like to be?
3 If you could live at another time in history, when would you like to live?

b *Now think of one more question for your partner.*

2 ▶ What are their names?

Answer your partner's questions about pictures 1–3.
Then find out from your partner the names of the robots, pets and people in pictures 4–6.
Ask like this: What's the name of the robot that is/has got …?

1

Jeff Tony

2

Barbie Pat

3

Rocky Robby

4

– jumping up and down
– climbing the wall

5

– sitting on the school bag
– standing on the book

6

– has got red hair
– has got short hair

13 ▶ What is it?

Explain the pictures to your partner. Use the phrases in the box below.
Can your partner guess who or what it is?

designs new gadgets • goes to school
keeps your food cold • plays CDs on the radio
takes people across water • shows you the time

B This is a person who … /
a thing which …
A Is it a/an …? / It must be …
B That's right. / No, sorry. Try again.

Unit 4

5 REVISION At a party → S 4: 2 (p. 130)

Look at the picture with food and drinks at a party. (Your partner has got a different picture.)
Answer your partner's questions. Use a little / a few / a lot / not … any.
Then ask about the things in the list below.

A Have you got any apples?
B Yes, I've got a few / a lot.
or:
No, I haven't got any.

B Have you got any sandwiches?
A Yes, … / No, …

Unit 5

3 ▶ Each other or themselves?

Look at these pictures. You and your partner have the same pictures, but in a different order. Tell your partner about your pictures and write down the order of your partner's pictures.

A In my picture 1, two kids are taking photos of each other.
B Oh, that's my picture 6. In *my* picture 1, a girl and a boy are thinking …

5 B

Unit 5

8 ▶ Can you play chess with me?

You are Layla. It is Friday evening and you phone your friend Tim. You want to play chess with him. Try and arrange a time for a game with him. Think of what you have planned already.

LAYLA What are you doing on Saturday morning, Tim? Can you play chess with me?
TIM No, sorry, …
LAYLA What about the afternoon?
TIM … . But I'm not … in the evening.
LAYLA Oh, I'm …
TIM …

7 B

Unit 7

ACTIVITY (p. 90)

b *Read the police interview with Dave and add the new information to your table. Your partner has the police interview with Tina. He/She will tell you what he/she has found out about Tina. Add this information, too. Then tell your partner what you have found out about Dave.*

POLICE And when did you start work today, Mr Smith?
DAVE I'm not sure when I got in – about half past nine, I think – I don't wear a watch.
POLICE Did you meet anyone else when you arrived?
DAVE Not meet, no. I saw Eddie – he was up in the lights. Oh, and I saw Tina. She was going to make-up with some guests.
POLICE What did you do then?
DAVE I went to the storeroom and read my newspaper. And at 10.30 Tina fetched me.
POLICE What did you do next, sir?
DAVE I fixed the step, of course – I always have to do things quickly for that floor manager. I'm not sorry that this is my last day – even if I haven't got another job yet.
POLICE Did you leave the studio at any time after that?
DAVE No, … oh, maybe I went to the toilet …
POLICE When was that?
DAVE I can't remember. Well, you don't look at the clock every time you go to the toilet, do you?
POLICE No, sir, I don't – you're right!

LANGUAGE SUMMARY

Die folgenden **LANGUAGE SUMMARY**-Seiten geben einen Überblick über das, was du in den Units dieses Buches gelernt oder wiederholt hast.

Links stehen grammatische Regeln und Hinweise sowie Lerntipps und Merkkästen. **Rechts** stehen Beispiele und Übersichten. Warndreiecke (⚠) weisen auf Fehlerquellen und wichtige Regeln hin. Ein Hinweis wie → P 3a (p. 14) bedeutet, dass zu diesem Abschnitt die Übung 3a von Seite 14 gehört.

Die mit **REMEMBER** gekennzeichneten Stellen enthalten Stoff, den du bereits kennst und an den du dich erinnern solltest.

Zwischendurch findest du immer wieder kurze englische Zusammenfassungen der wichtigsten Regeln, damit du auch auf Englisch über die neue Grammatik sprechen kannst.

Am Ende jeder Unit zeigt eine kleine Übersicht, was du schon auf Englisch ausdrücken kannst („In Unit 1 hast du gelernt …“).

Übrigens: Alexander und Dilek lernen wieder mit – ihre Fragen und Hinweise können auch dir helfen. Und wenn du Probleme mit grammatischen Begriffen hast, schau in der Liste auf den Seiten 197–198 nach.

Unit 1

1 Wiederholung: Die Zeitformen der Verben

Revision: The tenses of the verbs

a Die einfache Form der Gegenwart
Wenn etwas **regelmäßig**, immer, oft oder nie geschieht.

The simple present
My parents **watch** TV every evening.
Does it often **rain** here in the summer?

b Die Verlaufsform der Gegenwart
Wenn etwas gerade **im Verlauf** und noch nicht abgeschlossen ist.

The present progressive
What **are** the Owens **doing**? – They**'re watching** TV.
Look, we can't play outside. It**'s raining**. → P 3a (p. 14)

c Das *present perfect*
Wenn man sagen will, **dass** (nicht: wann!) etwas geschehen ist. Oft hat die Handlung oder das Geschehen Auswirkungen auf die Gegenwart.

The present perfect
Sue **has broken** her leg. She can't go to the disco.
Have you **listened** to your new CDs yet? → P 2, 3b (p. 14)

d Die einfache Form der Vergangenheit
Wenn man sagt, **wann** etwas geschah.

The simple past
Sue **broke** her leg when she **fell** off her bike yesterday.
Did you **listen** to your new CDs last night?
Mr Owen has gone to Wales. He **left** two days ago.
→ P 1, 3b (p. 14)

e Die Verlaufsform der Vergangenheit
Wenn etwas zu einer bestimmten Zeit in der Vergangenheit gerade **im Verlauf** war.

The past progressive
What **were** you **doing** at 10 o'clock last night?
Miss Picken **was having** a bath when the lights went out.

f Das Futur mit *will*
Wenn man **Vermutungen** über die Zukunft äußert oder **Vorhersagen** macht.

The *will*-future
The weather **will be** fine tomorrow.
I don't think you**'ll like** it at Tony's party.

g Das Futur mit *going to*
Wenn man **Absichten** oder **Pläne** beschreibt.

The *going to*-future
We**'re going to have** a party next weekend.
What **are** you **going to do** tonight?

S

Unit 1

2 Das *present perfect* mit *since* und *for*

Das *present perfect* kann verwendet werden, um über **Zustände** zu sprechen, die in der Vergangenheit begonnen haben und in der Gegenwart noch andauern.

The present perfect with *since* and *for*

My family **has lived** in London since last summer.
Meine Familie **lebt** seit dem letzten Sommer in London.
We**'ve had** this old house for twenty years.
Wir **haben** dieses alte Haus seit 20 Jahren.
Tom's mother **has been** out of work since May last year.
Toms Mutter **ist** seit Mai letzten Jahres arbeitslos.

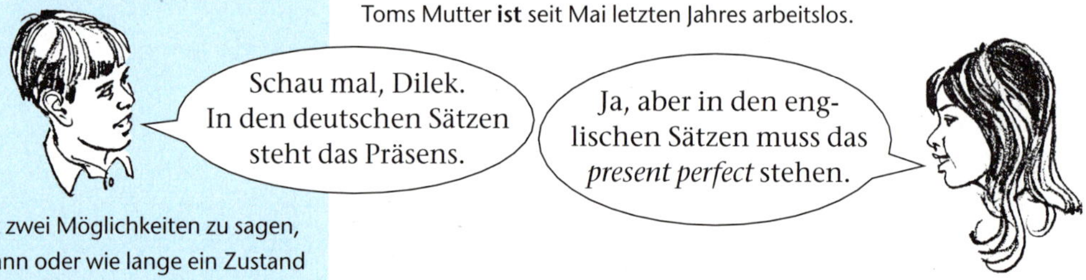

Es gibt zwei Möglichkeiten zu sagen, seit wann oder wie lange ein Zustand schon andauert:

– Man verwendet *since* mit dem *present perfect*, wenn man sagen will, **wann** der Zustand begonnen hat *(since 1996, since April, since last year)*.

since + *Zeitpunkt*

My mother **has been** a teacher | since 1996. / since April. / since last year.

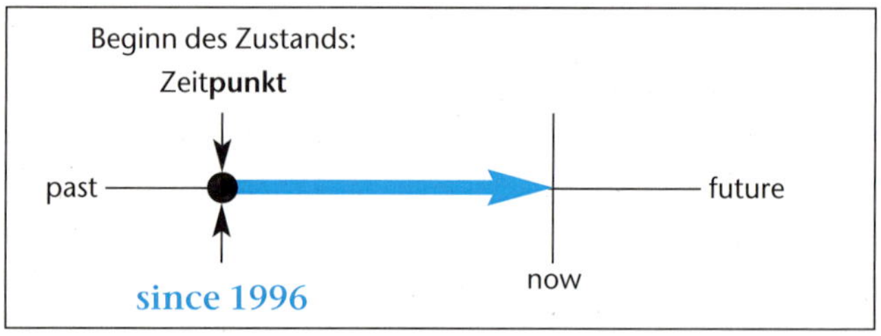

– Man verwendet *for* mit dem *present perfect*, wenn man sagen will, **wie lange** der Zustand schon andauert *(for three months, for years, for a long time)*.

for + *Zeitraum*

My mother **has been** a teacher | for three months. / for years. / for a long time.

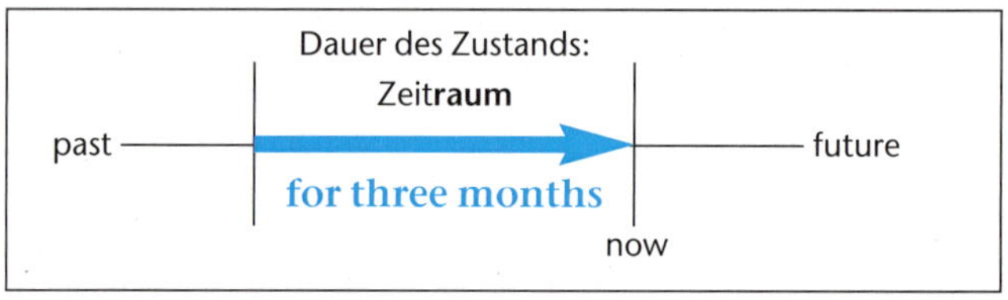

Wenn man danach fragen will, seit wann oder wie lange ein Zustand schon andauert, lautet die Frage *How long ...?* + *present perfect*.
Darauf kann man mit *since* + Zeitpunkt oder *for* + Zeitraum antworten.

How long has Megan **lived** in London?
– Since last month. – For a few weeks.
Wie lange / Seit wann wohnt Megan (schon) in London?
– Seit letztem Monat. – Seit ein paar Wochen.

→ P 4, 5, 6 (p. 15)

In English: The present perfect with *since* and *for*

1 We use the present perfect to describe a state[1] or situation that started in the past and has gone on up to the present.

2 We use *since* with the present perfect to say **when** the situation started (= a point of time).

3 We use *for* with the present perfect to say **how long** the situation has lasted[2] (= a period of time).

[1]state *Zustand* [2](to) last *(an)dauern*

3 Die Verlaufsform des *present perfect*

a Gebrauch

Mit dem *present perfect progressive* drückt man aus, dass eine **Handlung** oder ein **Vorgang** in der Vergangenheit begonnen hat und bis (oder fast bis) in die Gegenwart andauert.

⚠ Im Deutschen benutzt man in diesem Fall meist das Präsens. Aber in den englischen Sätzen muss das *present perfect progressive* stehen.

The present perfect progressive

Use

The kids **have been playing** football since two o'clock.
Die Kinder **spielen** (schon) seit zwei Uhr Fußball.
(Die Kinder haben um zwei Uhr mit dem Fußballspielen begonnen und spielen jetzt, d.h. zum Zeitpunkt des Sprechens, immer noch.)

You**'ve been driving** for three hours. Shall I drive now?
Du **fährst** schon seit drei Stunden. …
How long **has** it **been raining**? – Since lunch.
Wie lange **regnet** es schon? – Seit dem Mittagessen.

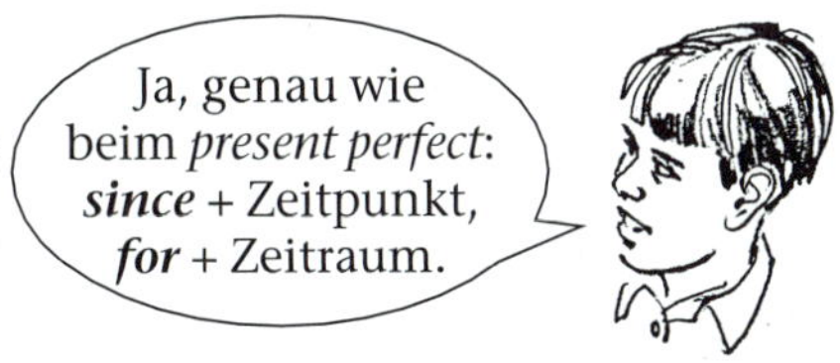

b Form

Das *present perfect progressive* wird mit *have/has been* + *-ing*-Form gebildet.

Form

Statements:

I/You/We/They **have been** | **reading**.
He/She **has been** | **reading**.

I/You/We/They **haven't been** | **playing**.
He/She **hasn't been** | **playing**.

Questions:

How long **have** I/you/we/they **been** | **watching** TV?
How long **has** he/she **been** | **watching** TV?

c Verben, die **Zustände** beschreiben, können nicht in der *progressive form* verwendet werden. Solche Verben sind z.B. *know, like, need.*

How long **have** you **known** Megan?
Nicht: How long ~~have you been knowing~~ Megan?

→ P 8, 9 (p. 16)

In English: The present perfect progressive

1 We form the present perfect progressive with *have/has been* + *-ing* form.
2 We use the present perfect progressive to say that an action began in the past and is still going on now.

4 *since* + Nebensatz

Zur Angabe des Zeitpunktes kann nach ***since*** entweder ein **Nomen** *(Sunday; ten o'clock)* oder ein **Satz im *simple past*** *(he left; I came home)* stehen.

since + sub-clause

We haven't seen Mark | **since Sunday**. / **since he left**.
seit Sonntag / seit er gegangen ist.

I've been writing letters | **since ten o'clock**. / **since I came home**.

In Unit 1 hast du gelernt ...

– zu sagen, ob und wann jemand etwas getan hat.	▶ I've been to Florida. We went there last summer.
– zu sagen, seit wann oder wie lange ein Zustand oder ein Vorgang bereits andauert.	▶ I've known Claudia since 1996. Mary and I have been friends for many years. I've been watching television since I came home. Mr Owen has been waiting for two hours.
– Personen zu beschreiben.	▶ Liz has got black hair, brown eyes and a friendly face.
– zu sagen, wie sich jemand fühlt.	▶ On her first day Megan was nervous about her new school, but now she feels good about it.

Unit 2

1 Wiederholung: Modale Hilfsverben und ihre Ersatzverben — Revision: Modal auxiliaries and their substitutes

a Fähigkeit: *can/could – be able to* — Ability: *can/could – be able to*

Present: *can – be able to*	My mother **can speak** / **is able to speak** English but she **can't speak** / **isn't able to speak** French.
Past: *could – was/were able to*	**Could** you **swim** when you were five? – No, I **couldn't**. The shop was open. So I **was able to get** some bread.
Andere Zeiten: *have/has been able to, will be able to*	I**'ve** always **been able to sing** well. In a few years you**'ll be able to speak** English well.

b Erlaubnis: *can/could, may ▸◂ mustn't – be allowed to* — Permission: *can/could, may ▸◂ mustn't – be allowed to*

Bitte um Erlaubnis: *can, may, could*	**Can/May/Could** we **use** your phone, please? – Yes, of course.
Ausdrückliches Verbot: *mustn't*	You **mustn't leave** your bike here.
Present: *can – be allowed to*	My friend **can** always **do** what she likes. We **can't go** / **aren't allowed to go** to school discos. Our parents say we aren't old enough.
Past: *could, was/were allowed to*	When we were children, we **could watch** / **were allowed to watch** TV until 9 o'clock.
Andere Zeiten: *have/has been allowed to, will be allowed to*	Our dog **has** always **been allowed to sleep** on the sofa. **Will** you **be allowed to go** to the disco next week?

c Notwendigkeit, Zwang: *must ▸◂ needn't – have (got) to* — Necessity, strong obligation: *must ▸◂ needn't – have (got) to*

Present: *must, needn't – have (got) to*	I **must leave** / **have to leave** now. I don't want to be late. You **needn't do** / **don't have to do** your homework now. You can do it later.
Past und andere Zeiten: *had to, have/has had to, will have to*	**Did** you **have to wait** long? – No, I didn't. Emma **has** always **had to help** her parents. I'm sure people **won't have to work** all day in the future.

→ P 3 (p. 28)

2 Bedingungssätze

Ein Bedingungssatz besteht aus einem **Nebensatz mit *if* (*if-clause*)** und einem **Hauptsatz** *(main clause)*.
Im Nebensatz wird eine Bedingung genannt. Im Hauptsatz steht, was geschieht, wenn diese Bedingung erfüllt wird.
Wenn der Hauptsatz vor dem *if*-Satz steht, verwendet man im Englischen kein Komma.

⚠ Beachte den Unterschied zwischen *if* und *when*:
If leitet einen **Nebensatz der Bedingung** ein.

When leitet einen **Nebensatz der Zeit** ein.

Conditional sentences

REMEMBER

if-clause	Main clause
If it rains,	we'll watch TV.
Wenn (= Falls) es regnet,	sehen wir fern.

Main clause	*if*-clause
We'll watch TV	if it rains.

If my father comes home, we'll have lunch together.
Wenn (= Falls) mein Vater nach Hause kommt/kommen sollte, …
(Ich bin nicht sicher, ob mein Vater heute zum Mittagessen kommt.)

When my father comes home, we'll have lunch together.
Wenn (= Sobald/Dann wenn) mein Vater nach Hause kommt, …
(Ich bin sicher, dass mein Vater zum Mittagessen kommt.)

a* Bedingungssätze I

Bedingungssätze des Typs I drücken aus, dass die **Bedingung offen, d.h. erfüllbar** ist. Es ist gut möglich, dass das im *if*-Satz Gesagte eintritt.
Der *if*-Satz kann sich auch auf eine Tatsache in der Gegenwart beziehen.

Conditional sentences, type I

If the boys **play** well, they **will win**.
Wenn die Jungen gut spielen, gewinnen sie/werden sie gewinnen.
(Die Jungen sind eine gute Mannschaft. Es ist durchaus möglich, dass sie gut spielen.)
If Emma **likes** football, she **should go** to the match.
(Emma hat Interesse an Fußball. Also sollte sie zu dem Match gehen.)

Im *if*-Satz steht das ***simple present***.
Im Hauptsatz stehen häufig
- das ***will-future***
- ein **Modalverb** (z.B. *can, must, should*) + Infinitiv
- ein **Imperativ**.

If you **come** to my party, you**'ll meet** Sue and Pete.
Emma is a vegetarian. **If** she **comes** for dinner, we **shouldn't have** meat.
If you **need** the police in Britain, **phone** 999.

Kein „will" im if-Satz!

In allgemeingültigen Aussagen steht auch im Hauptsatz das ***simple present***.

If you **add** blue to yellow, you **get** green.
If I **miss** the last bus home, I always **take** a taxi.
(*If* bedeutet hier „jedes Mal, wenn …")

→ P 4, 5, 6 (pp. 28/29)

* In Bundesländern, in denen das Thema „Bedingungssätze I" bereits in Klassenstufe 6 zum Pflichtstoff gehörte, ist dieser Abschnitt als Wiederholung zu betrachten.

b Bedingungssätze II

Bedingungssätze des Typs II drücken aus, dass man es für **unwahrscheinlich (oder unmöglich)** hält, dass das im *if*-Satz Gesagte eintritt.

Conditional sentences, type II

If the boys **played** well, they **would win**.
Wenn die Jungen gut spielten/spielen würden, würden sie gewinnen. (Die Jungen sind zurzeit nicht in Form. Es ist nicht zu erwarten, dass sie gut spielen.)

Im *if*-Satz des Typs II steht das ***simple past***. (Der *if*-Satz bezieht sich aber trotzdem auf die Zukunft oder die Gegenwart.)
Im Hauptsatz steht ***would/could/ might*** + Infinitiv.

If I **won** £100,000, I'**d** (= I **would**) **fly** round the world.
Wenn ich 100.000 Pfund gewänne/gewinnen würde, …
If Emma **had** more time, she **might read** more.
Wenn Emma mehr Zeit hätte, …
If Grandma **was** 30 years younger, she **would buy** a motorbike. Wenn Oma 30 Jahre jünger wäre, …

Statt *was* steht im *if*-Satz manchmal *were*.

If Grandma **were** 30 years younger, …

Um Ratschläge zu erteilen, wird die Wendung ***If I were you, …*** benutzt.

If I **were** you, I'**d take** the job.
Wenn ich du wäre, würde ich … / Ich an deiner Stelle würde …

Statt des *simple past* kann im *if*-Satz auch ***could*** + Infinitiv stehen.

If you **could meet** a famous person, who **would** you **like** to meet?
Wenn du einen berühmten Menschen treffen könntest, …?

Kein „would" im if-Satz!

→ P 8, 9, 10, 11 (p. 30)

In English: Conditional sentences

1 Conditional sentence, type I: We think the condition may come true[1]. We use the simple present in the *if*-clause and the *will*-future, a modal auxiliary or the imperative in the main clause.
If one thing always follows from another, we use the simple present in the main clause.

2 Conditional sentence, type II: We think the condition won't or can't come true. We use the simple past in the *if*-clause and *would/could/might* in the main clause.

[1](to) come true *hier: erfüllt werden*

In Unit 2 hast du gelernt …

- über Spielregeln zu sprechen. ▶ Players must kick the ball over the goalposts.
- zu sagen, was vielleicht der Fall ist oder vielleicht geschehen könnte. ▶ You may be right. They say it might rain tomorrow.
- zu sagen, was unter bestimmten Bedingungen geschieht oder geschehen könnte. ▶ If we win today, we'll go to the championships. If we won today, we'd go to the championships.
- Landschaften zu beschreiben. ▶ My part of Germany has lots of small lakes.
- Notizen zu machen und übersichtlich anzuordnen. ▶ Cardiff = capital: exciting

Unit 3

Bestimmende Relativsätze
Defining relative clauses

a* **Gebrauch**

Bestimmende Relativsätze werden verwendet, um ein Nomen genauer zu bestimmen. Ohne diese Relativsätze wäre unklar, wer oder was genau gemeint ist (welcher Mann? welcher Apparat?).
Relativsätze werden durch **Relativpronomen** eingeleitet: *who, which, that, whose.*
⚠ Relativsätze haben die übliche Wortstellung: **S – V – O**.

Use

The man who invented radar was from Scotland.
Der Mann, der das Radar erfunden hat, kam aus Schottland.

Is that **the gadget** which feeds the cat automatically?
Ist das der Apparat, der die Katze automatisch füttert?

	Subject	Verb	Object
	That girl	helped	me.
That's the girl	who	**helped**	me.

Das ist das Mädchen, das mir **geholfen hat**.

b* **Die Relativpronomen *who, which, that***

The relative pronouns *who, which, that*

Die Relativpronomen *who, which, that* werden unterschiedlich gebraucht:
- ***who*** und (weniger häufig) ***that*** für **Personen**
- ***which*** und ***that*** für **Dinge** (und Tiere).

I know **the woman** who/that wrote this book.
Ich kenne **die Frau, die** dieses Buch geschrieben hat.
It's about **a spaceship** which/that goes to Mars.
Es handelt von **einem Raumschiff, das** zum Mars fliegt.

- *who für Personen*
- *which für Dinge*
- *that für Dinge oder Personen*

Who, which und *that* können sowohl **Subjekt** als auch **Objekt** des Relativsatzes sein.

	Subject		
That's **the boy**	who/that	was at the party.	
Das ist **der Junge,**	der	auf der Fete war.	
	Object	**Subject**	
That's **the boy**	who/that	I	saw at the party.
Das ist **der Junge,**	den	ich	auf der Fete gesehen habe.

→ P 2, 3 (p. 40)

c **Das Relativpronomen *whose***

The relative pronoun *whose*

Das Relativpronomen *whose* entspricht dem deutschen „dessen, deren". Es bezieht sich meist auf Personen, kann aber auch für Dinge (und Tiere) verwendet werden.
Auf *whose* folgt immer ein Nomen.

Andrew is **the boy** whose mother works for the BBC.
Andrew ist **der Junge,** dessen Mutter bei der BBC arbeitet.
Mrs McKenna is **the woman** whose daughter designed a cat feeder.
Frau McKenna ist **die Frau,** deren Tochter einen Fütterungsautomaten für Katzen entworfen hat.

⚠ Verwechsle *whose* nicht mit der Kurzform *who's (= who is).*

The boy whose **picture** is in the magazine is my friend.
The boy who's **standing** at the front is my brother.

→ P 4 (p. 40)

* In Bundesländern, in denen das Thema „Relativsätze" bereits in Klassenstufe 6 zum Pflichtstoff gehörte, sind die Abschnitte a und b als Wiederholung zu betrachten.

d Relativsätze ohne Relativpronomen

Wenn *who, which, that* **Objekt** des Relativsatzes sind, werden sie meistens **weggelassen**.

Relativsätze ohne Relativpronomen nennt man ***contact clauses***, weil das näher zu bestimmende Nomen (im ersten Beispielsatz: *man*) und das Subjekt des Relativsatzes (im ersten Beispielsatz: *we*) **Kontakt** haben: Es steht kein Relativpronomen dazwischen.

Contact clauses

	Object	Subject	
Is that the man	who	we	met last week?

oder:

Is that the man	><	we	met last week?
…,	den	wir	letzte Woche getroffen haben?

who = **Objekt: kann weggelassen werden**

aber:

	Subject	
Is Mr Croft the man	who	had the accident?
…,	der	den Unfall hatte?

who = **Subjekt: darf nicht weggelassen werden**

→ P 5, 7 (p. 41)

e Relativsätze mit Präpositionen

Anders als im Deutschen steht eine Präposition in englischen Relativsätzen an derselben Stelle wie im Hauptsatz, d.h. **hinter dem Verb.**

Relative clauses with prepositions

The hotel which we **stayed at** was expensive.

Das Hotel, in dem wir **wohnten**, war teuer.

Vergleiche: We **stayed at** a hotel. (Hauptsatz)

Auch wenn das Relativpronomen **Objekt einer Präposition** ist, kann es weggelassen werden.

The hotel we **stayed at** was expensive.

→ P 6, 8 (pp. 41/42)

In English: Relative clauses

1 A defining relative clause adds important information about a noun. It does not have commas.
2 The relative pronouns are *who/that* for people, and *which/that* for things.
The relative pronoun *whose* means 'deren', 'dessen'.
3 Contact clauses: When the relative pronoun is the object of the relative clause, we can leave it out.
4 A preposition stays in the same place as in the main clause – that means after the verb.

In Unit 3 hast du gelernt …

- über die Funktionsweise von Geräten zu sprechen.
  ▶ When you open the box, the cassette starts.
  When you push the button, the motor stops.
- zusätzliche Informationen zu geben, die für das Verständnis notwendig sind.
  ▶ Bob is the boy who told me about the café.
  That's the gadget that feeds the cat.
  I met a girl whose sister knows you.
  Who was the man you met in the museum?
- eine Geschichte zu erzählen.
  ▶ I was working in the control room when suddenly the phone rang. So I … . Then I …

Unit 4

1 Das Passiv / The passive

a Aktiv und Passiv / Active and passive

Man kann einen Vorgang oder eine Handlung mit einem Aktivsatz oder mit einem Passivsatz beschreiben:

Mit einem **Aktivsatz** sagt man, wer oder was etwas **tut**.

Active – for example in a text about important inventors:

Alexander Graham Bell **invented** the telephone in 1876.

Im Aktivsatz führt das Subjekt die Handlung aus: Alexander Graham Bell erfand das Telefon.

Bei einem **Passivsatz** liegt die Betonung darauf, mit wem oder womit etwas **getan wird**.

Passive – for example in a text about important inventions:

The telephone **was invented** in 1876.

Im Passivsatz wird mit dem Subjekt etwas getan: Das Telefon wurde 1876 erfunden.

b Form / Form

Man bildet das Passiv mit einer **Form von *be* + Partizip Perfekt** *(past participle)*. Also:

- **Simple present passive:** *am/is/are* + past participle

		Form of *be*	Past participle	
Simple present	Our dog	is	fed	at six.
	Unser Hund wird um sechs gefüttert.			
	Lots of bikes	are	stolen	here.
	Hier werden viele Räder gestohlen.			

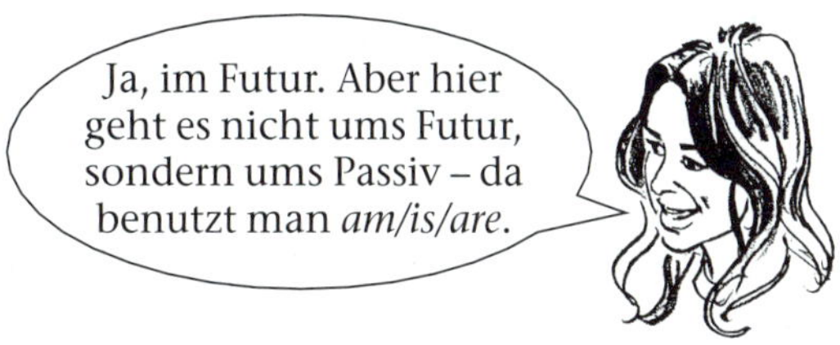

- **Simple past passive:** *was/were* + past participle
- **Present perfect passive:** *have been/has been* + past participle

		Form of *be*	Past participle	
Simple past	The match	was	shown	on TV.
	Das Spiel wurde im Fernsehen gezeigt.			
Present perfect	The money	has not been	found	yet.
	Das Geld ist noch nicht gefunden worden. / Man hat das Geld noch nicht gefunden.			

Passiv: Form von „be“ + Partizip Perfekt

Für die Verwendung der Zeitformen im Passiv gelten dieselben Regeln wie im Aktiv.

⚠ Eine zum Verb gehörende Präposition steht an derselben Stelle wie im Aktivsatz, d.h. **hinter dem Verb** (→ S 3: e).

This problem **was** **talked about** all night.

Über dieses Problem **wurde** die ganze Nacht **geredet**.

Vergleiche: We **talked about** this problem. (Aktiv)

→ P 1, 2, 7a/b (pp. 55, 57)

c **Das Passiv nach *will* und modalen Hilfsverben**

In Passivsätzen mit Hilfsverben (z.B. *will, can, must, should*) folgt auf das Hilfsverb der Infinitiv ***be* + Partizip Perfekt** *(be built, be bought, be left)*.

The passive after *will* and modal auxiliaries

***Will*-future**	A new road **will be built** soon. Bald wird eine neue Straße gebaut (werden).
Modal auxiliaries	Stamps **cannot be bought** here. Briefmarken können hier nicht gekauft werden. / Man kann hier keine Briefmarken kaufen. Hats and coats **should be left** at the door. Hüte und Mäntel sollten am Eingang abgegeben werden. / … sollte man am Eingang abgeben.

→ P 7c (p. 57)

d **Gebrauch**

Mit einem Passivsatz kann man Handlungen beschreiben, ohne zu sagen, wer die Handlung ausführt. Das Passiv steht daher z.B. oft in Berichten über Unfälle oder Verbrechen sowie in historischen Berichten oder technischen Beschreibungen.

Wenn man in einem Passivsatz hervorheben will, **von wem** etwas getan wird oder **wodurch** etwas geschieht, verwendet man die Präposition *by*.

Use

Two men **were killed** in a road accident near Chester. Seven people **were** badly **hurt** and **had to be taken** to hospital.
The earliest parts of the Tower **were built** more than 900 years ago. It **was planned** as a castle and **was used** as a palace. Later many famous people **were executed** there.

St Paul's Cathedral **was built by Christopher Wren.**
… von Christopher Wren …
The restaurant **was destroyed by fire.**
… durch einen Brand …

→ P 3, 4 (pp. 55/56)

In English: The passive

1 The passive is formed with a form of *be* + past participle.
2 The passive is used to say what is done to people or things. Often we do not say who does the action.
3 In a passive sentence, *by* is used when we want to say who does the action.

2 **Wiederholung: Mengenbezeichnungen mit zählbaren und nicht zählbaren Nomen**

- ***much*** („viel") + nicht zählbares Nomen
  many („viele") + zählbares Nomen im Plural
- ***a little*** („ein bisschen, (ein) wenig") + nicht zählbares Nomen
  a few („ein paar, einige") + zählbares Nomen im Plural
- ***lots of / a lot of / some / any*** + nicht zählbares oder zählbares Nomen

Revision: Quantifiers with countable and uncountable nouns

Nicht zählbare Nomen	Plural von zählbaren Nomen
How **much money** have you got? – Not **much**.	How **many T-shirts** did you buy? – Not **many**.
I've got **a little money**. I've got **a little time**. I've got **a little homework**.	I've got **a few pounds**. I've got **a few minutes**. I've got to do **a few exercises**.
Tim has got **a lot of money**. Debbie hasn't got **any homework**.	Tim has got **a lot of pounds**. Debbie hasn't got to do **any exercises**.

→ P 5 (p. 56)

In Unit 4 hast du gelernt ...

- über öffentliche Verkehrsmittel und Verkehrsverbindungen zu sprechen.
  ▶ What's the best route to Eaton Square?
  – Take the number 4 bus to Oak Street, then get off and change to the number 19.
- zu sagen, was gemacht wird oder wurde oder was jemandem passiert ist.
  ▶ I'm driven to school every day.
  The school was built last year.
  I've been robbed.
- zu sagen, von wem etwas gemacht wird oder wurde.
  ▶ Madame Tussaud's is visited by two million people every year.
  Tom Sawyer was written by Mark Twain.
- Empfehlungen zu geben.
  ▶ A new swimming-pool should be built.

Unit 5

1 Das Reflexivpronomen
a Formen und Gebrauch

The reflexive pronoun
Forms and use

Das Reflexivpronomen (*myself, yourself, himself* usw.) ist **„rückbezüglich"**: Es bezieht sich auf das Subjekt des Satzes und bezeichnet dieselbe Person oder Sache wie das Subjekt (*I, you, Leroy* usw.).

I taught **myself** French. — Ich habe **mir** Französisch beigebracht.
Be careful or **you**'ll hurt **yourself**. — ... oder du verletzt **dich**.
Leroy can look after **himself**. — ... auf **sich (selbst)** aufpassen.
She often talks to **herself**. — Sie spricht oft mit **sich (selbst)**.
The cat is clean. **It** washes **itself** all day. — ... Sie putzt **sich** ...
We can teach **ourselves** the new game. — ... **uns** das neue Spiel beibringen.
Did **you** listen to **yourselves** on cassette? — ... **euch** auf Cassette angehört?
They can look after **themselves**. — ... auf **sich (selbst)** aufpassen.

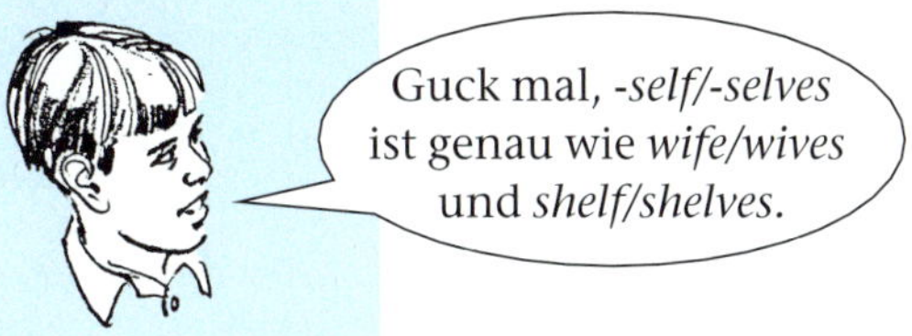

⚠ Beachte den Unterschied zwischen Reflexivpronomen *(himself)* und Personalpronomen *(him)*.

Aled fell off his bike.
He hurt **himself**.
Er (Aled) hat **sich (selbst)** verletzt.

Aled rode into David.
He hurt **him**.
Er (Aled) hat **ihn** (David) verletzt.

Merke dir die Wendungen:

Enjoy yourself. „Viel Spaß!" („Amüsier dich gut!")
Help yourself. „Greif zu!" („Bedien dich!")

Did you **enjoy yourselves** at the party?
Habt ihr auf der Party Spaß gehabt?
The food is on the table – just **help yourself**.
Das Essen steht auf dem Tisch – bedien dich einfach.

⚠ Viele Verben, die im Deutschen reflexiv sind, sind im Englischen **nicht reflexiv**:

(to) change	*sich (ver)ändern; sich umziehen*
(to) complain	*sich beschweren, sich beklagen*
(to) decide	*sich entscheiden*
(to) feel	*sich fühlen*
(to) hide	*sich verstecken*
(to) imagine sth.	*sich etwas vorstellen*
(to) listen to sth.	*sich etwas anhören*
(to) meet	*sich treffen (mit)*
(to) move	*sich bewegen*
(to) open	*sich öffnen*
(to) refer to	*sich beziehen auf*
(to) relax	*sich entspannen*
(to) remember	*sich erinnern (an)*
(to) sit down	*sich (hin)setzen*
(to) turn (around)	*sich umdrehen*
(to) watch sth.	*sich etwas ansehen*
(to) worry	*sich Sorgen machen*

(to) buy kann mit Reflexivpronomen verwendet werden. Häufiger steht es jedoch ohne.

Megan **felt** miserable after her mother died.
Megan **fühlte sich** elend ...
Mrs Mir and I **met** at the station.
Frau Mir und ich **haben uns** am Bahnhof **getroffen**.
Can you **remember** when we first met?
Kannst du **dich** daran **erinnern**, ...?

I'**ve bought (myself)** a new computer.

→ P 1, 2 (p. 66)

b Reflexivpronomen oder *each other*?

Reflexivpronomen:
„sich" (= sich selbst)
each other:
„sich" (= sich gegenseitig, einander)
Statt *each other* kann man auch *one another* verwenden.

-self/-selves = *sich selbst*
each other = *einander, sich gegenseitig*

Reflexive pronoun or *each other*?

Ann and Dan are looking at **themselves**.

Ann and Dan are looking at **each other**.

→ P 3, 4 (pp. 66/67)

In English: Reflexive pronouns and *each other*

1. The reflexive pronoun *(myself, herself, ourselves, ...)* refers to the subject.
2. There are some verbs that are reflexive in German, but not reflexive in English (e.g. *imagine, meet, worry*).
3. *-selves* means 'sich (selbst)', *each other* means 'sich (gegenseitig)'.

2 Das verstärkende Pronomen

Man kann *myself, yourself, himself* usw. auch verwenden, um ein Nomen oder Pronomen **hervorzuheben**. Im Deutschen verwenden wir dafür „selbst" oder „selber".
Wenn das Subjekt hervorgehoben werden soll, rückt das verstärkende *-self*-Pronomen oft an das Satzende.

The emphasizing pronoun

The house itself is quite ordinary, but the garden is fantastic. Das Haus **selbst** ist ziemlich gewöhnlich, …

I rang the number and spoke to **Madonna** herself.
Ich habe die Nummer gewählt und mit Madonna **selbst** gesprochen.

We're going to build the garage ourselves.
Wir haben vor, die Garage **selbst** zu bauen.

Sorry, but I can't help you. **I**'m a stranger here myself.
… Ich bin hier **selbst** fremd.

In English: Emphasizing pronouns

Myself, yourself, etc. can be used to emphasize[1] a noun or pronoun. Their meaning is 'selbst', 'selber'.
[1](to) emphasize ['emfəsaɪz] *betonen, hervorheben*

3 Der Infinitiv mit *to* nach Fragewörtern

Der Infinitiv mit *to* kann **nach Fragewörtern** *(how, what, when, where, which, who)* verwendet werden. Er entspricht einem Nebensatz mit einem modalen Hilfsverb *(can, could, might, must, should)*. Im Englischen wird jedoch die Konstruktion „Fragewort + *to*-Infinitiv" bevorzugt.

The *to*-infinitive after question words

I don't know | **what** to do / **what I should do** | in my free time.
…, was ich in meiner Freizeit machen soll.

Can you tell me | **how** to get / **how I can get** | to the station?
…, wie ich zum Bahnhof komme?

I've got no idea | **which way** to go. / **which way I must go.**
…, welchen Weg ich gehen muss.

→ P 6 (p. 67)

In English: The *to*-infinitive after question words

After question words *(how, what, when, where, which, who)* we often use the *to*-infinitive, not a sub-clause.

4 Wiederholung: Die Steigerung der Adjektive und Adverbien

Revision: The comparison of adjectives and adverbs

- Steigerung mit ***-er/-est***:
  - einsilbige Adjektive und Adverbien

clean – cleaner – cleanest
thin – thinner – thinnest
nice – nicer – nicest
fast – faster – fastest

  - zweisilbige Adjektive auf *-y*

happy – happier – happiest

- Steigerung mit ***more/most***:
  - die meisten zweisilbigen Adjektive
  - alle Adjektive mit mehr als zwei Silben

careful – more careful – most careful
expensive – more expensive – most expensive

  - Adverbien auf *-ly*

quickly – more quickly – most quickly

- **unregelmäßige Steigerung**:
  - *good/well*
  - *bad/badly*

good/well – better – best
bad/badly – worse – worst

→ P 7 (p. 68)

5 Das *present progressive* für Pläne und Verabredungen

Wie du weißt, benutzt man das *present progressive*, wenn jemand gerade etwas tut oder wenn etwas gerade stattfindet.

Du kannst das *present progressive* auch verwenden, wenn eine Handlung für die Zukunft **fest geplant** bzw. **verabredet** ist. Dabei muss klar sein, dass es sich um etwas Zukünftiges handelt.

The present progressive for plans and arrangements

REMEMBER

I'm busy. I'**m making** a poster for my Art class.
Please stop! You'**re hurting** me.
Leroy can't come to the phone. He'**s washing** his hair.
The dogs **are playing** in the garden now.

Jenny **is having** a party **on Saturday**. **Are** you **going**?
– I can't. I'**m visiting** my grandma **this weekend**.
Jenny gibt Samstag eine Party. Gehst du hin? / Wirst du hingehen?
– Ich kann nicht. Ich besuche dieses Wochenende meine Oma.

→ P 8, 9 (p. 68)

In English: The present progressive for plans and arrangements
We can use the present progressive to say that something has been arranged for the future.

In Unit 5 hast du gelernt ...

- zu sagen, dass jemand sich verletzt hat, sich selbst zugesehen hat usw. ▶ I've hurt myself with a knife. We watched ourselves on video.
- zu sagen, dass jemand etwas selbst gemacht hat. ▶ I made this dress myself.
- zu sagen, dass man sich gegenseitig hilft, sich etwas zeigt usw. ▶ The kids in my class all help each other.
- etwas anzubieten. ▶ Can I get something for you?
- über feste Verabredungen und Pläne für die Zukunft zu sprechen. ▶ What are you doing tonight? – I'm seeing my friends.
- jemanden für etwas zu interessieren. ▶ It's the best street festival ever. They've got some really good live bands.

Unit 6

1 Frageanhängsel
a* Gebrauch

Frageanhängsel *(aren't you? / can he? / don't they?)* werden häufig in der gesprochenen Sprache verwendet, wenn man vom Gesprächspartner **Zustimmung** erwartet. Deutsche Frageanhängsel sind zum Beispiel *nicht wahr? / oder? / ne? / gell? / woll?*

Auf Aussagen mit Frageanhängseln kann man mit Zustimmung oder Widerspruch reagieren.

Question tags
Use

You're German, **aren't you?**
Du bist Deutsche, nicht wahr?
Mark can't play the guitar, **can he?**
Mark kann nicht Gitarre spielen, oder?
Your friends live in London, **don't they?**
Deine Freunde leben in London, nicht wahr?

You go to Heinrich-Heine-Schule, **don't you?**

Yes, I do. / Yes, that's right.	No, I don't. (I go to ...)
Zustimmung („Ja."/„Stimmt.")	**Widerspruch** („Nein.")

You aren't from Germany, **are you?**

No, I'm not. / That's right.	I am! / Oh yes, I am!
Zustimmung („Nein."/„Stimmt.")	**Widerspruch** („Doch!")

* In Bundesländern, in denen das Thema „Frageanhängsel" bereits in Klassenstufe 6 zum Pflichtstoff gehörte, sind die Abschnitte 1a und 1b als Wiederholung zu betrachten.

b* **Form**

Ist der Hauptsatz **bejaht**, so ist das Frageanhängsel **verneint**.
Ist der Hauptsatz **verneint**, so ist das Frageanhängsel **bejaht**.

Hauptsatz **+** → *Anhängsel* **–**
Hauptsatz **–** → *Anhängsel* **+**

Form

You'**re** 13, **aren't you?**
bejaht → verneint
Hannah **isn't** 14 yet, **is she?**
verneint → bejaht

Frageanhängsel bestehen aus einem (verneinten oder bejahten) **Hilfsverb + Personalpronomen**.

Melissa is waiting for the bus, **isn't she?**

Wird im Hauptsatz ein Hilfsverb verwendet, so benutzt man dasselbe Hilfsverb im Frageanhängsel.

We **must** be home by 10 o'clock, **mustn't we?**
Winston **isn't** enjoying himself, **is he?**
You'**ve** got a cat, **haven't you?**
The party **will** finish by 10.30, **won't it?**
Your mum **doesn't** like loud music, **does she?**

Wird im Hauptsatz **kein** Hilfsverb verwendet, so benutzt man im Frageanhängsel *don't/doesn't/didn't*.

That boy and girl **look** good together, **don't they?**
He **spends** a lot of time at her house, **doesn't he?**
They **danced** most of the evening, **didn't they?**

⚠ Beachte folgende Sonderfälle:
- Hauptsatz: *this/that*
  → Frageanhängsel: *… it?*
- Hauptsatz: *there*
  → Frageanhängsel: *… there?*

That's right, **isn't it?**
There weren't many people at the party, **were there?**

c **Intonation**

Um auszudrücken, dass man vom Gesprächspartner Zustimmung zur eigenen Aussage erwartet, werden Frageanhängsel mit fallender Intonation *(falling intonation)* gesprochen, d. h., die Stimme geht am Satzende **nach unten** – wie bei einer Aussage.

Intonation

You can't see very well, can you?
You need help with your homework, don't you?

He spends a lot of time at his computer, doesn't he?

→ P 4, 5 (pp. 78/79)

In English: Question tags

1 We use question tags in spoken English when we are asking the listener to agree with us.
2 If the main clause is positive, the question tag is negative.
If the main clause is negative, the question tag is positive.

2 Das Gerundium

a Form

Das Gerundium *(gerund)* wird durch Anfügen von *-ing* an das Vollverb gebildet.

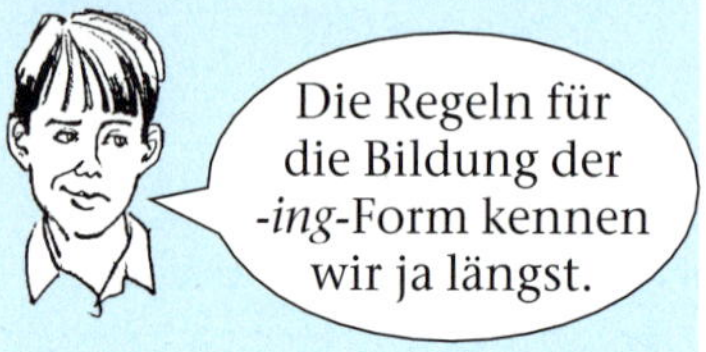

The gerund

Form

REMEMBER

read + -ing = **reading**

Stummes *-e* fällt weg:

make + -ing = making

write + -ing = writing

Nach einem einzelnen, betonten Vokal wird ein Endkonsonant verdoppelt:

sit + -ing = sitting

run + -ing = running

b Gebrauch

Das Gerundium hat im Satz die Funktion eines **Nomens**.

Use

Reading / **Football** | is fun. — Lesen / Fußball | macht Spaß.

Stop | **reading**. / **the car**. — Hör auf zu lesen. / Halt das Auto an.

Wie ein Verb kann das Gerundium erweitert werden, und zwar durch

- ein **Objekt**
- eine **adverbiale Bestimmung**.

Reading comics is fun.
Comics zu lesen / Das Lesen von Comics macht Spaß.

Reading in bed is fun.
Im Bett zu lesen macht Spaß.

c Das Gerundium als Subjekt

Das Gerundium kann Subjekt eines Satzes sein. Im Deutschen wird es oft durch einen Infinitiv oder ein Nomen wiedergegeben.

The gerund as subject

Swimming is good for your back.
Schwimmen ist gut für deinen Rücken.

Taking a taxi can be expensive.
Mit dem Taxi zu fahren / Eine Taxifahrt / Taxifahren kann teuer sein.

→ P 9 (p. 80)

d Das Gerundium als Objekt

Nach den Verben *enjoy, finish/stop, give up, go on, imagine, miss, practise, suggest* und einigen anderen steht ein zweites Verb als Gerundium, **nicht** als Infinitiv.

The gerund as object

Tim **suggested inviting** Yasmin to the party.
Tim schlug vor, Yasmin zur Party einzuladen.

I can't **imagine living** in England.
Ich kann mir nicht vorstellen, in England zu leben. / Ich kann mir ein Leben in England nicht vorstellen.

Es gibt auch eine Reihe von Verben, nach denen entweder ein Gerundium oder ein Infinitiv mit *to* stehen kann:

begin/start	„anfangen"	We **began/started** | **learning** / **to learn** | English in the fifth class.
continue	„fortfahren mit", „weiter (tun)"	Dr Willis **continued** | **working** / **to work** | late into the night.
hate	„sehr ungern tun"	Melissa **hates** | **taking** / **to take** | the bus.
like/love	„(sehr) gern tun"	I **like/love** | **riding** / **to ride** | my bike in the rain.

⚠ Nach *would like, would love, would hate* steht in der Regel der *to*-Infinitiv.

I **wouldn't like to ride** my new bike in the rain.

→ P 7, 8, 10 (pp. 79/80)

e **Das Gerundium nach Präpositionen**

Nach einer **Präposition** steht ein Verb als Gerundium. Die Präposition kann
- mit einem **Adjektiv** verbunden sein, z.B. *afraid of, famous for, frightened of, good/bad at, interested in, worried about.*

The gerund after prepositions

I'm **afraid of** going out alone at night.
Ich habe Angst davor, spät abends allein wegzugehen.
Are you **good at** cooking?
Kannst du gut kochen?

- mit einem **Nomen** verbunden sein, z.B. *chance of, choice between … and …, danger of, idea of, reason for.*

Mr Owen didn't like **the idea of** moving to London.
Herrn Owen gefiel der Gedanke nicht, nach London umzuziehen.
There were good **reasons for** not going to the party.
Es gab gute Gründe, nicht zur Party zu gehen.

- mit einem **Verb** verbunden sein, z.B. *dream of/about, look forward to, talk about/of, think about/of, thank sb. for, worry about.*

Selima often **dreams of** being a film star.
Selima träumt oft davon, ein Filmstar zu sein.

Are you **looking forward to** seeing Yasmin again?
Freust du dich darauf, Yasmin wiederzusehen? → P 11 (p. 80)

In English: The gerund

An *-ing* form which is used like a noun is called a gerund.
We use the gerund
- as the subject of a sentence,
- as the object after some verbs,
- after prepositions.

In Unit 6 hast du gelernt …

- auszudrücken, dass du Zustimmung zu deiner Aussage erwartest.
  ▶ Dr Willis is nice, isn't she?
  You haven't got a dog, have you?
- zu sagen, was jemand gern oder ungern tut.
  ▶ I like watching TV.
  I'm interested in learning Spanish.
  I enjoy surfing the Internet.
  She dreams of making a lot of money.
  I hate getting up early.
- zu sagen, worin jemand gut oder schlecht ist.
  ▶ Melissa is good at drawing.
  Melissa is bad at dancing.
- über das Leben in der Vergangenheit zu sprechen.
  ▶ The baths were built around 70 AD.
  The objects tell us that people used oil-lamps.

Unit 7

1 Vorhersagen und Vermutungen über die Zukunft

Predictions and suppositions about the future

a Das Futur mit *will*

Wie du weißt, werden allgemeine **Vorhersagen** und **Vermutungen** über die Zukunft mit dem *will-future* ausgedrückt.

The *will*-future

REMEMBER

The weather **will be** fine tomorrow.
Das Wetter wird morgen gut sein.
I'm sure the rain **will stop** soon.
Ich bin sicher, dass der Regen bald aufhört/aufhören wird.

b Das Futur mit *going to*

Man verwendet das *going to-future*, wenn man sagen will, dass etwas mit **großer Wahrscheinlichkeit** geschehen wird, weil es bereits **Anzeichen** dafür gibt (Wolken, lautes Verhalten usw.).

The *going to*-future

Look at those clouds. It**'s going to rain**.
Sieh dir die Wolken an. Es wird (bald) regnen. / Es gibt Regen.
The kids are very noisy. The teacher **is going to be** angry.
The tree house doesn't look safe. It**'s going to fall** down one day.

2 Pläne und Fahrpläne

Plans and timetables

a Das Futur mit *going to*

Das *going to-future* wird verwendet, wenn man sagen will, was jemand **vorhat**.

The *going to*-future

REMEMBER

I**'m going to visit** my grandma this afternoon.
Ich habe vor, heute Nachmittag meine Oma zu besuchen.
Tina's friends **are going to have** a birthday party for her.
Tinas Freunde haben vor, eine Geburtstagsparty für sie zu geben.

b Die Verlaufsform der Gegenwart

Um auszudrücken, dass etwas für die Zukunft **fest geplant** oder **verabredet** ist, verwendet man das *present progressive*.

The present progressive

REMEMBER

I**'m visiting** friends in Scotland next summer.
– **Are** you **staying** at a hotel?
Ich besuche nächsten Sommer Freunde in Schottland. / Ich werde … besuchen.
– Übernachtest du in einem Hotel? / Wirst du … übernachten?

[c] Die einfache Form der Gegenwart

Wenn ein zukünftiges Geschehen durch einen **Fahrplan**, ein **Programm**, einen **Kalender** oder Ähnliches festgelegt ist, verwendet man das *simple present*.

The simple present

Come on! The play **starts** at 8.
… Das Stück fängt um 8 an.
When **does** the next train to Manchester **leave**?
Wann fährt der nächste Zug …?
The meeting **is** in 20 minutes, and I'm not ready.
Das Treffen ist in 20 Minuten …

[ ] in einigen Bundesländern nicht obligatorisch

3 **Angebote, Versprechen und spontane Entschlüsse**
Das Futur mit *will*

Wenn man **anbietet** oder **verspricht**, etwas zu tun, oder sich **spontan zu etwas entschließt**, verwendet man das *will-future*.

Offers, promises and spontaneous decisions

The *will*-future

I'm really thirsty.
– I'**ll** **make** you some tea.
  Ich mach dir Tee.

I **won't** **tell** anyone what happened. I promise.
Ich sag niemandem, was passiert ist. Ich versprech's.

Would you like to order now?
– Hmm, I'**ll** **have** the fish, please.
  Ich nehme den Fisch, bitte.

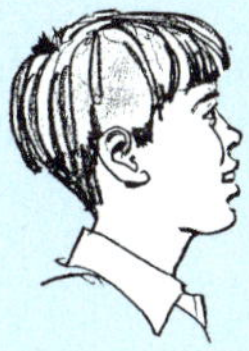

In English: Talking about the future

will-future	– for predictions
	– for spontaneous decisions, promises or offers
going to-future	– for plans or intentions[1]
	– for predictions which are based on a present situation
simple present	– for future events which are part of a timetable or a calendar
present progressive	– for something that has been arranged for the future

[1]intention *Absicht*

In Unit 7 hast du gelernt ...

- Vorhersagen aufgrund von äußeren Anzeichen zu machen. ▶ There's a lot of traffic. It's going to be a long journey.
- über Fahrpläne u.Ä. zu sprechen. ▶ Mum's plane arrives in half an hour.
- spontane Entschlüsse auszudrücken und Angebote zu machen. ▶ Who's that at the door? – I'll go and look.
- Schlussfolgerungen auszudrücken. ▶ Dave may/might/must be the saboteur. It can't be Tina because ...

VOCABULARY

Das *VOCABULARY* (Vokabelverzeichnis) enthält die neuen Wörter dieses Buches in der Reihenfolge, in der sie in den Units vorkommen.

- **Fett** gedruckte Wörter musst du verstehen und benutzen können.
  ➨ **brave** [breɪv] tapfer, mutig
- Normal gedruckte Wörter sollst du verstehen können, wenn du sie hörst oder liest.
  ➨ special ['speʃl] Sonderprogramm, -sendung
- Wörter aus Arbeitsanweisungen sind *kursiv* gedruckt. Du brauchst sie nur zu verstehen.
  ➨ *(to) explain erklären, erläutern*

Symbole

° Wörter und Ausdrücke mit einem **Kringel** sind nur in der Unit wichtig, in der sie vorkommen. *Beispiel:*
°busker ['bʌskə] Straßenmusikant/in

* Wörter und Ausdrücke mit einem **Sternchen** sind nur für Schüler und Schülerinnen neu, die bisher mit der Ausgabe *D2 plus* gearbeitet haben.

[ ] **Eckige Klammern** bedeuten, dass dieser Teil der Unit nicht Pflicht ist. Dein Lehrer/Deine Lehrerin wird dir sagen, ob du die Wörter lernen sollst.

~ Die **Tilde** in der dritten Spalte steht für das neue Wort. *Beispiel:*
hero – Batman and Superwoman are famous comic *~es*. (= … comic *heroes*.)

▸◂ Dies ist das „**Gegenteil**"-Zeichen.
Beispiel: (to) **sell** ▸◂ (to) **buy**
(to) buy („kaufen") ist das Gegenteil von *(to) sell („verkaufen")*.

⚠ Achtung, aufpassen – hier macht man leicht Fehler.

Betonung

['] und [ˌ] sind Betonungszeichen. Sie stehen vor der betonten Silbe.
['] zeigt die Hauptbetonung, [ˌ] die Nebenbetonung. *Beispiel:* **situation** [ˌsɪtʃu'eɪʃn]

Abkürzungen

p. = page
pp. = pages
pl = *plural*
no pl = *no plural*
adj = *adjective*
adv = *adverb*
conj = *conjunction*
n = *noun*
prep = *preposition*
v = *verb*
sb. = somebody/someone
sth. = something
jd. = jemand
jm. = jemandem
jn. = jemanden
infml = *informal* (umgangssprachlich, informell)

Vor- und Nachnamen, Ortsnamen und Ländernamen (und davon abgeleitete Adjektive) findest du auf den Seiten 195/196.
Grammatische Fachbegriffe stehen gesammelt auf den Seiten 197/198.

Auf der hinteren Umschlaginnenseite findest du eine Liste von Wendungen und Sätzen, die du häufig im Englischunterricht hören – und benutzen – wirst *(Classroom phrases)*.

Englische Wörter wie *jazz, toast* oder *training*, die du ohne Weiteres verstehst, werden nicht im *VOCABULARY* erklärt. Alle diese Wörter findest du aber mit Angabe ihrer Aussprache im *DICTIONARY*.

▶▶▶ Our Heroes

pp.6/7	**hero** ['hɪərəʊ], *pl* **heroes** ['hɪərəʊz]	Held, Heldin; Idol, Vorbild	Batman and Superwoman are famous comic *~es*. When I was a little boy, my grandpa was my ~.
	everyday *(adj)* ['evrideɪ]	Alltags-; alltäglich	Are you going to wear anything special tonight? – No, just my ~ clothes: jeans and a T-shirt.
	brave [breɪv]	tapfer, mutig	She was very ~: she jumped into the river and saved the child's life.
	***kind** [kaɪnd]	freundlich, nett, gütig	It was ~ of you to help me yesterday.
	thoughtful ['θɔːtfəl]	aufmerksam, rücksichtsvoll; nachdenklich	Thank you for the present. That was very ~ of you. She had a ~ expression on her face.
	***perhaps** [pə'hæps, præps]	vielleicht	maybe
	special (on) ['speʃl]	Sonderprogramm, Sondersendung (über)	Watch tonight's TV ~ *on* German players in British football clubs!
	by 31st May	bis spätestens 31. Mai	We need your report ~ next Monday. (= not later than next Monday)
	office ['ɒfɪs]	Büro	My father works in a factory and my mother in an ~.
	album ['ælbəm]	Album	
	(to) **belong to** [bɪ'lɒŋ]	gehören (zu)	Who *does* this book ~ *to*? – I think it's Julia's book.

▸▸▸ Unit 1: New Places, New Faces

pp.8/9	**timetable** ['taɪmteɪbl]	Fahrplan	⚠ *timetable* = **1.** Fahrplan; **2.** Stundenplan
	headteacher [ˌhed'ti:tʃə]	Schulleiter/in	
	(to) welcome (to) ['welkəm]	willkommen heißen (in)	When Liz and Pete arrived, Susan ~*d* them. ⚠ *(to) welcome* is a regular verb: *welcome – welcomed – welcomed*
	secretary ['sekrətri]	Sekretär, Sekretärin	She works in an office. She's a ~.
	choir ['kwaɪə]	Chor	a group of singers choir Chor
	(to) **include** [ɪn'klu:d]	(mit) einschließen, enthalten	*Does* the trip ~ a tour of London? The team ~*s* two women. (= Zum Team gehören zwei Frauen.)
	art [ɑ:t]	Kunst	⚠ English *art* = „Kunst" • German „Art, Sorte" = *sort*
	athletics [æθ'letɪks]	Leichtathletik	I'm an ~ fan, I love sports like running and jumping.
	journey ['dʒɜ:ni]	Reise, Fahrt, Weg	Is it a long ~ from your home to your school?
p.10/A1	***until** [ən'tɪl]	bis	I'll have to work ~ 5 o'clock today.

until / till – by

until / till *(prep; conj)* = **„bis"**

(prep) I'll have to work **until/till** 5 o'clock today.
*Ich muss heute **bis** 5 Uhr arbeiten.*

(conj) Megan lived in Wales **until/till** she was 13.
*Megan lebte in Wales, **bis** sie 13 war.*

till is more informal than ***until***.

by *(prep)* = **„bis spätestens", „nicht später als"**

We needed your report **by** Friday **(= on or before Friday)**. Now it's too late.
*Wir brauchten Ihren Bericht **bis** Freitag.*

All letters must be with us **by** 31st May.
*Alle Briefe müssen **bis** zum 31. Mai bei uns sein.*

	even ['i:vn]	sogar, selbst	Everyone helped, ~ the children.
	miserable ['mɪzrəbl]	unglücklich, elend; erbärmlich, armselig	I felt very sad when my cat died. I was really ~. The weather was ~ – really cold and wet.
	a year and a half	eineinhalb Jahre, anderthalb Jahre	*a year and a half* = one and a half year<u>s</u>
	(to) **sell** [sel], **sold, sold** [səʊld]	verkaufen	▸◂ (to) buy
	(to) **move** [mu:v]	(um)ziehen	After 18 months we ~*d* to London. We ~*d* to a small flat in Camden. – When *did* you ~ in? ⚠ *(to) move* = **1.** (sich) bewegen; **2.** (um)ziehen
A2	(to) **be scared (about; of)** [skeəd]	Angst haben (wegen; vor)	(to) be frightened What's wrong? – *I'm ~ about* the Maths test. My little brother *is ~ of* ghosts.

Verbs with two objects

Im Englischen gibt es wie im Deutschen Verben, nach denen zwei Objekte stehen können:
– ein **indirektes Objekt** (meist eine Person – daher auch **Personenobjekt**)
– ein **direktes Objekt** (meist eine Sache – daher auch **Sachobjekt**).

• Die normale Wortstellung ist wie im Deutschen: **<u>P</u>ersonenobjekt vor <u>S</u>achobjekt** (also wie im Alphabet: P vor S), d.h. **indirektes Objekt vor direktem Objekt**:

Mr Owen gave **Megan some money**.	*Herr Owen gab Megan etwas Geld.*
They showed **us their new flat**.	*Sie zeigten uns ihre neue Wohnung.*

• Die Wortstellung **Sachobjekt + *to* + Personenobjekt** wird verwendet, wenn

– das **Sachobjekt ein Pronomen** *(it, them)* ist:	Megan bought a CD and showed **it *to*** Sally. *Megan kaufte eine CD und zeigte sie Sally.*
– das **Personenobjekt sehr lang** ist:	She gave the CD ***to* her new friend at school**. *Sie gab die CD ihrer neuen Schulfreundin.*
– das **Personenobjekt betont** werden soll:	Megan sent a letter ***to* Sally** (not to Sarah). *Megan schickte Sally (nicht Sarah) einen Brief.*

⚠ Nach *describe, explain, present* und *suggest* wird ein Personenobjekt immer mit ***to*** angeschlossen:
I want to **describe** my dream ***to* you**. The assistant **explained** the computer ***to* us**.
Present your report ***to* the class**. 'Let's play a game,' Grandma **suggested *to* Ben**.

	nervous ['nɜːvəs]	nervös, aufgeregt	Are you scared before a test? – No, just a bit ~.
	Good luck. [lʌk]	Viel Glück.	
	***Shall I ...?** [ʃæl, ʃəl]	Soll ich ...?	It's cold in here. – ~ I close the window?
A3	**this way**	*hier:* so, auf diese Weise	Let's do it *this* ~: you draw and I'll write. ⚠ It's better *this way.* = *So* ist es besser. Come on, *this way.* = Los, komm, *hier entlang.*
	(to) **miss** [mɪs]	vermissen; verpassen, verfehlen	It was great in London, but I ~*ed* my friends. She got up late today, so she ~*ed* the bus.
	since July [sɪns]	seit Juli	Alison has lived (⚠ *nicht:* ~~lives~~) in Jena ~ 1996.
	(to) **get dressed** [ˌget 'drest]	sich anziehen	(to) put on your clothes *Do* you *get* ~ before breakfast or after breakfast?
A4	**for** a few seconds	seit einigen Sekunden	Ron has lived in Jena ~ two years. ⚠ *for* one year = **1.** seit einem Jahr; **2.** ein Jahr lang
	strange [streɪndʒ]	seltsam, sonderbar; fremd	I ate too much and now I feel ~. Jane's mother said, 'Never get in a ~ car.'
	midday [ˌmɪd'deɪ]	Mittags-; Mittagszeit	
	form [fɔːm]	Formular, Vordruck	
	on your own	allein, selbstständig	
	(to) **sign** [saɪn]	unterschreiben	Please don't forget to ~ the form.
	(to) cross out [ˌkrɒs_'aʊt]	aus-, durchstreichen	
	(to) **return** [rɪ'tɜːn]	zurückkehren; zurücksenden, -bringen	I left London on 3rd May and ~*ed* on 14th May. Fill in the form and ~ it to the school secretary.

TIPP **Das Wichtigste zuerst ...**

- **Nimm dir nicht zu viel vor** – 10 bis 15 neue Vokabeln auf einmal genügen! (Das ist wie beim Essen – wer zu viel auf einmal isst, kriegt Bauchschmerzen!)
- **Lerne nicht zu lange, aber regelmäßig!** Beim Lernen sind 6 mal 10 Minuten mehr als eine Stunde!
- **Lerne nicht nur mündlich** – wenn du die Vokabeln aufschreibst, behältst du sie besser.
- **Wiederholung ist wichtig** – sieh dir regelmäßig auch die „alten" Wörter wieder an.

p.11/A5	corridor ['kɒrɪdɔː]	Gang, Korridor	
	stairs *(pl)* [steəz]	Treppe; Treppenstufen	⚠ Geh *diese Treppe* hinauf. = Go up *these stairs.*
	floor [flɔː]	Stock(werk)	*first floor* = *erster Stock* *ground floor* = *Erdgeschoss*  ⚠ *im* ersten Stock = *on* the first floor
	toilet ['tɔɪlət]	Toilette	
	cloakroom ['kləʊkruːm]	Garderobe	
	assembly hall [ə'sembli hɔːl]	Aula	
	staff room ['stɑːf ruːm]	Lehrerzimmer	
	main [meɪn]	Haupt-	the ~ question = the most important question There's always a lot of traffic on ~ roads.
	entrance ['entrəns]	Eingang	Let's meet at the main ~ to the disco. 

A6 **Adverb oder Adjektiv nach bestimmten Verben**

verb + adverb

Wie du weißt, werden nach Verben **Adverbien der Art und Weise** verwendet, um zu sagen, **wie jemand etwas tut:**

- Megan waited **nervously.**
  Megan wartete nervös.
  (Wie wartete sie? – Nervös.)

verb + adjective

Es gibt auch Verben, die nicht Tätigkeiten beschreiben, sondern **Zustände oder Eigenschaften (wie jemand oder etwas ist).** Nach diesen Verben stehen **Adjektive:**

- Megan felt **nervous.**
  Megan fühlte sich nervös / war nervös.
  (Wie fühlte sie sich? Wie war sie? – Nervös.)
- The choir sang a song. It sounded **beautiful.**
  Der Chor sang ein Lied. Es klang wunderschön.
- Megan seems **sad** today. What's wrong?
  Megan scheint heute traurig zu sein. Was fehlt ihr?

Vergleiche:

(1) Megan looked **angrily** at Susan.
Megan sah Susan wütend an. (Tätigkeit)

(2) Megan looked **angry.**
Megan sah wütend aus. (Zustand)

	focus on grammar/on words ['fəʊkəs]	*etwa:* Blickpunkt „Grammatik"/ „Wörter"	
	table ['teɪbl]	*Tabelle*	
p.12/A7	***quite** [kwaɪt]	ziemlich; ganz	⚠ *quite* [kwaɪt] = ziemlich; ganz *quiet* ['kwaɪət] = ruhig, leise, still
	different from	anders als	
A8	(to) **be good at** sth.	gut in etwas sein; etwas gut können	Megan likes Maths – and she*'s good* ~ it. ◂▸ (to) be bad at sth.

Some more school subjects

Biology [baɪ'ɒlədʒi]	Biologie	**History** ['hɪstri]	Geschichte
Chemistry ['kemɪstri]	Chemie	**Social Studies** [ˌsəʊʃl 'stʌdiz]	Sozialkunde, Gemeinschaftskunde
Physics *(no pl)* ['fɪzɪks]	Physik		
Design and Technology [dɪ'zaɪn], [tek'nɒlədʒi]	Design und Technologie/Technik	**RE (Religious Education)** [ˌɑːr_'iː (rɪˌlɪdʒəs_edʒu'keɪʃn)]	Religion(sunterricht)

I'm **good/bad at** Maths.	Ich bin **gut/schlecht in** Mathematik.
My **favourite subject** is English.	Mein **Lieblingsfach** ist Englisch.
I **like** Biology **best**.	Ich **mag** Biologie **am liebsten**.
We **have** Mrs Neumann **for Spanish**.	Wir **haben Spanisch bei** Frau Neumann.
We **have two** History **lessons** every week.	Wir **haben zwei Stunden** Geschichte jede Woche.

	e.g. [ˌiː_'dʒiː]	*z.B. (= zum Beispiel)*	for example (Latin *exempli gratia*)
	*(to) **enjoy** [ɪn'dʒɔɪ]	mögen, genießen, gernhaben, gern tun	Did you like the film? – Yes, I really *~ed* it.
	(to) **study** ['stʌdi]	studieren; lernen; sorgfältig durchlesen	She's a professor now, but she had to ~ a long time. There's a test tomorrow so I have to ~ tonight. My father *studies* the sports page every morning.
	mark [mɑːk]	(Zeugnis-)Note, Zensur	Sue's French is very good. She has got very good *~s*. ⚠ *mark* = Note, Zensur – *note* = Notiz
	period ['pɪəriəd]	Unterrichtsstunde; Zeitdauer, Periode	What is your third ~ today? – Social Studies. We use 'for', not 'since', with *~s* of time.
A9	**at last** [ˌət 'lɑːst]	schließlich, endlich	It was a long train ride, but *at* ~ we arrived in Paris.
	***everywhere** ['evriweə]	überall	I can't find my ball. I've looked ~.
	(to) **introduce** sb. **to** sb. [ˌɪntrə'djuːs]	jn. jm. (anderen) vorstellen, jn. mit jm. bekanntmachen	You don't know him? Let me ~ you *to* him.
	for the first time	zum ersten Mal	Today I'm going to play tennis *for the first* ~ in my life. (I've never played tennis before.)
p.13/A10	*(to) **ring** [rɪŋ], **rang** [ræŋ], **rung** [rʌŋ]	läuten, klingeln	I think the phone *is ~ing*.
	not … until/till	erst (um)	Our guests did*n't* go ~ 10 pm.
A11	***rule** [ruːl]	Regel, Vorschrift	Do you know the *~s* of American football? You can't run in this area. It's against the *~s*.
	°vandalism ['vændəlɪzəm]	Wandalismus	
	fault [fɔːlt]	Schuld; Fehler	You didn't wake me up this morning. It's your ~ that I'm late for school.
	(to) **play a trick on** sb. [trɪk]	jm. einen Streich spielen	
	(to) **smile (at** sb.**)** [smaɪl]	(jn. an)lächeln	The man *~d at* his baby. 
	market ['mɑːkɪt]	Markt	My parents go and buy vegetables at the ~ every Saturday.
	°lock [lɒk]	Schleuse	
	excited (about) [ɪk'saɪtɪd]	aufgeregt (wegen, über)	⚠ (to) be *excited* = *aufgeregt* sein an *exciting* trip = ein *aufregender* Ausflug
	kind (of) [kaɪnd]	*Art*	
	(to) be called [kɔːld]	*heißen, genannt werden*	
	action ['ækʃn]	*Handlung, Tat*	
	(to) go on	*im Gange sein, vorgehen*	
	feeling ['fiːlɪŋ]	Gefühl	I feel funny. I've got a funny ~ in my head. verb: '(to) feel' – noun: *'feeling'*

P 3	**last** [lɑːst]	zuletzt, das letzte Mal	►◄ first
P 6	******(to) be missing* ['mɪsɪŋ]	*fehlen*	
P 8	**earth** [ɜːθ]	Erde	⚠ *auf der Erde = on earth*
	billion ['bɪljən]	Milliarde(n)	1,000,000,000
P 9	*(to) be/feel **thirsty** ['θɜːsti]	durstig sein, Durst haben	I'm not just hungry, I'm ~, too. Can I have a glass of milk, please?
P 11	******drawing* ['drɔːɪŋ]	*Zeichnung*	
	at least [ət 'liːst]	*mindestens*	
	description [dɪ'skrɪpʃn]	*Beschreibung*	
P 12	*wall display* [dɪ'spleɪ]	*Wandzeitung, Wandbild*	
	(to) leave room	*Platz lassen*	

The Boy with Green Hair

p.18	**bacon** ['beɪkən]	Schinkenspeck	We had ~ and eggs for breakfast.
	stranger ['streɪndʒə]	Unbekannte(r), Fremde(r)	No one in the village knew her. She was a ~.
	***noisy** ['nɔɪzi]	laut, lärmend	noun: 'noise' – adjective: *'noisy'*
	***full (of)** [fʊl]	voll (mit/von)	There's so much traffic, all the roads are ~ *of* cars.
	empty ['empti]	leer	►◄ full
	just then	genau in dem Moment; gerade dann	At three o'clock we wanted to go swimming in the lake, and *just* ~ it started to rain.
	stall [stɔːl]	Stand	I bought this T-shirt at a ~ at the market yesterday.
	canal [kə'næl]	Kanal	
	path [pɑːθ]	Pfad, Weg	a *path* along a *canal* 
	°busker ['bʌskə]	Straßenmusikant/in	
p.19	frantic ['fræntɪk]	verzweifelt, aufgeregt, in Panik	
	(to) **look after** sb. [ˌlʊk‿'ɑːftə]	sich um jn. kümmern, auf jn. aufpassen	Paul's sister is only three. He often ~*s after* her.
	worried (about) ['wʌrid]	beunruhigt (wegen), besorgt (wegen/um)	Sandra is ~ *about* her grandfather. He's very ill.
	***not … anywhere** ['enɪweə]	nirgendwo; nirgendwohin	I can*'t* find my homework ~. We aren*'t* going ~ at the weekend.
	the two of them	die beiden; alle beide	Hannah and Tony met at the stall, and then *the ~ of them* ran to the canal.
	half a mile [ˌhɑːf‿ə 'maɪl]	eine halbe Meile	⚠ Wortstellung: *half a* mile – eine halbe Meile; *half an* hour – eine halbe Stunde

half

You need ***half* an apple** and ***half* a kilo** of grapes. ***Half* an hour** later we met at our favourite café.	… einen halben Apfel und ein halbes Kilo Trauben. Eine halbe Stunde später …
After **a year and a *half*** he found a new job. (= After **one and a *half* years** …)	Nach eineinhalb Jahren …
Look at **the first *half*** of page 9 again. Then match the **sentence *halves*.**	… die erste Hälfte von Seite 9 … . … die Satzhälften …
At ***half*-time** all the players had some orange juice. Then **the second *half*** of the match began.	In der Halbzeit(pause) … … die zweite Halbzeit …
It's ***half* past eight**, I have to go now.	Es ist halb neun, …

	side [saɪd]	Seite	How can we get to the other ~ of the river? ⚠ Seite *(im Buch)* = page
	°aviary ['eɪviəri]	Vogelhaus	
	for ages ['eɪdʒɪz] *(infml)*	eine Ewigkeit, ewig	I haven't seen you *for* ~ – where have you been?
	***age** [eɪdʒ]	Alter	
	panic ['pænɪk]	Panik	
	(to) **be over** ['əʊvə]	vorbei sein, zu Ende sein	At 5.30 the match *was* ~. Everyone went home.

p.20 How to describe people

	how to do sth.	wie man etwas tun kann/soll	You can ask your teacher or your parents ~ *to do* your homework.
1	(to) **tell**	erkennen, feststellen	Can you ~ the difference between these pictures? – Yes, in one it's summer, in the other winter.

as *(conj; adv)*	wie	*As* you know, there's a test tomorrow.

as

'wie'

As you know, Chester is a town in England.
***Wie** ihr wisst, ist Chester eine Stadt in England.*
Traffic is a problem here, **as** in all big cities.
*… ein Problem hier, **wie** in allen großen Städten.*

'als'

'Hi,' he said **as** (= when) she opened the door.
*„Hi", sagte er, **als** sie die Tür öffnete.*
My uncle works **as** a taxi driver.
*Mein Onkel arbeitet **als** Taxifahrer.*

⚠ **as** a child = ***als** Kind* – **As** a child, I couldn't speak English.
like a child = ***wie** ein Kind* – Sometimes I'm frightened at night **like** a little child.

(to) **imagine** sth. [ɪ'mædʒɪn]	sich etwas vorstellen	I can't ~ why some people like punk music.
*(to) **join** [dʒɔɪn]	beitreten, eintreten in *(einen Klub usw.)*	All my friends ~*ed* the football club last year.
character ['kærəktə]	Charakter; Person, Figur *(in Roman, Film usw.)*	They're twins, but their ~*s* are very different.
°incident ['ɪnsɪdənt]	Vorfall, Begebenheit	
opinion (of) [ə'pɪnjən]	Meinung (von, zu)	What do you think about him? – I don't have an ~. *In my opinion …* (= Meiner Meinung nach …)
2 *apart from* [ə'pɑːt]	*außer, abgesehen von*	
relative ['relətɪv]	*Verwandte(r)*	
entry ['entri]	*Beitrag, Einsendung*	
etc. [et'setərə]	usw.	and so on
order ['ɔːdə]	Reihenfolge; (An-)Ordnung	Put the following words in the right ~: 'you – help – Can – me?'.
beginning [bɪ'gɪnɪŋ]	Anfang, Beginn	*at the ~* = 'am Anfang'

TIPP

Und jetzt ganz entspannt …

Am besten lernt man, wenn man ganz entspannt ist und den Kopf frei hat von anderen Dingen.

- Mach es dir gemütlich: Setz oder leg dich mit deinem Englischbuch ungestört hin.
- Wähle etwa 10 neue Vokabeln aus, die du lernen willst.
- Schau dir ein neues englisches Wort und dessen deutsche Entsprechung an. Dann schließ die Augen und stell dir bildhaft vor, was das Wort bezeichnet (es kann ein Einzelbild oder eine ganze Situation sein). Sag das englische Wort mehrmals laut, dann wird sich der Klang des Wortes fest mit deinem Bild verbinden und besser im Gedächtnis bleiben.

▶▶▶ Unit 2: On the Move

p.22 on the move [muːv]	unterwegs, auf Achse	
°freak [friːk]	Freak, Fanatiker/in	
°couch potato [ˌkaʊtʃ pə'teɪtəʊ] *(infml)*	„Dauerglotzer" *(wörtlich:* Sofakartoffel)	
score [skɔː]	Spielstand, (Spiel-)Ergebnis, Punktestand	The English team lost the match. The ~ was Italy 3, England 1. / The ~ was 3–1 to Italy.
none [nʌn]	keine(r, s)	
winter ['wɪntə]	Winter	
spring [sprɪŋ]	Frühling	
autumn ['ɔːtəm]	Herbst	

spring *summer* *autumn* *winter*

Sports

aerobics [eə'rəʊbɪks]	Aerobic	**jogging** ['dʒɒgɪŋ]	*(das)* Joggen, Jogging
American football ['fʊtbɔːl]	Football	**racing** ['reɪsɪŋ]	Rennsport
baseball ['beɪsbɔːl]	Baseball	**riding** ['raɪdɪŋ]	*(das)* Reiten, Reitsport
cricket ['krɪkɪt]	Kricket	**rugby** ['rʌgbi]	Rugby
cycling ['saɪklɪŋ]	*(das)* Radfahren	**running** ['rʌnɪŋ]	*(das)* Laufen
football ['fʊtbɔːl]	Fußball	**sailing** ['seɪlɪŋ]	*(das)* Segeln
golf [gɒlf]	Golf	**skiing** ['skiːɪŋ]	*(das)* Skilaufen, Skisport
ice-hockey ['aɪs hɒki]	Eishockey	**table tennis** ['teɪbl tenɪs]	Tischtennis
ice skating ['aɪs skeɪtɪŋ]	*(das)* Eislaufen	**windsurfing** ['wɪndsɜːfɪŋ]	*(das)* Windsurfen

⚠ Remember: You **do** aerobics/judo/… • You **go** cycling/jogging/… • You **play** baseball/cricket/…

	a **cup of** chocolate/tea [kʌp]	eine Tasse Schokolade/ Tee	
	Who cares? [keəz]	*etwa:* Wen interessiert das? / Ist doch egal!	... and her parents have got a lot of money. – *Who ~?* Money isn't everything.
	called [kɔːld]	*hier:* mit (dem) Namen	
p.116	**Your score**		
	less [les]	weniger	◂▸ more
	(to) **spend** time/money (**on**) [spend], **spent, spent** [spent]	Zeit verbringen (mit) / Geld ausgeben (für)	I *spent* three hours at the chess club yesterday. My brother *~s* a lot of money *on* clothes.
	healthy ['helθɪ]	gesund	It's very ~ to do sports. ◂▸ unhealthy
	attitude (towards) ['ætɪtjuːd]	Haltung (gegenüber), Einstellung (zu)	What's your ~ *towards* alternative energy?
	exercise *(no pl)* ['eksəsaɪz]	(körperliche) Bewegung, Training, Gymnastik	⚠ **1.** *exercise (no pl, no article)* = Bewegung: My parents say I need more *exercise.* **2.** *exercise(s)* = Übung(en): Which *exercises* have we got for homework?
	(to) **relax** [rɪ'læks]	(sich) entspannen, sich ausruhen	
p.23/A1	**rubbish** ['rʌbɪʃ] *(infml)*	*hier:* Quatsch, Blödsinn	⚠ *rubbish* = **1.** Abfall, Müll; **2.** Quatsch, Blödsinn
	(to) **be interested (in)** ['ɪntrəstɪd]	interessiert sein (an), sich interessieren (für)	David is a sports freak. He *is* very *interested ~* sports. ⚠ (to) be *interested* (in) = *interessiert* (an); an *interesting* book = ein *interessantes* Buch
	(to) **get ready** ['redi]	sich bereitmachen, sich fertig machen	It's half past eight. You must *get ~* for school now.
	county ['kaʊnti]	Grafschaft, Verwaltungsbezirk	
	***both** [bəʊθ]	beide, beides	

both

both + noun:	Let's listen to **both** CDs.	He lost **both** parents in 1984.
both the/my/these + noun:	Let's listen to **both the** CDs.	He lost **both his** parents in 1984.
⚠ Word order: die *beiden* CDs = *both* the CDs • seine *beiden* Eltern = *both* his parents		
both of us/you/them:	Tidy up your rooms now – **both of you**! Did you invite David or Colin? – **Both of them**.	
both:	David and Emma **both** want to go on a bike trip. Can we watch these two videos? They're **both** great!	

	championship ['tʃæmpiənʃɪp]	Meisterschaft	
A2	oval ['əʊvl]	oval	 
	round [raʊnd]	rund	
	(to) **last** [lɑːst]	(an-, fort)dauern	A football match *~s* 90 minutes.
	(to) **kick** [kɪk]	treten	The football player *~ed* the ball.
	*(to) **carry** ['kæri]	tragen; befördern, transportieren	I need some help with these suitcases. Can you ~ this one for me, please?
	forward(s) ['fɔːwəd(z)]	vorwärts, nach vorn	
	°(to) tackle ['tækl]	angreifen, fassen	
	(to) **give** sth. **up**	etwas aufgeben	I had to ~ *up* football. I didn't have the time.
	°goal-line ['gəʊl laɪn]	Torlinie	
	***goal** [gəʊl]	Tor *(im Sport)*	
	°try [traɪ]	„Versuch" *(beim Rugby erzieltes Tor)*	
	type (of) [taɪp]	Art, Sorte, Typ	What ~ of person is he? Noisy? Quiet? Funny?
	°goalpost ['gəʊlpəʊst]	Torpfosten	
	°conversion [kən'vɜːʃn]	Platztritt *(Rugby)*	
	also ['ɔːlsəʊ]	auch	Bill paid and John paid, too. = John ~ paid.
	°(to) drop-kick ['drɒpkɪk]	*(beim Rugby)* einen Sprungtritt machen	
	°crossbar ['krɒsbɑː]	Querlatte	
	°penalty goal	Tor *(nach einem Foul)*	
	penalty ['penəlti]	Strafe, Strafstoß	
	above [ə'bʌv]	*oben*	

p.24/A3	(to) **beat** [bi:t], **beat, beaten** ['bi:tn]	schlagen; besiegen	I ~ my brother at tennis last Sunday.
	tired ['taɪəd]	müde	tired
	he **may be** the best … [meɪ]	er ist vielleicht der beste …	
	athlete ['æθli:t]	Athlet/in, Sportler/in	
	You **might be** right. [maɪt]	Du könntest (vielleicht) Recht haben.	

Möglich? Wahrscheinlich? Sicherlich?

My parents	**may**	be at home now.	Meine Eltern	sind jetzt **vielleicht** zu Hause.
	might			**könnten** jetzt **vielleicht** zu Hause sein.
	could			**könnten** jetzt zu Hause sein.
	should			**sollten/müssten eigentlich** jetzt zu Hause sein.
	must			**müssen** jetzt zu Hause sein.

A4	coach [kəʊtʃ]	Trainer, Trainerin	⚠ *coach* = **1.** (Reise-)Bus; **2.** Trainer/in
	everything/everyone **else** [els]	alles andere/alle anderen	Have you got the drinks? I've got *everything* ~. Have you finished? *Everyone* ~ has finished.

… else

Let's go to the park. We've been **everywhere else**.	… Wir sind **überall sonst schon** gewesen.
I met Jo at the party. – Did you meet **anyone else**?	… – Hast du **sonst noch jemanden** getroffen?
Do you need **anything else** from the shop?	Brauchst du **sonst noch etwas** …?
So you went to Paris. Did you go **anywhere else**?	… Bist du **sonst noch irgendwo** hingefahren?
I'm tired. **Someone else** will have to tidy up.	… **Jemand anders** muss aufräumen.
Let's play football. – Can't we do **something else**?	… – Können wir nicht **etwas anderes** machen?
We always go there. Let's go **somewhere else**.	… Lasst uns **woanders** hingehen.
Who else did you meet?	**Wen** hast du **(sonst) noch** getroffen?
What else do you know about Scotland?	**Was** weißt du **(sonst) noch** über Schottland?

	°league [li:g]	Liga	
p.25/A6	**popular (with)** ['pɒpjələ]	beliebt (bei)	Swimming is very ~ *with* girls in Wales.
	(to) prepare [prɪ'peə]	*vorbereiten*	
	enough [ɪ'nʌf]	*genug*	
	encyclopedia [ɪn,saɪklə'pi:dɪə]	Enzyklopädie, Lexikon	
	(to) **be born** [bi 'bɔ:n]	geboren sein/werden	When *were* you ~? – I *was* ~ on 15th March, 1987. ⚠ Wann *bist* du geboren? = When *were* you born? Never: I ~~am born~~ in 1987.
	transparency [træns'pærənsi]	Folie	
	at the back of the book	*hinten im Buch*	
	**clear(ly)* [klɪə], ['klɪəli]	*klar, deutlich*	
p.26/A7	**I'd** (= I **would**) fly to … .	Ich würde nach … fliegen.	*Would* you help me, please? – Yes, of course.
	wish [wɪʃ]	Wunsch	If I had a ~, I'd travel around the world.
	sensible ['sensəbl]	vernünftig	My pupils are very ~. They usually work hard.
	guidebook ['gaɪdbʊk]	Reiseführer	
	***guide** [gaɪd]	(Fremden-)Führer/in, Reiseleiter/in	

A8 **Numbers**

11,400 = eleven thousand four hundred
⚠ 11.4 = eleven point four (*deutsch:* 11,4 – elf Komma vier)
1,100,000 = one million one hundred thousand
⚠ 1.1 million = one point one million (*deutsch:* 1,1 Millionen)

Im Englischen steht oft ein Komma in Zahlen, die größer als 1000 sind.

A9	**valley** ['væli]	Tal	the land between two mountains or hills
	rest (of) [rest]	Rest	After lunch we spent the ~ *of* the day at the beach.

'of' in place phrases

the **city of** Glasgow	die Stadt Glasgow
the **town of** Carlisle	die Stadt Carlisle
the **Isle of** Skye off the coast of Scotland	die Insel Skye vor der Küste Schottlands

p.27/A10	**hilly** ['hɪli]	hügelig	
	countryside ['kʌntrɪsaɪd]	Landschaft, (ländliche) Gegend	The ~ in Wales is very beautiful.
	railway ['reɪlweɪ]	Eisenbahn	
	fact [fækt]	*Tatsache, Fakt*	
	present ['preznt]	*Gegenwart*	
	optimist ['ɒptɪmɪst]	*Optimist/in*	
	pessimist ['pesɪmɪst]	*Pessimist/in*	
	(to) **grow** [grəʊ], **grew** [gruː], **grown** [grəʊn]	wachsen	Orange trees ~ only in hot countries. I*'ve ~n* a lot. I'm almost as tall as my father now.
	Now that …	*Jetzt, wo … / Jetzt, da …*	
	section ['sekʃn]	*Abschnitt, Teil*	
	tourist board ['tʊərɪst bɔːd]	Fremdenverkehrsbüro	
	Dear Sir or Madam [sɜː], ['mædəm]	Sehr geehrte Damen und Herren	
	(to) **look forward to** sth. [ˌlʊk 'fɔːwəd]	sich auf etwas freuen	School this week has been boring. I*'m* really *looking ~ to* the weekend. ⚠ Wir *freuen uns darauf*, von Ihnen *zu hören*. = We *look forward to hearing* from you.
	Yours faithfully ['feɪθfəli]	Mit freundlichen Grüßen / Hochachtungsvoll	

Letters

Name des Empfängers / der Empfängerin bekannt	Dear **Mrs Barker**, … **Yours sincerely,** (Your name)	Name des Empfängers / der Empfängerin unbekannt	Dear **Sir or Madam**, … **Yours faithfully,** (Your name)

P 1	*lost-property office* ['prɒpəti]	*Fundbüro*	
P 4	**concert** ['kɒnsət]	Konzert	⚠ Betonung auf der ersten Silbe: *concert* ['kɒnsət]
P 5	**chain* [tʃeɪn]	*Kette*	
	***hat** [hæt]	Hut	
[P 7]	*radio commentaries* ['kɒməntriz]	*Rundfunkreportagen*	
P 8	youth hostel ['juːθ hɒstl]	Jugendherberge	
	festival ['festɪvl]	Festival, Fest	
P 9	**reason* ['riːzn]	*Grund*	
P 11	on fire	in Brand	
P 12	°word building	*etwa:* das „Bauen"/ Bilden von Wörtern	
	*(to) **build** [bɪld], **built** [bɪlt], **built**	bauen	verb: *'(to) build'* – noun: 'building' (= Gebäude)
	suffix ['sʌfɪks]	Nachsilbe, Suffix	
P 13	**(to) fit (-tt-)*[1] [fɪt]	*passen*	
P 14	trouble spot ['trʌbl spɒt]	*hier etwa:* Falle	
P 15	in the open air	im Freien	

The Race

p.32	**article** ['ɑːtɪkl]	(Zeitungs-)Artikel	There was an ~ in the newspaper about the race.
	(to) have sth. in common ['kɒmən]	etwas miteinander gemein haben	We're not interested in the same things – we *have* nothing *in ~*.
	win [wɪn]	Sieg	A football team gets three points for every ~.
	stadium ['steɪdiəm]	Stadion	
	***pass** [pɑːs]	Pass, Ballabgabe	
	team-mate ['tiːmmeɪt]	Mannschaftskamerad/in	After games my *~s* and I usually eat something.
	***surprised (at/by)** [sə'praɪzd]	überrascht (über)	People say it usually rains in Scotland. So I was *~ at* the weather there – it was great!
	°(to) go/run for the try	*etwa:* versuchen Punkte zu erzielen	
	local ['ləʊkl]	örtlich, Lokal-; am/vom Ort	Find out what's happening in your town! Buy your ~ newspaper!

[1] Die Angabe „(-tt-)" zeigt, dass der Endkonsonant bei der Bildung von *-ing*-Form, *simple past*-Form und *past participle* verdoppelt wird: *fitting, fitted.*

	(to) take third place	den dritten Platz belegen	
	junior ['dʒuːniə]	Junioren-, Jugend-	
	(to) come (in) third	als Dritter ins Ziel kommen; Dritter werden	David *came (in) third* in the race, after Tom and Nathan. (= He took third place.)
	favourite ['feɪvrɪt]	Favorit, Favoritin	
	16-year-old	16-Jährige(r, s)	We've got a *2-year-old* cat. *13-year-old* Ben lives here. (= Der 13-jährige Ben …)
	(to) be ahead (of sb.) [ə'hed]	führen, in Führung liegen (vor jm.); jm. voraus sein	Sometimes David *was ~ of* Aled, sometimes Aled *was ~ of* David.
	°checkpoint ['tʃekpɔɪnt]	Kontrollpunkt	
	°finish ['fɪnɪʃ]	Ziel; Finish	
	rival ['raɪvl]	Rivale, Rivalin; Konkurrent, Konkurrentin	David and Aled are *~s* – they both want to win the race.
	(to) **do so**; (to) **say so**	es/das tun; es/das sagen	Buy now. If you *do ~*, you'll save a lot of money. Mark is very bad at Maths. – Who *said ~*?
	tail [teɪl]	Schwanz	
	explanation [ˌeksplə'neɪʃn]	*Erklärung*	

p.33 How to take notes

	(to) **take notes** [nəʊts]	sich Notizen machen	(to) **take notes** = sich Notizen machen *(von einem Lese-/Hörtext)* (to) **make notes** = sich Notizen machen *(als Vorbereitung für einen Aufsatz/Bericht)*
1	*mostly* ['məʊstli]	*hauptsächlich*	
	population [ˌpɒpju'leɪʃn]	Bevölkerung, Einwohner(zahl)	the number of people who live in a country or city: Wales has got a ~ of about three million people.
	programme ['prəʊgræm]	(Radio-, Fernseh-)Sendung; Programm	
	c. (= circa) ['sɜːkə]	ca. (= zirka)	
	per cent (%) [pə'sent]	Prozent	Two ~ ~ of two hundred is four.
	symbol ['sɪmbl]	Symbol	⚠ Betonung auf der ersten Silbe: *symbol* ['sɪmbl]
	and so on	und so weiter	
	abbreviation [əˌbriːvi'eɪʃn]	Abkürzung	
3	*if*	*ob*	
	heading ['hedɪŋ]	Überschrift	

TIPP **Das Vokabelpuzzle**

- **Du brauchst:** einen Bogen weißen Karton (DIN A4 reicht für den Anfang), ein Lineal, eine Schere, Schreibzeug.
- Unterteile den Karton mit Lineal und Bleistift wie im Beispiel rechts in Drei- und Vierecke.
- Trage jetzt – wie im Beispiel rechts – die Vokabeln und ihre Übersetzung ein.
- Schneide nun die einzelnen Puzzleteile aus. Beim Puzzeln helfen dir die Form der Teile und deine Vokabelkenntnis.

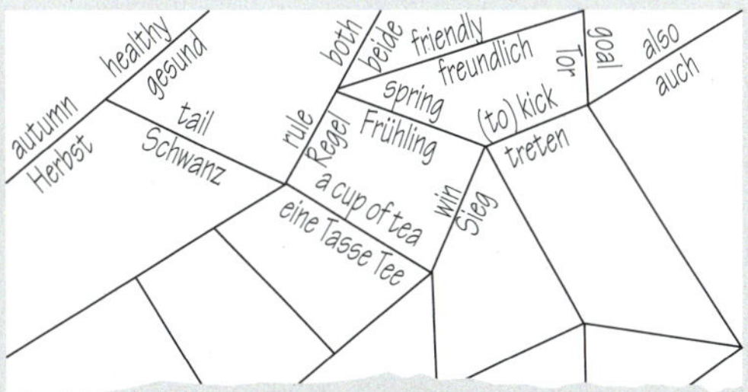

Am besten, du arbeitest mit einem Partner/einer Partnerin, dann könnt ihr eure Puzzles tauschen.

▶▶▶ Unit 3: A Great Idea!

pp.34/35	burglar ['bɜːglə]	Einbrecher, Einbrecherin	A ~ came into our house and stole everything.
	(to) **catch** [kætʃ], **caught** [kɔːt], **caught**	fangen; erwischen	You throw the ball, and I'*ll ~* it. The assistant *caught* the thief and called the police.
	bell [bel]	Glocke, Klingel	*bells* 
	wheel [wiːl]	Rad	A bike has two *~s*.
	°boxing glove ['bɒksɪŋ glʌv]	Boxhandschuh	

	glove [glʌv]	Handschuh	
	(to) **turn** [tɜːn]	drehen	
	(to) **push** [pʊʃ]	drücken, schieben, stoßen	⧓ (to) pull Susan *~ed* Mike, and he fell into the water.
	(to) **be on**	an sein, laufen *(Fernseher, Licht usw.)*	That's strange. The TV *is ~*, but there's no one in the room. ⧓ (to) be off
	invention [ɪn'venʃn]	Erfindung	
	(to) **invent** [ɪn'vent]	erfinden	Alexander Graham Bell *~ed* the telephone in 1876.
	inventor [ɪn'ventə]	Erfinder, Erfinderin	⚠ *driver, reader, …* – but: *inventor, sailor, visitor*
	discovery [dɪ'skʌvəri]	Entdeckung	The ~ of penicillin [ˌpenɪ'sɪlɪn] has saved many lives.
	(to) **discover** [dɪ'skʌvə]	entdecken; herausfinden, feststellen	Alexander Fleming *~ed* penicillin in 1928. Yesterday I *~ed* that there's a new café in Elm Street.
	fridge [frɪdʒ]	Kühlschrank	Food and drinks stay cold in a ~.
	°penicillin [ˌpenɪ'sɪlɪn]	Penizillin	
	difficult ['dɪfɪkəlt]	schwierig, schwer	⧓ easy
	television ['telɪvɪʒn]	Fernsehen; Fernsehgerät	TV
	radar ['reɪdɑː]	Radar	
	(to) **get**	bringen, befördern	The taxi *got* us to the station just before the train left.
	gadget ['gædʒɪt]	Gerät, Apparat	
	cooker ['kʊkə]	Herd	
	answering machine ['ɑːnsərɪŋ məˌʃiːn]	Anrufbeantworter	
	clock [klɒk]	(Wand-, Stand-, Turm-)Uhr	
	fax machine ['fæks məˌʃiːn]	Faxgerät	
	microwave ['maɪkrəweɪv]	Mikrowelle, Mikrowellengerät	
	stereo ['steriəʊ]	Stereoanlage; Stereo	
	washing-machine ['wɒʃɪŋ məˌʃiːn]	Waschmaschine	

fridge

cooker

microwave

a stereo

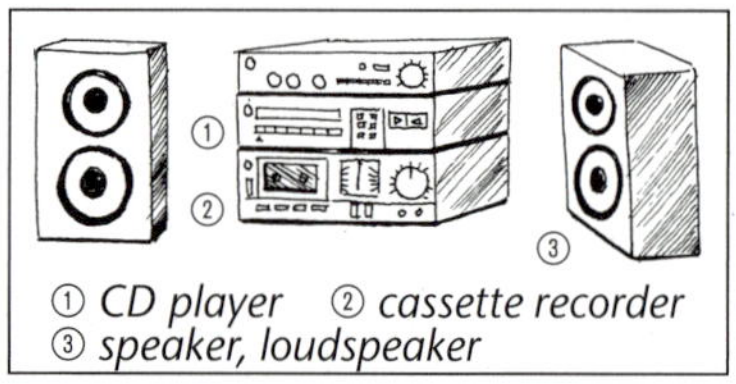

pp.36/37

A1	(to) **complain (to** sb. **about** sth.) [kəm'pleɪn]	sich (bei jm. über etwas) beschweren, beklagen	The food wasn't very good. – If you didn't like it, you should ~ *to* the waiter.
	instruction [ɪn'strʌkʃn]	Anweisung, Anleitung	Read the *~s* carefully before you use the microwave.
	design [dɪ'zaɪn]	Entwurf; Design, Gestaltung, Konstruktion	The town planners looked at the *~s* for the new shopping centre.
	(to) design [dɪ'zaɪn]	entwerfen, konstruieren	Jill's parents *~ed* and built their own house.
A2	***who** [huː]	der/die/das, die *(Relativpronomen)*	The man/woman/child ~ wants to talk to you is waiting in my office.
	***which** [wɪtʃ]	der/die/das, die *(Relativpronomen)*	We don't have any restaurants here ~ are open all night.
	first of all	zuallererst	
	***that** [ðæt, ðət]	der/die/das, die *(Relativpronomen)*	The people ~ work in this restaurant are nice. And the food ~ they've got is very good, too.
	next [nekst]	als Nächstes	We've read the text. What do we do ~?
	useful ['juːsfəl]	nützlich	
	(to) **leave** [liːv], **left, left** [left]	(zurück)lassen, hinterlassen	You can ~ your bag in the classroom. *Don't ~* the door open, please.
	automatic [ˌɔːtə'mætɪk]	automatisch	This is an ~ door: it opens *~ally*. adjective: *'automatic'* – adverb: *'automatically'*
	(to) **go away**	verreisen	
	(to) **hold on (to)** [həʊld], ***held**, ***held** [held]	sich festhalten (an)	
	*(to) **hold** [həʊld], **held, held** [held]	(fest)halten	Can you ~ my bag, please?
	board [bɔːd]	Brett	You need *~s* to make a bookshelf.

	engineer [ˌendʒɪˈnɪə]	Ingenieur/in, Techniker/in	My father is an ~. He designs cars.

Jobs ⚠ Im Englischen mit **unbestimmtem Artikel**: My mum is **an** engineer / **a** teacher / **a** police officer. My dad works as **a** shop assistant / **a** taxi driver.

What do you want to **be** when you leave school? *Was willst du **werden**, wenn du von der Schule abgehst?*

	(to) underline [ˌʌndəˈlaɪn]	*unterstreichen*	
	arrow [ˈærəʊ]	*Pfeil*	
	body [ˈbɒdi]	Körper	Arms, legs and hands are parts of the ~ .
A3	(to) **notice** [ˈnəʊtɪs]	(be)merken	Sally was at the party, too, but I *didn't* ~ her. ⚠ *(to) notice* = bemerken – *note* = Notiz
	oil rig [ˈɔɪl rɪg]	(Öl-)Bohrinsel	
	whose [hu:z]	deren, dessen *(Relativpronomen)*	Jane is the girl ~ mother is a bus driver.
p.38/A4	**industry** [ˈɪndəstri]	Industrie	There's no ~ in our area, but there are a lot of farms. ⚠ Betonung auf der ersten Silbe: *industry* [ˈɪndəstri]
	down south	unten im Süden	⧓ up north (= oben im Norden)
	parliament [ˈpɑ:ləmənt]	Parlament	The German ~ is called the 'Bundestag'. ⚠ Schreibung: *parliament*
	***wonderful** [ˈwʌndəfl]	wunderbar	very nice, great, fantastic
	°Highland Games [ˌhaɪlənd ˈgeɪmz]	*Festival mit Musik und Sportwettkämpfen im schottischen Hochland*	
	°hydroelectric [ˌhaɪdrəʊɪˈlektrɪk]	hydroelektrisch *(elektrische Energie mit Wasserkraft erzeugend)*	
p.39/A5	**nobody** [ˈnəʊbədi]	niemand	no one

-one/ -body

everyone/everybody [ˈevribɒdi]	jeder, alle		
someone/somebody [ˈsʌmbədi]	jemand	**anyone?/anybody?** [ˈenibɒdi]	(irgend)jemand?
no one/nobody [ˈnəʊbədi]	niemand	**not … anyone/not … anybody**	niemand

	(to) **be/feel cold**	frieren	⚠ *Mir war kalt. = I was cold. / I felt cold.* *Mir war heiß. = I was hot. / I felt hot.*
	coat [kəʊt]	Mantel	It's cold today. You'll need a pullover and a ~.
	post [pəʊst]	Post(sendungen)	⚠ Kannst du bitte mal zur *Post* (= zum Postamt) gehen? = Can you go to the *post office*, please?
	*(to) **be pleased (with/about)** [pli:zd]	zufrieden sein (mit), sich freuen (über)	I got good marks in History. My parents *are* very ~.
	thin (-nn-) [θɪn]	dünn	Tom eats almost nothing. He's very ~. thin – dünn
	useless [ˈju:sləs]	nutzlos, zu nichts nütze	⧓ useful
	umbrella [ʌmˈbrelə]	Regenschirm	
	store(room) [ˈstɔ:ru:m]	Lager(raum)	
	heavy [ˈhevi]	schwer *(von Gewicht)*	Can you help me with this box? It's very ~. ⚠ eine *schwere* Kiste = a *heavy* box eine *schwere* Übung = a *difficult* exercise
	*(to) **pass** [pɑ:s]	vorbeifahren, vorbeigehen an; überholen	*Do* we ~ a post office on the way to the station? There's too much traffic. You can't ~ here.
	enough [ɪˈnʌf]	genug	
A6	button [ˈbʌtn]	Knopf	Which ~ do I push to turn the radio on?
	gate [geɪt]	Tor, Pforte	Close the ~ so the dog can't get out of the garden.
P1	**present** [ˈpreznt]	Gegenwart	the past – the *present* (now) – the future
P4	(to) **be called** [kɔ:ld]	heißen, genannt werden	Obelix has got a little dog. It*'s* ~ 'Idefix'.
P5	*(to) join sth. together*	*etwas miteinander verbinden*	
	(to) **hold** [həʊld], **held, held** [held]	veranstalten, abhalten	The Highland Games in Braemar – do they ~ them every year?

	(to) **keep** [ki:p], **kept**, **kept** [kept]	aufbewahren, aufheben	Where *do* you ~ all your photos? – In my album. You should ~ your notes, you might need them again.
	copy ['kɒpi]	Kopie, Abschrift	
P 6	timer ['taɪmə]	Zeitmesser	
	(to) **contact** sb. ['kɒntækt]	sich mit jm. in Verbindung setzen; mit jm. Kontakt aufnehmen	I *~ed* Mrs Turner about a job in her company. I phoned her, and we're going to meet tomorrow. ⚠ Betonung auf der ersten Silbe: *contact* ['kɒntækt]
P 8	(to) frighten ['fraɪtn]	ängstigen, erschrecken	The film *~ed* Tom so much that he couldn't sleep.
	little ['lɪtl]	wenig	This cactus ['kæktəs] needs very ~ water.
P 9	(to) run **after** sb.	hinter jm. herrennen	'Come back,' shouted the boy as he *ran* ~ his dog.
	(to go/drive/move) **along** [ə'lɒŋ]	weiter…, vorwärts…; dahin…	Move ~ or we'll be late. I was driving ~ in my car when I heard a funny noise.
[P 11]	*(to) translate (into)* [træns'leɪt]	*übersetzen (in)*	
P 12	*(to) end* [end]	*enden*	
P 14	***cinema** ['sɪnəmə]	Kino	

Verbs and their nouns

	-ion / -tion / -ation			*-ing*	
(to) collect [kə'lekt]	**collection** [kə'lekʃn]	Sammlung	(to) begin	**beginning**	Anfang, Beginn
(to) decide [dɪ'saɪd]	**decision** [dɪ'sɪʒn]	Entscheidung	(to) build	**building**	Gebäude
(to) describe [dɪ'skraɪb]	**description** [dɪ'skrɪpʃn]	Beschreibung	(to) feel	**feeling**	Gefühl
(to) discuss [dɪ'skʌs]	**discussion** [dɪ'skʌʃn]	Diskussion	(to) meet	**meeting**	Treffen; Versammlung; Besprechung
(to) explain [ɪk'spleɪn]	**explanation** [ˌeksplə'neɪʃn]	Erklärung	(to) train	**training**	Training, Ausbildung
(to) imagine [ɪ'mædʒɪn]	**imagination** [ɪˌmædʒɪ'neɪʃn]	Vorstellungskraft, Fantasie			
(to) invent [ɪn'vent]	**invention** [ɪn'venʃn]	Erfindung			
(to) invite [ɪn'vaɪt]	**invitation** [ˌɪnvɪ'teɪʃn]	Einladung			
(to) pollute [pə'lu:t]	**pollution** [pə'lu:ʃn]	(Umwelt-)Verschmutzung			
(to) suggest [sə'dʒest]	**suggestion** [sə'dʒestʃn]	Vorschlag			

⚠ Be careful with spelling and pronunciation!

Dr Joe's Antiseptic

p.44	**below** *(adv; prep)* [bɪ'ləʊ]	unten; unter, unterhalb (von)	From the plane, we could see London ~. Your mouth is ~ your nose.
	above *(adv; prep)* [ə'bʌv]	oben; über, oberhalb (von)	The clouds ~ began to get darker. Your eyes are ~ your nose. ◂▸ below
	°antiseptic [ˌænti'septɪk]	Antiseptikum *(Mittel, das Bakterienwachstum hemmt)*	
	*(to) **cross** [krɒs]	überqueren, kreuzen	
	cart [kɑ:t]	Karren, Wagen	
	crowd [kraʊd]	(Menschen-)Menge	
	wound [wu:nd]	Wunde	
	operation [ˌɒpə'reɪʃn]	Operation *(auch medizinisch)*	He was in hospital for one week after the ~. The doctor did an ~ on the girl's broken leg.
	(to) **operate (on** sb.) ['ɒpəreɪt]	(jn.) operieren	The woman was badly hurt in the accident so the doctors decided to ~ *on* her.
	patient ['peɪʃnt]	Patient, Patientin	My doctor has lots of *~s*.
	°the wound became infected [bɪˌkeɪm‿ɪn'fektɪd]	die Wunde entzündete sich	
	(to) **become** [bɪ'kʌm], **became** [bɪ'keɪm], **become**	werden	Kate Walker *became* a pop singer five years ago. She *became* famous after her second CD. ⚠ Was willst du mal *werden*? = What do you want to *be*? ⚠ 'False friend': *(to) become* = werden • bekommen = *(to) get*
	°bandage ['bændɪdʒ]	Verband, Bandage	
	surgeon ['sɜ:dʒən]	Chirurg, Chirurgin	
	(to) **marry** ['mæri]	heiraten	Ann is married now. She *married* Tom Dean last year.

mad [mæd]	verrückt, wahnsinnig	
(to) **cut** sth. **off** [ˌkʌt‿ˈɒf]	etwas abschneiden; *hier:* amputieren	
He **didn't think so.**	Er glaubte das nicht.	'Perhaps we'll be late,' he said, but he *didn't think* ~.
I think so.	Ich glaube (ja).	'Is she Scottish?' – 'I *think* ~, but I'm not quite sure.'
I don't think so.	Das finde/glaube ich nicht.	'Glasgow will lose.' – I *don't think* ~. They're a very good team.'
subject [ˈsʌbdʒekt]	Thema, Gegenstand	What's the ~ of your report? – Famous inventors. ⚠ *subject* = **1.** Thema; **2.** Schulfach; **3.** Subjekt
because of	wegen	

Giving reasons

Dr Lister worked hard **to** save lives.	..., **um** Leben **zu** retten.
In his time many people died in hospitals **because** their wounds became infected.	..., **weil** ihre Wunden sich entzündeten.
The wounds became infected **because of** bacteria.	... **wegen** Bakterien.
He wanted to help people, **so** he read a lot about bacteria.	..., **deshalb/daher** las er eine Menge ...
The reason (**why** many people died) **was that** wounds became infected.	**Der Grund** (**dafür, dass** ...) **war, dass** ...
Dr Lister read everything about bacteria **so (that)** he could help people who needed an operation.	..., **damit** er Leuten helfen konnte, ...

°bacteria *(pl)* [bækˈtɪəriə]	Bakterien	
inside *(prep)* [ˌɪnˈsaɪd]	innerhalb, im Innern (von); in (... hinein)	It's raining. Let's wait ~ the boutique.
***inside** *(adv)*	drinnen; nach drinnen	Shall we have the party in the garden, or ~?
outside *(prep)* [ˌaʊtˈsaɪd]	außerhalb (von); aus (... heraus)	Gwen lives ~ the city, on a farm. ▸◂ inside
***outside** *(adv)*	draußen; nach draußen	▸◂ inside
p.45 **at that time**	damals, zu jener/dieser Zeit	⚠ *zu jener Zeit, in dieser Zeit (in der Vergangenheit)* = *at that time* (nicht: ~~*in this time*~~)
(to) **cut** sth. **up** [ˌkʌt‿ˈʌp]	etwas zerschneiden, in Stücke schneiden	The string is one metre long. *Cut* it ~ into five pieces, each 20 cm long.
°carbolic acid [kɑːˌbɒlɪk‿ˈæsɪd]	Karbol(säure), Phenol	
°drain [dreɪn]	Abflussrohr	Smell
(to) **smell** [smel]	riechen	I could ~ the cake that my mum was making. 'Mmmm, that ~*s* good,' I said.

Verbs and nouns with the same form

(to) **cry**	schreien; weinen	(to) **report**	berichten, melden
cry	Schrei, Ruf	**report**	Bericht, Reportage
(to) **drive**	*(ein Auto, einen Bus)* fahren	(to) **return**	zurückkehren; zurücksenden
drive	(Auto-)Fahrt	**return**	Rückkehr, Wiederkehr
(to) **end**	enden; beenden	(to) **scream**	schreien, kreischen
end	Ende, Schluss	**scream**	Schrei, Aufschrei
(to) **guide**	führen, lenken, leiten	(to) **smell**	riechen
guide	(Fremden-)Führer/in	**smell**	Geruch
(to) **hope**	hoffen	(to) **smile**	lächeln
hope	Hoffnung	**smile**	Lächeln
(to) **interview**	befragen, interviewen	(to) **start**	anfangen, beginnen (mit)
interview	Interview	**start**	Anfang, Beginn, Start
(to) **list**	auflisten, aufzählen	(to) **visit**	besuchen; besichtigen
list	Liste	**visit**	Besuch

(to) **add** [æd]	addieren, hinzufügen, ergänzen	*Add* blue water to yellow water and you get green water.
method [ˈmeθəd]	Methode	The new teaching ~*s* are better than the old ones.
9 out of 11	9 von 11	14 ~ *of* 25 pupils in our form are girls.
for other reasons [ˈriːznz]	aus anderen Gründen	The trip to Spain was very cheap, but that's not the reason why I went there. I went ~ *other reasons*.
°death sentence [ˈdeθ ˌsentəns]	Todesurteil	
unless [ənˈles]	wenn ... nicht, außer wenn, sofern ... nicht	You'll get into trouble with your parents ~ you work harder.
especially [ɪˈspeʃli]	besonders, insbesondere	I love chocolate, ~ chocolate from Switzerland and Belgium.

	result [rɪ'zʌlt]	Ergebnis, Resultat	Have you heard the football ~*s*? Barcelona lost. There was lots of traffic and as a ~ I was late.
	(to) **fill** sth. (**with** sth.) [fɪl]	etwas (mit etwas) füllen	
	although [ɔːl'ðəʊ]	obwohl	*Although* I studied hard, I got a bad mark.
	well *(adj)*	gesund, wohlauf	Yesterday I felt ill, but today I'm (feeling) ~ again. ⚠ *well* = **1.** *(adv)* gut: She sang *well. (adv zu 'good')* **2.** *(adj)* gesund: I'm *well* again.
	based on ['beɪst‿ɒn]	basierend auf	
	by accident	zufällig, versehentlich	I found the house *by* ~. I wasn't looking for it.
	accident	Zufall	⚠ *accident* = **1.** Unfall; **2.** Zufall
	scientist ['saɪəntɪst]	*Wissenschaftler/in*	
p.46	*(to) make sure*	*sicherstellen, sichergehen*	
	(to) **persuade** sb. **(to do** sth.) [pə'sweɪd]	jn. überzeugen/überreden (etwas zu tun)	Sita didn't want to go at first, but then we were able to ~ her *to* come with us.
	(to) **let** sb. **do** sth. **(-tt-)**, **let, let** [let]	jm. erlauben, etwas zu tun; jn. etwas tun lassen	*Do* your parents ~ you watch late films? That bag is so heavy. *Let* me carry it for you.
	polite [pə'laɪt]	höflich	Remember to say 'please' and 'thank you'. Be ~.
	What do you mean by that?	Was verstehst du darunter?	
	(to) work closely with sb. ['kləʊsli]	eng mit jm. zusammenarbeiten	
	(to) **support** [sə'pɔːt]	unterstützen	(to) help
	(to) **disagree (with)** [ˌdɪsə'griː]	anderer Meinung sein (als), nicht übereinstimmen (mit)	▸◂ agree
	at first	zuerst, anfangs, am Anfang	I was very bad at English *at* ~, but I'm getting better. ⚠ *zuerst* (= als Erstes) = *first:* *First* turn left, then right.
	(to) be grateful (to sb.) ['greɪtfəl]	(jm.) dankbar sein	Thank you very much. I*'m* very ~ *to* you.

p.47 How to tell a story

1	**thick** [θɪk]	dick; dicht	▸◂ thin
	smoke [sməʊk]	Rauch	(to) lie
	(to) **lie** [laɪ], **lay** [leɪ], **lain** [leɪn]	liegen	She *lay* on the bed and watched TV. liegen ⚠ -ing form: *lying* – She's *lying* on the sofa.
	(just) in time	(gerade) rechtzeitig	We arrived *just in* ~ – two minutes before the bus left.
2	*grandchild*	*Enkel, Enkelin*	
3	**grammar** ['græmə]	Grammatik	
	spelling ['spelɪŋ]	(Recht-)Schreibung, Schreibweise	Your story is interesting, but your ~ is terrible.

TIPP

Zu zweit gehts besser ...

Hier zwei Spielideen für das Lernen zu zweit oder in der Gruppe:

- Eine prima Sache für Freiarbeitsstunden ist das **Vokabel-Memory**. Ihr müsst dafür 10 bis 15 Kartenpaare anfertigen – es gehören immer zwei Karten zusammen. Als Paare könnt ihr wählen:
  - englisches Wort – deutsche Entsprechung ***(coat* - Mantel; *polite* - höflich)** *oder*
  - Gegensätze ***(useful - useless; easy - difficult)*** *oder*
  - unregelmäßige Verben, Infinitiv und *simple past*-Form ***(go - went; say - said)*** *oder*
  - Teile von Wörtern ***(home + work → homework)***

  Die Karten liegen verdeckt auf dem Tisch. Abwechselnd darf jeder zwei Karten aufdecken – wer zusammengehörige Karten aufdeckt, darf sie behalten.

Arbeitet ihr mit einer **Vokabelkartei**? Dann probiert mal dieses Spiel:

- Nehmt 10 bis 15 Vokabelkarten und legt sie offen auf den Tisch. Partner **B** schließt die Augen, Partner **A** entfernt eine Karte und fragt:
  What have I changed?
  Partner **B** sagt, welche Karte fehlt; Beispiel:
  *You've taken away '**unless**'.*
  Wenn die Antwort stimmt, kann **B** die Karte behalten.

  (In der Gruppe macht es noch mehr Spaß, weil es auf Schnelligkeit ankommt.)

▶▶▶ Unit 4: London

pp.48/49	***sights** *(pl)* [saɪts]	Sehenswürdigkeiten	Why do you want to go to London? – Because I want to see the ~.
	bank [bæŋk]	(Fluss-)Ufer	 ⚠ *(Sitz-)Bank = bench*
	complex ['kɒmpleks]	(Gebäude-)Komplex	There's a new stadium and sports ~ in our town.
	theatre ['θɪətə]	Theater	⚠ Betonung auf der ersten Silbe: *theatre* ['θɪətə]
	°Crown Jewels *(pl)* [ˌkraʊn 'dʒu:əlz]	Kronjuwelen	
	(to) learn about	etwas erfahren über/von, etwas herausfinden über	When *did* you ~ *about* their plans? Come to 'Water World' and ~ *about* dolphins and sea lions!
	violent ['vaɪələnt]	gewalttätig, gewaltsam	Some pupils become ~ and hit other pupils.
	(to) mention ['menʃn]	*erwähnen, nennen*	

Some places and sights in London

Big Ben *die Glocke der Turmuhr des Parlamentsgebäudes (umgangssprachlich auch für Turm und Uhr des Parlamentsgebäudes gebraucht)*
Buckingham Palace [ˌbʌkɪŋəm 'pæləs] *Londoner Wohnsitz der Königin/des Königs*
Chinatown ['tʃaɪnətaʊn] *Straßenviertel im Vergnügungsbezirk Soho mit vielen chinesischen Läden und Restaurants*
Covent Garden [ˌkɒvnt 'gɑ:dn] *ehemaliger Obst-, Blumen- und Gemüsegroßmarkt, jetzt bunter Treffpunkt mit Straßencafés, Lädchen, Straßentheater, Musikanten usw.*
the **Globe Theatre** [ˌgləʊb 'θɪətə] *das Globe-Theater* (globe = *Globus*)
the **Houses of Parliament** *das Parlamentsgebäude*
the **London Aquarium** [ə'kweəriəm] *das Londoner Aquarium (mit 30.000 Meerestieren u. -pflanzen)*
the **London Dungeon** ['dʌndʒən] *Stadtmuseum nahe der London Bridge* (dungeon = *Kerker, Verlies*)
Madame Tussaud's [ˌmædəm tə'sɔ:dz] *Madame Tussauds Wachsfigurenkabinett*
the **Museum of the Moving Image** ['ɪmɪdʒ] **(MOMI)** *Film- und Fernsehmuseum nahe der Waterloo Bridge*
Nelson's Column [ˌnelsnz 'kɒləm] *die Nelson-Säule (auf dem Trafalgar Square)*
Piccadilly Circus [ˌpɪkədɪli 'sɜ:kəs] *Platz im West End mit Eros-Statue, Touristentreffpunkt*
St Paul's (Cathedral) [sənt 'pɔ:lz] *die St.-Pauls-Kathedrale (im Zentrum Londons)*
the **Statue of Eros** [ˌstætʃu:‿əv‿'ɪərɒs] *die Eros-Statue am Piccadilly Circus*
the **(River) Thames** [temz] *die Themse*
Tower Bridge *Klappbrücke beim Tower*
the **Tower (of London)** *mittelalterliche Festung, heute Aufbewahrungsort der Kronjuwelen*
Trafalgar Square [trəˌfælgə 'skweə] *Platz im West End mit Nelson-Säule*
the **West End** [ˌwest‿'end] *vornehmer Stadtteil im Zentrum mit zahlreichen Einkaufsstraßen, Hotels, Kinos, Diskotheken und Theatern*
Westminster Abbey [ˌwestmɪnstər‿'æbi] *die Westminster-Abtei (Krönungskirche der englischen Könige und Königinnen)*

avenue ['ævənju:]	Allee, Boulevard
circus ['sɜ:kəs]	(runder) Platz *(in einer Stadt)*
column ['kɒləm]	Säule
palace ['pæləs]	Palast, Schloss
square [skweə]	Platz *(in einer Stadt)*
statue ['stætʃu:]	Statue

p.50/A1	**the underground** *(no pl)* ['ʌndəgraʊnd]	die U-Bahn	Take *the underground* / *the tube* to Oxford Street. There's an *underground* station / a *tube* station at Oxford Circus. 
	the tube *(no pl)* [tju:b] *(infml)*	die U-Bahn *(in London)* *(eigentlich:* Rohr, Röhre)	⚠ Wann fährt die nächste *U-Bahn* nach …? = When's the next *(underground) train* to …?
	ticket office ['tɪkɪt‿ˌɒfɪs]	(Fahr-)Kartenschalter; Kartenvorverkaufsstelle	I still have to buy my train ticket. Where's the ~ ~? You can get tickets for the concert next week at the ~ ~.
	over there [ˌəʊvə 'ðeə]	dort drüben, da drüben	
A2	**line** [laɪn]	(U-Bahn-)Linie	
	route [ru:t]	Route, Strecke	What's the best *route* from Queensway to Piccadilly Circus? – Well, take an *eastbound* Central *Line* train and *change* to the Bakerloo *Line* at Oxford Circus.
	southbound ['saʊθbaʊnd]	Richtung Süden	
	(to) **change** (trains)	umsteigen	

V

Unit 4

	(to) **get off** [ˌget‿ˈɒf]	aussteigen	This is Oxford Circus. We have to *get* ~ here. ⧓ (to) get in – There's the taxi. Let's *get in*.

German 'ein-/aus-steigen'

(to) **get on** / (to) **get off** – **a bus** / **a train** / **a plane** / **a bike**

She *got on* the bus at 2.30.
He *got off* the train at Euston Station.
We *got in(to)* the car and drove away.
The driver helped me to *get out of* the taxi.

(to) **get in(to)** / (to) **get out of** – **a car** / **a taxi**

p.51/A3	wax [wæks]	Wachs	At Madame Tussaud's you can see ~ figures of a lot of famous people.
	owner [ˈəʊnə]	Besitzer/in	Who's the ~ of that big car outside? Is it the Parkers' car?
	mask [mɑːsk]	Maske	*masks* 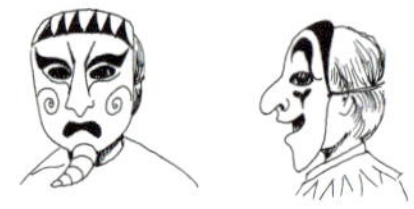
	revolution [ˌrevəˈluːʃn]	Revolution	
	successful [səkˈsesfl]	erfolgreich	
	all around [ˈɔːl‿əˌraʊnd]	überall in	People play football ~ ~ the world.
	known as [ˈnəʊn‿əz]	bekannt als	His real name is Schumacher, but he is ~ ~ Schumi.
	***century** [ˈsentʃəri]	Jahrhundert	Konrad Adenauer lived in the 20th ~.
	(to) execute [ˈeksɪkjuːt]	hinrichten	(to) kill because of a death sentence (= Todesstrafe)
A4	***visitor** [ˈvɪzɪtə]	Besucher/in, Gast	How many ~*s* does the museum have each year?
	Chinese *(adj; n)* [ˌtʃaɪˈniːz]	chinesisch; Chinesisch; Chinese/Chinesin	
	shadow [ˈʃædəʊ]	Schatten	I opened my eyes and saw the ~ of a man on the bedroom wall.
	modern [ˈmɒdən]	modern	⚠ Betonung auf der ersten Silbe: *modern* [ˈmɒdən]
	intelligent [ɪnˈtelɪdʒənt]	intelligent, klug	clever ⧓ stupid
	actor [ˈæktə]	Schauspieler	a man who acts in a film or play
	actress [ˈæktrəs]	Schauspielerin	a woman who acts in a film or play
	°tramp [træmp]	Land-, Stadtstreicher/in	
	newsreader [ˈnjuːzˌriːdə]	Nachrichtensprecher/in	The person who reads the *news* on the TV is the ~.
	news *(no pl)* [njuːz]	Nachricht(en), Neuigkeit(en)	Have you got any *news*? – Yes, and the *news* is good. ⚠ Nie: ~~a news~~ • Nie: *The news* ~~are~~ …
	°(to) bring to life [ˌbrɪŋ tə ˈlaɪf]	lebendig machen	
	(to) **be made of …**	aus … (gemacht) sein	*Is* the bottle ~ *of* plastic or glass?
p.52/A5	(to) pick sth. up [ˌpɪk‿ˈʌp]	etwas abholen, mitnehmen; etwas aufheben	You can come with me, my mother is going to drive me. We*'ll* ~ you *up* at 8.20. OK? Who dropped this paper on the floor? Come and ~ it *up*, please.
	°Changing of the Guard [gɑːd]	Wachablösung *(vor dem Buckingham Palace)*	
	ceremony [ˈserəməni]	Zeremonie; Feier(lichkeit)	The Changing of the Guard is a famous ~ at Buckingham Palace. ⚠ Betonung auf der ersten Silbe: *ceremony* [ˈserəməni]
	pigeon [ˈpɪdʒɪn]	Taube	
	°admiral [ˈædmərəl]	Admiral	
	°Lord [lɔːd]	Lord *(engl. Adelstitel)*	
	homeless [ˈhəʊmləs]	obdachlos	A person without a home is a ~ person.
	homelessness [ˈhəʊmləsnəs]	Obdachlosigkeit	adjective: 'homeless' – noun: *'homelessness'*
	issue [ˈɪʃuː]	(Streit-)Frage, Thema, Angelegenheit	Pollution is one of the big ~*s* of our time.
	paper [ˈpeɪpə]	Zeitung	another word for 'newspaper'

'jede(r,s)': each – every

each: jede(r,s) einzelne …

Each day is different. On Monday I go swimming,
on Tuesday I have my music lesson,
on Wednesday I …

⚠ Nur *each* kann vor einer *of-phrase* stehen:
Each of the lessons lasts 45 minutes.
Each of us got a present.

every: jede(r,s), d.h. alle zusammen

You can come when you like. I'll be at home **every** day.
= I'll be at home all week.

p.53/A6	**off** [ɒf]	von (… herunter/ hinunter)	We must help homeless people to get ~ the streets. The boy fell ~ the roof and broke his leg.
	(to) go a long way	viel erreichen, viel bewirken	£2 isn't much, but it can ~ *a long way* when you're hungry.
	(to) **mean** something **to** sb.	jm. etwas bedeuten	My job ~*s a lot to* me. (= My job is important to me.) The name ~*s nothing to* me. (= Der Name sagt mir nichts. / Ich kenne den Namen nicht.)
	paradise ['pærədaɪs]	Paradies	⚠ Aussprache: *paradise* ['pærədaɪs]
	transport *(no pl)* ['trænspɔːt]	Verkehrsmittel	Buses, trains and cars are all forms of ~.
	tram [træm]	Straßenbahn, Tram	 *a tram*
	town hall [ˌtaʊn 'hɔːl]	Rathaus	
	event [ɪ'vent]	Ereignis; Veranstaltung	The first day at school is a big ~ in a child's life.
	Continue to collect words. [kən'tɪnjuː]	*Sammle weiter Wörter.*	
A7	mime group ['maɪm gruːp]	Pantomimengruppe	We listened to a jazz group and watched a ~ *group*.
	°pickpocket ['pɪkpɒkɪt]	Taschendieb/in	
	pocket ['pɒkɪt]	Tasche *(an einem Kleidungsstück)*	
	(to) **rob** (-bb-) [rɒb]	berauben, ausrauben	Three men ~*bed* a supermarket and took £20,000. A man ~*bed* me on my way home. ⚠ (to) *steal* sth. (from sb.) = (jm.) etwas *stehlen* (to) *rob* sb. = jn. *berauben*
	(to) chase sb. (away) [tʃeɪs]	jn. (weg)jagen	The dog *is chasing* the cat. 
	°street entertainer [ˌstriːt‿entə'teɪnə]	Straßenkünstler/in	
	(to) save the day	die Situation retten, der Retter sein *(in einer bestimmten Situation)*	We wanted to play tennis, but we had no ball. Then John arrived and brought some tennis balls – he ~*d the day* for us.
p.54/A8	**New Year** [ˌnjuː 'jɪə]	Neujahr	
	parade [pə'reɪd]	Parade, Umzug	
	(to) **catch a train/bus**	einen Zug/Bus nehmen, erreichen	We don't have to walk, we can ~ *a bus*. We had to run to ~ *the bus*.
	(to) **care (about** sth.) [keə]	sich kümmern (um etwas), (etwas) wichtig nehmen	A lot of people *don't* ~ *about* the environment. Often, the only thing they ~ *about* is money.
	by the way [ˌbaɪ ðə 'weɪ]	übrigens, nebenbei (bemerkt)	*By the* ~, have you heard that Sally is moving?
	Look.	Pass auf. / Hör mal.	Perhaps we can play tennis tomorrow. – OK. *Look*, I'll phone you after school.
A9	(to) watch out	aufpassen	*Watch* ~. There's a lot of traffic on this road.
	about *(adv)* [ə'baʊt]	unterwegs	It was late at night, so there weren't many people ~.
	purse [pɜːs]	Portmonee, Geldbeutel	Don't leave the money on the table, put it in your ~ or your pocket.
	any ['eni]	jede(r/s) (beliebige)	It's so easy, ~ child could do it.

'any' in positive sentences

You can use this ticket on **any** train.	… in **jedem (beliebigen)** Zug
You can come **any** day you like.	… an **irgendeinem** Tag / an **jedem beliebigen** Tag
You're just as good as **anybody** else.	… wie **jeder** andere / wie **irgendein** anderer
You can have **anything** you like for Christmas.	… **(alles,) was** du willst
There is more traffic in London than **anywhere** else in Britain.	… als **irgendwo** sonst, als an **jedem** anderen Ort

any/anybody etc. is often used after *if*: If **anybody** has **any** questions, I'll do my best to answer them.

A10	**exactly** *(adv)* [ɪg'zæktli]	genau	Sue and John are ~ the same size.
	exact *(adj)* [ɪg'zækt]	genau	What's the ~ size of Germany?
	wherever [weər'evə]	wohin (auch) immer; wo (auch) immer	I'll come with you, ~ you go. We'll find you, ~ you are.
P 2	*(to) **steal** [sti:l], **stole** [stəʊl], **stolen** ['stəʊlən]	stehlen	Where's your new bike? – Someone *stole* it yesterday.
P 3	prince [prɪns]	Prinz	
	(to) surprise [sə'praɪz]	überraschen	Dennis ~*d* me. I never thought he could run, but he won the race.
	rich [rɪtʃ]	reich	Someone who has a lot of money is ~. ▸◂ poor
	future ['fju:tʃə]	zukünftige(r, s)	What will ~ years bring, do you think?
	the only … ['əʊnli]	der/die/das einzige …	This is *the* ~ big hotel. All the others are small.
P 4	(to) crown [kraʊn]	krönen	Queen Elizabeth became queen in 1952. She *was* ~*ed* in 1952.
P 7	(to) **put** sth. **in**	etwas hineintun, einfügen, einsetzen	
	(to) make sth. sth.	*etwas zu etwas machen*	
P 8	(to) get sb. into trouble	jn. in Schwierigkeiten bringen	You*'ll* ~ me *into* ~ if I let you take my brother's bike.
	mystery *(n; adj)* ['mɪstri]	Rätsel; rätselhafte(r, s)	How the car got in the swimming-pool is a ~. She's got a ~ illness. Nobody knows what it is.

Save the Crown Jewels

p.58	maze [meɪz]	Irrgarten, Labyrinth	
	agent ['eɪdʒənt]	Agent/in	
	step [step]	Schritt; Stufe	Try to do the exercise ~ by ~. (= Schritt für Schritt) 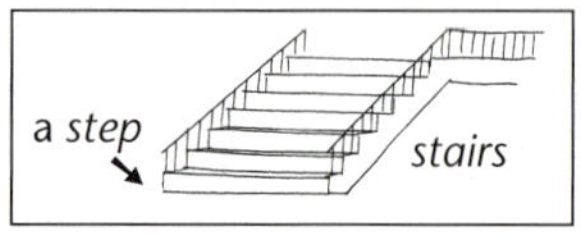
	table ['teɪbl]	Tabelle	
	*(to) **take**	dauern, *(Zeit)* brauchen	It ~*s* about 20 minutes to do this exercise. How long *does* it ~ to get from Euston to Victoria? ⚠ (to) *take* = *dauern* (Zeit in Anspruch nehmen) (to) *last* = *andauern, fortdauern* (im Gang sein)
	total ['təʊtl]	Gesamtbetrag, Summe	
	°Secret Service [ˌsi:krət 'sɜ:vɪs]	Geheimdienst	
	bomb [bɒm]	Bombe	⚠ Stummes „b": *bomb* [bɒm]
	°(to) defuse [di:'fju:z]	entschärfen	
	code [kəʊd]	(Geheim-)Kode	I can't read the letter, it's in ~.
	(to) **be alive** [ə'laɪv]	leben, am Leben sein	▸◂ (to) be dead ⚠ Aussprache: *alive* [ə'laɪv] – *(to) live* [lɪv] — alive am Leben
	°Put that in your pipe and smoke it. *(infml)*	*etwa:* Lass dir das gesagt sein. / Schreib dir das hinter die Ohren.	 
	pipe [paɪp]	Pfeife	
	(to) **smoke** [sməʊk]	rauchen	When you see this sign, you mustn't ~.
	(to) **pass** [pɑ:s]	vergehen, vorübergehen *(Zeit)*	The lesson was so interesting that the time ~*ed* really quickly.
	directions *(pl)* [də'rekʃnz]	Anweisung(en)	
	information desk [ˌɪnfə'meɪʃn ˌdesk]	Informationsschalter	When's the next train? – I don't know. Let's ask at the ~ ~.
p.59	°hologram ['hɒləgræm]	Hologramm *(mithilfe eines Lasers erzeugtes dreidimensionales Bild)*	
	university [ˌju:nɪ'vɜ:səti]	Universität, Hochschule	⚠ Betonung auf der dritten Silbe: *university* [ˌju:nɪ'vɜ:səti] ⚠ *a university* (nicht: ~~*an university*~~)
	(to) **hide** [haɪd], **hid** [hɪd], **hidden** ['hɪdn]	(sich) verstecken	Let's ~ behind that tree. They won't see us there.
	poor things [ˌpʊə 'θɪŋz]	die Armen	They're all wet, *poor* ~.

	platform ['plætfɔ:m]	Bahnsteig, Gleis	The train to London leaves from ~ 3.
	microchip ['maɪkrəʊtʃɪp]	Mikrochip	
p.60	**gun** [gʌn]	Schusswaffe	The police officer pulled out his ~ and shouted, 'Stop!'
	manager ['mænɪdʒə]	Geschäftsführer/in, Manager/in	

How to scan a text

	(to) scan (-nn-) [skæn]	*(einen Text)* überfliegen *(um bestimmte Informationen zu finden)*	
	technique [tek'ni:k]	(Arbeits-)Verfahren, Technik, Methode	How do you learn new words? Do you have a special ~? ⚠ Betonung auf der zweiten Silbe: *technique* [tek'ni:k]
1	*specific* [spə'sɪfɪk]	*bestimmte(r, s)*	
2	*past* [pɑ:st]	*vorbei an, vorüber an*	
	(to) note sth. down	*etwas aufschreiben, notieren*	
	wavy lines [ˌweɪvi 'laɪnz]	*Wellenlinien, Schlangenlinien*	
	edge [edʒ]	*Rand, Kante*	

TIPP **Werbung für Vokabeln!**

Ist dir schon mal aufgefallen, dass du dir jede Menge neue Namen für Schokoriegel oder Eissorten merkst, ohne dass du dich dafür anstrengen musst? Das liegt sicher daran, dass du diese Produktnamen so oft zu sehen bekommst, auch wenn dir das gar nicht bewusst ist.

Diesen Effekt kannst du beim Vokabellernen ausnutzen:

Das Vokabel-Werbeplakat – Gib den Popstars oder Fußballern auf deinen Postern Sprechblasen. Oder nimm ein A3-Blatt, Filzstifte und ein paar Fotos und gestalte dein eigenes Vokabelplakat.

Wenn du deine Plakate so aufhängst, dass du sie ständig siehst, werden sich die Vokabeln ganz nebenbei einprägen – wie die Produktnamen.

▶▶▶ Unit 5: All British!

p.61	Asian *(adj; n)* ['eɪʃn, 'eɪʒn]	asiatisch; Asiat/in	
	°bazaar [bə'zɑ:]	Basar	
	Enjoy yourself … [ɪn'dʒɔɪ jəˌself]	Amüsier dich … / Vergnüg dich …	I'm going to the theatre tonight. – Well, ~ *yourself!* (= Viel Spaß! / Amüsier dich gut!)
	ethnic ['eθnɪk]	ethnisch, Volks-	There are people from lots of different ~ groups in our city: people from Turkey, Russia, Bosnia, …
	minority [maɪ'nɒrəti]	Minderheit	There are 16 girls and 11 boys in my class. The boys are in the ~. minority Minderheit
	religion [rɪ'lɪdʒn]	Religion	⚠ Betonung auf der zweiten Silbe: *religion* [rɪ'lɪdʒn]
	Pakistani [ˌpɑ:kɪ'stɑ:ni]	Pakistani, Pakistaner/in	someone from Pakistan
	Bangladeshi [ˌbæŋglə'deʃi]	Bangale/Bangalin *(jd. aus Bangladesch)*	someone from Bangladesh
	Afro-Caribbean [ˌæfrəʊ kærə'bi:ən]	Afro-Karibe/-Karibin *(Schwarze/r karibischer Herkunft)*	a black person from the Caribbean (a group of small islands east of Central America, for example Jamaica, Trinidad and Tobago, Barbados)
	foreigner ['fɒrənə]	Ausländer/in, Fremde(r)	someone from another country ⚠ *a stranger* = someone you haven't met before
	foreign ['fɒrən]	ausländisch, fremd	Lots of ~ tourists come here, from Japan, Spain, … .
	mainly ['meɪnli]	hauptsächlich	The tourists were ~ from Germany, but there were some from other countries, too.
	Christian *(adj; n)* ['krɪstʃən]	christlich; Christ/in	People who believe in Jesus ['dʒi:zəs] are ~.

	Muslim *(adj; n)* ['mʊzlɪm, 'mʌzlɪm]	moslemisch; Moslem	People whose religion is Islam are ~.
	Hindu *(adj; n)* [ˌhɪn'du:]	Hindu-; Hindu	
p.62/A1	**I'm afraid** [ə'freɪd]	leider	I have to go now, *I'm ~*. Sorry, but I can't stay.
	(to) **be afraid (of)**	sich fürchten (vor), Angst haben (vor)	Don *is ~ of* big dogs. I*'m ~ of* mice.
	°Urdu ['ʊədu:]	Urdu *(in Pakistan und Indien gesprochene Sprache)*	

A2 **Reflexive pronouns (Reflexivpronomen)**

I've hurt **myself**.	Ich habe **mir** wehgetan.	/ **mich** verletzt.	
You've hurt **yourself**.	Du … **dir** … .	/ **dich** … .	
He has hurt **himself**.	Er … **sich** … .	/ **sich** … .	
She has hurt **herself**.	Sie … **sich** … .	/ **sich** … .	
It has hurt **itself**.	Es … **sich** … .	/ **sich** … .	
We've hurt **ourselves**.	Wir … **uns** … .	/ **uns** … .	
You've hurt **yourselves**.	Ihr … **euch** … .	/ **euch** … .	
They've hurt **themselves**.	Sie … **sich** … .	/ **sich** … .	

⚠ Aussprache/Betonung:
-self [-'self]
-selves [-'selvz]

	hardly ['hɑ:dli]	kaum	The roads were so quiet. I saw ~ anyone. ⚠ She works *hard*. = Sie arbeitet *hart*. She *hardly* works. = Sie arbeitet *kaum*.
	lady ['leɪdi]	Dame	My grandma is a lovely old ~.
	instrument ['ɪnstrəmənt]	Instrument	⚠ Betonung auf der ersten Silbe: *instrument* ['ɪnstrəmənt]
	musical ['mju:zɪkl]	Musik-, musikalisch	⚠ a *musical* instrument/person/voice/event a *music* teacher/lesson/festival/room/shop
p.63/A3	**even** worse/better/taller ['i:vn]	(sogar) noch schlechter/besser/größer	I'm very tall, but my brother is ~ *taller*.
	each other [i:tʃ_'ʌðə]	einander, sich (gegenseitig)	Paul likes Linda and Linda likes Paul. Linda and Paul like ~ *other*.
	origin ['ɒrɪdʒɪn]	Herkunft, Ursprung, Entstehung	
	celebration [ˌselɪ'breɪʃn]	(Gedenk-)Feier	My grandpa will be 90 next week and we're going to have a ~.
	relative ['relətɪv]	Verwandte(r)	Uncles, aunts and cousins are all ~*s*.
	total ['təʊtl]	Gesamt-, gesamt, völlig, total	⚠ Betonung auf der ersten Silbe: *total* ['təʊtl]
	builder ['bɪldə]	Bauarbeiter/in	someone who builds houses
	herself [hɜ:'self]	selbst, selber	Where did Sally buy that dress? – She made it ~!
	And they were pretty dresses, **too**.	Und schöne Kleider waren es außerdem/noch dazu.	She broke her leg last week – and on her birthday, *too*! (= … und noch dazu an ihrem Geburtstag!)
	(to) translate (into) [træns'leɪt]	*übersetzen (in)*	
p.64/A4	UN (United Nations) [ˌju:_'en, juˌnaɪtɪd 'neɪʃnz]	UN (Vereinte Nationen)	
	killing ['kɪlɪŋ]	Tötung	
	racist *(adj; n)* ['reɪsɪst]	rassistisch; Rassist/in	He said, 'Blacks go home.' That's stupid and ~. People who say they don't like black people are ~*s*.
	racism ['reɪsɪzəm]	Rassismus	
	(to) **beat** sb. **up** [bi:t]	jn. zusammenschlagen	Some young men *beat* ~ a taxi driver last night. He was badly hurt and had to go to hospital.
	headline ['hedlaɪn]	Schlagzeile	I don't have time to read the whole newspaper. I just read the ~*s*. ⚠ *headline* = Schlagzeile • *heading* = Überschrift
	(to) **fight (against)** sb./sth. [faɪt], **fought, fought** [fɔ:t]	jn./etwas bekämpfen, gegen jn./etwas kämpfen	Look, those two dogs *are ~ing* again. We must ~ *against* all sorts of racism.
	brain [breɪn]	Gehirn	Your ~ is inside your head. You think with it.
	anti-(racist) ['ænti]	anti(rassistisch)	

Der Infinitiv mit *to*

Der **Infinitiv mit *to*** kann stehen:

• nach **Adjektiven** und ihren gesteigerten Formen, z.B. *difficult, easy, good, happy, hard, important, interesting, nice, right, wrong*	I'm so **happy to see** you! *Ich bin so glücklich, dich zu sehen.* I'm **happiest to be** with you. *Ich bin am glücklichsten, wenn ich mit dir zusammen bin.* It's **good to read** your letters, but it's **better to hear** your voice. Maybe it's **best to eat** first.
• nach **Nomen**, z.B. *decision, fun, plan, time*	It's **time to go** home. *Es ist Zeit, nach Hause zu gehen.* I think your **decision to leave** school now is wrong.
• nach **Verben**, z.B. *agree, begin, decide, forget, hope, learn, plan, remember, start, try*	I'**m learning to play** the guitar. *Ich lerne gerade, Gitarre zu spielen.* I'**ve decided to do** judo. We'**re planning to go** to England this year.

Der Infinitiv mit ***to*** entspricht meist dem deutschen Infinitiv mit **„zu"**. (Beachte die Wortstellung!)

A5	**perfect** ['pɜːfɪkt]	perfekt, einwandfrei, vollkommen; ideal	This little park is the ~ place for a picnic. ⚠ Betonung auf der ersten Silbe: *perfect* ['pɜːfɪkt]
	(to) **wonder** ['wʌndə]	sich fragen, gern wissen wollen	(to) ask yourself I don't know that boy over there. I ~ who he is. ⚠ Aussprache: *wonder* ['wʌndə]
	strict (with sb.**)** [strɪkt]	streng (mit/zu jm.)	Peter mustn't watch TV after 6 o'clock. His parents are very ~ with him. strict streng
	construction [kən'strʌkʃn]	*Konstruktion*	
A6	**usual** ['juːʒuəl]	gewöhnlich, üblich	10 o'clock is my ~ time to go to bed. Yesterday I went to bed at 10 o'clock, as ~. adjective: *'usual'* – adverb: 'usually'
p.65/A7	(to) blush [blʌʃ]	rot werden, erröten	I ~*ed* after I noticed my big mistake.
	shy [ʃaɪ]	scheu, schüchtern	I find it hard to meet new people because I'm so ~.

'some' and 'something' in questions

Wir verwenden ***some*** (nicht *any*) **in Fragen,**

a) wenn wir jemandem **etwas anbieten**:	Would you like **some** cola? Do you want **something** to eat, too?
b) wenn wir **um etwas bitten**:	Can I ask you **something**? May I have **some** more bread, please?

	°samosa [sə'məʊsə]	*dreieckige Teigtaschen mit würziger Gemüse- oder Fleischfüllung*	
A8	rude (to sb.) [ruːd]	unhöflich, grob (zu jm.)	She was ~ *to* me: she called me stupid and silly.
	upset (about) [ˌʌp'set]	aufgebracht, aufgeregt; betrübt (wegen)	very nervous Jim was very ~ when he heard about your accident.
	(to) **go on** [ˌgəʊ‿'ɒn]	fortfahren, weitermachen; weiterreden	The speaker stopped and drank a glass of water. Then she *went* ~: 'And we should …'
	anyway ['eniweɪ]	jedenfalls, wie dem auch sei; außerdem, und überhaupt; sowieso	We'll be here at 7.30 or 7.45, ~, before 8. No, you can't go out now. *Anyway*, didn't you want to wash the dishes? Don't try and phone. Ann isn't at home ~.
	definite ['defɪnət]	*bestimmt, festgelegt, definitiv*	
	Should he even ask?	*Sollte er überhaupt fragen?*	
	°ebony ['ebəni]	Ebenholz	
	°ivory ['aɪvəri]	Elfenbein	
P1	**guitar** [gɪ'tɑː]	Gitarre	⚠ Sarah spielt *Gitarre.* = Sarah plays *the guitar.*
P2	(to) **run**	verkehren, fahren *(Zug, Bus)*	Buses *don't* ~ very often in the evening.
	good	artig, brav	⚠ 'False friend': *brave* = tapfer • brav = *good*
P4	**free time** [ˌfriː 'taɪm]	Freizeit, freie Zeit	What do you do in your *free* ~?

	***free** [friː]	frei; kostenlos	Animals don't like cages. They want to be ~. How much did the disco cost last night? – It was ~!
P 8	*(to) arrange* [ə'reɪndʒ]	*vereinbaren, ausmachen*	
P 9	*(to) be out*	*ausgeschieden sein*	
P 10	**nationality** [ˌnæʃə'næləti]	Staatsangehörigkeit, Nationalität	My husband and I have different *nationalities*. He's French and I'm British.
	nation ['neɪʃn]	Nation, Volk	⚠ *nation (n)* ['neɪʃn] – *national (adj)* ['næʃnəl]
	alphabetical [ˌælfə'betɪkl]	*alphabetisch*	

P 11 **Singular and plural nouns**

English singular	All this **information is** interesting. That's too much **homework**. Sandra's **hair is** brown. No **news is** good news.	All diese **Informationen sind** interessant. Das **sind** zu viele **Hausaufgaben**. Sandras **Haare sind** braun. Keine **Nachrichten sind** gute Nachrichten.	**German plural**
English plural	These **stairs go** up to my room. These **clothes/trousers are** nice. The **police are looking** for a thief.	Diese **Treppe geht** hinauf zu meinem Zimmer. Diese **Kleidung/Hose ist** schön. Die **Polizei sucht** einen Dieb.	**German singular**

P 12	*(to) feel about*	*halten von, denken über*	
	***fishing** ['fɪʃɪŋ]	*(das)* Angeln	
	soft [sɒft]	weich	Do you like a ~ or a hard bed? ▸◂ hard

'I Felt like a Monster'

p. 70	(to) **grow up** [ˌgrəʊ_'ʌp]	aufwachsen; erwachsen werden	When my grandparents *were ~ing up*, they had no television. Dave is 12. When he *~s up,* he wants to be a doctor.

TIPP **So unregelmäßig sind die unregelmäßigen Verben gar nicht!**

Wenn du dir die Liste der unregelmäßigen Verben (S. 199/200) einmal genauer ansiehst, wirst du feststellen, dass man Gruppen bilden kann, die sich viel leichter lernen lassen.

- Gruppe 1:

A	A	A
cost	*cost*	*cost*
let	*let*	*let*
…		

- Gruppe 2:

A	B	A
become	*became*	*become*
run	*ran*	*run*
…		

- Gruppe 3:

A	B	B
bring	*brought*	*brought*
feel	*felt*	*felt*
…		

- Gruppe 4:

A	B	C
begin	*began*	*begun*
grow	*grew*	*grown*
…		

Welche der unregelmäßigen Verben, die dir bekannt sind, passen in welche Gruppe?

°the Midlands ['mɪdləndz]	Mittelengland	
in fact [ɪn 'fækt]	eigentlich, genau gesagt; in Wirklichkeit	I think she's fifteen. Well, *in ~* I know she is. Ken says Sue lives in Chester, but *in ~* she lives in Bradford.
childhood ['tʃaɪldhʊd]	Kindheit	your ~ = your years as a child
°Punjabi [pʌn'dʒɑːbi]	Pandschabi *(im Pandschab – einer Gegend in Nordpakistan und Nordindien – gesprochene Sprache)*	
heat [hiːt]	Hitze	It's so hot. I can't sleep *in this ~*. (= bei dieser Hitze.) adjective: 'hot' – noun: *'heat'*
firstly, …; secondly, …; thirdly, …	erstens …; zweitens …; drittens …	*Firstly,* we need something to eat. *Secondly,* we have to buy some lemonade. And *thirdly,* …
education [ˌedʒu'keɪʃn]	(Schul-, Aus-)Bildung; Erziehung	My school ~ started when I was 5 and finished when I was 16.
gift [gɪft]	Geschenk, Gabe	a present
kind (of) [kaɪnd]	Art	What ~ *of* music do you like? – Pop music. ⚠ *Was für ein* Auto …? = *What kind of* car …?
once [wʌns]	einmal; einst	I've only met him ~. That was two years ago. Our house was ~ the village school.

blood [blʌd]	Blut	Have you cut your hand? You've got ~ on it. 
***whole** [həʊl]	ganze(r, s), gesamte(r, s)	I spent the ~ morning (= all morning) in bed today. ⚠ Stummes „w": *whole* [həʊl] (klingt wie *hole* = Loch)
just like	genau wie	

just

I like all sorts of stories, not **just** cowboy stories.	…, nicht **nur** Cowboygeschichten.
(In a shop) I'm **just** looking.	Ich sehe mich **nur** mal um.
You look **just like** your mother.	… **genau wie** deine Mutter.
I'm **just as** tired **as** you are.	Ich bin **genauso** müde **wie** du!
Just a moment!	Einen Moment **mal (eben)**!
Just imagine!	Stell dir **(nur) mal** vor!
They're **just** leaving. / They've **just** left.	Sie gehen **gerade**. / Sie sind **gerade** gegangen.
He could **just** move his legs.	Er konnte **gerade noch** seine Beine bewegen.
'Let's go', I said – **just then** the phone rang.	… – **genau in dem Moment** klingelte das Telefon.
I **just** can't understand why he's so silly.	Ich kann **einfach** nicht verstehen, warum …

script [skrɪpt]	Drehbuch	
p.71 *extract (from)* ['ekstrækt]	*Auszug, Ausschnitt (aus) (einem Film, Buch)*	
darling ['dɑːlɪŋ]	Liebling, Schatz	
°place setting ['pleɪs ˌsetɪŋ]	Gedeck	
***guest** [gest]	Gast	
(to) **be supposed to** (do/be) [sə'pəʊzd]	(tun) sollen / angeblich (sein) sollen	We *'re ~ to* learn all the new words for homework. This school *is ~ to* be one of the best in the country.
°Top of the Pops	*etwa:* Hitparade	
(to) **turn** sth. **up/down** [tɜːn]	*(Radio usw.)* lauter/leiser stellen; *(Heizung usw.)* aufdrehen/niedriger stellen	*Turn down* that music. It's too loud. *Turn up* the heat, or it won't cook properly.
volume ['vɒljuːm]	Lautstärke	
(to) yawn [jɔːn]	gähnen	
dish [dɪʃ]	Schale, Schüssel, Platte	*dishes* 
as if [əz‿'ɪf]	als ob	The sky is very grey. It looks ~ *if* it'll rain soon.
if	ob	Ann wants to know ~ you need help.
proud (of sb./sth.) [praʊd]	stolz (auf jn./etwas)	Our daughter is the best pupil in her class. We're ~ *of* her.
pea [piː]	Erbse	*peas* 
curry ['kʌri]	*scharfes, mit Curry gewürztes Gericht*	⚠ 'False friend': English *curry* = *ein Gericht* German „Curry" = *ein Gewürz*
°…, haven't you?	oder? / nicht wahr?	
stuff [stʌf] *(infml)*	Zeug, Kram	What's that red ~ on your shirt? Ketchup?
gravy ['greɪvi]	(Braten-)Soße	
onion ['ʌnjən]	Zwiebel	⚠ Aussprache: *onion* ['ʌnjən] an *onion* 
garlic ['gɑːlɪk]	Knoblauch	 *garlic*
fish finger [ˌfɪʃ 'fɪŋgə]	Fischstäbchen	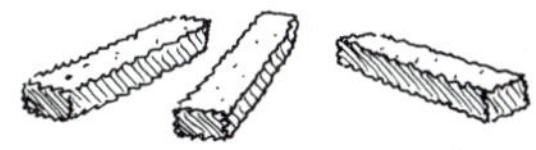 *fish fingers*
birth [bɜːθ]	Geburt	Please fill in your address, nationality, date of ~ (= Geburtsdatum) and place of ~ (= Geburtsort).
How do you know …?	*Woher weißt du …?*	

p.72 How to interest people in something

	(to) interest sb. in sth. ['ɪntrəst]	jn. an/für etwas interessieren	
1	(to) **make** sb. **do** sth.	jn. dazu bringen, etwas zu tun; jn. zwingen, etwas zu tun	Our teacher ~*s* us *speak* English in our lessons. I like comics. They ~ me *laugh* and they ~ me *feel good*.
	the best festival **ever**	das beste Fest, das es je gegeben hat	
2	(to) put sth. down	etwas aus der Hand legen, hinlegen, hinstellen	
	(to) **get lost**	sich verlaufen	I couldn't remember the way and *got* ~.
	snow [snəʊ]	Schnee	
	finally ['faɪnəli]	*schließlich, endlich*	
3	*in different ways*	*auf verschiedene Weise(n)*	
	(to) learn by heart [hɑ:t]	*auswendig lernen*	
	(to) try sth. on sb.	*etwas an jm. ausprobieren*	
	(to) **mention** ['menʃn]	erwähnen, nennen	I'm sure they'll help you if you ~ my name.

TIPP

Nun aber fix ...

Folgende Wortschatzspiele könnt ihr in der Gruppe **nach Zeit** spielen:

- Eine/r von euch gibt einen **Oberbegriff** vor, die anderen müssen in der vorgegebenen Zeit – probiert es mal mit 2 oder 3 Minuten – so viele **Unterbegriffe** aufschreiben wie möglich.
  Beispiel:
  family*: mother, father, sister, uncle, ...*
- Eine/r von euch gibt einen **Anfangsbuchstaben** vor, die anderen müssen in der vorgegebenen Zeit so viele Wörter mit diesem Anfangsbuchstaben aufschreiben wie möglich.
  Beispiel:
  „c"*: clean, clothes, cold, colour, come, ...*
- Eine/r von euch gibt ein **langes Wort** vor, die anderen müssen in der vorgegebenen Zeit so viele Wörter aus den Buchstaben des vorgegebenen Wortes bilden wie möglich.
  Beispiel:
  breakfast*: a, as, are, eat, sea, tea, best, east, fast, rest, break, ...*

▶▶▶ Unit 6: When the Romans Ruled Britannia

p.73	**Roman** ['rəʊmən]	römisch; Römer/in	
	(to) **rule** [ru:l]	(be)herrschen, regieren	Although Britain has a queen, parliament ~*s* the country.
	archaeologist [ˌɑ:kɪ'ɒlədʒɪst]	Archäologe/Archäologin	someone who looks for very old things ⚠ Betonung auf der dritten Silbe: [ˌɑ:kɪ'ɒlədʒɪst]
	70 **AD** [ˌeɪ'di:]	70 n. Chr.	70 *AD* = 70 years after the birth of Christ[1] *(Christus)* [1][kraɪst]
	70 **BC** [ˌbi:'si:]	70 v. Chr.	70 *BC* = 70 years before the birth of Christ ⚠ Wortstellung: *70* ***AD*** or ***AD*** *70;* but only: *70* ***BC***
	remains *(pl)* [rɪ'meɪnz]	(Über-)Reste	What shall I do with the ~ of the meal? Throw them away?
	object ['ɒbdʒɪkt]	*Gegenstand*	
	°amphora ['æmfərə]	Amphore *(Krug mit Henkeln)*	
	comb [kəʊm]	Kamm	a *comb*  ⚠ Stummes „b": *comb* [kəʊm]
	(to) **comb**	kämmen	⚠ Vergiss nicht, <u>*dich*</u> *zu kämmen.* = Don't forget *to comb* <u>*your hair*</u>.
	°hairpin ['heəpɪn]	Haarnadel	
	spoon [spu:n]	Löffel	*knife and fork*  *spoons* 
	fork [fɔ:k]	Gabel	
	lamp [læmp]	Lampe	It's getting dark. Can you turn the ~ on, please?
	coin [kɔɪn]	Münze	I tried to make a phone call, but it was one of those old phone boxes where you still need ~*s*.

p.74/A1	(to) **run out**	knapp werden, zu Ende gehen, ausgehen	There's only five more minutes before the match finishes; time *is running* ~.
	I've **run out** of money.	Mir ist das Geld ausgegangen.	
	site [saɪt]	Ausgrabungsstätte; Bauplatz	a place where a building, town, etc. was or will be built
	unfortunately [ʌn'fɔːtʃnətli]	leider, unglücklicherweise	Janet is giving a party on Saturday, but ~ I can't go. ⧓ fortunately
	valuable ['væljuəbl]	wertvoll	This amphora is Roman. It's very ~.
	grave [greɪv]	Grab	
	(to) dig (up) (-gg-) [dɪg], dug, dug [dʌg]	(aus-, um)graben	In the garden last week my mother *dug* ~ an old shoe.
A2	bulldozer ['bʊldəʊzə]	Planierraupe, Bulldozer	
	(to) **wish** [wɪʃ]	wünschen	We all want to ~ you 'Happy Birthday'.

(to) wish

I wish I **knew** the answer to this question. — Ich wünschte, ich **wüsste** die Antwort …
I wish it **wasn't raining**. — Ich wünschte, es **regnete nicht/würde nicht regnen**.

In Wunschsätzen mit ***I wish*** (= „Ich wünschte“) steht das folgende Verb im *simple past* oder im *past progressive*, obwohl sich die Sätze nicht auf die Vergangenheit beziehen, sondern auf die Gegenwart oder die Zukunft. Im Deutschen steht der Konjunktiv.

	rubbish dump ['rʌbɪʃ ˌdʌmp]	Müllhalde, Müllkippe	the place where rubbish is taken
	(to) **continue** [kən'tɪnjuː]	weitergehen/-reden/-machen, weiter (tun); fortsetzen, fortfahren (mit)	(to) go on I stopped, but the others ~*d*. The teacher ~*d* (to talk) after the bell rang. She ~*d* the lesson.
	fence [fens]	Zaun	*a fence* 
A3	tile [taɪl]	Ziegel, Fliese	
	It's a tile, **isn't it**?	Es ist ein Ziegel, nicht wahr?/oder?	
	(to) **promise** ['prɒmɪs]	versprechen	I don't want any presents. *Promise* that you won't bring one. ⚠ Versprich *es (mir)*! = Promise *(me)*! (nicht: ~~Promise it~~!)
A4	**experience** [ɪk'spɪərɪəns]	Erlebnis, Erfahrung	How was your holiday? – It was a wonderful ~. Bob didn't get the job because he hasn't got enough ~. ⚠ Sie *hat* heute eine neue Erfahrung *gemacht*. = She *had* (nicht: ~~made~~) a new experience today.
	fleet [fliːt]	Flotte	
	***expert (on)** ['ekspɜːt]	Experte, Expertin, Fachmann, Fachfrau (für)	
	genuine ['dʒenjuɪn]	echt	The coin is what we thought it is, a ~ Roman one.
	Dr = Doctor ['dɒktə]	Dr. = Doktor	
	encounter [ɪn'kaʊntə]	Begegnung	
	while *(conj)* [waɪl]	während	I can learn some vocabulary ~ I'm waiting.
	(to) express [ɪk'spres]	*ausdrücken, äußern*	
	piano [pi'ænəʊ]	Klavier	⚠ Sarah spielt *Klavier.* = Sarah plays the *piano*.

German 'Doch!'

You don't like cats, do you? – **I do!** I love them.
*Du magst keine Katzen, oder? – **Doch!** Ich liebe sie.*

That coin isn't genuine, is it? – **Oh yes, it is!**
*Diese Münze ist nicht echt, oder? – **Oh doch!***

You can't play the piano, can you? – **Yes, I can.**
*Du kannst nicht Klavier spielen, oder? – **Doch!***

You haven't got a computer, have you? – **I have!**
*Du hast keinen Computer, nicht wahr? – **Doch!***

Im Deutschen widerspricht man einer verneinten Aussage meist mit „Doch!“.

Im Englischen benutzt man – wie bei den Kurzantworten – das Hilfsverb aus dem Aussagesatz, also:

You don't … → **(Oh yes,)** I **do!**
It isn't … → **(Oh yes,)** It **is!**
You can't … → **(Oh yes,)** I **can!**
You haven't … → **(Oh yes,)** I **have!**

p.75/A5	**right** *(adv)*	ganz, völlig; genau, direkt; gerade	They live ~ at the end of the street, in the last house. The accident happened ~ in front of the hotel. I'll help you later; I'm busy ~ now.
	empire ['empaɪə]	Reich, Weltreich	a group of countries that is ruled by one country
	***soldier** ['səʊldʒə]	Soldat	
	Celtic ['keltɪk]	keltisch; Keltisch	⚠ Aussprache: *Celtic* ['keltɪk]
	tribe [traɪb]	Stamm, Volksstamm	
	(to) last [lɑ:st]	halten *(Obst, Gemüse; Ehe usw.)*	It's a very cheap radio. It *won't* ~ very long.
A6	°What's cooking? *(infml)*	Was liegt an? / Was ist los?	
	pot [pɒt]	Topf, Kochtopf	
	°charcoal ['tʃɑ:kəʊl]	Holzkohle	
	(to) bake [beɪk]	backen	
	oven ['ʌvn]	Backofen	⚠ Aussprache: *oven* ['ʌvn]
	sauce [sɔ:s]	Soße	Do you want some tomato ~ on your chips?
	olive ['ɒlɪv]	Olive; Oliven-	⚠ Betonung auf der ersten Silbe: *olive* ['ɒlɪv]
	perfume ['pɜ:fju:m]	Parfüm	⚠ Betonung auf der ersten Silbe: *perfume* ['pɜ:fju:m]
	(to) rub (-bb-) [rʌb]	reiben, einreiben	If your hands are cold, you must ~ them (together).
	skin [skɪn]	Haut	Do 'white' people really have a white ~?
p.76/A7	slave [sleɪv]	Sklave, Sklavin	
	(to) **enter** ['entə]	betreten; einreisen in	When the new teacher ~*ed* the room, everyone stopped talking. Do Germans need a passport when they ~ Britain?
p.77/A8	(to) **interrupt** [ˌɪntə'rʌpt]	unterbrechen	Don't ~ me when I'm talking. Wait till I've finished.
A9	(to) **organize** ['ɔ:gənaɪz]	organisieren, veranstalten	to plan something and get ready for it
	demonstration [ˌdemən'streɪʃn]	Demonstration	⚠ Betonung auf der dritten Silbe: *demonstration* [ˌdemən'streɪʃn]
	unhappy (about) [ʌn'hæpi]	unglücklich, traurig (über/wegen)	sad ◂▸ happy
A10	(to) **thank** sb. [θæŋk]	jm. danken, sich bei jm. bedanken	to say 'thank you'
	marriage ['mærɪdʒ]	Ehe; Hochzeit	verb: '(to) marry' – noun: *'marriage'*
	(to) **get married (to** sb.**)** [ˌget 'mærɪd]	(sich ver)heiraten (mit jm.), (jn.) heiraten	(to) marry
	Bad luck.	Pech (gehabt)!	
	anyway ['eniweɪ]	trotzdem	

anyway	No, you can't go out now. **Anyway**, didn't you promise to wash the dishes?	… . **Außerdem/Und überhaupt**, hast du nicht versprochen, das Geschirr abzuwaschen?
	I'm not sure when we'll arrive: perhaps 7.30 or 7.45 – **anyway**, we'll be there before 8 o'clock.	…: vielleicht um 7 Uhr 30 oder 7 Uhr 45. **Wie dem auch sei**, wir werden vor 8 Uhr da sein.
	It was raining, but I didn't want to go out **anyway**.	…, aber ich wollte **sowieso** nicht rausgehen.
	It was raining, but I went out **anyway**.	…, aber ich ging **trotzdem** raus.

	sum [sʌm]	Rechenaufgabe; Summe	I hate maths. I hate doing ~*s* (= rechnen).
	straight *(adj; adv)* [streɪt]	gerade; gerade(wegs), direkt	a ~ line ——— a ~ road 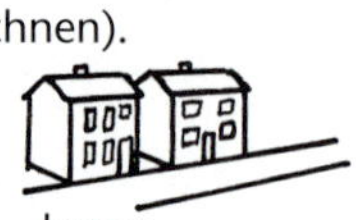 When I saw how late it was, I went ~ home.
	corner ['kɔ:nə]	Ecke	Anita rode down the street and disappeared round the ~. ⚠ Sand Street, *Ecke* London Road = *on the corner of* Sand Street and London Road
P1	**farmer** ['fɑ:mə]	Bauer/Bäuerin, Landwirt/in	
	object ['ɒbdʒɪkt]	Gegenstand	
	Latin ['lætɪn]	Latein	

	Briton ['brɪtn]	Britannier *(keltische Urbevölkerung Großbritanniens)*	⚠ *the Britons* = die Britannier die Briten = *the British*
P 3	***false** [fɔːls]	falsch, unecht	⧓ true
[P 6]	*mine* [maɪn]	*Bergwerk*	
P 10	(to) **do well/badly (in)**	gut/schlecht sein (in), gut/schlecht abschneiden (in)	Tina always *~es well* in her English tests.
	chance [tʃɑːns]	Chance, Gelegenheit	You have only one ~ to guess the right answer.
[P 12]	*sign* [saɪn]	*(An-)Zeichen*	
	opening times	*Öffnungszeiten*	
	personal ['pɜːsənl]	*persönlich*	
P 13	prefix ['priːfɪks]	Vorsilbe	
	(to) **get a** friendly **welcome** / (to) **give** sb. **a** friendly **welcome**	freundlich empfangen werden / jn. freundlich empfangen	When we arrived, we *got a* very friendly ~.
P 14	*(to) replace sth. (with)* [rɪ'pleɪs]	*etwas ersetzen (durch)*	
P 15	**communication** [kəˌmjuːnɪ'keɪʃn]	Kommunikation	⚠ Betonung auf der vierten Silbe: *communication* [kəˌmjuːnɪ'keɪʃn]
	planet ['plænɪt]	*Planet*	
	°alien ['eɪliən]	außerirdisches Wesen	

The Golden Hairpin

p.82	**past** *(prep; adv)* [pɑːst]	vorbei, vorüber (an)	We drove ~ houses, farms and forests. I was waiting at the bus stop when Don's mother drove ~. ⚠ She walked *past* me. = She passed me.
	°lead [led]	Blei	
	mine *(n)* [maɪn]	Bergwerk	
	fat (-tt-) [fæt]	dick	a *fat* cat   a *thin* cat ⚠ 1. *fat* bei Menschen, Tieren, Büchern: *a fat man, a fat dog, a fat book* 2. *thick* bei Sachen: *a thick wall, a thick book*
	horse [hɔːs]	Pferd	
	(to) **run** sth.	etwas leiten, betreiben, (durch)führen, veranstalten	

(to) run

John can't **run** very fast.	**laufen**	Sonia's parents **run** a hotel by the sea.	**betreiben**
Buses don't **run** very often on Sundays.	**verkehren**	They **run** training courses for windsurfers.	**durchführen**

	secret *(adj; n)* ['siːkrət]	geheim; Geheimnis	We had a ~ meeting; we didn't tell anyone about it. I'm sorry I can't tell you. It's a ~.
	tax (on) [tæks]	Steuer (auf)	
	that's why	deshalb, darum	that's the reason why
	(to) **be/feel bored** [bɔːd]	gelangweilt sein, sich langweilen	I*'m* ~. I don't have anything to do. I didn't enjoy Pete's party. I left early because I *felt* ~. ⚠ *boring* = *langweilig* – a *boring* party
	°commander [kə'mɑːndə]	Kommandant/in, Führer/in, Leiter/in	
	°legion ['liːdʒn]	Legion	
p.83	°mansio *(Latin)*	Bleibe; Hotel	
	senator ['senətə]	Senator/in	⚠ Betonung auf der ersten Silbe: *senator* ['senətə]
	handsome ['hænsəm]	gut aussehend	

'gut aussehen'

• **good-looking** is used for men and women:	*a good-looking man/woman*
• **beautiful** is used for women and children:	*a beautiful woman/child/girl*
• **handsome** is used mainly for men:	*a handsome man*
• **pretty** is used for women, girls, babies and young boys:	*a pretty woman/girl/baby/little boy*

°covered cart ['kʌvəd]	Planwagen	
(to) cover ['kʌvə]	bedecken, zudecken	The teacher~*ed* the piece of paper with her hand so I couldn't read what was on it.
°ingot ['ɪŋgət]	Ingot *(Barren Gold, Silber, Blei usw.)*	
(to) **tie (to)** [taɪ]	binden, anbinden (an)	Sometimes we ~ our dog *to* a tree in the garden. ⚠ -ing form: *tying*
(to) **be up**	auf(gestanden) sein	
back *(n)* [bæk]	Rückseite, hinterer Teil	The *back* of the house is dark, …
front *(n)* [frʌnt]	Vorderseite, vorderer Teil	… but the *front* isn't.
writing	Geschriebenes; (Hand-)Schrift	
(to) kidnap (-pp-) ['kɪdnæp]	entführen, kidnappen	
(to) **touch** [tʌtʃ]	berühren, anfassen	*Don't* ~ the plates! They're hot.
blond [blɒnd]	blond	She has ~ hair, not dark hair! ⚠ Aussprache: [blɒnd]
god, goddess [gɒd, 'gɒdes]	Gott, Göttin	
God	Gott	⚠ *God* (= christlicher Gott) wird großgeschrieben.
tear [tɪə]	Träne	His eyes were full of ~*s*. He was crying.
p.84 (to) stab (-bb-) [stæb]	(zu)stechen	
moon [mu:n]	Mond	
(to) take sb. **by** the hand	jn. an die Hand nehmen	
diagram ['daɪəgræm]	*Diagramm, grafische Darstellung*	

TIPP

Make your own WORD GAMES

Selbst gestaltete Vokabelrätsel eignen sich prima zum Wiederholen von Vokabeln in Partner- oder Gruppenarbeit – hier sind zwei Vorschläge:

- **VERSTECKTE WÖRTER:**
  1) Zeichne ein Rätselgitter mit 10 mal 10 Feldern.
  2) Wähle einen Oberbegriff, z.B. *clothes*, und suche 8 bis 10 Unterbegriffe dazu *(shirt, trousers, socks, …)*.
  3) Trage die Unterbegriffe in das Gitter ein – waagerecht, senkrecht oder diagonal, vorwärts oder rückwärts.
  4) Ergänze die noch leeren Felder mit beliebig gewählten Buchstaben. (Achtung, es dürfen keine neuen Wörter entstehen!)

  Nun tausche dein Rätsel mit einem Partner/einer Partnerin – wer findet am schnellsten die versteckten Wörter?
  (Im Beispiel rechts sind die Lösungen hervorgehoben.)

clothes

C	E	A	N	O	R	A	K	B	J
K	S	B	L	H	O	S	Q	E	K
M	H	O	X	A	S	D	K	S	A
P	I	B	C	O	A	T	W	U	E
G	R	A	O	K	C	H	K	O	L
D	T	N	S	J	S	N	D	L	K
A	F	L	S	K	R	D	S	B	H
Q	Z	B	E	V	C	V	N	D	A
W	R	S	R	E	S	U	O	R	T
E	T	B	D	O	P	S	D	F	G

- **KAMMRÄTSEL:**
  1) Zeichne einen „Kamm" wie im Beispiel rechts und lege ein Lösungswort mit 8 bis 10 Buchstaben fest, z.B. *br<u>e</u>a<u>k</u>f<u>a</u>s<u>t</u>*.
  2) Suche Wörter, die mit dem 2., 4., 6. und 8. Buchstaben deines Lösungsworts beginnen. Diese Wörter sollten alle gleich viele Buchstaben haben, damit das Rätsel die Form eines Kamms bekommt, z.B. *road; aunt; fast; shop*.
  3) Gib deinem Partner/deiner Partnerin Hinweise, welche senkrechten Wörter gesucht sind, z.B. 2: *another word for 'street'* 4: *your mother's or your father's sister* 6: *not slow, but …* 8: *Here you can buy things.*
  4) Gib deinem Partner/deiner Partnerin einen Hinweis auf dein Lösungswort, z.B. _ _ _ _ _ _ _ _ _ *is the first meal of the day.*

  Kann dein Partner/deine Partnerin dein Lösungswort finden?

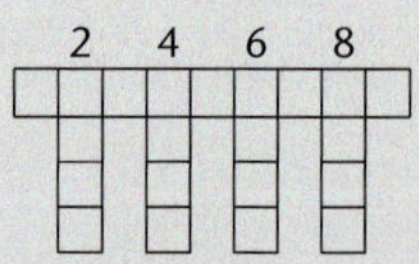

p.85 How to listen for information

(to) **listen for** sth.	auf etwas horchen, auf etwas achten	
1 *audio* ['ɔ:dɪəʊ]	*Audio-*	

	(to) **prepare (for)** [prɪ'peə]	(sich) vorbereiten (auf); *(Mahlzeit)* zubereiten	(to) get ready (for)
2	°furnace ['fɜ:nɪs]	Ofen	
	mind [maɪnd]	*Geist, Verstand*	
	detail ['di:teɪl]	*Detail, Einzelheit*	
	changing room	Umkleideraum	
3	*(to) sketch* [sketʃ]	*skizzieren*	
	(to) panic ['pænɪk]	in Panik geraten	When the fire started, people began to ~. ⚠ -ing form: *panicking* • simple past form: *panicked*

▶▶▶ Unit 7: A Very Special TV Special

pp.86/87	°set [set]	Bühnenbild, Kulisse	
	stage [steɪdʒ]	Bühne	At 9 o'clock the band came on ~ and started to play.
	***tool** [tu:l]	Werkzeug	
	cable ['keɪbl]	Kabel	
	°gallery ['gæləri]	Regie(raum)	
	(to) nominate ['nɒmɪneɪt]	*nominieren, vorschlagen*	
	carpenter ['kɑ:pəntə]	Zimmermann, Tischler/in	
	electrician [ɪˌlek'trɪʃn]	Elektriker/in	 There's a problem with the lights. We need an ~.
	presenter [prɪ'zentə]	Moderator/in	Thomas Gottschalk is the ~ of 'Wetten, dass ...'.
	make-up ['meɪkʌp]	Make-up	⚠ Betonung auf der ersten Silbe: *make-up* ['meɪkʌp]
	°floor manager ['flɔ: ˌmænɪdʒə]	Aufnahmeleiter/in	
	director [də'rektə]	Regisseur/in	
	assistant	stellvertretende(r, s)	
	(to) work **in** television	beim Fernsehen arbeiten	
p.88	rehearsal [rɪ'hɜ:sl]	Probe *(Theater, Film)*	
	mirror ['mɪrə]	Spiegel	Peter looked at himself in the ~. 
	walkie-talkie [ˌwɔ:ki 'tɔ:ki]	Walkie-Talkie *(tragbares Funksprechgerät)*	
	(to) **fix** [fɪks]	reparieren, in Ordnung bringen	The chair is broken. – Well, you're a carpenter, ~ it!
	(to) **be glad (about)** **(-dd-)** [glæd]	froh sein, sich freuen (über)	(to) be happy, (to) be pleased
	meanwhile ['mi:nwaɪl]	inzwischen, währenddessen	I went to bed at 10 pm. *Meanwhile* in Japan, people were getting up.
	coffee shop	Kaffeestube, Café	
	just after/before 10.30	kurz nach/vor 10.30	Do I have to go to bed now? It's only ~ *after* 9!
	°(to) sabotage ['sæbətɑ:ʒ]	sabotieren	
p.89	anonymous [ə'nɒnɪməs]	anonym	Many old songs are ~: we don't know who wrote them. ⚠ Betonung auf der zweiten Silbe: *anonymous* [ə'nɒnɪməs]
	a **six-week** trip	eine sechswöchige Reise	
	(to) **be in a bad mood** [mu:d]	schlechte Laune haben, in schlechter Stimmung sein	◂▸ (to) be in a good mood
	whoever [hu:'evə]	wer (auch) immer, wen/wem (auch) immer	Well, it's your birthday party, you can invite ~ you like.

wherever, whenever, whoever, whatever

Wherever you go, I'll come with you.	**Wo auch immer** du hingehst, ...
Visit me **whenever** you like.	..., **wann immer** du willst.
I won't open the door, **whoever** you are.	..., **wer immer** Sie **auch** sind.
Whoever told you that was wrong.	**Wer immer** dir das **auch** erzählt hat, hatte Unrecht.
I'll help you **whatever** happens.	..., **was immer auch** geschieht.

suspect ['sʌspekt]	*Verdächtige(r)*	
(to) put the phone down	den Hörer auflegen	
°sound engineer ['saʊnd_endʒɪˌnɪə]	Toningenieur/in, Tontechniker/in	
tape [teɪp]	(Ton-)Band	
incident ['ɪnsɪdənt]	*Zwischenfall, Vorkommnis*	
(to) **take a break**	eine Pause machen	You've worked for four hours, you should ~ *a break.*

German 'machen'

die Hausaufgaben **machen**	(to) **do** your homework	eine Pause **machen**	(to) **take** a break
Einkäufe **machen**	(to) **do** the shopping	Fotos **machen**	(to) **take** photos
einen Vorschlag **machen**	(to) **make** a suggestion	einen Spaziergang **machen**	(to) **go for** a walk
einen Fehler **machen**	(to) **make** a mistake	eine Radtour **machen**	(to) **go on** a bike tour
einen Plan **machen**	(to) **make** a plan	einen Ausflug **machen**	(to) **go on** a trip
eine Entdeckung **machen**	(to) **make** a discovery	Urlaub **machen**	(to) **go/be** on holiday
		ein Picknick **machen**	(to) **have** a picnic

	°saboteur [ˌsæbə'tɜː]	Saboteur/in	
	witness ['wɪtnəs]	Zeuge, Zeugin	
	suspect ['sʌspekt]	Verdächtige(r)	
p.90	*column* ['kɒləm]	*Spalte*	
	so far [səʊ 'fɑː]	*bis hierher, bis jetzt*	
	strong [strɒŋ]	stark	⚠ 'False friend': *strong* = stark • streng = *strict*
	(to) **lift** [lɪft]	(an-, hoch)heben	
	chaos ['keɪɒs]	Chaos	⚠ Aussprache: *chaos* ['keɪɒs]
p.91	(to) **break loose (from)** [luːs]	sich losreißen, sich lösen (von)	We tied the dog to a tree, but it *broke* ~ and ran away. ⚠ *loose* [luːs] *(= locker, lose)* is an adjective *(to) lose* [luːz] *(= verlieren)* is a verb
	(to) **take a step towards** sb.	einen Schritt auf jn. zugehen	
	(to) crash [kræʃ]	krachen	
	centimetre ['sentɪmiːtə]	Zentimeter	There are 100 ~*s* in a metre.
	(to) **lead** [liːd], **led, led** [led]	führen, leiten	This road ~*s* to the next village. You ~ and we'll follow.
	policeman/policewoman	Polizist/Polizistin	police officer
	(to) take sb. away	*hier:* jn. abführen	

TIPP

Reim dich oder ich fress dich!

Du kannst dir schwierige Wörter, z.B. unregelmäßige Verben, besser merken, wenn du sie in Reimform bringst und dann rhythmisch sprichst – du kannst dabei im Rhythmus klatschen, dann wird daraus so eine Art Rap.

Probier's mal mit diesen Verben:
blow, break, fly, wake.

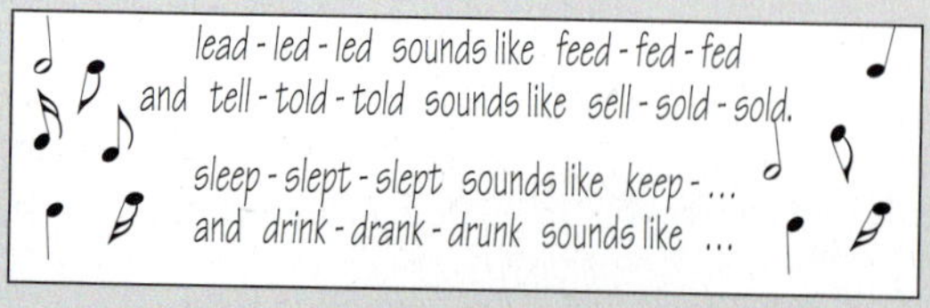

In der Liste der unregelmäßigen Verben (S. 199/200) findest du sicher noch weitere Paare.

Das *DICTIONARY* enthält den Wortschatz der Bände 1 bis 3.

° – Wörter, die mit einem kleinen Kringel (°) markiert sind, gehören nicht zum Lernwortschatz.
* – Unregelmäßige Verben sind mit einem Stern (*) gekennzeichnet (vgl. *List of irregular verbs*, S. 199/200).

Abkürzungen

jm. = jemandem	sb. = somebody/someone	*Part. Perf. = Partizip Perfekt*	*pl = plural*
jn. = jemanden	sth. = something	*si. past = simple past (form)*	*no pl = no plural*

A

a, an [ə, ən] ein, eine • °**seven days a week** sieben Tage die/pro Woche
abbey ['æbi] Abtei
abbreviation [əˌbriːvi'eɪʃn] Abkürzung
able ['eɪbl]: **be able to do sth.** etwas tun können; fähig sein, etwas zu tun
°**Aboriginal** [ˌæbə'rɪdʒənl] Ureinwohner/in
about [ə'baʊt] **1.** *(adv)* ungefähr; **2.** *(adv)* unterwegs; **3.** *(prep)* über; wegen • **It's about Mrs McCann.** Es ist wegen Mrs McCann. • **a question about your book** eine Frage über dein Buch/zu deinem Buch • **this book is about** dieses Buch handelt von • °**That's not what friends are about.** *etwa:* Unter Freunden stelle ich mir aber etwas anderes vor! **dream/hear/know about** träumen/hören/wissen von °**move about the country** sich im Land umherbewegen **tell about** erzählen von, berichten über • **think about** halten von, denken über **What about a calendar?** Wie wär's mit einem Kalender? **What about Jenny?** Was ist mit Jenny? / Und Jenny? **What was funny about the docks?** Was war komisch an den Docks?
above [ə'bʌv] **1.** *(adv)* oben; **2.** *(prep)* über, oberhalb (von)
abroad [ə'brɔːd] ins Ausland; im Ausland
accident ['æksɪdənt] **1.** Unfall; **2.** Zufall • **by accident** zufällig, versehentlich
acid rain [ˌæsɪd 'reɪn] saurer Regen
across [ə'krɒs] **1.** *(prep)* (quer) über, durch; **2.** *(adv)* hinüber, herüber
act [ækt] **1.** spielen, schauspielern • **act out** vorspielen °**2.** handeln
°**action** ['ækʃn] Handlung, Tat
activity [æk'tɪvəti] Aktivität, Tätigkeit
actor ['æktə] Schauspieler **actress** ['æktrəs] Schauspielerin
AD [ˌeɪ'diː]: **70 AD** 70 n. Chr.
adapted from [ə'dæptɪd] eine Bearbeitung von, frei nach
add [æd] addieren, hinzufügen, ergänzen
address [ə'dres] Adresse, Anschrift
°**admiral** ['ædmərəl] Admiral
adopt [ə'dɒpt] adoptieren, die Patenschaft übernehmen für
°**advantage** [əd'vɑːntɪdʒ] Vorteil
adventure [əd'ventʃə] Abenteuer
°**advert** ['ædvɜːt] Anzeige, Reklame
aerobics [eə'rəʊbɪks] Aerobic
afraid [ə'freɪd]: **be afraid (of)** sich fürchten (vor), Angst haben (vor) • **I'm afraid** leider
Afro-Caribbean [ˌæfrəʊ kærə'biːən] Afro-Karibe/Afro-Karibin *(Schwarze/r karibischer Herkunft)*
after ['ɑːftə] **1.** *(prep)* nach **after that** danach • **look after sb.** sich um jn. kümmern, auf jn. aufpassen • **run after sb.** hinter jm. herrennen **2.** *(conj)* nachdem
afternoon [ˌɑːftə'nuːn] Nachmittag • **Good afternoon.** Guten Tag. *(nachmittags)* **in the afternoon(s)** am Nachmittag, nachmittags **that afternoon** an jenem Nachmittag • **this afternoon** heute Nachmittag • **tomorrow afternoon** morgen Nachmittag
afterwards ['ɑːftəwədz] danach
again [ə'gen] wieder, noch einmal • **again and again** immer wieder
against [ə'genst] gegen
age [eɪdʒ] Alter • **for ages** *(infml)* eine Ewigkeit (lang), ewig
agent ['eɪdʒənt] Agent/in
ago [ə'gəʊ]: **a long time ago** vor langer Zeit • **a minute/week ago** vor einer Minute/Woche
agree [ə'griː] sich einigen, beschließen • **agree with sb.** mit jm. übereinstimmen; jm. zustimmen
ahead [ə'hed]: **be ahead (of sb.)** führen, in Führung liegen (vor jm.); jm. voraus sein
air [eə] Luft • **in the open air** im Freien
airport ['eəpɔːt] Flughafen
album ['ælbəm] Album
alcohol ['ælkəhɒl] Alkohol
°**alien** ['eɪliən] außerirdisches Wesen
alive [ə'laɪv]: **be alive** leben, am Leben sein
all [ɔːl] alle; alles • **all the kids** alle Kinder • **all day/morning/summer** den ganzen Tag/Morgen/Sommer (lang) **all the time/money/food** die ganze Zeit (lang)/das ganze Geld/Essen • **all alone** ganz allein • **all around …** überall in … • **all over the world** auf der ganzen Welt, überall auf der Welt • **all right** gut, in Ordnung • **all wet** ganz nass, völlig nass • **first of all** zuallererst
allowed [ə'laʊd]: **be allowed to do sth.** etwas tun dürfen
almost ['ɔːlməʊst] fast, beinahe
alone [ə'ləʊn] allein
along [ə'lɒŋ]: **1.** *(prep)* **along the street** entlang der Straße, die Straße entlang; **2.** *(adv)* **(go/drive/move) along** weiter…, vorwärts…; dahin…
alphabet ['ælfəbet] Alphabet °**alphabetical** [ˌælfə'betɪkl] alphabetisch
already [ɔːl'redi] schon, bereits
also ['ɔːlsəʊ] auch
alternative *(n; adj)* [ɔːl'tɜːnətɪv] **1.** Alternative; **2.** Alternativ-
although [ɔːl'ðəʊ] obwohl
always ['ɔːlweɪz] immer
am [ˌeɪ_'em] … Uhr morgens/vormittags
ambulance ['æmbjələns] Krankenwagen

D

American *(n; adj)* [ə'merɪkən] 1. Amerikaner/in; 2. amerikanisch • **American football** Football

°amphora ['æmfərə] Amphore *(Krug mit Henkeln)*

an [ən] ein, eine

and [ənd, *betont:* ænd] und **And so on.** Und so weiter.

°Angles ['æŋglz]: **the Angles** die Angeln *(Angehörige des Volksstammes der Angeln)*

°Anglo-Saxons [,æŋgləʊ 'sæksnz]: **the Anglo-Saxons** die Angelsachsen

angry (with) ['æŋgri] böse, zornig, wütend (auf)

animal ['ænɪml] Tier

anonymous [ə'nɒnɪməs] anonym

anorak ['ænəræk] Anorak

another [ə'nʌðə] ein(e) andere(r, s); noch ein(e) • **one another** einander, sich (gegenseitig)

answer *(v; n)* ['ɑːnsə] 1. antworten; beantworten **answering machine** Anrufbeantworter 2. **answer (to)** Antwort (auf)

anti-(racist) ['ænti] anti-(rassistisch) • **anticlockwise** [,ænti'klɒkwaɪz] entgegen dem Uhrzeigersinn

°antiseptic [,ænti'septɪk] Antiseptikum *(Mittel, das Bakterienwachstum hemmt)*

any ['eni] jede(r/s) (beliebige) **not … any** kein(e) • °**not … any more** nicht mehr; kein(e,n) … mehr • **any?** (irgend)welche?

anybody ['enibɒdi] jede(r) (beliebige) • **not … anybody** niemand • **anybody?** (irgend)jemand?

anyone ['eniwʌn] jede(r) (beliebige) • **not … anyone** niemand • **anyone?** (irgend)jemand?

anything ['eniθɪŋ] irgendetwas (beliebiges) • **not … anything** nichts • **anything?** (irgend)etwas?

anyway ['eniweɪ] 1. jedenfalls, wie dem auch sei; 2. außerdem, und überhaupt; 3. sowieso; 4. trotzdem

anywhere ['enɪweə] irgendwo(hin) • **not … anywhere** nirgendwo(hin)

°apart from [ə'pɑːt] außer, abgesehen von

appear [ə'pɪə] erscheinen, auftauchen

apple ['æpl] Apfel

April ['eɪprəl] April

archaeologist [,ɑːkɪ'ɒlədʒɪst] Archäologe/Archäologin

are [ə, *betont:* ɑː] bist; sind; seid • **How much are …?** Was kosten …? / Wie viel kosten …?

area ['eəriə] Bereich; Gebiet, Gegend

°argue ['ɑːgjuː] streiten

arm [ɑːm] Arm

around [ə'raʊnd] um … herum; in … umher • **all around …** überall in … • **around Ashton** in Ashton umher, durch Ashton • **be around** *(infml)* in der Nähe sein, da sein • **Look around (you).** Sieh dich um. • **run around** umherrennen, herumrennen **stand around** herumstehen

arrange [ə'reɪndʒ] 1. (an)ordnen; °2. vereinbaren, ausmachen

arrive [ə'raɪv] ankommen, eintreffen

°arrow ['ærəʊ] Pfeil

art [ɑːt] Kunst

article ['ɑːtɪkl] (Zeitungs-)Artikel

as [əz, *betont:* æz] 1. *(conj)* als, während • **as you know** wie du weißt • **as if** als ob 2. *(prep)* **as a child** als Kind 3. *(adv)* **as in London** wie in London • **as quick as** so schnell wie • **as bad as this** so schlimm, so schlecht

Asia ['eɪʃə, 'eɪʒə] Asien • **Asian** *(adj; n)* ['eɪʃn, 'eɪʒn] asiatisch; Asiat/in

ask [ɑːsk] fragen • **ask sb. for sth.** jn. um etwas bitten **ask questions** Fragen stellen

assembly [ə'sembli] Schulversammlung *(oft mit Andacht)* **assembly hall** Aula

assistant [ə'sɪstənt] 1. Assistent/Assistentin; 2. Verkäufer/in; 3. stellvertretende(r, s)

astronaut ['æstrənɔːt] Astronaut/in

at [ət, *betont:* æt] an, bei • **at a travel agent's** in einem Reisebüro • **at all times** immer, jederzeit • **at dinner** beim Abendessen • **at first** zuerst, anfangs, am Anfang • **at home** zu Hause, daheim • **at Kingsway High School** an/auf der Kingsway High School **at last** schließlich, endlich °**at least** mindestens • **at lunch-time** zur Mittagszeit, mittags • **at night** nachts, in der Nacht • **at once** sofort, (so)gleich • **at school** in der Schule • **at sea** auf See • **at six** um sechs • **at that time** damals, zu jener/dieser Zeit **at the door** an der Tür • **at the end** am Ende, am Schluss **at the front** vorn • **at the moment** im Moment, gerade, zurzeit • **at the restaurant** im Restaurant • **at the same time** zur gleichen Zeit **at the weekend** am Wochenende • **at weekends** an Wochenenden • **at work** bei der Arbeit, am Arbeitsplatz

ate [et, eɪt] *si. past von „eat"*

athlete ['æθliːt] Athlet/in, Sportler/in • **athletics** [æθ'letɪks] Leichtathletik

atlas ['ætləs] Atlas

°attack [ə'tæk] angreifen

attitude (towards) ['ætɪtjuːd] Haltung (gegenüber), Einstellung (zu)

au pair [,əʊ 'peə] Aupair-Mädchen, Aupair-Junge

°audio ['ɔːdɪəʊ] Audio-

August ['ɔːgəst] August

°Auld Lang Syne [,ɔːld læŋ 'saɪn] *etwa:* Die gute, alte Zeit

aunt [ɑːnt] Tante

authentic [ɔː'θentɪk] authentisch

automatic *(adj)* [,ɔːtə'mætɪk] automatisch • **automatically** *(adv)* automatisch

autumn ['ɔːtəm] Herbst

avenue ['ævənjuː] Allee, Boulevard

°aviary ['eɪviəri] Vogelhaus

away [ə'weɪ] weg, fort

°awesome ['ɔːsəm] überwältigend

B

back *(n; adv)* [bæk] 1. Rücken; Rückseite, hinterer Teil • °**at the back of the book** hinten im Buch 2. zurück • **Get back!** (Geh/Tritt) Zurück! • **back in Chester** daheim in Chester

bacon ['beɪkən] Schinkenspeck

°bacteria *(pl)* [bæk'tɪəriə] Bakterien

bad [bæd] schlecht, schlimm **be bad at sth.** schlecht in etwas sein; etwas schlecht können • **Bad luck.** Pech (gehabt)! • **do badly (in)** schlecht sein (in), schlecht abschneiden (in)

badminton ['bædmɪntən] Badminton, Federball

bag [bæg] Tasche, Beutel, Tüte; Sack

bake [beɪk] backen

ball [bɔːl] Ball

banana [bə'nɑːnə] Banane

band [bænd] Band, (Musik-)Gruppe

°bandage ['bændɪdʒ] Verband, Bandage

bang [bæŋ] Knall

Bangladeshi [ˌbæŋglə'deʃi] Bangale/Bangalin *(jd. aus Bangladesch)*
bank [bæŋk] **1.** Bank, Sparkasse **bottle bank** Altglascontainer **2.** (Fluss-)Ufer
°**barbarian** [bɑː'beərɪən] Barbar/in
barbecue ['bɑːbɪkjuː] Grillparty
baseball ['beɪsbɔːl] Baseball
based on ['beɪst_ɒn] basierend auf
basket ['bɑːskɪt] Korb
basketball ['bɑːskɪtbɔːl] Basketball
bath [bɑːθ] Bad • **have/take a bath** ein Bad nehmen, *(in der Wanne)* baden • **bathhouse** Badehaus • **bathroom** ['bɑːθruːm] Badezimmer
°**battle** ['bætl] Schlacht
°**bazaar** [bə'zɑː] Basar
BC [ˌbiː'siː]: **70 BC** 70 v. Chr.
be* [bi, *betont:* biː] sein • **be called** heißen, genannt werden • **be cold** frieren • **be in trouble** in Schwierigkeiten sein; Ärger kriegen • **be late** zu spät sein/kommen • **be on holiday** in Urlaub sein; Ferien haben/machen • **be right** Recht haben • **be wrong** **1.** sich irren, Unrecht haben; **2.** nicht in Ordnung sein, nicht stimmen
beach [biːtʃ] Strand • **on the beach** am Strand
beat* [biːt] besiegen; schlagen **beat sb. up** jn. zusammenschlagen
beat [biːt] *si. past von „beat"*
beaten ['biːtn] *Part. Perf. von „beat"*
beautiful ['bjuːtɪfl] (wunder-) schön
became [bɪ'keɪm] *si. past von „become"*
because [bɪ'kɒz] weil • **that's because** das kommt daher, weil • **because of** wegen
become* [bɪ'kʌm] werden
become [bɪ'kʌm] *Part. Perf. von „become"*
bed [bed] Bett
bedroom ['bedruːm] Schlafzimmer
been [biːn, bɪn] *Part. Perf. von „be"* • **I've been to …** Ich war (schon mal) in … / Ich bin (schon) in … gewesen.
before [bɪ'fɔː] **1.** *(prep)* vor; **2.** *(conj)* bevor; **3.** *(adv)* vorher; vorher schon mal
began [bɪ'gæn] *si. past von „begin"*
begin* **(-nn-)** [bɪ'gɪn] beginnen, anfangen (mit) • **beginning** Anfang, Beginn • **at the beginning** am Anfang
begun [bɪ'gʌn] *Part. Perf. von „begin"*

behind [bɪ'haɪnd] hinter
believe (in) [bɪ'liːv] glauben (an)
bell [bel] Glocke, Klingel
belong to [bɪ'lɒŋ] gehören (zu)
below [bɪ'ləʊ] **1.** *(adv)* unten; **2.** *(prep)* unter, unterhalb (von)
bench [bentʃ] Bank *(zum Sitzen)*
best [best]: **(the) best** (der/die/das) beste …; am besten
bet* **(-tt-)** [bet] wetten
bet [bet] **1.** *si. past von „bet"*; **2.** *Part. Perf. von „bet"*
better (than) ['betə] besser (als)
between [bɪ'twiːn] zwischen
beyond [bɪ'jɒnd] über … hinaus, jenseits (von)
bicycle ['baɪsɪkl] Fahrrad
big **(-gg-)** [bɪg] groß
bike [baɪk] Fahrrad • **ride a bike** Rad fahren • **bike ride** Radfahrt, Radtour
bikini [bɪ'kiːni] Bikini
billion ['bɪljən] Milliarde(n)
bin [bɪn] Papierkorb, Mülleimer
bingo ['bɪŋgəʊ] Bingo
biology [baɪ'ɒlədʒi] Biologie
bird [bɜːd] Vogel
biro ['baɪrəʊ] Kugelschreiber
birth [bɜːθ] Geburt • **date of birth** Geburtsdatum • **place of birth** Geburtsort
birthday ['bɜːθdeɪ] Geburtstag **birthday card** Geburtstagskarte • **Happy birthday!** Herzlichen Glückwunsch zum Geburtstag! • **It's my birthday next week.** • Ich habe nächste Woche Geburtstag. **When's your birthday?** Wann hast du Geburtstag?
biscuit ['bɪskɪt] Keks, Plätzchen
bit: **a bit** [ə 'bɪt] ein bisschen, etwas
black [blæk] schwarz
blew [bluː] *si. past von „blow"*
°**blindfold sb.** ['blaɪndfəʊld] jm. die Augen verbinden • **One person is blindfolded.** Einer Person sind die Augen verbunden.
blond [blɒnd] blond
blood [blʌd] Blut
blouse [blaʊz] Bluse
blow* [bləʊ] wehen, blasen
blown [bləʊn] *Part. Perf. von „blow"*
blue [bluː] blau
blush [blʌʃ] rot werden, erröten
board *(n; v)* [bɔːd] **1.** Brett; (Wand-)Tafel • **board-game** Brettspiel • **notice board** Anschlagtafel, Schwarzes Brett °**2.** Spielbrett; **3. on board (the ship)** an Bord (des Schiffes) • **go on board** an Bord gehen **4. board a plane/ship** an Bord eines Flugzeugs/Schiffes gehen

boat [bəʊt] Boot, Schiff
body ['bɒdi] Körper
°**bold print** [ˌbəʊld 'prɪnt] Fettdruck
bomb [bɒm] Bombe
bone [bəʊn] Knochen
book [bʊk] Buch • **bookshop** Buchhandlung, Buchladen **bookshelf** ['bʊkʃelf], *pl* **bookshelves** ['bʊkʃelvz] Bücherregal • **exercise book** Heft, Schulheft
border ['bɔːdə] Grenze
bored [bɔːd]: **be/feel bored** gelangweilt sein, sich langweilen • **boring** ['bɔːrɪŋ] langweilig
born [bɔːn]: **be born** geboren sein/werden
boss [bɒs] *(infml)* Boss, Chef/Chefin
both [bəʊθ] beide, beides **both of you** alle beide; ihr beide
bottle ['bɒtl] Flasche • **a bottle of …** eine Flasche … **bottle bank** ['bɒtl bæŋk] Altglascontainer
bottom ['bɒtəm] Boden *(eines Gefäßes usw.)*; unteres Ende **bottom row** untere Reihe
bought [bɔːt] **1.** *si. past von „buy"*; **2.** *Part. Perf. von „buy"*
boutique [buː'tiːk] Boutique
bowling ['bəʊlɪŋ] Bowling
box [bɒks] Kasten, Kiste **a box of chocolates** eine Schachtel Pralinen
°**boxing glove** ['bɒksɪŋ glʌv] Boxhandschuh
boy [bɔɪ] Junge
boyfriend ['bɔɪfrend] (fester) Freund
°**brackets** ['brækɪts] Klammern
brain [breɪn] Gehirn
°**brass** [brɑːs] Blechbläser
brave [breɪv] tapfer, mutig
bread *(no pl)* [bred] Brot
break [breɪk] Pause • **take a break** eine Pause machen
break* [breɪk] (zer)brechen; kaputt machen; kaputt gehen **break loose (from)** sich losreißen, sich lösen (von)
breakfast ['brekfəst] Frühstück **for breakfast** zum Frühstück **have breakfast** frühstücken
bridge [brɪdʒ] Brücke
bright [braɪt] leuchtend, hell **brightness** ['braɪtnəs] Helligkeit, *(das)* Leuchten
brilliant ['brɪliənt] toll, glänzend, großartig
bring* [brɪŋ] (mit-, her)bringen • °**bring to life** lebendig machen
British ['brɪtɪʃ] britisch • **He's/She's British.** Er ist Brite./Sie ist Britin. • **the British** die Briten

Briton ['brɪtn] Britannier *(keltische Urbevölkerung Großbritanniens)*
brochure ['brəʊʃə] Prospekt, Broschüre
broke [brəʊk] *si. past von „break"*
broken ['brəʊkən] **1.** *Part. Perf. von „break"*; **2.** *(adj)* gebrochen; zerbrochen
brother ['brʌðə] Bruder
brought [brɔ:t] **1.** *si. past von „bring"*; **2.** *Part. Perf. von „bring"*
brown [braʊn] braun
brush *(n; v)* [brʌʃ] **1.** (Haar-)Bürste; **2.** bürsten • **brush your teeth** sich die Zähne putzen
budgie ['bʌdʒi] Wellensittich
°**buffet** ['bʊfeɪ] Büfett
build* [bɪld] bauen • **builder** Bauarbeiter/in
building ['bɪldɪŋ] Gebäude
built [bɪlt] **1.** *si. past von „build"*; **2.** *Part. Perf. von „build"*
bulldozer ['bʊldəʊzə] Planierraupe, Bulldozer
burglar ['bɜ:glə] Einbrecher/in
burn [bɜ:n] (ver)brennen; anbrennen lassen
bus [bʌs] Bus • **on the bus** im Bus • **bus stop** Bushaltestelle
business ['bɪznəs] Unternehmen, Geschäft(e)
°**busker** ['bʌskə] Straßenmusikant/in
busy ['bɪzi] beschäftigt; belebt, verkehrsreich, hektisch
but [bət, *betont:* bʌt] aber
butter ['bʌtə] Butter
button ['bʌtn] Knopf
buy* [baɪ] kaufen
by [baɪ] **1.** von; durch • **by accident** zufällig, versehentlich • **What do you mean by that?** Was verstehst du darunter?
2. an, neben; (nahe) bei • **by the way** übrigens, nebenbei (bemerkt)
3. by bike/car/… mit dem Rad/Auto/… • **take sb. by the hand** jn. an die Hand nehmen
4. by 31st May bis spätestens 31. Mai
Bye bye! [baɪ 'baɪ] Tschüs!

C

c. (= circa) ['sɜ:kə] ca. (= zirka)
cable ['keɪbl] Kabel
café ['kæfeɪ] (kleines) Restaurant, Imbissstube; Café
cage [keɪdʒ] Käfig
cake [keɪk] Kuchen, Torte
calendar ['kælɪndə] Kalender
call *(v; n)* [kɔ:l] **1.** nennen; rufen; anrufen; aufrufen • **call for help** um Hilfe rufen
What do you call this? Wie nennt man dies? • **called** mit (dem) Namen • **be called** heißen, genannt werden
caller Anrufer/in
2. (An-)Ruf
camcorder ['kæmkɔ:də] Camcorder *(Videokamera mit eingebauter Abspielfunktion)*
came [keɪm] *si. past von „come"*
camera ['kæmərə] Kamera, Fotoapparat
camp-site ['kæmpsaɪt] Campingplatz, Zeltplatz
can [kæn] Dose, Büchse
can [kən, *betont:* kæn] **1.** können; **2.** dürfen • **you can't** [kɑ:nt] **(= cannot)** ['kænɒt] du kannst nicht / darfst nicht
canal [kə'næl] Kanal
candle ['kændl] Kerze
canteen [kæn'ti:n] Kantine, Schulmensa
canyon ['kænjən] Cañon, Schlucht
capital ['kæpɪtl] Hauptstadt
captain ['kæptɪn] Kapitän/in
°**caption** ['kæpʃn] Bildunterschrift
car [kɑ:] Auto
°**carbolic acid** [kɑ:ˌbɒlɪk‿'æsɪd] Karbol(säure), Phenol
card [kɑ:d] Karte
°**cardboard** ['kɑ:dbɔ:d] Pappe, Karton
care (about) [keə] sich kümmern (um), wichtig nehmen
I don't care. Das ist mir egal.
Who cares? *etwa:* Wen interessiert das? / Ist doch egal!
careful *(adj)* ['keəfl] **1.** vorsichtig; **2.** sorgfältig • **carefully** *(adv)* ['keəfəli] **1.** vorsichtig; **2.** sorgfältig
carpenter ['kɑ:pəntə] Zimmermann, Tischler/in
carry ['kæri] **1.** tragen; **2.** befördern, transportieren
cart [kɑ:t] Karren, Wagen
carton ['kɑ:tn] Karton, (Milch-, Saft-)Packung
cashier [kæ'ʃɪə] Kassierer/in
cassette [kə'set] Kassette
cassette recorder Kassettenrecorder
castle ['kɑ:sl] Burg, Schloss
cat [kæt] Katze, Kater
°**catalogue** ['kætəlɒg] Katalog
catch* [kætʃ] fangen; erwischen • **catch a train/bus** einen Zug/Bus nehmen, erreichen
cathedral [kə'θi:drəl] Kathedrale, Dom
caught [kɔ:t] **1.** *si. past von „catch"*; **2.** *Part. Perf. von „catch"*
cause [kɔ:z] verursachen
°**cave** [keɪv] Höhle
CD [ˌsi:'di:] CD • **CD player** CD-Spieler • **CD-ROM** [ˌsi:di:'rɒm] CD-ROM *(nur lesbare, nicht überschreibbare Computer-CD)*
°**ceilidh** ['keɪli] *lockeres Beisammensein mit Musik und Tanz*
celebration [ˌselɪ'breɪʃn] (Gedenk-)Feier
Celtic ['keltɪk] keltisch; Keltisch
centimetre ['sentɪmi:tə] Zentimeter
central ['sentrəl] Zentral-, Mittel-
centre ['sentə] Zentrum; Mitte
century ['sentʃəri] Jahrhundert
ceremony ['serəməni] Zeremonie; Feier(lichkeit)
chain [tʃeɪn] Kette
chair [tʃeə] Stuhl
champion ['tʃæmpiən] Wettkampfsieger/in, Champion, Meister/in • **championship** ['tʃæmpiənʃɪp] Meisterschaft
chance [tʃɑ:ns] Chance, Gelegenheit
change *(v; n)* [tʃeɪndʒ] **1.** ändern • **change into** (ver)ändern, umwandeln in; sich verändern in, werden zu
change (trains) umsteigen
2. *(Geld)* wechseln, umtauschen; **3.** wechseln *(Kleidung)*; sich umziehen • **changing room** Umkleideraum
4. (Ver-)Änderung, Wechsel
°**Changing of the Guard** [gɑ:d] Wachablösung *(vor dem Buckingham Palace)*
Channel Tunnel [ˌtʃænl 'tʌnl] Kanaltunnel *(Tunnel zwischen England und Frankreich)*
chaos ['keɪɒs] Chaos
character ['kærəktə] Charakter; Person, Figur *(in Roman, Film)*
°**charcoal** ['tʃɑ:kəʊl] Holzkohle
°**chart** [tʃɑ:t] Tabelle
chase sb. (away) [tʃeɪs] jn. (weg)jagen
cheap [tʃi:p] billig, preiswert
check [tʃek] (über)prüfen, kontrollieren • **check in** einchecken *(Flughafen)*; sich anmelden, sich eintragen *(Hotel)*
°**checkpoint** ['tʃekpɔɪnt] Kontrollpunkt
°**cheek** [tʃi:k]: **have the cheek** die Frechheit/Stirn haben
cheer [tʃɪə] jubeln, Beifall klatschen
cheese [tʃi:z] Käse
chemistry ['kemɪstri] Chemie
chess [tʃes] Schach
chicken ['tʃɪkɪn] Huhn; (Brat-)Hähnchen
child [tʃaɪld], *pl* **children** ['tʃɪldrən] Kind • **childhood** ['tʃaɪldhʊd] Kindheit

Chinese *(adj; n)* [ˌtʃaɪ'ni:z] chinesisch; Chinesisch; Chinese/Chinesin
chips *(pl)* [tʃɪps] Pommes frites
chocolate ['tʃɒklət] **1.** Schokolade; **2.** Praline
choice [tʃɔɪs] (Aus-)Wahl
choir ['kwaɪə] Chor
choose* [tʃu:z] aussuchen, (aus)wählen
chose [tʃəʊz] *si. past von „choose"*
chosen ['tʃəʊzn] *Part. Perf. von „choose"*
Christ [kraɪst] Christus
Christian *(adj; n)* ['krɪstʃən] christlich; Christ/in
Christmas ['krɪsməs] Weihnachten • **for Christmas** zu Weihnachten
church [tʃɜ:tʃ] Kirche
cinema ['sɪnəmə] Kino
circus ['sɜ:kəs] **1.** Zirkus; **2.** (runder) Platz *(in einer Stadt)*
city ['sɪti] Stadt, Großstadt
clap **(-pp-)** [klæp] (Beifall) klatschen
class [klɑ:s] Klasse, Kurs • **in class** in der Klasse, im Unterricht • °**classmate** ['klɑ:smeɪt] Klassenkamerad/in, Mitschüler/in • **classroom** Klassenzimmer • **classroom phrases** [ˌklɑ:sru:m 'freɪzɪz] *Redewendungen für das Klassenzimmer; Unterrichtssprache*
classical ['klæsɪkl] klassisch
clause [klɔ:z] (Teil-, Glied-)Satz **main clause** Hauptsatz
clean *(adj; v)* [kli:n] **1.** sauber; **2.** sauber machen
clear *(adj)* [klɪə] klar, deutlich **clearly** *(adv)* ['klɪəli] eindeutig, klar
clever ['klevə] schlau, klug **cleverness** ['klevənəs] Klugheit, Cleverness
cliff [klɪf] Klippe
climb [klaɪm] klettern; hinaufklettern (auf)
cloakroom ['kləʊkru:m] Garderobe
clock [klɒk] (Wand-, Stand-, Turm-)Uhr • **clockwise** ['klɒkwaɪz] im Uhrzeigersinn
close [kləʊz] schließen, zumachen
close (to) [kləʊs] nahe (bei, an)
closely ['kləʊsli]: **work closely with sb.** eng mit jm. zusammenarbeiten
clothes *(pl)* [kləʊðz, kləʊz] Kleidung, „Klamotten"
cloud [klaʊd] Wolke • **cloudy** ['klaʊdi] bewölkt, wolkig
clown [klaʊn] Clown
club [klʌb] Klub; Verein
clue [klu:] Hinweis, Anhaltspunkt

coach [kəʊtʃ] **1.** Reisebus; **2.** Trainer/in
°**coal** [kəʊl] Kohle
coast [kəʊst] Küste • **on the coast** an der Küste
coat [kəʊt] Mantel
cocoa ['kəʊkəʊ] Kakao
code [kəʊd] (Geheim-)Kode
coffee ['kɒfi] Kaffee • **coffee shop** Kaffeestube, Café
coin [kɔɪn] Münze
cola ['kəʊlə] Cola
cold [kəʊld] kalt • **be/feel cold** frieren • **I was/felt cold.** Mir war kalt.
°**collage** ['kɒlɑ:ʒ] Collage
collect [kə'lekt] (ein)sammeln **collection** [kə'lekʃn] Sammlung
colour *(n; v)* ['kʌlə] **1.** Farbe **What colour is it?** Welche Farbe hat es (er, sie)? °**2.** bunt anmalen
column ['kɒləm] **1.** Säule; °**2.** Spalte
comb *(n; v)* [kəʊm] **1.** Kamm; **2.** kämmen • **Comb your hair.** Kämm dich.
°**combination** [ˌkɒmbɪ'neɪʃn] Kombination, Verbindung
come* [kʌm] kommen • **Come here.** Komm her. • **come in** hereinkommen • **come (in) third** als Dritter ins Ziel kommen; Dritter werden • **Come on.** Komm schon! Los, komm!
come [kʌm] *Part. Perf. von „come"*
comic ['kɒmɪk] Comic-Heft
°**commander** [kə'mɑ:ndə] Kommandant/in, Führer/in, Leiter/in
common ['kɒmən]: **have sth. in common** etwas miteinander gemein haben
communication [kəˌmju:nɪ'keɪʃn] Kommunikation
compare (to) [kəm'peə] vergleichen (mit) • °**make comparisons** [kəm'pærɪsnz] Vergleiche anstellen, vergleichen
competition [ˌkɒmpə'tɪʃn] Wettbewerb, Wettkampf
complain (to sb. about sth.) [kəm'pleɪn] sich (bei jm. über etwas) beschweren, beklagen
complete [kəm'pli:t] vervollständigen, ergänzen
complex ['kɒmpleks] (Gebäude-)Komplex
computer [kəm'pju:tə] Computer, Rechner
°**concentrate** ['kɒnsəntreɪt] (sich) konzentrieren
concert ['kɒnsət] Konzert
°**conqueror** ['kɒŋkərə] Eroberer/Eroberin
°**construction** [kən'strʌkʃn] Konstruktion

contact sb. ['kɒntækt] sich mit jm. in Verbindung setzen; mit jm. Kontakt aufnehmen
context ['kɒntekst] Zusammenhang, Kontext
continue [kən'tɪnju:] weitergehen/-reden/-machen, weiter (tun); fortsetzen, fortfahren (mit)
control [kən'trəʊl] Kontrolle; *hier:* Kontrollzentrum
°**conversation** [ˌkɒnvə'seɪʃn] Gespräch, Unterhaltung
°**conversion** [kən'vɜ:ʃn] Platztritt *(Rugby)*
cook *(v; n)* [kʊk] **1.** kochen, zubereiten • °**What's cooking?** *(infml)* Was liegt an? / Was ist los? **2.** Koch, Köchin
cooker ['kʊkə] Herd
cool [ku:l] cool, scharf, stark
copy *(v; n)* ['kɒpi] **1.** übertragen, kopieren, abschreiben; **2.** Kopie, Abschrift
corner ['kɔ:nə] Ecke • **on the corner** an der Ecke
cornflakes ['kɔ:nfleɪks] Cornflakes
Cornish ['kɔ:nɪʃ] kornisch *(aus Cornwall, zu Cornwall gehörig)*
correct *(v; adj)* [kə'rekt] **1.** verbessern, korrigieren; **2.** richtig, korrekt
corridor ['kɒrɪdɔ:] Gang, Korridor
cost* *(v; n)* [kɒst] **1.** kosten; **2.** Kosten
cost [kɒst] **1.** *si. past von „cost"*; **2.** *Part. Perf. von „cost"*
costume ['kɒstju:m] Kostüm, Verkleidung
°**couch potato** [ˌkaʊtʃ pə'teɪtəʊ] *(infml)* „Dauerglotzer" (*wörtlich:* Sofakartoffel)
could [kəd, *betont:* kʊd] **1.** konnte(n); **2.** könnte(n)
count [kaʊnt] zählen
country ['kʌntri] Land • **in the country** auf dem Land
countryside ['kʌntrɪsaɪd] Landschaft, (ländliche) Gegend
county ['kaʊnti] Grafschaft, Verwaltungsbezirk
°**couple** ['kʌpl]: **a couple of** ein paar
course: **of course** [əv 'kɔ:s] natürlich, selbstverständlich
cousin ['kʌzn] Cousin/Cousine
cover ['kʌvə] **1.** bedecken, zudecken • °**covered cart** Planwagen °**2.** Umschlag
cow [kaʊ] Kuh
Crack! [kræk] Knacks!
crash [kræʃ] **1.** krachen **crash (into)** zusammenstoßen (mit), hineinfahren (in) **2.** abstürzen *(Computer)*
°**crazy** ['kreɪzi] verrückt

cricket ['krɪkɪt] Kricket
crisps [krɪsps] Kartoffelchips
cross [krɒs] überqueren; (sich) kreuzen • **cross out** aus-, durchstreichen
°**crossbar** ['krɒsbɑː] Querlatte
crowd [kraʊd] (Menschen-) Menge
crown [kraʊn] krönen
°**Crown Jewels** *(pl)* [ˌkraʊn 'dʒuːəlz] Kronjuwelen
cry *(v; n)* [kraɪ] **1.** weinen; schreien; **2.** Schrei, Ruf
cup [kʌp] Tasse • **a cup of chocolate/tea** eine Tasse Schokolade/Tee
cupboard ['kʌbəd] Schrank
°**curly** ['kɜːli] kraus, gelockt
curry ['kʌri] *scharfes, mit Curry gewürztes Gericht*
customer ['kʌstəmə] Kunde, Kundin
cut* **(-tt-)** [kʌt] (aus)schneiden • **cut off** abschneiden; *hier:* amputieren • **cut out** ausschneiden • **cut up** zerschneiden, in Stücke schneiden
cut [kʌt] **1.** *si. past von „cut";* **2.** *Part. Perf. von „cut"*
cycle ['saɪkl] Rad fahren
cycling *(das)* Radfahren
cycle lane, cycle track ['saɪkl leɪn, 'saɪkl træk] Radweg
cyclist ['saɪklɪst] Radfahrer/in

D

dad [dæd] Vati, Papa; Vater
dance *(v; n)* [dɑːns] **1.** tanzen
dancing *(das)* Tanzen
dancer Tänzer/in
2. Tanz
danger ['deɪndʒə] Gefahr
dangerous ['deɪndʒərəs] gefährlich
dark [dɑːk] dunkel • **darkness** ['dɑːknəs] Dunkelheit
darling ['dɑːlɪŋ] Liebling, Schatz
date [deɪt] Datum • **date of birth** Geburtsdatum
What's the date? Welches Datum haben wir?
daughter ['dɔːtə] Tochter
day [deɪ] Tag • **one day** eines Tages • **that day** an jenem Tag • **the next day** der nächste Tag; am nächsten Tag
What day is 1st January? Was für ein Tag ist der 1. Januar? • **day of the week** Wochentag
°**dazzled** ['dæzld] überwältigt
dead [ded] tot
dear [dɪə] Liebling, Schatz
Dear Katrin and Julia Liebe Katrin, liebe Julia • **Dear Sir or Madam** Sehr geehrte Damen und Herren

°**death sentence** ['deθ ˌsentəns] Todesurteil
December [dɪ'sembə] Dezember
decide (on) [dɪ'saɪd] sich entscheiden (für), beschließen
decision [dɪ'sɪʒn] Entscheidung • °**make a decision** eine Entscheidung treffen
°**definite** ['defɪnət] bestimmt, festgelegt, definitiv
°**definition** [ˌdefɪ'nɪʃn] Definition
°**defuse** [diː'fjuːz] entschärfen
delay [dɪ'leɪ] Verzögerung
delicious [dɪ'lɪʃəs] lecker, köstlich
demonstration [ˌdemən'streɪʃn] Demonstration
department store [dɪ'pɑːtmənt stɔː] Kaufhaus
departure [dɪ'pɑːtʃə] Abfahrt, Abreise
describe [dɪ'skraɪb] beschreiben • **description** [dɪ'skrɪpʃn] Beschreibung
design *(v; n)* [dɪ'zaɪn] **1.** entwerfen, konstruieren; **2.** Entwurf; Design, Gestaltung, Konstruktion • **Design and Technology** Design und Technologie/Technik *(engl. Schulfach)*
desk [desk] **1.** Schreibtisch, Schülertisch; **2.** *(Informations-)* Schalter
destroy [dɪ'strɔɪ] zerstören, vernichten
°**detail** ['diːteɪl] Detail, Einzelheit
°**detective** [dɪ'tektɪv] Detektiv
°**diagram** ['daɪəgræm] Diagramm, grafische Darstellung
dialogue ['daɪəlɒg] Dialog
diary ['daɪəri] Tagebuch; Terminkalender
°**dictation** [dɪk'teɪʃn] Diktat
dictionary ['dɪkʃənri] Wörterbuch, *(alphabetisches)* Wörterverzeichnis
did [dɪd] *si. past von „do"*
die (of) [daɪ] sterben (an)
difference ['dɪfrəns] Unterschied • **different (from)** ['dɪfrənt] anders (als); verschieden, unterschiedlich; andere(r, s)
difficult ['dɪfɪkəlt] schwierig, schwer
dig* (up) **(-gg-)** [dɪg] (aus-, um)graben
°**dining room** ['daɪnɪŋ ruːm] Esszimmer
dinner ['dɪnə] Abendessen
at dinner beim Abendessen
for dinner zum Abendessen
have dinner Abendbrot essen
directions *(pl)* [də'rekʃnz] Anweisung(en)
director [də'rektə] Regisseur/in

dirty ['dɜːti] schmutzig
disabled [dɪs'eɪbld] (körper)behindert
°**disadvantage** [ˌdɪsəd'vɑːntɪdʒ] Nachteil
disagree (with) [ˌdɪsə'griː] anderer Meinung sein (als), nicht übereinstimmen (mit)
disappear [ˌdɪsə'pɪə] verschwinden
disc jockey ['dɪsk dʒɒki] Diskjockey
disco ['dɪskəʊ] Disko
discover [dɪ'skʌvə] entdecken; herausfinden, feststellen
discovery [dɪ'skʌvəri] Entdeckung
discuss [dɪ'skʌs] besprechen, diskutieren über • **discussion** [dɪ'skʌʃn] Diskussion
°**disguised: disguised voice** [dɪsˌgaɪzd 'vɔɪs] verstellte Stimme
dish [dɪʃ] Schale, Schüssel, Platte • **dishes** *(pl)* Geschirr
wash the dishes das Geschirr abwaschen
divorced [dɪ'vɔːst] geschieden
DJ [ˌdiː'dʒeɪ], **disc jockey** ['dɪsk dʒɒki] Diskjockey
do* [duː] tun, machen • **do so** es/das tun • **do well/badly (in)** gut/schlecht sein (in), gut/schlecht abschneiden (in)
do your homework die Hausaufgabe(n) machen, Schularbeiten machen • **do jobs** Arbeiten/Aufträge erledigen • **do sport(s)** Sport treiben • **do sums** rechnen
do the shopping Einkäufe machen/erledigen, einkaufen
dock [dɒk] Dock, Anlegestelle
doctor ['dɒktə] Arzt/Ärztin; Doktor
dog [dɒg] Hund
dollar ($) ['dɒlə] Dollar *(US-Währung)*
dolphin ['dɒlfɪn] Delfin
done [dʌn] *Part. Perf. von „do"*
door [dɔː] Tür • **at the door** an der Tür • **front door** [ˌfrʌnt 'dɔː] Wohnungstür, Haustür
doorbell ['dɔːbel] Türklingel
ring the doorbell (an der Tür) klingeln
down [daʊn] hinunter, herunter, nach unten • **down south** unten im Süden
down the tree den Baum hinunter • **put down** hinstellen, hinlegen • **sit down** sich hinsetzen • **write down** aufschreiben, notieren
downstairs [ˌdaʊn'steəz] nach unten; unten
Dr = Doctor ['dɒktə] Dr. = Doktor
°**drain** [dreɪn] Abflussrohr

drama ['drɑ:mə] Drama, Schauspiel
drank [dræŋk] *si. past von „drink"*
draw* [drɔ:] zeichnen °**drawing** ['drɔ:ɪŋ] Zeichnung
drawn [drɔ:n] *Part. Perf. von „draw"*
dream *(n; v)* [dri:m] **1.** Traum; **2. dream (about/of)** träumen (von)
dress [dres] Kleid
dressed: **get dressed** [ˌget 'drest] sich anziehen
drew [dru:] *si. past von „draw"*
drink* *(v; n)* [drɪŋk] **1.** trinken; **2.** Getränk
drive* *(v; n)* [draɪv] **1.** *(ein Auto, einen Bus)* fahren • **drive off** wegfahren • **drive on** weiterfahren • **driver** Fahrer/in °**driving-licence** ['draɪvɪŋ ˌlaɪsəns] Führerschein **2.** (Auto-)Fahrt
driven ['drɪvn] *Part. Perf. von „drive"*
drop **(-pp-)** [drɒp] fallen lassen
°**drop-kick** ['drɒpkɪk] einen Sprungtritt machen *(Rugby)*
drove [drəʊv] *si. past von „drive"*
drum [drʌm] Trommel; Schlagzeug • **play the drums** Schlagzeug spielen
drunk [drʌŋk] *Part. Perf. von „drink"*
dry [draɪ] trocken
duck [dʌk] Ente
dug [dʌg] **1.** *si. past von „dig"*; **2.** *Part. Perf. von „dig"*
dump [dʌmp] Müllkippe

E

each [i:tʃ] jeder, jede, jedes (einzelne) • **each other** einander, sich (gegenseitig)
ear [ɪə] Ohr
early ['ɜ:li] früh; zu früh
earth [ɜ:θ] Erde
east [i:st] östlich; (nach) Osten **eastbound** ['i:stbaʊnd] Richtung Osten
easy ['i:zi] leicht, einfach
eat* [i:t] essen
eaten ['i:tn] *Part. Perf. von „eat"*
°**ebony** ['ebəni] Ebenholz
°**edge** [edʒ] Rand, Kante
education [ˌedʒu'keɪʃn] (Schul-, Aus-)Bildung; Erziehung
°**e.g.** [ˌi:‿'dʒi:] z.B. (= zum Beispiel)
egg [eg] Ei
either ['aɪðə, 'i:ðə]: **not (...) either** auch nicht; auch kein
electric [ɪ'lektrɪk] elektrisch **electrician** [ɪˌlek'trɪʃn] Elektriker/in
electronic [ɪˌlek'trɒnɪk] elektronisch

elephant ['elɪfənt] Elefant
else [els]: **anyone/anything else** sonst (noch) jemand / sonst (noch) etwas • **anywhere else** sonst (noch) irgendwo(hin) • **everyone/everything else** alle anderen/alles andere • **everywhere else** überall sonst • **someone/something else** (noch) jemand anderes / (noch) etwas anderes • **somewhere else** woanders(hin), sonst irgendwo(hin) • **who/what/where/... else?** wer/was/wo/... sonst (noch)?
°**elsewhere** [ˌels'weə] woanders
e-mail ['i:meɪl] E-Mail, elektronische Post
emergency [i'mɜ:dʒənsi] Notfall
°**emperor** ['empərə] Kaiser
empire ['empaɪə] Reich, Weltreich
empty ['empti] leer
encounter [ɪn'kaʊntə] Begegnung
encyclopedia [ɪnˌsaɪklə'pi:dɪə] Enzyklopädie, Lexikon
end *(v; n)* [end] **1.** enden; beenden; **2.** Ende, Schluss • **at the end** am Ende, am Schluss
ending ['endɪŋ] Ende, Schluss; Endung • **happy ending** Happy End
°**enemy** ['enəmi] Feind/in
energy ['enədʒi] Energie
engine ['endʒɪn] Motor, Maschine
engineer [ˌendʒɪ'nɪə] Ingenieur/in, Techniker/in
England ['ɪŋglənd] England
English ['ɪŋglɪʃ] englisch; Englisch • **He's/She's English.** Er ist Engländer./Sie ist Engländerin. • **in English** auf Englisch • **What's this in English?** Wie heißt das auf Englisch?
enjoy [ɪn'dʒɔɪ] mögen, genießen, gernhaben, gern tun • **Enjoy yourself!** Viel Spaß! / Amüsier dich gut!
enough [ɪ'nʌf] genug
enter ['entə] betreten; einreisen in
entrance ['entrəns] Eingang
°**entry** ['entri] Beitrag, Einsendung
environment [ɪn'vaɪrənmənt] Umwelt, Umgebung **environment-friendly** umweltfreundlich
°**escape** [ɪ'skeɪp] fliehen; entkommen
especially [ɪ'speʃli] besonders, insbesondere
etc. [et'setərə] usw.
ethnic ['eθnɪk] ethnisch, Volks-
euro (€) ['jʊərəʊ] Euro
Europe ['jʊərəp] Europa

even ['i:vn] sogar, selbst **even if** selbst wenn, auch wenn • **even worse/better/taller** (sogar) noch schlechter/besser/größer • °**Should he even ask?** Sollte er überhaupt fragen?
evening ['i:vnɪŋ] Abend • **Good evening.** Guten Abend. • **in the evening(s)** am Abend, abends • **this evening** heute Abend • **tomorrow evening** morgen Abend
event [ɪ'vent] Ereignis; Veranstaltung
ever ['evə] je, jemals, schon mal **the best festival ever** das beste Fest, das es je gegeben hat
every ['evri] jede, jeder, jedes
everybody ['evribɒdi] jeder, alle
everyday *(adj)* ['evrideɪ] Alltags-; alltäglich
everyone ['evriwʌn] jeder, alle
everything ['evriθɪŋ] alles
everywhere ['evriweə] überall
exact *(adj)* [ɪg'zækt] genau **exactly** *(adv)* [ɪg'zæktli] genau
example [ɪg'zɑ:mpl] Beispiel **for example** zum Beispiel
°**exchange rate** [ɪks'tʃeɪndʒ reɪt] Wechselkurs
excited (about) [ɪk'saɪtɪd] aufgeregt (wegen, über) **exciting** [ɪk'saɪtɪŋ] aufregend, spannend
excuse *(n; v)* **1.** [ɪk'skju:s] Ausrede, Entschuldigung; **2. Excuse me.** [ɪk'skju:z] Entschuldigung. / Entschuldigen Sie.
execute ['eksɪkju:t] hinrichten
exercise ['eksəsaɪz] **1.** Übung **exercise book** Übungsheft, Schulheft **2.** *(no pl)* (körperliche) Bewegung, Training, Gymnastik
°**expect** [ɪk'spekt] erwarten
expensive [ɪk'spensɪv] teuer
experience [ɪk'spɪərɪəns] Erlebnis, Erfahrung
experiment [ɪk'sperɪmənt] Experiment
expert ['ekspɜ:t] Experte, Expertin, Fachmann, Fachfrau
explain sth. to sb. [ɪk'spleɪn] jm. etwas erklären, erläutern **explanation** [ˌeksplə'neɪʃn] Erklärung
°**express** [ɪk'spres] ausdrücken, äußern • **expression** [ɪk'spreʃn] Ausdruck
°**extract (from)** ['ekstrækt] Auszug, Ausschnitt (aus) *(einem Film, Buch)*
eye [aɪ] Auge

F

face [feɪs] Gesicht
°**fact** [fækt] Tatsache, Fakt • **in fact** eigentlich, genau gesagt; in Wirklichkeit
factory ['fæktri] Fabrik
fair [feə] fair, gerecht
°**fairy** ['feəri] Fee
faithfully ['feɪθfəli]: **Yours faithfully** Mit freundlichen Grüßen / Hochachtungsvoll
fall* [fɔ:l] fallen
fallen ['fɔ:lən] *Part. Perf. von „fall"*
false [fɔ:ls] falsch, unecht
family ['fæməli] Familie °**family member** ['membə] Familienangehörige(r) **family name** Familienname, Nachname
famous (for) ['feɪməs] berühmt (für, wegen)
fan [fæn] Fan
fantastic [fæn'tæstɪk] fantastisch, toll
far [fɑ:] weit (entfernt)
farm [fɑ:m] Bauernhof, Farm **farmer** Bauer/Bäuerin, Landwirt/in
farther ['fɑ:ðə] weiter (entfernt)
farthest ['fɑ:ðɪst] am weitesten (entfernt)
fashion ['fæʃn] Mode
fast *(adj; adv)* [fɑ:st] schnell
fat **(-tt-)** [fæt] dick
father ['fɑ:ðə] Vater
fault [fɔ:lt] Schuld; Fehler
favourite ['feɪvərɪt] Favorit/in; Lieblings-
fax [fæks] (Tele-)Fax • **fax machine** Faxgerät
February ['februəri] Februar
fed [fed] **1.** *si. past von „feed"*; **2.** *Part. Perf. von „feed"*
fed up [ˌfed_'ʌp]: **get fed up (with sth.)** etwas satt haben/bekommen; die Nase voll haben (von etwas)
feed* [fi:d] füttern • **feeding times** Fütterungszeiten
feel* [fi:l] fühlen; sich fühlen °**feel about** halten von, denken über • **feel bored** sich langweilen • **feel cold** frieren • **I felt cold/hot.** Mir war kalt/heiß. • **feel sorry for sb.** jn. bedauern • **feeling** ['fi:lɪŋ] Gefühl
feet [fi:t] *pl von „foot"*
fell [fel] *si. past von „fall"*
felt [felt] **1.** *si. past von „feel"*; **2.** *Part. Perf. von „feel"*
felt-tip ['felttɪp] Filzstift
fence [fens] Zaun
ferry ['feri] Fähre
festival ['festɪvl] Fest, Festival
fetch (from) [fetʃ] holen, abholen (von)
few [fju:] wenige • **a few** ein paar, einige
field [fi:ld] Feld, Wiese, Weide **in the field** auf dem Feld, der Wiese, der Weide
fight* (against) sb./sth. [faɪt] jn./etwas bekämpfen, gegen jn./etwas kämpfen
figure ['fɪgə] Gestalt, Figur
fill (with) [fɪl] füllen (mit) **fill in** **1.** einsetzen; °**2.** ausfüllen
film *(n; v)* [fɪlm] **1.** Film; **2.** filmen
°**finally** ['faɪnəli] schließlich, endlich
find* [faɪnd] finden; suchen **find out** herausfinden
fine [faɪn] gut, fein, schön **I'm fine.** Mir geht's gut. / Es geht mir gut.
finger ['fɪŋgə] Finger
finish ['fɪnɪʃ] **1.** beenden, zu Ende machen; enden **finished** fertig, vollendet °**2.** Ziel; Finish
fire ['faɪə] Feuer, Brand • **on fire** in Brand • **fire brigade** ['faɪə brɪˌgeɪd] Feuerwehr **firework** ['faɪəwɜ:k] Feuerwerkskörper • **fireworks** *(pl)* Feuerwerk
first [fɜ:st] **1.** erste(r, s) • **first floor** erster Stock **2.** zuerst, als Erstes, erstens **first of all** zuallererst • **at first** zuerst, anfangs, am Anfang • **firstly; ...** erstens, ... °**3.** zum ersten Mal, das erste Mal • **The first time he saw Mark's room ...** Als er Marks Zimmer das erste Mal sah, ...
fish, *pl* **fish** [fɪʃ] Fisch • **fish finger** Fischstäbchen **fisherman** ['fɪʃəmən], *pl* **fishermen** ['fɪʃəmən] Fischer **fishing** ['fɪʃɪŋ] *(das)* Angeln **fishing village** Fischerdorf
fit **(-tt-)** [fɪt] *(in der Größe)* passen
fitness ['fɪtnəs] Fitness
fix [fɪks] reparieren, in Ordnung bringen
flag [flæg] Fahne, Flagge
flash [flæʃ] aufleuchten, blinken
flat [flæt] Wohnung • **in the flats** *hier:* in unserem Wohnblock
fleet [fli:t] Flotte
flew [flu:] *si. past von „fly"*
flight [flaɪt] Flug
float [fləʊt] *(auf dem Wasser)* schwimmen, treiben
floor [flɔ:] **1.** Fußboden; **2.** Stock(werk) • **first floor** erster Stock • **ground floor** Erdgeschoss • **on the first floor/ground floor** im ersten Stock/Erdgeschoss
°**floor manager** ['flɔ: ˌmænɪdʒə] Aufnahmeleiter/in
°**flour** ['flaʊə] Mehl
flown [fləʊn] *Part. Perf. von „fly"*
fly* [flaɪ] fliegen
focus on grammar/on words ['fəʊkəs] *etwa:* Blickpunkt „Grammatik"/„Wörter"
follow ['fɒləʊ] folgen; verfolgen • °**the following words** die folgenden Wörter
food [fu:d] Essen; Lebensmittel; Futter
foot [fʊt], *pl* **feet** [fi:t] Fuß °**on foot** zu Fuß
football ['fʊtbɔ:l] Fußball
for [fə, *betont:* fɔ:] für • **for breakfast/lunch/dinner** zum Frühstück/Mittagessen/Abendessen • **for Christmas** zu Weihnachten • **for example** zum Beispiel • **for other reasons** aus anderen Gründen • **for the first time** zum ersten Mal • **for ages** *(infml)* eine Ewigkeit (lang), ewig • **for a few seconds** einige Sekunden (lang); seit einigen Sekunden • **for a long time** seit langem; lange Zeit • **for an hour** seit einer Stunde; eine Stunde lang **for hours/weeks** stundenlang/wochenlang
°**force** [fɔ:s] zwingen
forecast ['fɔ:kɑ:st] Vorhersage, Voraussage
foreign ['fɒrən] ausländisch, fremd • **foreigner** ['fɒrənə] Ausländer/in, Fremde(r)
forest ['fɒrɪst] Wald
forget* **(-tt-)** [fə'get] vergessen
forgot [fə'gɒt] *si. past von „forget"*
forgotten [fə'gɒtn] *Part. Perf. von „forget"*
fork [fɔ:k] Gabel
form [fɔ:m] **1.** *(englische)* (Schul-)Klasse; **2.** Form; **3.** Formular, Vordruck; °**4.** bilden, formen
fort [fɔ:t] Fort
fortunately ['fɔ:tʃnətli] glücklicherweise
°**fortune-teller** ['fɔ:tʃu:n ˌtelə] Wahrsager/in
forward(s) ['fɔ:wədz] vorwärts, nach vorn • **look forward to sth.** sich auf etwas freuen
fought [fɔ:t] **1.** *si. past von „fight"*; **2.** *Part. Perf. von „fight"*
foul [faʊl] Foul, Regelverstoß
found [faʊnd] **1.** *si. past von „find"*; **2.** *Part. Perf. von „find"*
frantic ['fræntɪk] verzweifelt, aufgeregt, in Panik
°**freak** [fri:k] Freak, Fanatiker/in
free [fri:] **1.** kostenlos; **2.** frei **free time** Freizeit, freie Zeit
French [frentʃ] französisch; Französisch
Friday ['fraɪdeɪ, 'fraɪdi] Freitag

fridge [frɪdʒ] Kühlschrank
friend [frend] Freund/in • **be friends with sb.** mit jm. befreundet sein
friendly ['frendli] freundlich, nett • **friendliness** ['frendlɪnəs] Freundlichkeit
frighten ['fraɪtn] ängstigen, erschrecken • **be frightened (of)** ['fraɪtnd] Angst haben (vor), sich fürchten (vor)
from [frəm, *betont:* frɒm] aus; von • **I'm from ...** Ich bin aus ... / Ich komme aus ... **from Monday to Friday** von Montag bis Freitag
front [frʌnt] Vorderseite, vorderer Teil • **at the front** vorn **in front of** vor • **front door** [ˌfrʌnt 'dɔ:] Wohnungstür, Haustür
fruit [fru:t] Obst, Früchte; Frucht
full (of) [fʊl] voll (mit/von)
fun [fʌn] Spaß • **have fun** Spaß haben, sich amüsieren **Have fun!** Viel Spaß! **Shopping is (great) fun.** Einkaufen macht (viel/großen) Spaß. • **funny** ['fʌni] witzig, komisch, merkwürdig
°**furnace** ['fɜ:nɪs] Ofen
future ['fju:tʃə] **1.** Zukunft; **2.** zukünftige(r, s)

G

gadget ['gædʒɪt] Gerät, Apparat
°**gallery** ['gæləri] Regie(raum)
game [geɪm] Spiel
garage ['gærɪdʒ] Garage
garden ['gɑ:dn] Garten
garlic ['gɑ:lɪk] Knoblauch
gate [geɪt] **1.** Tor, Pforte; **2.** Flugsteig
gave [geɪv] *si. past von „give"*
genuine ['dʒenjuɪn] echt
geography [dʒi'ɒgrəfi] Geografie, Erdkunde
German ['dʒɜ:mən] deutsch; Deutsch; Deutsche(r)
Germany ['dʒɜ:məni] Deutschland
get* **(-tt-)** [get] **1.** bekommen, kriegen • **get a friendly welcome** freundlich empfangen werden
2. holen, besorgen
3. gelangen, (hin)kommen **Get back!** (Geh/Tritt) Zurück!
4. bringen, befördern • **get sb. into trouble** jn. in Schwierigkeiten bringen
5. get angry, cold, ... wütend, kalt, ... werden • **get dressed** sich anziehen • **get fed up (with sth.)** etwas satt haben/ bekommen; die Nase voll haben (von etwas) • **get in** einsteigen • **get in(to) a car/ taxi** in ein Auto/Taxi einsteigen • **get lost** sich verlaufen **get married (to sb.)** (sich ver)heiraten (mit jm.), (jn.) heiraten • **get off** aussteigen **get off a bus/train/bike** aus einem Bus/Zug aussteigen; von einem Fahrrad absteigen **get on a bus/train/bike** in einen Bus/Zug einsteigen; auf ein Fahrrad aufsteigen • **get out of a car/taxi** aus einem Auto/Taxi aussteigen • **get ready** sich bereitmachen, sich fertig machen • °**get rid of** loswerden • **get sth. right/ wrong** etwas richtig/falsch machen • **get through** durchkommen, Verbindung bekommen *(am Telefon)* • **get up** aufstehen
ghost [gəʊst] Geist, Gespenst
giant ['dʒaɪənt] riesig, gigantisch
gift [gɪft] Geschenk, Gabe
giraffe [dʒə'rɑ:f] Giraffe
girl [gɜ:l] Mädchen
girlfriend ['gɜ:lfrend] (feste) Freundin
give* [gɪv] geben • **give sb. a friendly welcome** jn. freundlich empfangen • **give sb. $3 off** jm. eine Ermäßigung von 3 Dollar geben • **Give Susan my love.** Grüß Susan von mir. **give sth. up** etwas aufgeben
given ['gɪvn] *Part. Perf. von „give"*
glad (-dd-) [glæd]: **be glad (about)** froh sein, sich freuen (über)
glass [glɑ:s] Glas
glove [glʌv] Handschuh
°**glue** [glu:] Klebstoff
go* [gəʊ] **1.** gehen; fahren **2.** (hin)gehören, (hin)kommen **Let's go.** Auf geht's! • **go away** verreisen • **go climbing/surfing/swimming** klettern/wellenreiten/schwimmen gehen • **go shopping/ go to the shops** einkaufen gehen • **go a long way** viel erreichen, viel bewirken • **go for a walk** einen Spaziergang machen • **go for help** Hilfe holen gehen • °**go for the try** *etwa:* versuchen Punkte zu erzielen • **go in** hineingehen **go on** °**1.** weitergehen; **2.** weitermachen; **3.** fortfahren, weiterreden; **4.** angehen *(Licht)*; °**5.** im Gange sein, vorgehen **go on a trip** einen Ausflug/ eine Reise machen • **go on board** an Bord gehen • **go on holiday** in Urlaub fahren; Ferien machen • **go out** **1.** ausgehen, weggehen; **2.** ausfahren, auslaufen; **3.** ausgehen *(Licht)* • **go under** untergehen • **go up** steigen, in die Höhe gehen • **I'm going to phone.** Ich werde anrufen. / Ich habe vor anzurufen.
goal [gəʊl] Tor *(im Sport)* °**goal-line** ['gəʊl laɪn] Torlinie °**goalpost** ['gəʊlpəʊst] Torpfosten
god, God [gɒd] Gott **goddess** ['gɒdes] Göttin
gold [gəʊld] Gold • **golden** ['gəʊldən] golden • **goldfish**, *pl* **goldfish** Goldfisch
golf [gɒlf] Golf
gone [gɒn] *Part. Perf. von „go"* °**be gone** weg sein
good [gʊd] **1.** gut • **Good luck.** Viel Glück. • **Good morning/afternoon/evening/night.** Guten Morgen/ Tag/Abend/Gute Nacht. **Goodbye.** [ˌgʊd'baɪ] Auf Wiedersehen. • **be good at sth.** gut in etwas sein; etwas gut können • **good-looking** gut aussehend • **be no good** zu nichts zu gebrauchen sein, nichts taugen
2. artig, brav
got [gɒt] **1.** *si. past von „get"*; **2.** *Part. Perf. von „get"* **have got*** haben, besitzen
graffiti *(pl)* [grə'fi:ti] Graffiti *(Wandkritzeleien)*
grammar ['græmə] Grammatik
grand- ['græn-]: **grandad** Opa °**grandchild** Enkel/in **grandfather** Großvater **grandma** Oma • **grandmother** Großmutter **grandpa** Opa • **grandparents** Großeltern
grape [greɪp] Weintraube
grateful ['greɪtfəl]: **be grateful (to sb.)** (jm.) dankbar sein
grave [greɪv] Grab
gravy ['greɪvi] (Braten-)Soße
great [greɪt] großartig, toll **look great** toll aussehen
°**great-grandmother** [ˌgreɪt 'grænmʌðə] Urgroßmutter
green [gri:n] grün
grew [gru:] *si. past von „grow"*
grey [greɪ] grau
grim *(adj)* [grɪm] grimmig **grimly** *(adv)* grimmig
ground [graʊnd] (Erd-)Boden **ground floor** Erdgeschoss °**grounds** *(pl)* Gelände
group [gru:p] Gruppe • **a group of girls** eine Gruppe (von) Mädchen • **in groups of four** in Vierergruppen
grow* [grəʊ] wachsen • **grow up** aufwachsen, erwachsen werden

grown [grəʊn] *Part. Perf. von „grow"*
guess [ges] raten, erraten
guest [gest] Gast
guide *(v; n)* [gaɪd] **1.** führen, lenken, leiten; **2.** (Fremden-) Führer/in, Reiseleiter/in **guidebook** Reiseführer
guitar [gɪ'tɑ:] Gitarre • **play the guitar** Gitarre spielen
gun [gʌn] Schusswaffe
gym [dʒɪm] Sport-, Turnhalle

H

had [hæd] **1.** *si. past von „have got" und „have"*; **2.** *Part. Perf. von „have got" und „have"*
hair *(no pl)* [heə] Haar, Haare **Comb your hair.** Kämm dich.
°**hairpin** ['heəpɪn] Haarnadel
half [hɑ:f], *pl* **halves** [hɑ:vz] Hälfte • **a year and a half** eineinhalb Jahre, anderthalb Jahre • **the first half** die erste Hälfte/Halbzeit • **half-time** [ˌhɑ:f'taɪm] Halbzeitpause **half an hour/mile** eine halbe Stunde/Meile • **half past eight** halb neun (8.30/20.30) °**half-price** zum halben Preis
hamburger ['hæmbɜ:gə] Hamburger
hamster ['hæmstə] Hamster
hand [hænd] Hand • **handbag** Handtasche
handsome ['hænsəm] gut aussehend
happen (to sb.) ['hæpən] (jm.) geschehen, passieren **What's happening?** Was ist los? / Was geht hier vor?
happy ['hæpi] glücklich, froh **Happy birthday!** Herzlichen Glückwunsch zum Geburtstag! • **happy ending** Happy End • **happiness** Glück
harbour ['hɑ:bə] Hafen
hard [hɑ:d] **1.** *(adj)* hart; schwierig, schwer; **2.** *(adv)* heftig, kräftig, sehr • **try hard** sich sehr bemühen, sich anstrengen
hardly ['hɑ:dli] kaum
°**harp** [hɑ:p] Harfe
hat [hæt] Hut
hate [heɪt] hassen, gar nicht mögen • **hate shopping** gar nicht gern einkaufen gehen
have* [hæv] haben • **have breakfast/lunch/dinner** frühstücken/Mittag essen/ Abendbrot essen • **have a cola/a hamburger** eine Cola trinken/einen Hamburger essen • **have a bath** ein Bad nehmen, *(in der Wanne)* baden **have a shower** (sich) duschen • **have a look at** ansehen, einen Blick werfen auf **have a party** eine Party veranstalten, feiern • **have fun** Spaß haben, sich amüsieren **Have a nice weekend.** Schönes Wochenende. • **have sth. in common** etwas miteinander gemein haben
have got* haben, besitzen **have got to do sth.** etwas tun müssen
have* to do sth. ['hæf tə, 'hæv tə] etwas tun müssen
he [hi, *betont:* hi:] er
head [hed] Kopf
heading ['hedɪŋ] Überschrift
headline ['hedlaɪn] Schlagzeile
headteacher [ˌhed'ti:tʃə] Schulleiter/in
healthy ['helθɪ] gesund
hear* [hɪə] hören
heard [hɜ:d] **1.** *si. past von „hear"*; **2.** *Part. Perf. von „hear"*
°**heart** [hɑ:t]: **learn sth. by heart** etwas auswendig lernen
heat [hi:t] Hitze • **in this heat** bei dieser Hitze
heavy ['hevi] schwer *(von Gewicht)*
held [held] **1.** *si. past von „hold"*; **2.** *Part. Perf. von „hold"*
helicopter ['helɪkɒptə] Hubschrauber, Helikopter
Hello. [hə'ləʊ] Hallo. / Guten Tag. • **Say hello to …** Grüß …
helmet ['helmɪt] Helm
help *(v; n)* [help] **1.** helfen **Help yourself.** Greif zu! / Bedien dich! • **May I help you?** Sie wünschen? **2.** Hilfe • **shout for help** um Hilfe rufen
her [hə, *betont:* hɜ:] **1.** ihr, ihre; **2.** sie; ihr
here [hɪə] hier; hierher • **Here you are.** Hier bitte. Bitte sehr.
hero ['hɪərəʊ], *pl* **heroes** ['hɪərəʊz] Held, Heldin; Idol, Vorbild
hers [hɜ:z] ihre(r, s)
herself [hə'self, *betont:* hɜ:'self] sich (selbst); selbst, selber
hid [hɪd] *si. past von „hide"*
hidden ['hɪdn] *Part. Perf. von „hide"*
hide* [haɪd] (sich) verstecken
high [haɪ] hoch
°**Highland Games** [ˌhaɪlənd 'geɪmz] *Festival mit Musik und Sportwettkämpfen im schottischen Hochland*
hill [hɪl] Hügel, Berg • **hilly** ['hɪli] hügelig
him [hɪm] ihn; ihm
himself [hɪm'self] sich (selbst); selbst, selber
Hindu *(adj; n)* [ˌhɪn'du:] Hindu-; Hindu
his [hɪz] **1.** sein, seine; **2.** seine(r, s)
history ['hɪstri] Geschichte, Vergangenheit
hit [hɪt] Hit
hit* sb./sth. **(-tt-)** [hɪt] jn./ etwas anfahren; gegen etwas stoßen; jn./etwas schlagen, treffen
hit [hɪt] **1.** *si. past von „hit"*; **2.** *Part. Perf. von „hit"*
hobby ['hɒbi] Hobby
hockey ['hɒki] Hockey
°**Hogmanay** ['hɒgməneɪ] Silvester *(in Schottland)*
hold* [həʊld] **1.** (fest)halten; **2.** veranstalten, abhalten **hold on (to)** sich festhalten (an) • °**hold up** hochhalten
hole [həʊl] Loch
holiday(s) ['hɒlədeɪ(z)] Ferien, Urlaub • **be/go on holiday** in Urlaub sein/fahren; Ferien haben/machen • **holidaymaker** Urlauber/in
°**hologram** ['hɒləgræm] Hologramm *(mit einem Laser erzeugtes dreidimensionales Bild)*
home [həʊm] **1.** Heim, Zuhause; **2.** nach Hause • **at home** zu Hause, daheim • **We're home.** Wir sind (wieder) zu Hause. • **homeless** obdachlos • **homelessness** Obdachlosigkeit
homepage ['həʊmpeɪdʒ] Homepage *(Einstiegs- und Informationsseite von Firmen/ Institutionen im Internet)*
homework *(no pl)* ['həʊmwɜ:k] Hausaufgabe(n) • **do your homework** die Hausaufgabe(n) machen
hope *(v; n)* [həʊp] **1.** hoffen; **2.** Hoffnung
horrible ['hɒrəbl] scheußlich, grauenhaft, furchtbar
horse [hɔ:s] Pferd
hospital ['hɒspɪtl] Krankenhaus
hot **(-tt-)** [hɒt] heiß • **hot dog** ['hɒt dɒg] Hotdog
hotel [həʊ'tel] Hotel • **stay at a hotel** in einem Hotel übernachten
hour ['aʊə] Stunde • **for an hour** eine Stunde lang • **for hours** stundenlang • **half an hour** eine halbe Stunde
house [haʊs] Haus
how [haʊ] wie • **How are you?** Wie geht es dir/euch/ Ihnen? • **How did they like it?** Wie gefiel es ihnen? / Wie fanden sie es? • **how many?** wie viele? • **how much?** wie viel? • **How much is/are …?** Was kostet/kosten …? Wie viel kostet/kosten …? • **how to do sth.** wie man etwas tun kann/soll • °**How do you know …?** Woher weißt du …?

hungry ['hʌŋgri] hungrig • **be hungry** hungrig sein, Hunger haben
hurricane ['hʌrɪkən] Hurrikan, Orkan
hurry ['hʌri] °**1.** sich beeilen; *(jn)* antreiben; **2. be in a hurry** in Eile sein, es eilig haben
hurt* [hɜːt] verletzen; wehtun **She wasn't hurt.** Sie war/ wurde nicht verletzt.
hurt [hɜːt] **1.** *si. past von „hurt"*; **2.** *Part. Perf. von „hurt"*
husband ['hʌzbənd] Ehemann
°**hydroelectric** [ˌhaɪdrəʊɪ'lektrɪk] hydroelektrisch *(elektrische Energie mit Wasserkraft erzeugend)*

I

I [aɪ] ich • **I'm fine.** Mir geht's gut. / Es geht mir gut. • **I'm afraid** leider
ice [aɪs] Eis • **ice-cream** (Speise-)Eis • **ice-hockey** ['aɪs hɒki] Eishockey • **ice skating** ['aɪs skeɪtɪŋ] *(das)* Eislaufen
idea [aɪ'dɪə] **1.** Idee, Einfall; **2. idea (of)** Vorstellung (von)
°**idiom** ['ɪdiəm] Ausdrucksweise, Sprachstil
if [ɪf] **1.** wenn, falls • **even if** selbst wenn, auch wenn **2.** ob • **as if** als ob
ill [ɪl] krank • **illness** ['ɪlnəs] Krankheit
imagine sth. [ɪ'mædʒɪn] sich etwas vorstellen • **imagination** [ɪˌmædʒɪ'neɪʃn] Vorstellungskraft, Fantasie
important (to) [ɪm'pɔːtnt] wichtig (für)
°**improve** [ɪm'pruːv] verbessern
in [ɪn] in • **in there** dort drinnen • **in 1645** (im Jahre) 1645 • **(just) in time** (gerade) rechtzeitig • °**in different ways** auf verschiedene Weise(n) • **in English** auf Englisch • **in fact** eigentlich, genau gesagt; in Wirklichkeit **in front of** vor • **in November** im November • **in bad weather** bei schlechtem Wetter • **in my opinion** meiner Meinung nach • **in the country** auf dem Land • **in the field** auf dem Feld/der Wiese/der Weide • **in the morning(s)/afternoon(s)/ evening(s)** am Morgen, morgens/am Nachmittag, nachmittags/am Abend, abends **in the open air** im Freien **in the photo/picture** auf dem Foto/Bild • **In the sky** am Himmel • **in the street** auf der Straße • **in the world** auf der Welt • **in this heat** bei dieser Hitze • **go/come in** hineingehen/hereinkommen **work in television** beim Fernsehen arbeiten
°**incident** ['ɪnsɪdənt] Vorfall, Begebenheit, Zwischenfall, Vorkommnis
include [ɪn'kluːd] (mit) einschließen, enthalten
Indian *(adj; n)* ['ɪndiən] **1.** indisch; Inder/in; **2.** indianisch; Indianer/in
industry ['ɪndəstri] Industrie
°**infected** [ɪn'fektɪd]: **the wound became infected** die Wunde entzündete sich
information *(no pl)* [ˌɪnfə'meɪʃn] Information(en); Auskunft, Auskünfte • **information desk** Informationsschalter
°**ingot** ['ɪŋgət] Ingot *(Barren Gold, Silber, Blei usw.)*
injury ['ɪndʒəri] Verletzung
inside [ˌɪn'saɪd] **1.** *(prep)* innerhalb, im Innern (von); in (… hinein); **2.** *(adv)* drinnen; nach drinnen
inspector [ɪn'spektə] *etwa:* Polizeiinspektor/in
instead [ɪn'sted] stattdessen, dafür
instruction [ɪn'strʌkʃn] Anweisung, Anleitung
instrument ['ɪnstrəmənt] Instrument
intelligent [ɪn'telɪdʒənt] intelligent, klug
interactive [ˌɪntər'æktɪv] interaktiv
interest sb. in sth. ['ɪntrəst] jn. an/für etwas interessieren **be interested (in)** ['ɪntrəstɪd] interessiert sein (an), sich interessieren (für) • **interesting** ['ɪntrəstɪŋ] interessant
international [ˌɪntə'næʃnəl] international
Internet ['ɪntənet] Internet **on the Internet** im Internet
interrupt [ˌɪntə'rʌpt] unterbrechen
interview *(v; n)* ['ɪntəvjuː] **1.** befragen, interviewen; **2.** Interview
into ['ɪntə, *betont:* 'ɪntuː] in (… hinein)
introduce sb. to sb. [ˌɪntrə'djuːs] jn. jm. (anderen) vorstellen, jn. mit jm. bekanntmachen
°**invade** [ɪn'veɪd] einfallen in, einmarschieren in • °**invader** Angreifer/in, Eindringling
invent [ɪn'vent] erfinden • **invention** [ɪn'venʃn] Erfindung **inventor** [ɪn'ventə] Erfinder/ Erfinderin
°**invertebrate** [ɪn'vɜːtɪbrət] wirbelloses Tier
invitation [ˌɪnvɪ'teɪʃn] Einladung • **invite** [ɪn'vaɪt] *(Gäste)* einladen
Irish ['aɪrɪʃ] irisch, Irisch
°**irregular** [ɪ'regjələ] unregelmäßig
is [ɪz] ist • **How much is …?** Was kostet …? / Wie viel kostet …? • **the felt-tip is 65p** der Filzstift kostet 65 Pence
island ['aɪlənd] Insel
issue ['ɪʃuː] (Streit-)Frage, Thema, Angelegenheit
it [ɪt] es *(bei Sachen und Tieren auch:* er, sie) • **It's me – Sita.** Ich bin es – Sita. • **its** [ɪts] sein, seine *(bei Sachen und Tieren auch:* ihr, ihre)
itself [ɪt'self] sich (selbst); selbst, selber
°**ivory** ['aɪvəri] Elfenbein

J

jacket ['dʒækɪt] Jacke; Jackett, Sakko
January ['dʒænjuəri] Januar
jar [dʒɑː] Glas, Topf
jazz [dʒæz] Jazz
jeans *(pl)* [dʒiːnz] Jeans
job [dʒɒb] Beruf, Arbeit, Job; Aufgabe • **do jobs** Arbeiten/ Aufträge erledigen
jogging ['dʒɒgɪŋ] *(das)* Joggen, Jogging
join [dʒɔɪn] beitreten, eintreten in *(einen Klub usw.)* • °**join together** miteinander verbinden
joke [dʒəʊk] Witz
journey ['dʒɜːni] Reise, Fahrt, Weg
judo ['dʒuːdəʊ] Judo
juice [dʒuːs] Saft
July [dʒu'laɪ] Juli
jump [dʒʌmp] springen
June [dʒuːn] Juni
junior ['dʒuːniə] Junioren-, Jugend-
just [dʒʌst] **1.** nur, bloß • **I'm just looking.** Ich sehe mich nur um. • **Just a moment!** Einen Moment mal (eben)! **just after/before 10.30** kurz nach/vor 10.30 **2.** einfach • **Just imagine.** Stell dir (nur) mal vor! **3.** gerade (eben), soeben **just in time** (gerade) rechtzeitig • **just then** genau in dem Moment; gerade dann **4. just as tired (as you are)** genauso müde (wie du) • **just like** genau wie

K

karaoke [ˌkærə'əʊkeɪ] Karaoke
kayaking ['kaɪækɪŋ] *(das)* Kajakfahren
keep* [ki:p] (be)halten; aufbewahren, aufheben • **keep sb./sth. away (from)** jn./etwas fernhalten (von)
kept [kept] **1.** *si. past von „keep"*; **2.** *Part. Perf. von „keep"*
ketchup ['ketʃəp] Ketschup
key [ki:] Schlüssel
kick [kɪk] treten (gegen)
kid [kɪd] Kind, Jugendliche(r)
kidnap **(-pp-)** ['kɪdnæp] entführen, kidnappen
kill [kɪl] töten • **killer** Killer/in, Mörder/in • **killing** Tötung
kilo ['ki:ləʊ] Kilo(gramm) **2 kilos of meat** 2 Kilo Fleisch
kilometre ['kɪləmi:tə] Kilometer
kind [kaɪnd] freundlich, gütig, nett
kind (of) [kaɪnd] Art • **What kind of …?** Was für ein/e …?
kindergarten ['kɪndəgɑ:tn] Kindergarten; Vorschule
king [kɪŋ] König
kiss [kɪs] küssen
kitchen ['kɪtʃɪn] Küche
kite [kaɪt] Drachen • **°fly a kite** einen Drachen steigen lassen
knew [nju:] *si. past von „know"*
knife [naɪf], *pl* **knives** [naɪvz] Messer
°knock [nɒk] klopfen
know* [nəʊ] **1.** wissen • **I don't know.** Ich weiß (es) nicht. • **you know** weißt du; nämlich **2.** kennen • **known as** bekannt als
known [nəʊn] *Part. Perf. von „know"*

L

°label ['leɪbl] beschriften, etikettieren
°ladder ['lædə] *(die)* Leiter
lady ['leɪdi] Dame • **ladies** meine Damen
lain [leɪn] *Part. Perf. von „lie"*
lake [leɪk] (Binnen-)See
lamb [læm] Lamm
lamp [læmp] Lampe
land *(n; v)* [lænd] **1.** Land, Grund und Boden; **2.** landen *(Flugzeug)*, anlegen *(Schiff)*
language ['læŋgwɪdʒ] Sprache **°bad language** Kraftausdrücke
large [lɑ:dʒ] groß
laser ['leɪzə] Laser
last [lɑ:st] **1.** (an-, fort)dauern; **2.** halten *(Obst, Gemüse usw.)*
last [lɑ:st] **1.** letzte(r, s) • **last year** letztes/im letzten Jahr **2.** zuletzt, das letzte Mal • **at last** schließlich, endlich
late [leɪt] spät; zu spät • **be late** zu spät sein/kommen **I'm late for school.** Ich komme zu spät zur Schule. **sleep late** lange schlafen **later** ['leɪtə] später
Latin ['lætɪn] Latein
laugh [lɑ:f] lachen • **laugh at** lachen über; auslachen
lay [leɪ] *si. past von „lie"*
lazy ['leɪzi] faul, träge
°lead [led] Blei
lead* [li:d] führen, leiten
°league [li:g] Liga
learn [lɜ:n] lernen • **°learn by heart** auswendig lernen **learn about** etwas erfahren über/von, etwas herausfinden über
°least [li:st]: **at least** mindestens
leave* [li:v] **1.** weggehen, abfahren; **2.** (zurück)lassen, hinterlassen; verlassen • **leave a message** eine Nachricht hinterlassen • **°leave room** Platz lassen • **leave school** von der Schule abgehen **leave sth. out** etwas auslassen, weglassen
led [led] **1.** *si. past von „lead"*; **2.** *Part. Perf. von „lead"*
left [left] **1.** *si. past von „leave"*; **2.** *Part. Perf. von „leave"*
left [left] nach links; linke(r, s) **on the left** links, auf der linken Seite
leg [leg] Bein
°legion ['li:dʒn] Legion
lemonade [ˌlemə'neɪd] Limonade
less [les] weniger
lesson ['lesn] Unterrichtsstunde • **lessons** *(pl)* Unterricht
let* sb. do sth. **(-tt-)** [let] jm. erlauben, etwas zu tun; jn. etwas tun lassen • **Let's …** Lass(t) uns … • **Let's swap.** Lass uns tauschen. / Tauschen wir. • **Let's go.** Auf geht's!
let [let] **1.** *si. past von „let"*; **2.** *Part. Perf. von „let"*
letter ['letə] **1.** Buchstabe; **2. letter (to)** Brief (an)
lettuce ['letɪs] (Kopf-)Salat
librarian [laɪ'breəriən] Bibliothekar/in • **library** ['laɪbrəri] Bibliothek, Bücherei
lie* [laɪ] liegen • **°lie down** sich hinlegen
life [laɪf], *pl* **lives** [laɪvz] (das) Leben • **°bring to life** lebendig machen • **°life-size** lebensgroß
lift [lɪft] (an-, hoch)heben
lift [lɪft] Lift, Aufzug, Fahrstuhl
light* *(v; n)* [laɪt] **1.** anzünden; **2.** Licht, Lampe • **°lighthouse** ['laɪthaʊs] Leuchtturm
like [laɪk] wie • **What's … like?** Wie ist …? • **blouses like this** solche Blusen • **Start like this: …** Fang so an: … **like that** so
like [laɪk] mögen, gern haben **How did they like …?** Wie gefiel ihnen …? / Wie fanden sie …? • **like shopping** gern einkaufen gehen • **I'd like (= I would like)** Ich hätte gern / Ich möchte gern • **I'd like to go.** Ich würde gern/möchte gehen.
line [laɪn] **1.** Zeile; **2.** (U-Bahn-)Linie
link *(v; n)* [lɪŋk] **1.** verbinden, verknüpfen; **2.** Verbindung **linking word** Bindewort
lion ['laɪən] Löwe
list *(v; n)* [lɪst] **1.** auflisten, aufzählen; **2.** Liste
listen ['lɪsn] zuhören; horchen **listen for sth.** auf etwas horchen, auf etwas achten **listen to sb./sth.** jm. zuhören / sich etwas anhören **listener** Zuhörer/in
lit [lɪt] **1.** *si. past von „light"*; **2.** *Part. Perf. von „light"*
litre ['li:tə] Liter • **2 litres of milk** 2 Liter Milch
little ['lɪtl] **1.** klein, jung; **2.** wenig • **a little** ein bisschen, ein wenig
live [lɪv] leben, wohnen; *(Patient usw.)* am Leben bleiben, überleben • **°living corals** ['kɒrəlz] lebende Korallen
live [laɪv] live, direkt
lives [laɪvz] *pl von „life"*
living-room ['lɪvɪŋru:m] Wohnzimmer
load [ləʊd] (auf-, ein)laden; beladen
local ['ləʊkl] örtlich, Lokal-; am/vom Ort
lock [lɒk] abschließen, zuschließen
°lock [lɒk] Schleuse
Londoner ['lʌndənə] Londoner, Londonerin
lonely ['ləʊnli] einsam • **loneliness** ['ləʊnlɪnəs] Einsamkeit
long [lɒŋ] lang • **a minute longer** noch eine Minute
look *(v; n)* [lʊk] **1.** schauen, sehen • **I'm just looking.** Ich sehe mich nur um. • **Look.** Pass auf. / Hör mal. • **Look out!** Pass auf! / Vorsicht! **look at** anschauen, ansehen **Look at the board.** Sieh an die Tafel. • **Look at the picture.** Sieh dir das Bild an. **look after sb.** sich um jn. kümmern, auf jn. aufpassen **look for** suchen • **look forward to sth.** sich auf etwas freuen • **look round**

sich umsehen • **look through sth.** etwas durchsehen, durchsuchen
2. aussehen • **look great** toll aussehen • **look like** aussehen wie • **Does this shirt look good on me?** Steht mir dieses Hemd?
3. Blick • **have a look at** ansehen, einen Blick werfen auf
loose [lu:s] locker, lose
break loose (from) sich losreißen, sich lösen (von)
°**Lord** [lɔ:d] Lord *(engl. Adelstitel)*
lose* [lu:z] verlieren • **loser** Verlierer/in
lost [lɒst] 1. *si. past von „lose"; 2. Part. Perf. von „lose";* 3. *(adj)* verloren • °**lost-property office** ['prɒpəti] Fundbüro • **get lost** sich verlaufen
lot [lɒt]: **a lot (of)** eine Menge, viel, viele • **lots (of)** eine Menge, viel, viele • **like sb. a lot** jn. sehr mögen
loud [laʊd] laut
love *(v; n)* [lʌv] 1. lieben, sehr mögen • **love shopping** sehr gern einkaufen gehen
2. Liebe • **Love, ...** Viele liebe Grüße (von) ... • **Give Susan my love.** Grüß Susan von mir.
love [lʌv] null *(Tennis)*
lovely ['lʌvli] schön, herrlich, hübsch
lower ['ləʊə] herab-, hinablassen
luck [lʌk]: **Good luck.** Viel Glück. • **Bad luck.** Pech (gehabt)! • **You're lucky.** ['lʌki] Du hast Glück. / Du bist gut dran. • **lucky day** Glückstag
lunch [lʌntʃ] Mittagessen
for lunch zum Mittagessen
have lunch Mittag essen

M

machine [mə'ʃi:n] Maschine, Gerät
mad [mæd] verrückt, wahnsinnig
Madam ['mædəm]: **Dear Sir or Madam** Sehr geehrte Damen und Herren
made [meɪd] 1. *si. past von „make"; 2. Part. Perf. von „make"* • **be made of ...** aus ... (gemacht) sein
magazine [,mægə'zi:n] Zeitschrift
magic *(adj; n)* ['mædʒɪk] magisch, Zauber-; Magie, Zauberkunst
°**magnet** ['mægnət] Magnet
main [meɪn] Haupt- • **main clause** Hauptsatz • **mainly** ['meɪnli] hauptsächlich
°**majesty** ['mædʒəsti] Majestät
make* [meɪk] machen, bilden, bauen; zubereiten • **be made of ...** aus ... (gemacht) sein
make sb. do sth. jn. dazu bringen, etwas zu tun; jn. zwingen, etwas zu tun
°**make sth. sth.** etwas zu etwas machen • °**make a decision** eine Entscheidung treffen • °**make comparisons** Vergleiche anstellen, vergleichen • **make notes** sich Notizen machen • °**make sure** sicherstellen, sichergehen
°**make up** sich ausdenken, erfinden
make-up ['meɪkʌp] Make-up
mama [mə'mɑ:] Mama
man [mæn], *pl* **men** [men] Mann
°**manager** ['mænɪdʒə] Geschäftsführer/in, Manager/in
°**mansio** *(Latin)* Bleibe; Hotel
many ['meni] viele • **how many?** wie viele?
map [mæp] Landkarte, Stadtplan
March [mɑ:tʃ] März
mark [mɑ:k] (Zeugnis-)Note, Zensur
°**mark** markieren
market ['mɑ:kɪt] Markt
marmalade ['mɑ:məleɪd] (Orangen-)Marmelade
marriage ['mærɪdʒ] Ehe; Hochzeit
marry ['mæri] heiraten • **married (to)** ['mærid] verheiratet (mit) • **get married (to sb.)** (sich ver)heiraten (mit jm.), (jn.) heiraten
mask [mɑ:sk] Maske
match *(n; v)* [mætʃ] 1. Spiel, Wettkampf; 2. Streichholz; 3. zuordnen • °**Match the answers to the questions.** Ordne die Antworten den Fragen zu.
mate [meɪt] Kumpel, Kamerad
material [mə'tɪəriəl] Material, Stoff
maths *(no pl)* [mæθs] Mathematik
May [meɪ] Mai
may [meɪ] dürfen • **May I help you?** Sie wünschen?
may [meɪ]: **he may be the best ...** er ist vielleicht der beste ...
maybe ['meɪbi] vielleicht
mayday ['meɪdeɪ] SOS-Ruf, Maydaysignal
maze [meɪz] Irrgarten, Labyrinth
me [mi, *betont:* mi:] mir; mich
It's me – Sita. Ich bin es – Sita. • **Me too.** Ich auch.
meal [mi:l] Mahlzeit, Essen
mean* [mi:n] 1. meinen (= sagen wollen) • **What do you mean by that?** Was verstehst du darunter?
2. bedeuten • **mean something to sb.** jm. etwas bedeuten • **The name means nothing to me.** Der Name sagt mir nichts. / Ich kenne den Namen nicht. • **meaning** ['mi:nɪŋ] Bedeutung
meant [ment] 1. *si. past von „mean"; 2. Part. Perf. von „mean"*
meanwhile ['mi:nwaɪl] inzwischen, währenddessen
meat [mi:t] Fleisch
meet* [mi:t] sich treffen; *jn.* treffen • **Nice to meet you.** Freut mich, euch (dich/Sie) kennenzulernen. • **meeting** Versammlung, Besprechung, Treffen
mega ['megə] mega-; Mega-
men [men] *pl von „man"*
mention ['menʃn] erwähnen, nennen
°**menu** ['menju:] Speisekarte
message ['mesɪdʒ] Nachricht
leave a message eine Nachricht hinterlassen
met [met] 1. *si. past von „meet"; 2. Part. Perf. von „meet"*
metal ['metl] Metall
method ['meθəd] Methode
metre ['mi:tə] Meter
mice [maɪs] *pl von „mouse"*
microchip ['maɪkrəʊtʃɪp] Mikrochip
microwave ['maɪkrəweɪv] Mikrowelle, Mikrowellengerät
midday [,mɪd'deɪ] Mittags-; Mittagszeit
°**middle** ['mɪdl] Mitte • **middle row** mittlere Reihe
°**Midlands** ['mɪdləndz]: **the Midlands** Mittelengland
midnight ['mɪdnaɪt] Mitternacht
might [maɪt]: **You might be right.** Du könntest (vielleicht) Recht haben.
mile [maɪl] Meile *(= ca. 1,6 km)*
milk [mɪlk] Milch • **milk shake** Milkshake
million ['mɪljən] Million
°**mime** [maɪm] vorspielen, pantomimisch darstellen
mime group Pantomimengruppe
°**mind** [maɪnd] Geist, Verstand
°**Mind the spelling.** [maɪnd] Gib Acht auf die Schreibung.
mine [maɪn] Bergwerk
mine [maɪn] meine(r, s)
mineral water ['mɪnərəl wɔ:tə] Mineralwasser
minority [maɪ'nɒrəti] Minderheit
minute ['mɪnɪt] Minute • **a minute longer** noch eine Minute • °**5 minutes' walk** 5 Minuten zu Fuß

mirror ['mɪrə] Spiegel
miserable ['mɪzrəbl] unglücklich, elend; erbärmlich, armselig
Miss [mɪs] Fräulein/Frau … *(unverheiratet)*
miss [mɪs] vermissen; verpassen, verfehlen • **be missing** fehlen • °**missing** fehlend
mistake [mɪ'steɪk] Fehler, Irrtum
°**mix up** [ˌmɪks 'ʌp] durcheinanderbringen • °**mixed up** durcheinander
model ['mɒdl] **1.** Modell, Modell-; **2.** Model, Mannequin
modern ['mɒdən] modern
moment ['məʊmənt]: **at the moment** im Moment, gerade, zurzeit • **Just a moment!** Einen Moment mal (eben)!
Monday ['mʌndeɪ, 'mʌndi] Montag
money ['mʌni] Geld
monitor ['mɒnɪtə] Bildschirm, Monitor
monkey ['mʌŋki] Affe
monster ['mɒnstə] Monster, Ungeheuer
month [mʌnθ] Monat
mood [mu:d] Laune, Stimmung • **be in a bad mood** in schlechter Stimmung sein, schlechte Laune haben • **be in a good mood** in guter Stimmung sein, gute Laune haben
moon [mu:n] Mond
more [mɔ:] mehr, weitere • **one more** noch ein(e), ein(e) weitere(r, s) • **no more school** keine Schule mehr • **more expensive (than)** teurer (als)
morning ['mɔ:nɪŋ] Morgen, Vormittag • **Good morning.** Guten Morgen. / Guten Tag. *(vormittags)* • **in the morning(s)** am Morgen, morgens **this morning** heute Morgen **tomorrow morning** morgen früh, morgen Vormittag
most [məʊst] (der/die/das) meiste …; am meisten • **most kids/cars/…** die meisten Kinder/Autos/… • **(the) most important** (der/die/das) wichtigste …; am wichtigsten
°**mostly** ['məʊstli] hauptsächlich
motel [məʊ'tel] Motel
mother ['mʌðə] Mutter
motor ['məʊtə] Motor • **motorbike** ['məʊtəbaɪk] Motorrad **motorcyclist** ['məʊtəsaɪklɪst] Motorradfahrer/in
mountain ['maʊntən] Berg
mouse [maʊs], *pl* **mice** [maɪs] Maus
mouth [maʊθ] Mund
move [mu:v] **1.** (sich) bewegen °**Move your counter.** Zieh deinen Spielstein. **2.** (um)ziehen • **move in** einziehen **3. on the move** unterwegs, auf Achse
Mr ['mɪstə] Herr …
Mrs ['mɪsɪz] Frau … *(verheiratet)*
much [mʌtʃ] **1.** viel • **How much?** Wie viel? • **How much is/are …?** Was kostet/kosten …? Wie viel kostet/kosten …? **2.** *(adv)* sehr, viel
mum [mʌm] Mutti, Mama; Mutter
museum [mju'zɪəm] Museum
music ['mju:zɪk] Musik **musical** ['mju:zɪkl] Musik-, musikalisch
Muslim *(adj; n)* ['mʊzlɪm, 'mʌzlɪm] moslemisch; Moslem
must [məst, *betont:* mʌst] müssen • **mustn't** ['mʌsnt] nicht dürfen
my [maɪ] mein, meine • **My name is …** Mein Name ist …/ Ich heiße …
myself [maɪ'self] mir/mich (selbst); selbst, selber
mystery *(n; adj)* ['mɪstri] Rätsel; rätselhafte(r, s)

N

name [neɪm] Name • **My name is …** Mein Name ist …/ Ich heiße … • **What's your name?** Wie heißt du?
narrow ['nærəʊ] schmal, eng
nation ['neɪʃn] Nation, Volk **national** ['næʃnəl] national **nationality** [ˌnæʃə'næləti] Staatsangehörigkeit, Nationalität
°**nature** ['neɪtʃə] Natur
near (to) [nɪə] in der Nähe von, nahe (bei) • **near there** dort in der Nähe; nicht weit von dort
nearly ['nɪəli] fast, beinahe
need [ni:d] brauchen, benötigen • **needn't** nicht brauchen, nicht müssen
negative ['negətɪv] negativ
°**neighbour** ['neɪbə] Nachbar/in
°**nephew** ['nefju:] Neffe
nervous ['nɜ:vəs] nervös, aufgeregt
net [net] Netz • **network** ['netwɜ:k] (Wörter-)Netz, „Wörterspinne"
never ['nevə] nie, niemals
new [nju:] neu • **New Year** Neujahr • °**New Year's Eve** [ˌnju: jɪəz‿'i:v] Silvester
news *(no pl)* [nju:z] Nachricht(en), Neuigkeit(en) **newspaper** ['nju:speɪpə] Zeitung • **newsreader** ['nju:zˌri:də] Nachrichtensprecher/in
next [nekst] **1.** nächste(r, s) *(zeitlich; Reihenfolge)* • **next Monday** (am) nächsten Montag • **next week** nächste Woche, in der nächsten Woche **the next day** der nächste Tag; am nächsten Tag **2.** als Nächstes
next to ['nekst tə] neben
nice [naɪs] schön, nett • **Nice to meet you.** Freut mich, Sie (dich/euch) kennenzulernen.
night [naɪt] Nacht, (später) Abend • **at night** in der Nacht, nachts • **that night** in jener Nacht
°**nightmare** ['naɪtmeə] Alptraum
nil [nɪl] null • **one nil to Kingsway** eins zu null für Kingsway
no [nəʊ] **1.** nein; **2.** kein, keine **no more school** keine Schule mehr • **no one** ['nəʊ‿wʌn] niemand
nobody ['nəʊbədi] niemand
noise [nɔɪz] Geräusch; Lärm **noisy** ['nɔɪzi] laut, lärmend
°**nominate** ['nɒmɪneɪt] nominieren, vorschlagen
none [nʌn] keine(r, s)
°**Normans** ['nɔ:mənz]: **the Normans** die Normannen
north [nɔ:θ] nördlich; (nach) Norden • **northbound** ['nɔ:θbaʊnd] Richtung Norden **north-east** [ˌnɔ:θ'i:st] nordöstlich; (nach) Nordosten **north-west** [ˌnɔ:θ'west] nordwestlich; (nach) Nordwesten
nose [nəʊz] Nase
not [nɒt] nicht • **I'm not German.** Ich bin kein Deutscher/ keine Deutsche. • °**not … any more** nicht mehr; kein(e,n) … mehr • **not (…) either** ['aɪðə, 'i:ðə] auch nicht; auch kein • **not … until/till** erst (um) • **not (…) yet** noch nicht
note [nəʊt] **1.** Notiz • **make notes** sich Notizen machen **take notes** sich Notizen machen °**2. note sth. down** etwas aufschreiben, notieren
nothing ['nʌθɪŋ] nichts
notice ['nəʊtɪs] **1.** (be)merken; °**2.** Mitteilung, Bekanntmachung
notice board ['nəʊtɪs bɔ:d] Anschlagtafel, Schwarzes Brett
nought [nɔ:t] null
November [nəʊ'vembə] November
now [naʊ] nun, jetzt • **right now** im Moment, jetzt gerade • °**Now that …** Jetzt,

wo … / Jetzt, da … • **Now what?** Was nun?
nuclear ['nju:kliə] nuklear, Kern-, Atom- • **nuclear power station** [ˌnju:kliə 'pauə steɪʃn] Atom-, Kernkraftwerk
number ['nʌmbə] Zahl, Ziffer **a small number of children** eine kleine Anzahl Kinder/von Kindern
nurse [nɜ:s] Krankenschwester, Krankenpfleger

O

object ['ɒbdʒɪkt] Gegenstand
o'clock [ə'klɒk]: **six o'clock** sechs Uhr
October [ɒk'təʊbə] Oktober
Odd word out [ˌɒd wɜ:d_'aʊt] *etwa:* Das unpassende Wort raus
of [əv, *betont:* ɒv] von • **a picture of Chester** ein Bild von Chester • **a group of girls** eine Gruppe (von) Mädchen • **a small number of children** eine kleine Anzahl Kinder/von Kindern • **in groups of four** in Vierergruppen • **one of you** eine/r von euch • **both of you** alle beide; ihr beide • **the two of them** die beiden; alle beide **the name of the street** der Name der Straße • **the city of Glasgow** die Stadt Glasgow **2 kilos of meat** 2 Kilo Fleisch **2 litres of milk** 2 Liter Milch **a piece of** ein Stück • **a lot of/lots of** eine Menge, viel, viele • **think of** halten von, denken über • **of course** natürlich, selbstverständlich
off [ɒf] aus; von (… herunter/hinunter) • **be off** aus(geschaltet) sein • **give sb. $3 off** jm. eine Ermäßigung von 3 Dollar geben • **take off** 1. ausziehen *(Kleidung)*; 2. starten, abfliegen, abheben *(Flugzeug)* • **turn off the light** das Licht ausschalten
°**offer** ['ɒfə] anbieten
office ['ɒfɪs] Büro
officer ['ɒfɪsə] Offizier/in **police officer** Polizist/in, Polizeibeamte(r)/Polizeibeamtin
often ['ɒfn] oft
oil [ɔɪl] Öl • **oil rig** ['ɔɪl rɪg] (Öl-)Bohrinsel
old [əʊld] alt • **16-year-old** 16-jährige(r, s)
oldie ['əʊldi] Oldie
olive ['ɒlɪv] Olive; Oliven-
Olympic Games [əˌlɪmpɪk 'geɪmz] Olympische Spiele
on [ɒn] auf • **report/show/film on** Reportage/Show/Film über • **straight on** geradeaus weiter • **on and on** immer weiter • **and so on** und so weiter • **on your own** allein, selbstständig **on board the ship** an Bord des Schiffes • **on fire** in Brand • °**on foot** zu Fuß **on the beach/coast** am Strand/an der Küste • **on the corner** an der Ecke • **on the bus/train/plane** im Bus/Zug/Flugzeug • **on the floor** auf dem Fußboden • **on the first floor** im ersten Stock • **on the Internet** im Internet **on the left** links, auf der linken Seite • **on the move** unterwegs, auf Achse • **on the phone** am Telefon • **on the radio/on TV** im Radio/im Fernsehen • **on the right** rechts, auf der rechten Seite **on the River Elbe** an der Elbe **on the show** in der Show/Sendung • **on the wall** an der Wand • **on 12th January** am 12. Januar • **on Monday** am Montag • **on Mondays** montags, jeden Montag • **on top (of sth.)** oben, obendrauf (auf etwas) • **be on** an sein, laufen *(Fernseher, Licht usw.)* • **go on** fortfahren, weitermachen; weiterreden **walk/drive on** weitergehen/weiterfahren • **turn on the light** das Licht einschalten
once [wʌns] einmal; einst • **at once** sofort, (so)gleich
one [wʌn]: **one another** einander, sich (gegenseitig) • **one more** noch ein(e), ein(e) weitere(r, s) • **one of you** eine/r von euch • **one morning/day** eines Morgens/Tages • **a yellow one** ein gelber, eine gelbe, ein gelbes • **the yellow ones** die gelben • **which one/ones** welche(r, s)/welche • **no one** niemand
onion ['ʌnjən] Zwiebel
only ['əʊnli] nur, bloß; erst **the only …** der/die/das einzige …
onto ['ɒntə, *betont:* 'ɒntu:] auf (… hinauf)
open *(v; adj)* ['əʊpən] 1. öffnen, aufmachen; sich öffnen; eröffnen; 2. geöffnet, offen
operate (on sb.) ['ɒpəreɪt] (jn.) operieren • **operating room** Operationssaal • **operation** [ˌɒpə'reɪʃn] Operation *(auch medizinisch)*
opinion (of) [ə'pɪnjən] Meinung (von, zu) • **in my opinion** meiner Meinung nach
opposite *(prep; n)* ['ɒpəzɪt] 1. gegenüber (von); 2. Gegenteil
°**optimist** ['ɒptɪmɪst] Optimist/Optimistin
or [ɔ:] oder
orange ['ɒrɪndʒ] Apfelsine, Orange • **orange juice** Orangensaft
order ['ɔ:də] 1. bestellen; °2. befehlen
order ['ɔ:də] Reihenfolge; (An-)Ordnung
ordinary ['ɔ:dnəri] gewöhnlich, normal
organize ['ɔ:gənaɪz] organisieren, veranstalten • **organizer** ['ɔ:gənaɪzə] Organisator/in
origin ['ɒrɪdʒɪn] Herkunft, Ursprung, Entstehung • **original** [ə'rɪdʒənl] Original-
Oscar ['ɒskə] Oscar *(Filmpreis)*
other ['ʌðə] andere • **the other** der/die/das andere, die anderen • **each other** einander, sich (gegenseitig)
our ['aʊə] unser, unsere
ours ['aʊəz] unsere(r, s)
ourselves [aʊə'selvz] uns (selbst); selbst, selber
out [aʊt] hinaus, heraus; draußen • **out there** dort draußen • **be out** 1. weg sein, nicht da sein; °2. ausgeschieden sein • **run out** knapp werden, zu Ende gehen, ausgehen • **I've run out of money.** Mir ist das Geld ausgegangen. • **out of …** aus … (heraus/hinaus) • **9 out of 11** 9 von 11 • °**out of cardboard** aus Pappe, aus Karton • **out of work** arbeitslos
outside [ˌaʊt'saɪd] 1. *(prep)* außerhalb (von); aus (… heraus); 2. *(adv)* draußen; nach draußen
oval ['əʊvl] oval
oven ['ʌvn] Backofen
over ['əʊvə] 1. über, oberhalb von; 2. über, mehr als • °**it's over to you** jetzt bist du dran **be over** vorbei sein, zu Ende sein • **all over the world** auf der ganzen Welt, überall auf der Welt • **over there** dort drüben, da drüben
overtake* [ˌəʊvə'teɪk] überholen
overtaken [ˌəʊvə'teɪkən] *Part. Perf. von „overtake"*
overtook [ˌəʊvə'tʊk] *si. past von „overtake"*
overwhelm [ˌəʊvə'welm] überwältigen
own [əʊn]: **your own bike** dein/Ihr/euer eigenes Fahrrad **on your own** allein, selbstständig
owner ['əʊnə] Besitzer/in

P

pack [pæk] packen, einpacken
packet ['pækɪt] Paket, Päckchen; Packung, Tüte
page [peɪdʒ] (Buch-, Heft-) Seite • **on page 25** auf Seite 25 • **Open your books at page 5.** Schlagt Seite 5 auf.
paid [peɪd] **1.** *si. past von „pay"*; **2.** *Part. Perf. von „pay"*
°**pairs of words** [peəz] Wortpaare
Pakistani [ˌpɑːkɪ'stɑːni] Pakistani, Pakistaner/in
palace ['pæləs] Palast, Schloss
panic *(n; v)* ['pænɪk] **1.** Panik; **2.** in Panik geraten
papa [pə'pɑː] Papa
paper ['peɪpə] **1.** Papier; **2.** Zeitung
parade [pə'reɪd] Parade, Umzug
paradise ['pærədaɪs] Paradies
paragraph ['pærəgrɑːf] Absatz, Abschnitt
paramedic [ˌpærə'medɪk] Sanitäter/in
parent ['peərənt] Elternteil (Vater oder Mutter) • **parents** Eltern
park [pɑːk] Park
parliament ['pɑːləmənt] Parlament
part [pɑːt] Teil
°**particular** [pə'tɪkjələ]: **in particular** insbesondere
partner ['pɑːtnə] Partner/in
party ['pɑːti] Party, Feier **have a party** eine Party veranstalten, feiern
pass [pɑːs] **1.** überholen; vorbeigehen, vorbeifahren an; **2.** vergehen, vorübergehen *(Zeit)*
pass [pɑːs] Pass, Ballabgabe
passenger ['pæsɪndʒə] Passagier/in, Fahrgast
passport ['pɑːspɔːt] (Reise-)Pass
past [pɑːst] **1.** *(n)* Vergangenheit; **2.** *(prep; adv)* vorbei, vorüber (an) • **half past eight** halb neun (8.30/20.30) **quarter past eight** Viertel nach acht (8.15/20.15)
path [pɑːθ] Pfad, Weg
patient ['peɪʃnt] Patient/in
°**pause** [pɔːz] Pause
pavement ['peɪvmənt] Gehweg, Fußweg
pay* (for) [peɪ] bezahlen
PE [ˌpiː‿'iː] **(Physical Education** [ˌfɪzɪkəl‿edʒu'keɪʃn]**)** Turnen, Sport(unterricht) *(in der Regel in der Halle)*
pea [piː] Erbse
°**peaceful** ['piːsfəl] friedlich
peanut ['piːnʌt] Erdnuss
pen [pen] Füller, Kugelschreiber • °**pen-friend** Brieffreund/in

penalty ['penəlti] Strafe, Strafstoß • °**penalty goal** Tor *(nach einem Foul)*
pence (p) *(pl)* [pens, piː] Pence
pencil ['pensl] Bleistift
pencil-case ['penslkeɪs] Federmäppchen
penguin ['peŋgwɪn] Pinguin
°**penicillin** [ˌpenɪ'sɪlɪn] Penizillin
penny ['peni] *kleinste britische Münze*
people *(pl)* ['piːpl] Leute, Menschen
per cent (%) [pə'sent] Prozent
perfect ['pɜːfɪkt] perfekt, einwandfrei, vollkommen; ideal
perfume ['pɜːfjuːm] Parfüm
perhaps [pə'hæps] vielleicht
period ['pɪəriəd] **1.** Zeitdauer, Periode; **2.** Unterrichtsstunde
person ['pɜːsn] Person
persuade sb. (to do sth.) [pə'sweɪd] jn. überzeugen/ überreden (etwas zu tun)
°**pessimist** ['pesɪmɪst] Pessimist/ Pessimistin
pet [pet] Haustier
phone *(v; n)* [fəʊn] **1.** anrufen; **2.** Telefon • **on the phone** am Telefon • **phone number** Telefonnummer • **phone box** Telefonzelle
photo ['fəʊtəʊ] Foto • **in the photo** auf dem Foto • **take photos** Fotos machen, fotografieren
phrase [freɪz] Ausdruck, (Rede-)Wendung
Physical Education [ˌfɪzɪkəl‿edʒu'keɪʃn] Turnen, Sport(unterricht) *(in der Regel in der Halle)*
physics *(no pl)* ['fɪzɪks] Physik
piano [pi'ænəʊ] Klavier • **play the piano** Klavier spielen
pick up [ˌpɪk‿'ʌp] abholen, mitnehmen; aufheben
°**pickpocket** ['pɪkpɒkɪt] Taschendieb/in
picnic ['pɪknɪk] Picknick • **have a picnic** ein Picknick machen
picture ['pɪktʃə] Bild • **in the picture** auf dem Bild
piece: a piece of [ə 'piːs‿əv] ein Stück
pig [pɪg] Schwein
pigeon ['pɪdʒɪn] Taube
°**pillage** ['pɪlɪdʒ] (aus)plündern
pilot ['paɪlət] Pilot, Pilotin
pipe [paɪp] Pfeife • °**Put that in your pipe and smoke it.** *(infml) etwa:* Lass dir das gesagt sein. / Schreib dir das hinter die Ohren.
°**piper** ['paɪpə] Dudelsackspieler/in
pizza ['piːtsə] Pizza
place [pleɪs] Ort, Platz, Stelle **place of birth** Geburtsort
take third place den dritten Platz belegen • °**place setting** ['pleɪs ˌsetɪŋ] Gedeck
plan *(v; n)* [plæn] **1. (-nn-)** planen • **planner** Planer/in **2.** Plan
plane [pleɪn] Flugzeug • **plane ticket** Flugschein, Flugticket
°**planet** ['plænɪt] Planet
plant [plɑːnt] (ein)pflanzen
plastic ['plæstɪk] Plastik, Kunststoff
plate [pleɪt] Teller
platform ['plætfɔːm] Bahnsteig, Gleis
play *(v; n)* [pleɪ] **1.** spielen **play the drums/the piano/...** Schlagzeug/Klavier/... spielen **play a team** gegen eine Mannschaft spielen • **play a trick on sb.** jm. einen Streich spielen • **player** Spieler/in **2.** Spiel; Theaterstück
playground ['pleɪgraʊnd] Schulhof
please [pliːz] bitte *(in Fragen und Aufforderungen)*
pleased [pliːzd] erfreut, froh **be pleased (with/about)** sich freuen (über), zufrieden sein (mit)
plug [plʌg] Stecker
pm [ˌpiː‿'em] ... Uhr nachmittags/abends
pocket ['pɒkɪt] Tasche *(an einem Kleidungsstück)* **pocket money** Taschengeld
poem ['pəʊɪm] Gedicht
°**poetry** ['pəʊətri] Dichtung, Gedichte
point *(n; v)* [pɔɪnt] **1.** Punkt; **2. 10.4 (ten point four)** 10,4 (zehn Komma vier); **3. point (at/to)** zeigen, deuten (auf) **point sth. at sb.** etwas auf jn. richten
police *(pl)* [pə'liːs] Polizei **policeman/policewoman** Polizist/Polizistin • **police officer** Polizeibeamte(r)/ Polizeibeamtin, Polizist/in **police station** Polizeiwache, Polizeirevier
polite [pə'laɪt] höflich
pollute [pə'luːt] *(die Umwelt)* verschmutzen • **pollution** [pə'luːʃn] (Umwelt-)Verschmutzung
pool [puːl] Pool • **swimming-pool** Schwimmbecken
poor [pɔː, pʊə] arm • **poor Trundle** der arme Trundle **poor things** die Armen
pop [pɒp] Pop(musik)
popcorn ['pɒpkɔːn] Popcorn
popular (with) ['pɒpjələ] beliebt (bei)
population [ˌpɒpju'leɪʃn] Bevölkerung, Einwohner(zahl)
positive ['pɒzətɪv] positiv

post [pəʊst] Post(sendungen) **post office** Postamt • **postbox** Briefkasten • **postcard** Postkarte
poster ['pəʊstə] Poster
pot [pɒt] Topf, Kochtopf
potato, *pl* **potatoes** [pə'teɪtəʊ] Kartoffel
pound (£) [paʊnd] Pfund *(britische Währung)*
pound against [paʊnd] klatschen gegen
power ['paʊə] Strom, Energie **power station** ['paʊə ˌsteɪʃn] Kraftwerk, Elektrizitätswerk
practice *(no pl)* ['præktɪs] Praxis, Übung(en)
practise ['præktɪs] üben, trainieren
prefix ['pri:fɪks] Vorsilbe
prepare (for) [prɪ'peə] (sich) vorbereiten (auf); *(Mahlzeit)* zubereiten
present ['preznt] 1. Gegenwart; 2. Geschenk
present sth. (to sb.) [prɪ'zent] (jm.) etwas präsentieren, zeigen, vorstellen • **presenter** [prɪ'zentə] Moderator/in **presentation** [ˌprezn'teɪʃn] Präsentation, Darbietung, Vorstellung
pretty ['prɪti] hübsch
price [praɪs] (Kauf-)Preis
°**prime minister** [ˌpraɪm 'mɪnɪstə] Premierminister/in
prince [prɪns] Prinz
°**print** *(v; n)* [prɪnt] 1. (ab-)drucken; 2. **bold print** [ˌbəʊld 'prɪnt] Fettdruck
°**prison** ['prɪzn] Gefängnis
prize [praɪz] Preis, Gewinn
problem ['prɒbləm] Problem
professor [prə'fesə] Professor/in
programme ['prəʊgræm] (Radio-, Fernseh-) Sendung; Programm
project ['prɒdʒekt] Projekt
promise ['prɒmɪs] versprechen
°**pronunciation** [prəˌnʌnsi'eɪʃn] Aussprache
proof *(no pl)* [pru:f] Beweis(e), Nachweis(e)
properly ['prɒpəli] richtig, ordentlich, sachgemäß
proud (of) [praʊd] stolz (auf)
°**provincial** [prə'vɪnʃl] provinziell
°**pub** [pʌb] Kneipe, Lokal
°**public record office** [ˌpʌblɪk 'rekɔ:d ˌɒfɪs] *etwa:* Nationalarchiv
°**publish** ['pʌblɪʃ] veröffentlichen
pull [pʊl] ziehen
pullover ['pʊləʊvə] Pullover
°**Punjabi** [pʌn'dʒɑ:bi] Pandschabi *(im Pandschab – einer Gegend in Nordpakistan und Nordindien – gesprochene Sprache)*
pupil ['pju:pl] Schüler/in
purse [pɜ:s] Portmonee, Geldbeutel
push [pʊʃ] drücken, schieben, stoßen
put* (-tt-) [pʊt] legen, stellen, *(etwas wohin)* tun • °**Put that in your pipe and smoke it.** *(infml) etwa:* Lass dir das gesagt sein. / Schreib dir das hinter die Ohren. • **put down** hinstellen, hinlegen, aus der Hand legen • **put the phone down** den Hörer auflegen **put in** einsetzen, einfügen, hineintun • **put on** anziehen *(Kleidung)*
put [pʊt] 1. *si. past von „put“;* 2. *Part. Perf. von „put“*

Q

quarter ['kwɔ:tə] Viertel **quarter past eight** [ˌkwɔ:tə pɑ:st ˌ'eɪt] Viertel nach acht (8.15/20.15) • **quarter to nine** [ˌkwɔ:tə tə 'naɪn] Viertel vor neun (8.45/20.45)
quarterback ['kwɔ:təbæk] Quarterback *(American football)*
queen [kwi:n] Königin
question ['kwestʃn] Frage **ask questions** Fragen stellen
questionnaire [ˌkwestʃə'neə] Fragebogen
quick *(adj)* [kwɪk] schnell **quickly** *(adv)* ['kwɪkli] schnell
quiet ['kwaɪət] ruhig, leise, still
quite [kwaɪt] ziemlich; ganz
quiz [kwɪz] Quiz, Ratespiel

R

rabbit ['ræbɪt] Kaninchen
race [reɪs] Rennen, (Wett-)Lauf **racing** ['reɪsɪŋ] Rennsport
racism ['reɪsɪzəm] Rassismus **racist** *(adj; n)* ['reɪsɪst] rassistisch; Rassist/in
radar ['reɪdɑ:] Radar
radio ['reɪdiəʊ] 1. Radio • **on the radio** im Radio 2. Funk; Funkgerät
railway ['reɪlweɪ] Eisenbahn
rain *(v; n)* [reɪn] 1. regnen; 2. Regen • **acid rain** [ˌæsɪd 'reɪn] saurer Regen • **rainy** ['reɪni] regnerisch
ran [ræn] *si. past von „run“*
rang [ræŋ] *si. past von „ring“*
rap [ræp] Rap *(rhythmischer Sprechgesang)*
rattle ['rætl] rütteln; klappern
RE [ˌɑ:r ˌ'i:] **(Religious Education)** [rɪˌlɪdʒəs ˌedʒu'keɪʃn] Religion(sunterricht)
reach [ri:tʃ] erreichen
read* [ri:d] lesen • °**read out (loud)** (laut) vorlesen • **read sth. to sb.** jm. etwas vorlesen **reader** Leser/in
read [red] 1. *si. past von „read“;* 2. *Part. Perf. von „read“*
ready ['redi] bereit, fertig **get ready** sich bereitmachen, sich fertig machen
real [rɪəl] echt, wirklich **really** ['rɪəli] wirklich
reason (for …/why …) ['ri:zn] Grund, Begründung (für …/dafür, dass …) • **for other reasons** aus anderen Gründen
°**recipe** ['resəpi] Rezept
record [rɪ'kɔ:d] aufnehmen, aufzeichnen *(auf Band)*
record ['rekɔ:d] Schallplatte
°**recorder** [rɪ'kɔ:də] Blockflöte
recycle [ˌri:'saɪkl] wiederverwerten, wiederaufbereiten **recycling** [ˌri:'saɪklɪŋ] Wiederverwertung, Wiederaufbereitung
red (-dd-) [red] rot
°**reef** [ri:f] Riff
refer to (-rr-) [rɪ'fɜ:] sich beziehen auf
rehearsal [rɪ'hɜ:sl] Probe *(Theater, Film)*
relative ['relətɪv] Verwandte(r)
relax [rɪ'læks] (sich) entspannen, sich ausruhen
religion [rɪ'lɪdʒn] Religion **Religious Education** [rɪˌlɪdʒəs ˌedʒu'keɪʃn] Religion(sunterricht)
remains *(pl)* [rɪ'meɪnz] (Über-)Reste
remember sth. [rɪ'membə] sich an etwas erinnern; an etwas denken, sich etwas merken
°**repeat** [rɪ'pi:t] wiederholen
°**replace sth. (with)** [rɪ'pleɪs] etwas ersetzen (durch)
report *(v; n)* [rɪ'pɔ:t] 1. berichten, melden • **reporter** Reporter/in 2. **report (on)** Bericht, Reportage (über)
request [rɪ'kwest] Bitte, Wunsch
rescue ['reskju:] retten; befreien
rest (of) [rest] Rest
restaurant ['restrɒnt] Restaurant • **at the restaurant** im Restaurant
result [rɪ'zʌlt] Ergebnis, Resultat • **as a result** als Ergebnis, als Resultat
retell* [ˌri:'tel] nacherzählen
retold [ˌri:'təʊld] 1. *si. past von „retell“;* 2. *Part. Perf. von „retell“*
return *(v; n)* [rɪ'tɜ:n] 1. zurückkehren; zurücksenden, zurückbringen; 2. Rückkehr, Wiederkehr
revision [rɪ'vɪʒn] Wiederholung *(des Lernstoffs)*

revolution [ˌrevəˈluːʃn] Revolution
rich [rɪtʃ] reich
°**rid** [rɪd]: **get rid of** loswerden
ridden [ˈrɪdn] *Part. Perf. von „ride"*
ride* *(v; n)* [raɪd] **1.** reiten; **2.** fahren mit • **ride a bike** Rad fahren • **Let's ride our bikes to school.** Lass(t) uns mit dem Rad zur Schule fahren. • **rider** Reiter/in; (Fahrrad-, Motorrad-)Fahrer/in **riding** *(das)* Reiten, Reitsport **3. (bike) ride** (Rad-)Fahrt, (Rad-)Tour
rig [rɪg] Bohrinsel, Förderturm
right [raɪt] **1.** richtig • **get sth. right** etwas richtig machen **You're right.** Du hast Recht. / Stimmt. • **Right, Debbie?** Nicht wahr, Debbie? • **Right.** Gut. / In Ordnung. • **all right** gut, in Ordnung **2.** nach rechts; rechte(r, s) **on the right** rechts, auf der rechten Seite **3.** ganz, völlig; genau, direkt; gerade • **right now** im Moment, jetzt gerade
ring* [rɪŋ] klingeln, läuten **ring the doorbell** (an der Tür) klingeln
rival [ˈraɪvl] Rivale, Rivalin; Konkurrent, Konkurrentin
river [ˈrɪvə] Fluss • **on the River Elbe** an der Elbe
road [rəʊd] Straße, Landstraße **road sign** Verkehrszeichen
rob **(-bb-)** [rɒb] berauben, ausrauben
robot [ˈrəʊbɒt] Roboter
rock [rɒk] Fels, Felsen
rode [rəʊd] *si. past von „ride"*
role [rəʊl] Rolle • **role-play** [ˈrəʊl pleɪ] Rollenspiel
Roman *(adj; n)* [ˈrəʊmən] römisch; Römer/in
roof [ruːf] Dach
room [ruːm] Zimmer, Raum
rope [rəʊp] Seil
rose [rəʊz] Rose
round [raʊnd] **1.** rund; **2.** um … (herum) • **look round** sich umsehen • **the wrong way round** verkehrt herum
route [ruːt] Route, Strecke
row [rəʊ]: **top/middle/bottom row** obere/mittlere/untere Reihe
rub **(-bb-)** [rʌb] (ein)reiben
rubber [ˈrʌbə] Radiergummi
rubbish [ˈrʌbɪʃ] **1.** Abfall, Müll **rubbish dump** Müllhalde, Müllkippe **2.** *(infml)* Quatsch, Blödsinn
rucksack [ˈrʌksæk] Rucksack
rude (to sb.) [ruːd] unhöflich, grob (zu jm.)
rugby [ˈrʌgbi] Rugby
rule *(v; n)* [ruːl] **1.** (be)herrschen, regieren; **2.** Regel, Vorschrift
ruler [ˈruːlə] Lineal
run* **(-nn-)** [rʌn] **1.** laufen, rennen • **run around** umherrennen, herumrennen °**run for the try** *etwa:* versuchen, Punkte zu erzielen **runner** Läufer/in • **running** *(das)* Laufen **2.** verkehren, fahren *(Zug, Bus)* **3.** leiten, betreiben, (durch-)führen, veranstalten **4. run out** knapp werden, zu Ende gehen, ausgehen • **I've run out of money.** Mir ist das Geld ausgegangen.
run [rʌn] *Part. Perf. von „run"*
rung [rʌŋ] *Part. Perf. von „ring"*

S

°**sabotage** [ˈsæbətɑːʒ] sabotieren • °**saboteur** [ˌsæbəˈtɜː] Saboteur/in
sad **(-dd-)** [sæd] traurig **sadness** [ˈsædnəs] Traurigkeit
safe [seɪf] sicher, gefahrlos **safety** [ˈseɪfti] Sicherheit
said [sed] **1.** *si. past von „say"*; **2.** *Part. Perf. von „say"*
sail [seɪl] segeln • **sailing** *(das)* Segeln • **sailor** [ˈseɪlə] Seemann, Matrose
°**saint** [seɪnt] Heilige(r)
salad [ˈsæləd] Salat *(als Gericht oder Beilage)*
salt [sɒlt] Salz
same [seɪm]: **the same (as)** der-/die-/dasselbe, dieselben (wie) • **the same thing** der-, die-, dasselbe
°**samosa** [səˈməʊsə] *dreieckige Teigtaschen mit würziger Gemüse- oder Fleischfüllung*
sanctuary [ˈsæŋktʃuəri] (Natur-, Tier-, Vogel-)Schutzgebiet
sandal [ˈsændl] Sandale
sandwich [ˈsænwɪdʒ] *(zusammengeklapptes)* belegtes Brot, Sandwich
sang [sæŋ] *si. past von „sing"*
sank [sæŋk] *si. past von „sink"*
sat [sæt] **1.** *si. past von „sit"*; **2.** *Part. Perf. von „sit"*
Saturday [ˈsætədeɪ, ˈsætədi] Samstag, Sonnabend
sauce [sɔːs] Soße
sausage [ˈsɒsɪdʒ] (Brat-, Bock-) Würstchen, Wurst
save [seɪv] **1.** sparen; **2. save sb. from sth.** jn. vor etwas retten • **save the day** die Situation retten, der Retter sein *(in einer bestimmten Situation)*
saw [sɔː] *si. past von „see"*
°**Saxons** [ˈsæksnz]: **the Saxons** die Sachsen
say* [seɪ] sagen • **You say** Du sagst / Man sagt • **Say hello to …** Grüß … • **say so** es/das sagen
scan **(-nn-)** [skæn] *(einen Text)* überfliegen *(um bestimmte Informationen zu finden)*
scare [skeə] erschrecken, Angst machen • **be scared (about; of)** [skeəd] Angst haben (wegen; vor) • **scary** [ˈskeəri] unheimlich, gruselig
scarf [skɑːf], *pl* **scarves** [skɑːvz] Schal
°**scene** [ˈsiːn] Szene
school [skuːl] Schule • **at school** in der Schule • **leave school** von der Schule abgehen • **start school** eingeschult werden • **school bag** Schultasche • **school subject** [ˈskuːl ˌsʌbdʒɪkt] Schulfach
science [ˈsaɪəns] (Natur-)Wissenschaft • °**scientist** [ˈsaɪəntɪst] Wissenschaftler/in
°**scissors** *(pl)* [ˈsɪzəz] (eine) Schere
score *(v; n)* [skɔː] **1.** *(einen Treffer)* erzielen, *(ein Tor)* schießen; **2.** Spielstand, (Spiel-)Ergebnis, Punktestand
scrambled egg(s) [ˌskræmbld ˈeg(z)] Rührei, Rühreier
scrapbook [ˈskræpbʊk] Sammelalbum
scream *(v; n)* [skriːm] **1.** schreien, kreischen; **2.** Schrei, Aufschrei
screen [skriːn] Bildschirm; Leinwand
script [skrɪpt] Drehbuch
sea [siː] Meer, *(die)* See • **at sea** auf See
sea lion [ˈsiː laɪən] Seelöwe
seal [siːl] Robbe, Seehund
second [ˈsekənd] zweite(r, s) **secondly, …** zweitens …
second [ˈsekənd] Sekunde
secret *(adj; n)* [ˈsiːkrət] geheim; Geheimnis • °**Secret Service** [ˌsiːkrət ˈsɜːvɪs] Geheimdienst
secretary [ˈsekrətri] Sekretär/in
°**section** [ˈsekʃn] Abschnitt, Teil
see* [siː] sehen • **see the sights** sich die Sehenswürdigkeiten ansehen • **See, …** Siehst du, … • **See you.** Tschüs. / Bis bald. / Bis dann. **I see!** Ich verstehe! / Aha! / Ach so! • **you see** weißt du, nämlich • °**See for yourself!** *etwa:* Überzeug dich selbst! **2.** besuchen, aufsuchen
seem (to be/do) [siːm] (zu sein/tun) scheinen
seen [siːn] *Part. Perf. von „see"*
sell* [sel] verkaufen
senator [ˈsenətə] Senator/in

send* (to) [send] schicken, senden (an)
sensible ['sensəbl] vernünftig
sent [sent] **1.** *si. past von „send"*; **2.** *Part. Perf. von „send"*
sentence ['sentəns] Satz
September [sep'tembə] September
°**servant** ['sɜːvənt] Diener/in
service ['sɜːvɪs] Dienst, Service
°**set** [set] Bühnenbild, Kulisse
°**set free** [ˌset 'friː] freilassen, erlösen
shadow ['ʃædəʊ] Schatten
shake* [ʃeɪk] zittern; schütteln
shaken ['ʃeɪkən] *Part. Perf. von „shake"*
shall [ʃæl, ʃəl]: **Shall I …?** Soll ich …?
she [ʃi, *betont:* ʃiː] sie
sheep, *pl* **sheep** [ʃiːp] Schaf
°**sheer** ['ʃɪə] schier
shelf [ʃelf], *pl* **shelves** [ʃelvz] Regal
shelter (from) ['ʃeltə] Schutz (vor)
ship [ʃɪp] Schiff
shirt [ʃɜːt] (Ober-)Hemd
shoe [ʃuː] Schuh
shook [ʃʊk] *si. past von „shake"*
shop *(n; v)* [ʃɒp] **1.** Laden, Geschäft • **shop assistant** Verkäufer/in
2. **(-pp-)** einkaufen gehen
shopping ['ʃɒpɪŋ] *(das)* Einkaufen; Einkäufe • **go to the shops/go shopping** einkaufen gehen • **do the shopping** einkaufen, Einkäufe machen/erledigen • **like shopping** gern einkaufen gehen • **hate shopping** gar nicht gern einkaufen gehen • **shopper** Käufer/in • **shoplifter** ['ʃɒplɪftə] Ladendieb/in
short [ʃɔːt] kurz
shorts *(pl)* [ʃɔːts] Shorts, kurze Hose
should [ʃəd, *betont:* ʃʊd]: **they should …** sie sollten …
shout (at) [ʃaʊt] rufen, (an)schreien • **shout for help** um Hilfe rufen
show* *(v; n)* [ʃəʊ] **1.** zeigen; **2.** Schau, Show; Ausstellung; (Fernseh-, Radio-)Sendung **on the show** in der Show/Sendung
shower Dusche; Regenschauer **have a shower** (sich) duschen
shown [ʃəʊn] *Part. Perf. von „show"*
Shut up. [ˌʃʌt_'ʌp] Halt den Mund!
shuttle ['ʃʌtl] Shuttle, (Weltraum-)Fähre, Transporter
shy [ʃaɪ] scheu, schüchtern
°**sick** [sɪk] krank
side [saɪd] Seite

sights *(pl)* [saɪts] Sehenswürdigkeiten • **see the sights** sich die Sehenswürdigkeiten ansehen
sign [saɪn] Schild; Zeichen **road sign** Verkehrszeichen
sign [saɪn] unterschreiben
silly ['sɪli] albern, dumm **silliness** ['sɪlɪnəs] Albernheit, Dummheit
°**similar** ['sɪmɪlə] ähnlich
since [sɪns] seit • **since then** seitdem, seit damals
sincerely [sɪn'sɪəli]: **Yours sincerely,** Mit freundlichen/herzlichen Grüßen
sing* [sɪŋ] singen • **singer** Sänger/in
sink* [sɪŋk] sinken, untergehen
Sir [sɜː, sə] *engl. Adelstitel* **Dear Sir or Madam** [sɜː] Sehr geehrte Damen und Herren
sister ['sɪstə] Schwester
sit* **(-tt-)** [sɪt] sitzen; sich (hin)setzen • **sit down** sich hinsetzen
site [saɪt] Ausgrabungsstätte; Bauplatz
°**situation** [ˌsɪtʃu'eɪʃn] Situation
size [saɪz] Größe • **What size are you?** Welche Größe hast du/haben Sie?
°**sketch** [sketʃ] skizzieren
ski [skiː] Ski laufen/fahren **ski-lift** ['skiːlɪft] Skilift **skiing** ['skiːɪŋ] Skisport, *(das)* Skilaufen
skin [skɪn] Haut
skirt [skɜːt] Rock
sky [skaɪ] Himmel • **in the sky** am Himmel
slave [sleɪv] Sklave, Sklavin
sleep* *(v; n)* [sliːp] **1.** schlafen **sleep late** lange schlafen **2.** Schlaf
slept [slept] **1.** *si. past von „sleep"*; **2.** *Part. Perf. von „sleep"*
°**slogan** ['sləʊgən] Slogan, Werbespruch
slow [sləʊ] langsam
small [smɔːl] klein
smell *(v; n)* [smel] **1.** riechen; **2.** Geruch
smile *(n; v)* [smaɪl] **1.** Lächeln; **2.** **smile (at sb.)** (jn. an)lächeln
smoke *(v; n)* [sməʊk] **1.** rauchen; **2.** Rauch
°**snake** [sneɪk] Schlange
snow [snəʊ] Schnee
so [səʊ] **1.** deshalb, daher; also; **2.** so • **so boring** so langweilig • °**so far** bis hierher, bis jetzt • **do so** es/das tun **say so** es/das sagen • **I think so.** Ich glaube (ja). • **I don't think so.** Das finde/glaube ich nicht.
3. **so (that)** sodass, damit

Social Studies [ˌsəʊʃl 'stʌdiz] Sozial-, Gemeinschaftskunde
sock [sɒk] Socke, Strumpf
sofa ['səʊfə] Sofa
soft [sɒft] weich
solar energy [ˌsəʊlər'enədʒi] Sonnenenergie, Solarenergie **solar-powered** [ˌsəʊlə'paʊəd] mit Sonnenenergie betrieben
sold [səʊld] **1.** *si. past von „sell"*; **2.** *Part. Perf. von „sell"*
soldier ['səʊldʒə] Soldat/in
some [səm, *betont:* sʌm] einige, ein paar; etwas
somebody ['sʌmbədi] jemand
someone ['sʌmwʌn] jemand
something ['sʌmθɪŋ] etwas
sometimes ['sʌmtaɪmz] manchmal
somewhere ['sʌmweə] irgendwo(hin)
son [sʌn] Sohn
song [sɒŋ] Lied
soon [suːn] bald
sorry ['sɒri]: **Sorry. / I'm sorry.** Entschuldigung. Tut mir leid. **Sorry?** Wie bitte? • **feel sorry for sb.** jn. bedauern
sort (of) [sɔːt] Art, Sorte
sound *(v; n)* [saʊnd] **1.** klingen, sich *(gut usw.)* anhören; **2.** Laut, Geräusch, Ton, Klang °**sound engineer** Toningenieur/in, Tontechniker/in
soup [suːp] Suppe
south [saʊθ] südlich; (nach) Süden • **southbound** ['saʊθbaʊnd] Richtung Süden **south-east** [ˌsaʊθ'iːst] südöstlich; (nach) Südosten **south-west** [ˌsaʊθ'west] südwestlich; (nach) Südwesten
souvenir [ˌsuːvə'nɪə] Souvenir, Andenken
space [speɪs] (der) Weltraum; Raum, Platz • **spaceship** Raumschiff
Spanish ['spænɪʃ] Spanisch; spanisch
°**spare time** [ˌspeə 'taɪm] Freizeit
speak* [spiːk] sprechen **speaker** Sprecher/in
special *(adj; n)* ['speʃl] **1.** besondere(r, s) • **be special** etwas Besonderes sein **2.** **special (on)** Sonderprogramm, -sendung (über)
°**specific** [spə'sɪfɪk] bestimmte(r, s)
spell [spel] buchstabieren **spelling** ['spelɪŋ] (Recht-)Schreibung, Schreibweise
spend* time/money (on) [spend] Zeit verbringen (mit) / Geld ausgeben (für)
spent [spent] **1.** *si. past von „spend"*; **2.** *Part. Perf. von „spend"*
°**spicy** ['spaɪsi] scharf

spoke [spəʊk] *si. past von „speak"*
spoken ['spəʊkən] *Part. Perf. von „speak"*
spoon [spu:n] Löffel
sport [spɔ:t] Sport, Sportart **do sport(s)** Sport treiben
spot [spɒt]: **Spot the difference.** Entdecke den Unterschied.
spray [spreɪ] Spray
spring [sprɪŋ] Frühling
square [skweə] Platz *(in einer Stadt)*
stab **(-bb-)** [stæb] (zu)stechen
stadium ['steɪdɪəm] Stadion
staff room ['stɑ:f ru:m] Lehrerzimmer
stage [steɪdʒ] Bühne
stairs *(pl)* [steəz] Treppe; Treppenstufen
stall [stɔ:l] Stand
stamp [stæmp] Briefmarke
stand* [stænd] stehen; sich (hin)stellen • **stand around** herumstehen • **stand back (from)** zurücktreten (von); entfernt stehen (von)
star [stɑ:] (Film-, Pop-)Star
start *(v; n)* [stɑ:t] **1.** anfangen, beginnen (mit) • **start a car** ein Auto anlassen, starten **start school** eingeschult werden
2. Anfang, Beginn, Start
°**statement** ['steɪtmənt] Aussage
station ['steɪʃn] **1.** Bahnhof; **2.** Station • **police station** Polizeiwache, Polizeirevier **power station** Kraftwerk, Elektrizitätswerk
statue ['stætʃu:] Statue
stay [steɪ] bleiben; übernachten • **stay out** wegbleiben, nicht nach Hause kommen
steal* [sti:l] stehlen
step [step] Schritt; Stufe • **step by step** Schritt für Schritt **take a step towards sb.** einen Schritt auf jn. zugehen
stereo ['steriəʊ] Stereoanlage; Stereo
stick* [stɪk] kleben • **sticker** ['stɪkə] Sticker, Aufkleber
°**stick figure** ['stɪk fɪgə] Strichmännchen
still [stɪl] **1.** (immer) noch; **2.** trotzdem, dennoch
sting* [stɪŋ] stechen
stole [stəʊl] *si. past von „steal"*
stolen ['stəʊlən] *Part. Perf. von „steal"*
stone [stəʊn] Stein • °**Stone Age** ['stəʊn‿eɪdʒ] Steinzeit
stood [stʊd] **1.** *si. past von „stand"*; **2.** *Part. Perf. von „stand"*
stop *(v; n)* [stɒp] **1. (-pp-)** anhalten, stoppen; **2.** Halt; Haltestelle
store(room) ['stɔ:ru:m] Lager(raum)
storm [stɔ:m] Sturm; Gewitter
story ['stɔ:ri] Geschichte, Erzählung
straight *(adj; adv)* [streɪt] gerade; gerade(wegs), direkt; geradeaus • **straight on** geradeaus weiter
strange [streɪndʒ] **1.** seltsam, sonderbar; **2.** fremd **stranger** ['streɪndʒə] Unbekannte(r), Fremde(r)
stream [stri:m] Bach
street [stri:t] Straße *(in einer Stadt)* • **in the street** auf der Straße • °**street entertainer** [ˌstri:t‿entə'teɪnə] Straßenkünstler/in
°**stress** [stres] Betonung °**stressed syllable** [ˌstrest 'sɪləbl] betonte Silbe
strict (with sb.) [strɪkt] streng (mit/zu jm.)
string [strɪŋ] Schnur, Bindfaden
strong [strɒŋ] stark
stuck [stʌk] **1.** *si. past von „stick"*; **2.** *Part. Perf. von „stick"*
studio ['stju:diəʊ] Studio
study ['stʌdi] studieren; lernen; sorgfältig durchlesen
stuff [stʌf] *(infml)* Zeug, Kram
stung [stʌŋ] **1.** *si. past von „sting"*; **2.** *Part. Perf. von „sting"*
stupid ['stju:pɪd] blöd, dämlich
subject ['sʌbdʒɪkt] **1.** Thema, Gegenstand; **2.** (Unterrichts-)Fach
successful [sək'sesfl] erfolgreich
°**such as** ['sʌtʃ‿əz] wie zum Beispiel
suddenly ['sʌdnli] plötzlich, auf einmal
suffix ['sʌfɪks] Nachsilbe, Suffix
°**sugar** ['ʃʊgə] Zucker
suggest sth. (to sb.) [sə'dʒest] (jm.) etwas vorschlagen **suggestion** [sə'dʒestʃn] Vorschlag
suitcase ['su:tkeɪs] Koffer
sum [sʌm] Rechenaufgabe; Summe • **do sums** rechnen
summer ['sʌmə] Sommer **in (the) summer** im Sommer
sun [sʌn] Sonne • **sunny** ['sʌni] sonnig
Sunday ['sʌndeɪ, 'sʌndi] Sonntag
sung [sʌŋ] *Part. Perf. von „sing"*
sunk [sʌŋk] *Part. Perf. von „sink"*
super ['su:pə] super, toll
supermarket ['su:pəmɑ:kɪt] Supermarkt
support [sə'pɔ:t] unterstützen
suppose [sə'pəʊz] annehmen, vermuten • **be supposed to do/be** tun sollen / angeblich sein sollen
sure [ʃʊə] sicher(lich) • **Sure.** Sicher! / Natürlich! / Klar!
surfing ['sɜ:fɪŋ] *(das)* Wellenreiten, Surfen • **go surfing** wellenreiten gehen, surfen gehen
surgeon ['sɜ:dʒən] Chirurg/in
surprise [sə'praɪz] überraschen **surprised (at/by)** überrascht (über)
°**survey** ['sɜ:veɪ] Untersuchung, Vermessung
suspect ['sʌspekt] Verdächtige(r)
swam [swæm] *si. past von „swim"*
swap **(-pp-)** [swɒp] tauschen
sweatshirt ['swetʃɜ:t] Sweatshirt
swim* **(-mm-)** [swɪm] schwimmen • **swimming** *(das)* Schwimmen • **swimming-pool** Schwimmbad, Swimmingpool • **swimming-trunks** *(pl)* ['swɪmɪŋtrʌŋks] Badehose • **swimsuit** ['swɪmsu:t] Badeanzug
swum [swʌm] *Part. Perf. von „swim"*
°**syllable** ['sɪləbl] Silbe
symbol ['sɪmbl] Symbol
synthesizer ['sɪnθəsaɪzə] Synthesizer

T

table ['teɪbl] **1.** Tisch • **table tennis** Tischtennis
2. Tabelle
°**tackle** ['tækl] angreifen, fassen
tail [teɪl] Schwanz
take* [teɪk] **1.** nehmen; mitnehmen; (weg)bringen • **take sb. away** *hier:* jn. abführen • **take a bath** baden, ein Bad nehmen • **take a break** eine Pause machen • **take a step towards sb.** einen Schritt auf jn. zugehen • **take notes** sich Notizen machen • **take off** **1.** ausziehen *(Kleidung)*; **2.** starten, abfliegen, abheben *(Flugzeug)* • **take out** herausnehmen; ausleihen *(Bücher)* **take photos** Fotos machen, fotografieren • **take third place** den dritten Platz belegen
2. dauern; *(Zeit)* brauchen **Take a little time.** Nehmen Sie sich etwas Zeit.
taken ['teɪkən] *Part. Perf. von „take"*
talk (to) [tɔ:k] reden (mit), sich unterhalten (mit)
tall [tɔ:l] groß (gewachsen); hoch *(Bäume, Türme usw.)*
tape [teɪp] (Ton-)Band

tartan ['tɑ:tn] Schottenstoff, Schottenmuster
°**taste** [teɪst]: **a taste of ...** eine Kostprobe von ..., ein Vorgeschmack auf ...
taught [tɔ:t] **1.** *si. past von „teach"*; **2.** *Part. Perf. von „teach"*
tax (on) [tæks] Steuer (auf)
taxi ['tæksi] Taxi
tea [ti:] Tee
teach* [ti:tʃ] unterrichten, lehren • **teach sb. sth.** jm. etwas beibringen • **teacher** Lehrer/in
team [ti:m] Team, Mannschaft **team-mate** ['ti:mmeɪt] Mannschaftskamerad/in
tear [tɪə] Träne
technique [tek'ni:k] (Arbeits-)Verfahren, Technik, Methode
techno ['teknəʊ] Techno
technology [tek'nɒlədʒi] Technologie; Technik
teenager ['ti:neɪdʒə] Teenager, Jugendliche(r, s)
teeth [ti:θ] *pl von „tooth"*
telephone ['telɪfəʊn] Telefon **telephone box** Telefonzelle **telephone number** Telefonnummer
television ['telɪvɪʒn] Fernsehen; Fernsehgerät • **work in television** beim Fernsehen arbeiten
tell* [tel] **1. tell (about)** erzählen (von), berichten (über) **tell the way (to)** den Weg (zu/nach ...) beschreiben **Can you tell me the way to ...?** Können Sie mir sagen, wie ich zu/nach ... komme? **2.** erkennen; unterscheiden
tennis ['tenɪs] Tennis
tense [tens] Zeitform, Tempus
term [tɜ:m] Trimester
terrible ['terəbl] schrecklich, furchtbar
test *(v; n)* [test] **1.** testen, prüfen; **2.** Test, Prüfung, Klassenarbeit
text [tekst] Text
than: **slower than** ['sləʊə ðən] langsamer als
thank sb. [θæŋk] jm. danken, sich bei jm. bedanken **Thank you.** Danke (schön). **thanks** danke • **Thanks a lot.** Danke vielmals. Vielen Dank. • **thanks to Ben and Jenny** dank Ben und Jenny; wegen Ben und Jenny
that [ðət, *betont:* ðæt] **1.** dass **so (that)** sodass, damit **2.** der/die/das, die *(Relativpronomen)*
that [ðæt] jene(r, s); das (dort) **that afternoon/day/night** an jenem Nachmittag/Tag/in jener Nacht • **that's because** das kommt daher, weil **that's why** deshalb, darum **like that** so
the [ðə] der, die, das; die **the next day** der nächste Tag; am nächsten Tag • **the same** der-/die-/dasselbe, dieselben
theatre ['θɪətə] Theater
their [ðeə] ihr, ihre *(Plural)*
theirs [ðeəz] ihre(r, s)
them [ðəm, *betont:* ðem] sie; ihnen • **the two of them** die beiden; alle beide
themselves [ðəm'selvz] sich (selbst); selbst, selber
then [ðen] **1.** dann, danach **just then** genau in dem Moment; gerade dann **2.** damals, zu der Zeit
there [ðeə] da, dort; dahin, dorthin • **in there** dort drinnen • **out there** dort draußen • **near there** dort in der Nähe; nicht weit von dort **over there** dort drüben, da drüben • **up there** dort oben (hin), da oben (hin) • **there are** es sind (vorhanden); es gibt • **there's** = **there is** es ist (vorhanden); es gibt
these [ði:z] diese, die (hier)
they [ðeɪ] sie *(Plural)*
thick [θɪk] dick; dicht
thief [θi:f], *pl* **thieves** [θi:vz] Dieb, Diebin
thin (-nn-) [θɪn] dünn
thing [θɪŋ] Ding, Sache • **the same thing** der-, die-, dasselbe • **poor things** die Armen
think* [θɪŋk] glauben, meinen, denken • **think (about)** nachdenken (über) • **think about/of** halten von, denken über • **think of** denken an, sich ausdenken
third [θɜ:d] dritte(r, s) **thirdly, ...** drittens ...
thirsty ['θɜ:sti] durstig • **be thirsty** durstig sein, Durst haben
this [ðɪs] diese(r, s); dies (hier) **This is ...** Dies ist ... • **this morning/afternoon/evening** heute Morgen/Nachmittag/Abend • **this way** **1.** hier entlang; **2.** so, auf diese Weise
those [ðəʊz] die (da), jene (dort)
thought [θɔ:t] **1.** *si. past von „think"*; **2.** *Part. Perf. von „think"*
thoughtful ['θɔ:tfəl] aufmerksam, rücksichtsvoll; nachdenklich
threw [θru:] *si. past von „throw"*
°**throne** [θrəʊn] Thron
through [θru:] durch
throw* [θrəʊ] werfen °**Throw the dice.** Würfle.
thrown [θrəʊn] *Part. Perf. von „throw"*
Thursday ['θɜ:zdeɪ, 'θɜ:zdi] Donnerstag
°**tick** [tɪk] Häkchen
ticket ['tɪkɪt] **1.** Eintrittskarte; **2.** Fahrkarte, Fahrschein **ticket office** (Fahr-)Kartenschalter; Kartenvorverkaufsstelle
tidy ['taɪdi] ordentlich, aufgeräumt • **tidy up** aufräumen
tie (to) [taɪ] binden, anbinden (an)
°**tie** [taɪ] Krawatte
tiger ['taɪgə] Tiger
°**tight** [taɪt] fest
tile [taɪl] Ziegel, Fliese
till [tɪl] bis *(zeitlich)* • **not ... till** erst (um)
time [taɪm] **1.** Zeit • **What time is it?** Wie spät ist es? **What time is the film?** Wann fängt der Film an? • **(just) in time** (gerade) rechtzeitig **at all times** immer, jederzeit **at that time** damals, zu jener/dieser Zeit • **a long time ago** vor langer Zeit **for a long time** lange Zeit **Take a little time.** Nehmen Sie sich etwas Zeit. • **feeding times** Fütterungszeiten **free time** Freizeit, freie Zeit °**spare time** Freizeit • **timer** Zeitmesser • **timetable** Fahrplan **2. time(s)** Mal(e); -mal • **for the first time** zum ersten Mal **The first time Brian saw Mark's room ...** Als Brian Marks Zimmer das erste Mal sah, ... • **five times nought** fünf mal null
timetable ['taɪmteɪbl] Stundenplan
tin [tɪn] Dose, Büchse
tip [tɪp] Tipp
tired ['taɪəd] müde
°**title** ['taɪtl] Titel, Überschrift
to [tə, *betont:* tu:] **1.** zu, nach **letter to** Brief an • **Welcome to ...** Willkommen in ... **I've been to Husum.** Ich war (schon mal) in Husum. / Ich bin (schon) in Husum gewesen. • **quarter to nine** Viertel vor neun (8.45/20.45) **3.50 to 5.30** 3 Uhr 50 bis 5 Uhr 30 • **from Monday to Friday** von Montag bis Freitag • **next to** neben **one nil to Kingsway** eins zu null für Kingsway **2.** um zu; **3. try to do sth.** versuchen, etwas zu tun
toast [təʊst] Toast(brot)

today [tə'deɪ] heute • **today's match** das heutige Spiel
together [tə'geðə] zusammen
toilet ['tɔɪlət] Toilette
told [təʊld] **1.** *si. past von „tell"*; **2.** *Part. Perf. von „tell"*
tomato [tə'mɑ:təʊ], *pl* **tomatoes** [tə'mɑ:təʊz] Tomate
tomorrow [tə'mɒrəʊ] morgen **tomorrow morning/afternoon/evening** morgen Vormittag/Nachmittag/Abend
tonight [tə'naɪt] heute Nacht, heute Abend
too [tu:] **1.** auch • **and on her birthday, too!** und noch dazu an ihrem Geburtstag. • **And they were pretty dresses, too.** Und schöne Kleider waren es außerdem/noch dazu. **2. too little** zu klein
took [tʊk] *si. past von „take"*
tool [tu:l] Werkzeug • **tool box** Werkzeugkasten
tooth [tu:θ], *pl* **teeth** [ti:θ] Zahn • **brush your teeth** sich die Zähne putzen
top [tɒp] Spitze, oberes Ende **top row** obere Reihe • **on top (of sth.)** oben, obendrauf (auf etwas) • °**Top of the Pops** *etwa:* Hitparade
topic ['tɒpɪk] Thema, Themenbereich
tortoise ['tɔ:təs] Schildkröte
total *(n; adj)* ['təʊtl] **1.** Gesamtbetrag, Summe; **2.** Gesamt-, gesamt, völlig, total
touch [tʌtʃ] berühren, anfassen
tour (of) [tʊə] Tour, (Rund-)Reise (durch)
tourist ['tʊərɪst] Tourist/in **tourist board** ['tʊərɪst bɔ:d] Fremdenverkehrsbüro
towards Mark [tə'wɔ:dz] auf Mark zu, in Marks Richtung
tower ['taʊə] Turm
town [taʊn] Stadt • **town hall** [ˌtaʊn 'hɔ:l] Rathaus
toy [tɔɪ] Spielzeug
°**track** [træk] Pfad, Weg
tradition [trə'dɪʃn] Tradition
traffic ['træfɪk] Verkehr **traffic light(s)** ['træfɪk laɪts] Verkehrsampel
tragedy ['trædʒədi] Tragödie
train [treɪn] Zug • **on the train** im Zug
train [treɪn] üben; (jn.) trainieren; (jn.) ausbilden • **trainer** ['treɪnə] Trainer/in • **training** ['treɪnɪŋ] Training, Ausbildung
tram [træm] Straßenbahn, Tram
°**tramp** [træmp] Land-, Stadtstreicher/in
°**translate (into)** [træns'leɪt] übersetzen (in)
transparency [træns'pærənsi] Folie
transport *(no pl)* ['trænspɔ:t] Transport(mittel), Verkehrsmittel
travel *(v; n)* ['trævl] **1. (-ll-)** reisen; **2.** (das) Reisen • **travel agent** ['trævl‿ˌeɪdʒənt] Reisebürokaufmann/-kauffrau; *hier auch:* Reisebüro • °**travelcard** *Dauerkarte für den öffentlichen Nahverkehr*
tree [tri:] Baum
trend [trend] (Mode-)Trend
tribe [traɪb] (Volks-)Stamm
trick [trɪk]: **play a trick on sb.** jm. einen Streich spielen
trip (to) [trɪp] Ausflug, Reise (nach, zu) • **go on a trip** einen Ausflug/eine Reise machen
trouble ['trʌbl] Ärger, Schwierigkeiten • **be in trouble** in Schwierigkeiten sein; Ärger kriegen • **get sb. into trouble** jn. in Schwierigkeiten bringen • **trouble spot** ['trʌbl spɒt] *hier etwa:* Falle
trousers *(pl)* ['traʊzəz] (lange) Hose
true [tru:] wahr
try *(v; n)* [traɪ] **1.** versuchen, (aus)probieren • **try hard** sich sehr bemühen, sich anstrengen • **try on** anprobieren *(Kleidung)* • °**try sth. on sb.** etwas an jm. ausprobieren • **try to do sth./try and do sth.** versuchen, etwas zu tun °**2.** „Versuch" *(beim Rugby erzieltes Tor)*
T-shirt ['ti:ʃɜ:t] T-Shirt
tube [tju:b]: **the tube** *(no pl) (infml)* die U-Bahn *(in London) (eigentlich:* Rohr, Röhre)
Tuesday ['tju:zdeɪ, -di] Dienstag
°**tune** [tju:n] Melodie
tunnel ['tʌnl] Tunnel
Turkish ['tɜ:kɪʃ] türkisch
turn *(v; n)* [tɜ:n]: **1.** drehen **turn (around)** sich umdrehen • **turn right/left (into)** (nach) rechts/links abbiegen (in) • **turn (a vehicle)** (ein Fahrzeug) wenden • **turn to sb.** sich jm. zuwenden; sich an jn. wenden **2. turn on/off** ein-/ausschalten *(Licht, Gerät)* • **turn up/down** *(Radio usw.)* lauter/leiser stellen; *(Heizung usw.)* aufdrehen/niedriger stellen **3. It's my turn (to write/...)** Ich bin an der Reihe (zu schreiben/...)
TV [ˌti:'vi:] Fernsehgerät; Fernsehen • **on TV** im Fernsehen **watch TV** fernsehen
°**twice** [twaɪs] zweimal
twins [twɪnz] Zwillinge
type (of) [taɪp] Art, Sorte, Typ

U

umbrella [ʌm'brelə] Regenschirm
UN [ˌju:‿'en] **(United Nations)** [juˌnaɪtɪd 'neɪʃnz] UN (Vereinte Nationen)
uncle ['ʌŋkl] Onkel
under ['ʌndə] unter
underground ['ʌndəgraʊnd]: **the underground** *(no pl)* die U-Bahn
°**underline** [ˌʌndə'laɪn] unterstreichen • °**underlined** [ˌʌndə'laɪnd] unterstrichen
understand* [ˌʌndə'stænd] verstehen, begreifen
understood [ˌʌndə'stʊd] **1.** *si. past von „understand"*; **2.** *Part. Perf. von „understand"*
unfortunately [ʌn'fɔ:tʃnətli] leider, unglücklicherweise
unfriendly [ˌʌn'frendli] unfreundlich
unhappy (about) [ʌn'hæpi] unglücklich, traurig (über/wegen)
unhealthy [ʌn'helθi] ungesund
uniform ['ju:nɪfɔ:m] Uniform
unimportant [ˌʌnɪm'pɔ:tnt] unwichtig
unit ['ju:nɪt] Kapitel, Lektion
United Nations [juˌnaɪtɪd 'neɪʃnz] **(UN)** [ˌju:‿'en] Vereinte Nationen (UN)
university [ˌju:nɪ'vɜ:səti] Universität, Hochschule
unless [ən'les] wenn ... nicht, außer wenn, sofern ... nicht
unload [ˌʌn'ləʊd] ausladen, abladen
unlucky [ʌn'lʌki] unglückselig, Unglücks-
unpack [ˌʌn'pæk] auspacken
untidy [ˌʌn'taɪdi] unordentlich, unaufgeräumt
until [ən'tɪl] bis • **not ... until** erst (um)
unusual [ʌn'ju:ʒuəl] ungewöhnlich, außergewöhnlich
up [ʌp] hinauf, herauf, nach oben • **up north** oben im Norden • **up the tree** den Baum hinauf • **up there** dort oben (hin), da oben (hin) **be up** auf(gestanden) sein
upset (about) [ˌʌp'set] aufgebracht, aufgeregt; betrübt (wegen)
upstairs [ˌʌp'steəz] nach oben; oben
°**Urdu** ['ʊədu:] Urdu *(in Pakistan u. Indien gesprochene Sprache)*
us [əs, *betont:* ʌs] uns
use [ju:z] gebrauchen, verwenden, benutzen • **user** Benutzer/in, Anwender/in
useful ['ju:sfəl] nützlich
useless ['ju:sləs] nutzlos, zu nichts nütze

usual ['ju:ʒuəl] gewöhnlich, üblich • **usually** ['ju:ʒuəli] meistens, gewöhnlich, normalerweise

V

valley ['væli] Tal
valuable ['væljuəbl] wertvoll
van [væn] Lieferwagen
°**vandalism** ['vændəlɪzəm] Wandalismus
°**variety** [və'raɪəti] Vielfalt
vegetable ['vedʒtəbl] *(ein)* Gemüse
vegetarian [,vedʒə'teəriən] Vegetarier, Vegetarierin
vehicle ['vi:əkl] Fahrzeug
°**verse** [vɜ:s] Vers
very ['veri] sehr • **very funny** sehr witzig, sehr komisch
video ['vɪdiəʊ] Video • **video recorder** ['vɪdiəʊ rɪ,kɔ:də] Videorecorder
°**Vikings** ['vaɪkɪŋz]: **the Vikings** die Wikinger
villa ['vɪlə] Landhaus; Ferienhaus
village ['vɪlɪdʒ] Dorf
violent ['vaɪələnt] gewalttätig, gewaltsam
°**virus** ['vaɪrəs] Virus
visit *(v; n)* ['vɪzɪt] **1.** besuchen; besichtigen • **visitor** ['vɪzɪtə] Besucher/in, Gast
2. Besuch
vocabulary [və'kæbjələri] **1.** Vokabelverzeichnis, Wörterverzeichnis; **2.** Wortschatz, Vokabular
voice [vɔɪs] Stimme • °**disguised voice** [dɪs,gaɪzd 'vɔɪs] verstellte Stimme
volleyball ['vɒlibɔ:l] Volleyball
volume ['vɒlju:m] Lautstärke
volunteer [,vɒlən'tɪə] Freiwillige(r)
°**vote** [vəʊt] wählen

W

wait (for) ['weɪt fɔ:] warten (auf)
waiter ['weɪtə] Kellner
waitress ['weɪtrəs] Kellnerin
wake up* [,weɪk_'ʌp] aufwachen • **wake sb. (up)** jn. (auf)wecken
walk *(v; n)* [wɔ:k] **1.** (zu Fuß) gehen, laufen; spazieren gehen • °**walk about** herumlaufen • **walk on** weitergehen • **go walking** wandern
2. Spaziergang • **go for a walk** einen Spaziergang machen
walkie-talkie [,wɔ:ki 'tɔ:ki] Walkie-Talkie *(tragbares Funksprechgerät)*
walkman ['wɔ:kmən] Walkman
wall [wɔ:l] Wand; Mauer • **on the wall** an der Wand • °**wall display** ['wɔ:l dɪ,spleɪ] Wandzeitung, Wandbild
°**wallpaper** ['wɔ:lpeɪpə] Tapete
want [wɒnt] (haben) wollen
I want to go. Ich will/möchte gehen.
warm [wɔ:m] warm
was [wəz, *betont:* wɒz]: **(I/he/she/it) was** *si. past von „be"*
wash [wɒʃ] waschen • **wash the dishes** das Geschirr abwaschen
washing-machine ['wɒʃɪŋ mə,ʃi:n] Waschmaschine
wasp [wɒsp] Wespe
watch *(n; v)* [wɒtʃ] **1.** Armbanduhr; **2.** beobachten, sich *etwas* ansehen; zuschauen
watch out aufpassen
watch TV fernsehen
water ['wɔ:tə] Wasser
wave [weɪv] Welle • °**wavy lines** [,weɪvi 'laɪnz] Wellenlinien, Schlangenlinien
wax [wæks] Wachs
way [weɪ] **1.** Weg • **tell sb. the way (to)** jm. den Weg (zu/nach ...) beschreiben
Can you tell me the way to ...? Können Sie mir sagen, wie ich zu/nach ... komme?
on my way (to) auf dem Weg, unterwegs (nach/zu)
go a long way viel erreichen, viel bewirken • **by the way** übrigens, nebenbei (bemerkt)
2. Richtung • **this way** hier entlang • **the wrong way** in die falsche Richtung • **the wrong way round** verkehrt herum
3. Art und Weise • **in an intelligent way** auf intelligente Weise • **this way** so, auf diese Weise • °**in different ways** auf verschiedene Weise(n)
we [wi, *betont:* wi:] wir
wear* [weə] tragen, anhaben *(Kleidung)*
weather ['weðə] Wetter • **in bad weather** bei schlechtem Wetter
°**web site** ['web saɪt] *alle Seiten eines Anbieters im World Wide Web*
Wednesday ['wenzdeɪ, 'wenzdi] Mittwoch
week [wi:k] Woche • **next week** nächste Woche, in der nächsten Woche • **for weeks** wochenlang • **day of the week** Wochentag • **a six-week trip** eine sechswöchige Reise
weekend [,wi:k'end] Wochenende • **at the weekend** am Wochenende • **at weekends** an Wochenenden • **Have a nice weekend.** Schönes Wochenende.
welcome ['welkəm] **1.** willkommen • **Welcome to ...** Willkommen in ...
2. *(v)* **welcome sb. (to)** jn. willkommen heißen (in)
3. *(n)* **get a friendly welcome** freundlich empfangen werden
give sb. a friendly welcome jn. freundlich empfangen
well [wel] **1.** *(adj)* gesund, wohlauf; **2.** *(adv)* gut • **Well, ...** Nun, ...; Also, ... • **do well (in)** gut sein (in), gut abschneiden (in) • **You're doing well.** Du machst es gut.
Welsh [welʃ] Walisisch
went [went] *si. past von „go"*
were [wə, *betont:* wɜ:]: **(we/you/they) were** *si. past von „be"*
west [west] westlich; (nach) Westen • **westbound** ['westbaʊnd] Richtung Westen
wet (-tt-) [wet] nass, feucht
what [wɒt] **1.** was; **2.** welche, welcher, welches • **what a ...** was für ein(e) ... • **Now what?** Was nun? • **What about a calendar?** Wie wär's mit einem Kalender? • **What about Jenny?** Was ist mit Jenny? / Und Jenny? • **What are they talking about?** Worüber reden sie? • °**What's cooking?** *(infml)* Was liegt an? / Was ist los? • **What colour is it?** Welche Farbe hat es (er, sie)? • **What day is 1st January?** Was für ein Tag ist der 1. Januar? • **What do you call this?** Wie nennt man dies? • **What's ... like?** Wie ist ...? • **What kind of ...?** Was für ein/e ...? • **What size are you?** Welche Größe hast du/haben Sie? • **What time is it?** Wie spät ist es? • **What time is the film?** Wann fängt der Film an? • **What's the date?** Welches Datum haben wir? • **What's this in English?** Wie heißt das auf Englisch?
What's your name? Wie heißt du? / Wie heißen Sie?
whatever [wɒt'evə] was (auch) immer
wheel [wi:l] Rad
wheelchair ['wi:ltʃeə] Rollstuhl
when [wen] **1.** wann • **When is it?** Wann fängt es an?
When's your birthday? Wann hast du Geburtstag?
2. wenn; **3.** als
whenever [wen'evə] wann (auch) immer
where [weə] wo; wohin
Where are you from? Wo kommst du her?

wherever [weər'evə] wohin (auch) immer; wo (auch) immer
which … [wɪtʃ] 1. welche(r, s) … **which one(s)** welche(r, s); welche
2. der/die/das, die *(Relativpronomen)*
while *(conj)* [waɪl] während
whisper ['wɪspə] flüstern
whistle ['wɪsl] pfeifen
white [waɪt] weiß
who [hu:] 1. wer; 2. wen; wem; 3. der/die/das, die *(Relativpronomen)*
whoever [hu:'evə] wer (auch) immer, wen/wem (auch) immer
whole [həʊl] ganze(r, s), gesamte(r, s)
whose [hu:z] 1. wessen **Whose are these (CDs)?** Wem gehören die (CDs) hier? 2. deren, dessen *(Relativpronomen)*
why [waɪ] warum • **that's why** deshalb, darum
wife [waɪf], *pl* **wives** [waɪvz] Ehefrau
wild [waɪld] wild
will [wɪl]: **The world will be fantastic.** Die Welt wird fantastisch sein. • **You won't find many.** [wəʊnt] (= **You will not find many.**) Du wirst nicht viele finden.
win* *(v; n)* [wɪn] 1. **(-nn-)** gewinnen • **winner** Gewinner/in, Sieger/in 2. Sieg
wind [wɪnd] Wind • **windy** ['wɪndi] windig
window ['wɪndəʊ] Fenster
windsurfing ['wɪndsɜ:fɪŋ] *(das)* Windsurfen
°**wine** [waɪn] Wein
winter ['wɪntə] Winter
wish *(v; n)* [wɪʃ] 1. wünschen; 2. Wunsch
with [wɪð] mit (… zusammen), bei
without [wɪ'ðaʊt] ohne
witness ['wɪtnəs] Zeuge, Zeugin
wives [waɪvz] *pl von „wife"*
woke (up) [wəʊk] *si. past von „wake (up)"*
woken (up) ['wəʊkən] *Part. Perf. von „wake (up)"*
woman ['wʊmən], *pl* **women** ['wɪmɪn] Frau
won [wʌn] 1. *si. past von „win";* 2. *Part. Perf. von „win"*
wonder ['wʌndə] sich fragen, gern wissen wollen
wonderful ['wʌndəfəl] wunderbar
won't [wəʊnt]: **You won't (= will not) find many.** Du wirst nicht viele finden.

wood [wʊd] Holz
°**woodwind** ['wʊdwɪnd] Holzblasinstrument; Holzbläser
word [wɜ:d] Wort • °**word building** *etwa:* das „Bauen"/ Bilden von Wörtern • **word group** Wortgruppe • **word link** Wortverbindung °**word order** Wortstellung
wore [wɔ:] *si. past von „wear"*
work *(v; n)* [wɜ:k] 1. arbeiten **work on sth.** an etwas arbeiten • °**work sth. out** etwas ausarbeiten, etwas herausfinden • **worker** Arbeiter/in 2. funktionieren; 3. Arbeit **at work** bei der Arbeit, am Arbeitsplatz • **out of work** arbeitslos
world [wɜ:ld] Welt • **in the world** auf der Welt • **World Cup** [ˌwɜ:ld 'kʌp] Weltmeisterschaft
worn [wɔ:n] *Part. Perf. von „wear"*
worried (about) ['wʌrid] beunruhigt (wegen), besorgt (wegen/um)
worry *(n; v)* ['wʌri] 1. Sorge, Kummer; 2. **worry (about)** sich Sorgen machen (wegen, um) • **worry sb.** jn. beunruhigen, jm. Sorgen machen
worse [wɜ:s] schlechter, schlimmer
worst [wɜ:st]: **(the) worst** (der/die/das) schlechteste, schlimmste …; am schlechtesten, schlimmsten
would [wəd, *betont:* wʊd] würde, würdest, würden • **I'd (= I would) fly to …** Ich würde nach … fliegen. • **What would you like to do?** Was würdest/möchtest du gern machen? • **I'd like** Ich hätte gern / Ich möchte gern • **I'd like to go.** Ich würde gern/ möchte gehen.
wound [wu:nd] Wunde
write* (to) [raɪt] schreiben (an) **write down** aufschreiben, notieren • **writer** Schreiber/in, Schriftsteller/in **writing** Geschriebenes; (Hand-)Schrift
written ['rɪtn] *Part. Perf. von „write"*
wrong [rɒŋ] falsch • **What's wrong?** Was ist los? • **the wrong way** in die falsche Richtung • **the wrong way round** verkehrt herum • **be wrong** 1. sich irren, Unrecht haben; 2. nicht in Ordnung sein, nicht stimmen • **get sth. wrong** etwas falsch machen
wrote [rəʊt] *si. past von „write"*

Y

yawn [jɔ:n] gähnen
year [jɪə] Jahr; Jahrgangsstufe **a year and a half** eineinhalb Jahre, anderthalb Jahre • **16-year-old** 16-Jährige(r, s)
yellow ['jeləʊ] gelb
yes [jes] ja
yesterday ['jestədeɪ, -di] gestern
yet [jet]: **… yet?** … schon …? **not (…) yet** noch nicht
you [ju, *betont:* ju:] 1. du; ihr; Sie; 2. dich/dir; euch/euch; Sie/Ihnen; 3. man • **you know** weißt du; nämlich **You say** Du sagst / Man sagt **you see** weißt du, nämlich **How are you?** Wie geht es dir? / Wie geht es euch? / Wie geht es Ihnen? • **Thank you.** Danke (schön).
young [jʌŋ] jung
your [jɔ:] dein/deine; euer/ eure; Ihr/Ihre
yours [jɔ:z] deine(r, s); eure(r, s); Ihre(r, s)
Yours [jɔ:z] dein/deine; euer/ eure; Ihr/Ihre *(Briefschluss)* **Yours faithfully** ['feɪθfəli] Mit freundlichen Grüßen / Hochachtungsvoll • **Yours sincerely,** [sɪn'sɪəli] Mit freundlichen/herzlichen Grüßen
yourself [jə'self, *betont:* jɔ:'self] dir/dich (selbst); selbst, selber
yourselves [jə'selvz, *betont:* jɔ:'selvz] euch (selbst); selbst, selber
youth hostel ['ju:θ hɒstl] Jugendherberge
Yuck! [jʌk] Igitt! / Bäh!

Z

zebra ['zebrə] Zebra
zero ['zɪərəʊ] null
zoo [zu:] Zoo, Tierpark

LIST OF NAMES

Girls / Women

Angela ['ændʒələ]
Catherine ['kæθrɪn]
Chrissie ['krɪsi]
Diana [daɪ'ænə]
Donna ['dɒnə]
Emma ['emə]
Gloria ['glɔ:riə]
Gwen [gwen]
Jan [dʒæn]
Kate [keɪt]
Kathryn ['kæθrɪn]
Kim [kɪm]
Layla ['leɪlə]
Lorna ['lɔ:nə]
Maggie ['mægi]
Mandy ['mændi]
Marie [mə'ri:]
Marinetta [,mærɪ'netə]
Meena ['mi:nə]
Megan ['megən]
Melissa [mə'lɪsə]
Milly ['mɪli]
Moira ['mɔɪrə]
Nazreen [næz'ri:n]
Selima [sə'li:mə]
Shaila ['ʃaɪlə]
Sheena ['ʃi:nə]
Trisha ['trɪʃə]
Yasmin ['jæsmɪn]
Zahida [zæ'hi:də]

Boys / Men

Aled ['æled]
Ali ['æli]
Andrew ['ændru:]
Barry ['bæri]
Bert [bɜ:t]
Clive [klaɪv]
Eddie ['edi]
George [dʒɔ:dʒ]
Gerry ['dʒeri]
Jack [dʒæk]
Jason ['dʒeɪsn]
Leroy ['li:rɔɪ]
Nathan ['neɪθən]
Oliver ['ɒlɪvə]
Patrick ['pætrɪk]
Rob [rɒb]
Steve [sti:v]
Thomas ['tɒməs]
Winston ['wɪnstən]

Family names

Addison ['ædɪsən]
Ahram ['æxræm]
Alsford ['ɔ:lsfəd]
Anwar ['ænwɑ:]
Barnes [bɑ:nz]
Bates [beɪts]
Berwick ['berɪk]
Bhutto ['bʊtəʊ]
Clarke [klɑ:k]
Croaker ['krəʊkə]
Ellis ['elɪs]
Evans ['evnz]
Freeman ['fri:mən]
Gladstone ['glædstən]
Grant [grɑ:nt]
Hanson ['hænsn]
Harold ['hærəld]
Johnson ['dʒɒnsn]
Jones [dʒəʊnz]
Jordan ['dʒɔ:dən]
Khan [kɑ:n]
Kumar [ku:'mɑ:]
Logan ['ləʊgən]
Maceba [mæ'si:bə]
Masters ['mɑ:stəz]
McGough [mə'gɒf]
McGregor [mə'gregə]
McKenna [mə'kenə]
McPherson [mək'fɜ:sn]
Mir [mɪə]
Mitchell ['mɪtʃəl]
O'Hear [əʊ'hɪə]
Owen ['əʊɪn]
Patel [pə'tel]
Picken ['pɪkən]
Porter ['pɔ:tə]
Rice [raɪs]
Roberts ['rɒbəts]
Rosser ['rɒsə]
Stewart ['stju:ət]
Wells [welz]
Willis ['wɪlɪs]

Place names

Aberdeen [,æbə'di:n]
Adelaide Road [,ædəleɪd 'rəʊd]
Ankara ['æŋkərə]
Anson Road [,ænsn 'rəʊd]
Arran ['ærən]
Augustan Way [ɔ:,gʌstn 'weɪ]
Aviemore ['ævimɔ:]
Baker Street ['beɪkə stri:t]
Bangor ['bæŋgə]
Bass Rock High School [,bæs rɒk 'haɪ sku:l]
Bayswater ['beɪzwɔ:tə]
Birmingham ['bɜ:mɪŋəm]
Bradford ['brædfəd]
Braemar [,breɪ'mɑ:]
Brecon Beacons National Park [,brekən 'bi:kənz ,næʃnəl 'pɑ:k]
Britannia [brɪ'tæniə]
Burghley Road [,bɜ:li 'rəʊd]
Caernarfon [kə'nɑ:vn]
Camden ['kæmdən]
Cardigan ['kɑ:dɪgn]
the Caribbean [,kærə'bi:ən]
Carlisle [kɑ:'laɪl]
Chalk Farm [,tʃɔ:k 'fɑ:m]
Charing Cross [,tʃærɪŋ 'krɒs]
Chiltern Edge School [,tʃɪltən_edʒ 'sku:l]
Cilcain [kɪl'keɪn]
Culloden [kə'lɒdn]
Danelaw ['deɪnlɔ:]
Delhi ['deli]
Denbigh ['denbi]
Deva ['deɪvə]
Dover ['dəʊvə]
Downing Street ['daʊnɪŋ stri:t]
Dubris ['du:brɪs]
Eburacum [,i:bə'rɑ:kəm]
Euston Station [,ju:stən 'steɪʃn]
Gerrard Street ['dʒerɑ:d stri:t]
Graceland ['greɪslænd]
Hawaii [hə'waɪi:]
Inverness [,ɪnvə'nes]
Isle of Skye [,aɪl_əv 'skaɪ]
Jorvik ['jɔ:vɪk]
Kentucky [ken'tʌki]
Leicester Square [,lestə 'skweə]
Letocetum [,li:təʊ'si:təm]
Lister Park [,lɪstə 'pɑ:k]
Londinium [lɒn'dɪniəm]
Luguvalium [,lʊgʊ'væliəm]
Mamucium [mæ'mu:kiəm]
Manningham ['mænɪŋəm]
Louisville ['lu:ɪvɪl]
Paddington Station [,pædɪŋtən 'steɪʃn]
Peterpool ['pi:təpu:l]
Portsmouth ['pɔ:tsməθ]
Queensway ['kwi:nzweɪ]
Richborough ['rɪtʃbərə]
Snowdonia [snəʊ'dəʊniə]
St. Asaph [snt_'æsəf]
Thames [temz]
Tufnell Park School [,tʌfnl ,pɑ:k 'sku:l]
Westminster Pier [,westmɪnstə 'pɪə]
Wimbledon ['wɪmbldən]
Wolverhampton [,wʊlvə'hæmptən]

Other names

Agnes Syme Lister [,ægnəs saɪm 'lɪstə]
Alexander Fleming [ælɪg,zɑ:ndə 'flemɪŋ]
Alexander Graham Bell [ælɪg,zɑ:ndə ,greɪəm 'bel]
Anne Boleyn [,æn bə'lɪn]
Aquae Sulis [,ækwaɪ 'su:lɪs]
Bakerloo Line [,beɪkə'lu: laɪn]
Battle of Hastings [,bætl_əv 'heɪstɪŋz]
Baywatch ['beɪwɒtʃ]
BBC [,bi: bi: 'si:], British Broadcasting Corporation [,brɪtɪʃ 'brɔ:dkɑ:stɪŋ kɔ:pə,reɪʃn]
Betty Burke [,beti 'bɜ:k]
Birdoswald Fort [,bɜ:dəzwɔ:ld 'fɔ:t]
Bonnie Prince Charlie [,bɒni prɪns 'tʃɑ:li]
Caesar ['si:zə]
Cassita [kæ'si:tə]
Charlie Chaplin [,tʃɑ:li 'tʃæplɪn]
Christopher Columbus [,krɪstəfə kə'lʌmbəs]
Circle Line ['sɜ:kl laɪn]
Classis Britannica [,klæsɪs brɪ'tænɪkə]
Corinium Museum [kə,rɪniəm mju:'zi:əm]
Daedalus ['di:dələs]
Domesday Book ['du:mzdeɪ ,bʊk]
Flora Macdonald [,flɔ:rə mək'dɒnəld]
Gaius ['gaɪəs]
Gallus ['gæləs]
Hadrian's Wall [,heɪdrɪənz 'wɔ:l]
Henry VIII [,henri ði_'eɪtθ]
Hogmanay ['hɒgməneɪ]
Housesteads Fort [,haʊstedz 'fɔ:t]
James Greenlee [,dʒeɪmz 'gri:nli:]
James Syme [,dʒeɪmz 'saɪm]
James Thomson [,dʒeɪmz 'tɒmsən]
John Logie Baird [,dʒɒn ,ləʊgi 'beəd]
Joseph Lister [,dʒəʊzef 'lɪstə]
Jubilee Line ['dʒu:bɪli: laɪn]
Jupiter ['dʒu:pɪtə]
Juvena [dʒu:'vi:nə]
King Arthur [,kɪŋ_'ɑ:θə]
Lavinia [lə'vɪniə]
Lucius ['lu:siəs]
Madog ['mædɒg]
Marcus Flavius [,mɑ:kəs 'fleɪviəs]
Marie Tussaud [mə,ri: 'tu:səʊ]
Maximus ['mæksɪməs]
Meera Syal [,mɪərə saɪ'ɑ:l]
Mela ['meɪlə]
Metropolitan Line [,metrə'pɒlɪtn laɪn]
Nipius Ascanius [,nɪpiəs_æ'skeɪniəs]
Otho ['ɒθəʊ]
Prince Charles [,prɪns 'tʃɑ:lz]
Professor Brainstawm [prə,fesə 'breɪnstɔ:m]
Quintus Lavinius Timidus [,kwɪntəs lə,vɪniəs 'tɪmɪdəs]
Rautio ['rɔ:tiəʊ]
Scoobidoo [,sku:bi'du:]
Selgovae ['selgəvaɪ]
Serena [sə'ri:nə]
Sherlock Holmes [,ʃɜ:lɒk 'həʊmz]
Sir Christopher Wren [sə ,krɪstəfə 'ren]
Sir Robert Watson-Watt [sə ,rɒbət 'wɒtsn 'wɒt]
St. Mary in Castro [snt ,meəri_ɪn 'kæstrəʊ]
Stephen King [,sti:vn 'kɪŋ]
Techniquest Museum [,teknɪkwest mju:'zi:əm]
Ursus ['ɜ:səs]
Usk [ʌsk]
Victoria Line [vɪk'tɔ:riə laɪn]
Waterloo and City Line [,wɔ:təlu:_ənd 'sɪti laɪn]
William Shakespeare [,wɪljəm 'ʃeɪkspɪə]

COUNTRIES AND CONTINENTS (Länder und Kontinente)

Country/Continent	Person	People	Adjective
Africa ['æfrɪkə] *Afrika*	an African ['æfrɪkən]	the Africans	African
Albania [æl'beɪniə] *Albanien*	an Albanian [æl'beɪniən]	the Albanians	Albanian
America [ə'merɪkə] *Amerika*	an American [ə'merɪkən]	the Americans	American
Asia ['eɪʃə, 'eɪʒə] *Asien*	an Asian ['eɪʒn, 'eɪʃn]	the Asians	Asian
Australia [ɒ'streɪliə] *Australien*	an Australian [ɒ'streɪliən]	the Australians	Australian
Austria ['ɒstriə] *Österreich*	an Austrian ['ɒstriən]	the Austrians	Austrian
Bangladesh [,bæŋglə'deʃ] *Bangladesch*	a Bangladeshi [,bæŋglə'deʃi]	the Bangladeshis	Bangladeshi
Belgium ['beldʒəm] *Belgien*	a Belgian ['beldʒən]	the Belgians	Belgian
Bosnia-Herzegovina [,bɒzniə ,hɜ:tsəgə'vi:nə] *Bosnien-Herzegowina*	a Bosnian ['bɒzniən]	the Bosnians	Bosnian
Bulgaria [bʌl'geəriə] *Bulgarien*	a Bulgarian [bʌl'geəriən]	the Bulgarians	Bulgarian
(Great) Britain ['brɪtn] *Großbritannien*	a Briton ['brɪtn]	the British ['brɪtɪʃ]	British
China ['tʃaɪnə] *China*	a Chinese [,tʃaɪ'ni:z]	the Chinese	Chinese
Croatia [krəʊ'eɪʃə] *Kroatien*	a Croatian [krəʊ'eɪʃən]	the Croatians	Croatian
the **Czech Republic** [,tʃek rɪ'pʌblɪk] *Tschechien, die Tschechische Republik*	a Czech [tʃek]	the Czechs	Czech
Denmark ['denmɑ:k] *Dänemark*	a Dane [deɪn]	the Danes	Danish ['deɪnɪʃ]
England ['ɪŋglənd] *England*	an Englishman/-woman	the English ['ɪŋglɪʃ]	English
Estonia [es'təʊniə] *Estland*	an Estonian [es'təʊniən]	the Estonians	Estonian
Europe ['jʊərəp] *Europa*	a European [,jʊərə'pi:ən]	the Europeans	European
Finland ['fɪnlənd] *Finnland*	a Finn [fɪn]	the Finns	Finnish ['fɪnɪʃ]
France [frɑ:ns] *Frankreich*	a Frenchman/-woman	the French [frentʃ]	French
Germany ['dʒɜ:məni] *Deutschland*	a German ['dʒɜ:mən]	the Germans	German
Greece [gri:s] *Griechenland*	a Greek [gri:k]	the Greeks	Greek
Hungary ['hʌŋgəri] *Ungarn*	a Hungarian [hʌŋ'geəriən]	the Hungarians	Hungarian
India ['ɪndiə] *Indien*	an Indian ['ɪndiən]	the Indians	Indian
Ireland ['aɪələnd] *Irland*	an Irishman/-woman	the Irish ['aɪrɪʃ]	Irish
Italy ['ɪtəli] *Italien*	an Italian [ɪ'tæliən]	the Italians	Italian
Jamaica [dʒə'meɪkə] *Jamaika*	a Jamaican [dʒə'meɪkən]	the Jamaicans	Jamaican
Japan [dʒə'pæn] *Japan*	a Japanese [,dʒæpə'ni:z]	the Japanese	Japanese
Latvia ['lætviə] *Lettland*	a Latvian ['lætviən]	the Latvians	Latvian
Lithuania [,lɪθju'eɪniə] *Litauen*	a Lithuanian [,lɪθju'eɪniən]	the Lithuanians	Lithuanian
the **Netherlands** ['neðələndz] *die Niederlande, Holland*	a Dutchman/-woman	the Dutch [dʌtʃ]	Dutch
Norway ['nɔ:weɪ] *Norwegen*	a Norwegian [nɔ:'wi:dʒən]	the Norwegians	Norwegian
Pakistan [,pɑ:kɪ'stɑ:n] *Pakistan*	a Pakistani [,pɑ:kɪ'stɑ:ni]	the Pakistanis	Pakistani
Poland ['pəʊlənd] *Polen*	a Pole [pəʊl]	the Poles	Polish ['pəʊlɪʃ]
Portugal ['pɔ:tʃʊgl] *Portugal*	a Portuguese [,pɔ:tʃu'gi:z]	the Portuguese	Portuguese
Romania [ru'meɪniə] *Rumänien*	a Romanian [ru'meɪniən]	the Romanians	Romanian
Russia ['rʌʃə] *Russland*	a Russian ['rʌʃn]	the Russians	Russian
Scotland ['skɒtlənd] *Schottland*	a Scotsman/-woman, a Scot [skɒt]	the Scots, the Scottish	Scottish ['skɒtɪʃ]
Slovakia [sləʊ'vɑ:kiə, sləʊ'vækiə] *die Slowakei*	a Slovak ['sləʊvæk]	the Slovaks	Slovak
Slovenia [sləʊ'vi:niə] *Slowenien*	a Slovene ['sləʊvi:n], a Slovenian [sləʊ'vi:niən]	the Slovenes, the Slovenians	Slovenian, Slovene
Spain [speɪn] *Spanien*	a Spaniard ['spænɪəd]	the Spaniards	Spanish ['spænɪʃ]
Sweden ['swi:dn] *Schweden*	a Swede [swi:d]	the Swedes	Swedish ['swi:dɪʃ]
Switzerland ['swɪtsələnd] *die Schweiz*	a Swiss [swɪs]	the Swiss	Swiss
Turkey ['tɜ:ki] *die Türkei*	a Turk [tɜ:k]	the Turks	Turkish ['tɜ:kɪʃ]
the **United Kingdom** (the UK) [ju,naɪtɪd 'kɪŋdəm, ju:'keɪ] *das Vereinigte Königreich (Großbritannien und Nordirland)*	a Briton ['brɪtn]	the British ['brɪtɪʃ]	British
the **United States of America** **(the USA)** [ju,naɪtɪd ,steɪts‿əv‿ə'merɪkə, ju:‿es‿'eɪ] *die Vereinigten Staaten von Amerika*	an American [ə'merɪkən]	the Americans	American
Wales [weɪlz] *Wales*	a Welshman/-woman	the Welsh [welʃ]	Welsh
Yugoslavia [,ju:gəʊ'slɑ:viə] *Jugoslawien*	a Yugoslav ['ju:gəʊslɑ:v]	the Yugoslavs	Yugoslavian [ju:gəʊ'slɑ:viən]

GRAMMATICAL TERMS (Grammatische Fachbegriffe)

			Summary-Abschnitt
active ['æktɪv]	Aktiv	*The police **caught** the thief.*	**U4**: 1
adjective ['ædʒɪktɪv]	Adjektiv	*good, new, red, funny, boring*	
adverb ['ædvɜːb]	Adverb	*always, badly, here, really, today*	
adverb of frequency ['friːkwənsi]	Häufigkeitsadverb	*always, usually, often, sometimes, never*	
adverb of indefinite time [ɪnˌdefɪnət 'taɪm]	Adverb der unbestimmten Zeit	*already, always, before, ever, just, never, often, yet, not … yet*	
adverb of manner ['mænə]	Adverb der Art und Weise	*badly, nicely, happily, terribly, electronically, fast, hard, well*	
article ['ɑːtɪkl]	Artikel	*the, a/an*	
auxiliary [ɔːg'zɪliəri]	Hilfsverb		
comparative [kəm'pærətɪv]	Komparativ, erste Steigerungsform	*taller; more boring; more easily*	**U5**: 4
comparison [kəm'pærɪsn]	Steigerung; Vergleich	*tall – taller – tallest; boring – more boring – most boring* *easily – more easily – most easily*	**U5**: 4
conditional sentence [kənˌdɪʃənl 'sentəns]	Bedingungssatz	*If it rains, we won't see the mountains.*	**U2**: 2
conjunction [kən'dʒʌŋkʃn]	Konjunktion	*Let's play **when** you come home.* *Wash your hands **before** we eat.*	
contact clause ['kɒntækt klɔːz]	Relativsatz ohne Relativpronomen	*That's the man **we met** last week.* *The bike **I got** is great.*	**U3**
countable noun [ˌkaʊntəbl 'naʊn]	zählbares Nomen	*girl – girls, ruler – rulers*	**U4**: 2
defining relative clause [dɪˌfaɪnɪŋ ˌrelətɪv 'klɔːz]	bestimmender Relativsatz, notwendiger Relativsatz	*That's the girl **who helped me**.* *They invented a telephone **that really worked**.*	**U3**
definite article [ˌdefɪnət‿'ɑːtɪkl]	bestimmter Artikel	*the*	
emphasizing pronoun [ˌemfəsaɪzɪŋ 'prəʊnaʊn]	verstärkendes Pronomen	*I did it **myself**.*	**U5**: 2
future ['fjuːtʃə]	Futur, Zukunft		**U7**
gerund ['dʒerənd]	Gerundium (wie ein Nomen gebrauchte *-ing*-Form des Verbs)	*I like **dancing**. **Dancing** is fun.*	**U6**: 2
***going to*-future**	Futur mit *going to*	*I'**m going to watch** TV tonight.* *Look at the clouds. It'**s going to rain**.*	**U1**: 1g/ **U7**: 1b/2a
***if*-clause** ['ɪf klɔːz]	Nebensatz mit „if", „if"-Satz	***If it rains**, we won't see the mountains.*	**U2**: 2
imperative [ɪm'perətɪv]	Imperativ (Befehlsform)	***Open** your books. **Don't talk**.*	
indefinite article [ɪnˌdefɪnət‿'ɑːtɪkl]	unbestimmter Artikel	*a/an*	
infinitive [ɪn'fɪnətɪv]	Infinitiv	*(to) open, (to) see, (to) hear*	**U5**: 3
irregular verb [ɪˌregjələ 'vɜːb]	unregelmäßiges Verb	*(to) go – went – gone*	
main clause [ˌmeɪn 'klɔːz]	Hauptsatz	*If it rains, **we won't see the mountains**.*	**U2**: 2/ **U6**: 1b
modal auxiliary [ˌməʊdl‿ɔːg'zɪliəri]	modales Hilfsverb, Modalverb	*can, could, may, must, needn't, should, would*	**U2**: 1/ **U4**: 1c
negative statement [ˌnegətɪv 'steɪtmənt]	verneinter Aussagesatz	*I'm not ten. I haven't got a sister. I don't like pop songs.*	
noun [naʊn]	Nomen, Substantiv	*Nick, Debbie, girl, brother, time*	
object ['ɒbdʒɪkt]	Objekt	*Sita is cleaning **the kitchen**.*	**U6**: 2d
object question	Objektfrage, Frage nach dem Objekt	*Who do they help? What did you eat?*	
passive ['pæsɪv]	Passiv	*The thief **was caught** (by the police).*	**U4**: 1
past [pɑːst]	Vergangenheit		
past participle [ˌpɑːst 'pɑːtɪsɪpl]	Partizip Perfekt	*climbed, saved, stopped, tidied, bought, fallen, gone, written*	**U4**: 1b/1c
past progressive [ˌpɑːst prə'gresɪv]	Verlaufsform der Vergangenheit	*I **was washing** my hair at 8 o'clock yesterday evening.*	**U1**: 1e
personal pronoun [ˌpɜːsənəl 'prəʊnaʊn]	Personalpronomen (persönliches Fürwort)	*I, you, he, she, it, we, they, me, him, her, us, them*	

			Summary-Abschnitt
plural ['plʊərəl]	Plural		
positive statement [ˌpɒzətɪv 'steɪtmənt]	bejahter Aussagesatz	*I'm ten. I've got a sister. I like pop songs.*	
possessive determiner [pəˌzesɪv dɪ'tɜːmɪnə]	Possessivbegleiter (besitzanzeigender Begleiter)	*my, your, his, her, its, our, their*	
possessive pronoun [pəˌzesɪv 'prəʊnaʊn]	Possessivpronomen	*mine, yours, his, hers, ours, theirs*	
prefix ['priːfɪks]	Vorsilbe, Präfix	*in-, un-*	
preposition [ˌprepə'zɪʃn]	Präposition	*after, at, in, next to, on, to, under*	**U6**: 2e / **U3**: e
present ['preznt]	Präsens, Gegenwart		
present perfect [ˌpreznt 'pɜːfɪkt]	*present perfect* (Perfekt)	*I've* ***packed*** *my bag.* ***Have*** *you* ***packed*** *yours? – Yes, I* ***have****.* *Liz* ***has known*** *Megan for years.*	**U1**: 1c / 2
present perfect progressive [ˌpreznt ˌpɜːfɪkt prə'gresɪv]	Verlaufsform des *present perfect*	*Liz* ***has been waiting*** *for one hour.*	**U1**: 3
present progressive [ˌpreznt prə'gresɪv]	Verlaufsform der Gegenwart	*Debbie* ***is reading*** *a book. Nick* ***isn't reading****. He's* ***playing****.* *I'****m leaving*** *England tomorrow.*	**U1**: 1b / **U5**: 5 / **U7**: 2b
pronoun ['prəʊnaʊn]	Pronomen		
prop-word ['prɒpwɜːd]	Stützwort	*I've got three dogs, a black* ***one*** *and two brown* ***ones****.*	
quantifier ['kwɒntɪfaɪə]	Mengenbezeichnung	*some, any; much, many, a little, a few*	**U4**: 2
question tag ['kwestʃən tæg]	Frageanhängsel	*Ann lives in Chester,* ***doesn't she?*** *But she isn't British,* ***is she?***	**U6**: 1
question word ['kwestʃən wɜːd]	Fragewort	*who?, what?, when?, where?, why?, how?*	**U5**: 3
reflexive pronoun [rɪˌfleksɪv 'prəʊnaʊn]	Reflexivpronomen	*myself, yourself, himself, herself, itself, ourselves, yourselves, themselves*	**U5**: 1
regular verb [ˌregjələ 'vɜːb]	regelmäßiges Verb	*(to) help – helped – helped*	
relative clause [ˌrelətɪv 'klɔːz]	Relativsatz	*That's the girl* ***who helped me****.* *They invented a telephone* ***that really worked****.*	**U3**
relative pronoun [ˌrelətɪv 'prəʊnaʊn]	Relativpronomen	*who, that, which, whose*	**U3**
***s*-genitive** ['es ˌdʒenətɪv]	*s*-Genitiv	*Sue****'s*** *brother; my sister****'s*** *name*	
simple past [ˌsɪmpl 'pɑːst]	einfache Form der Vergangenheit	*I* ***didn't go*** *to school yesterday. I* ***stayed*** *at home.* ***Did*** *you* ***go****?*	**U1**: 1d
simple present [ˌsɪmpl 'preznt]	einfache Form der Gegenwart	*I* ***start*** *school at 8.45 every day. When* ***do*** *you* ***start*** *school?* *The next train to Leeds* ***leaves*** *in 10 minutes.*	**U1**: 1a / **U7**: 2c
singular ['sɪŋgjələ]	Singular		
sub-clause ['sʌbklɔːz], **subordinate clause** [səˌbɔːdɪnət 'klɔːz]	Nebensatz	***If it rains****, we won't see the mountains.* *I can't come* ***because I'm ill****.*	**U1**: 4 / **U2**: 2
subject ['sʌbdʒɪkt]	Subjekt	***My dog*** *is black.* ***His name*** *is Tim.*	**U6**: 2c
subject question	Subjektfrage, Frage nach dem Subjekt	*Who helped you? What woke you up?*	
suffix ['sʌfɪks]	Nachsilbe, Suffix	*-er, -ion, -ly*	
superlative [suː'pɜːlətɪv]	Superlativ, höchste Steigerungsform	*tallest; most boring; most easily*	**U5**: 4
tense [tens]	(grammatische) Zeitform, Tempus		**U1**: 1
uncountable noun [ʌnˌkaʊntəbl 'naʊn]	nicht zählbares Nomen	*music, water, butter, money, homework, information*	**U4**: 2
verb [vɜːb]	Verb	*count, hear, open, rain, see*	
***will*-future**	Futur mit *will*	*I'****ll be*** *13 next week.* *I'm thirsty. – I'****ll get*** *you a drink.*	**U1**: 1f / **U7**: 1a / 3
word order ['wɜːd‿ɔːdə]	Wortstellung		
yes/no question	Entscheidungsfrage	*Are you eleven? Have you got a sister?*	

LIST OF IRREGULAR VERBS

Infinitive	Simple past	Past participle	
(to) **be**	**was/were**	**been**	sein
(to) **beat**	**beat**	**beaten**	schlagen; besiegen
(to) **become**	**became**	**become**	werden
(to) **begin**	**began**	**begun**	beginnen, anfangen (mit)
(to) **bet**	**bet**	**bet**	wetten
(to) **blow**	**blew**	**blown**	wehen, blasen
(to) **break** [eɪ]	**broke**	**broken**	(zer)brechen; kaputt gehen
(to) **bring**	**brought**	**brought**	(mit-, her-)bringen
(to) **build**	**built**	**built**	bauen
(to) **buy**	**bought**	**bought**	kaufen
(to) **catch**	**caught**	**caught**	fangen; erwischen
(to) **choose** [uː]	**chose** [əʊ]	**chosen** [əʊ]	(aus)wählen, aussuchen
(to) **come**	**came**	**come**	kommen
(to) **cost**	**cost**	**cost**	kosten
(to) **cut**	**cut**	**cut**	(aus)schneiden
(to) **dig**	**dug**	**dug**	(aus-, um)graben
(to) **do**	**did**	**done** [ʌ]	tun, machen
(to) **draw**	**drew**	**drawn**	zeichnen
(to) **drink**	**drank**	**drunk**	trinken
(to) **drive** [aɪ]	**drove**	**driven** [ɪ]	*(ein Auto, einen Bus usw.)* fahren
(to) **eat**	**ate** [et, eɪt]	**eaten**	essen
(to) **fall**	**fell**	**fallen**	(hin)fallen
(to) **feed**	**fed**	**fed**	füttern
(to) **feel**	**felt**	**felt**	fühlen; sich fühlen
(to) **fight**	**fought**	**fought**	(be)kämpfen
(to) **find**	**found**	**found**	finden
(to) **fly**	**flew**	**flown**	fliegen
(to) **forget**	**forgot**	**forgotten**	vergessen
(to) **get**	**got**	**got**	bekommen; holen, besorgen; gelangen, hinkommen; werden
(to) **give**	**gave**	**given**	geben
(to) **go**	**went**	**gone** [ɒ]	gehen; fahren
(to) **grow**	**grew**	**grown**	wachsen
(to) **have (have got)**	**had**	**had**	haben
(to) **hear** [ɪə]	**heard** [ɜː]	**heard** [ɜː]	hören
(to) **hide**	**hid**	**hidden**	(sich) verstecken
(to) **hit**	**hit**	**hit**	schlagen, treffen
(to) **hold**	**held**	**held**	(fest)halten; veranstalten, abhalten
(to) **hurt**	**hurt**	**hurt**	verletzen, wehtun
(to) **keep**	**kept**	**kept**	(be)halten; aufbewahren, aufheben
(to) **know** [nəʊ]	**knew** [njuː]	**known** [nəʊn]	wissen; kennen
(to) **lead**	**led**	**led**	führen, leiten
(to) **leave**	**left**	**left**	(zurück)lassen; verlassen; weggehen, abfahren
(to) **let**	**let**	**let**	(zu)lassen, erlauben
(to) **lie** [aɪ]	**lay** [eɪ]	**lain** [eɪ]	liegen
(to) **light**	**lit**	**lit**	anzünden
(to) **lose** [uː]	**lost** [ɒ]	**lost** [ɒ]	verlieren
(to) **make**	**made**	**made**	machen
(to) **mean** [iː]	**meant** [e]	**meant** [e]	bedeuten; meinen, sagen wollen
(to) **meet**	**met**	**met**	(sich) treffen
(to) **overtake**	**overtook**	**overtaken**	überholen
(to) **pay**	**paid**	**paid**	bezahlen
(to) **put**	**put**	**put**	legen, stellen, *(wohin)* tun
(to) **read** [iː]	**read** [e]	**read** [e]	lesen
(to) **retell**	**retold**	**retold**	nacherzählen
(to) **ride**	**rode**	**ridden**	reiten; *(Rad)* fahren
(to) **ring**	**rang**	**rung**	klingeln, läuten; anrufen
(to) **run**	**ran**	**run**	laufen; verkehren; (durch)führen
(to) **say** [eɪ]	**said** [e]	**said** [e]	sagen
(to) **see**	**saw**	**seen**	sehen; besuchen
(to) **sell**	**sold**	**sold**	verkaufen
(to) **send**	**sent**	**sent**	schicken, senden
(to) **shake**	**shook**	**shaken**	zittern; schütteln

Infinitive	Simple past	Past participle	
(to) **show** [əʊ]	**showed** [əʊ]	**shown** [əʊ]	zeigen
(to) **sing**	**sang**	**sung**	singen
(to) **sink**	**sank**	**sunk**	sinken; versenken
(to) **sit**	**sat**	**sat**	sitzen; sich setzen
(to) **sleep**	**slept**	**slept**	schlafen
(to) **speak**	**spoke**	**spoken**	sprechen
(to) **spend**	**spent**	**spent**	*(Zeit)* verbringen; *(Geld)* ausgeben
(to) **stand**	**stood**	**stood**	stehen; sich (hin)stellen
(to) **steal**	**stole**	**stolen**	stehlen
(to) **stick**	**stuck**	**stuck**	kleben
(to) **sting**	**stung**	**stung**	stechen
(to) **swim**	**swam**	**swum**	schwimmen
(to) **take**	**took**	**taken**	(mit)nehmen; (weg)bringen; dauern
(to) **teach**	**taught**	**taught**	unterrichten, lehren
(to) **tell**	**told**	**told**	erzählen, berichten; erkennen
(to) **think**	**thought**	**thought**	(nach)denken; glauben, meinen
(to) **throw**	**threw**	**thrown**	werfen
(to) **understand**	**understood**	**understood**	verstehen, begreifen
(to) **wake up**	**woke up**	**woken up**	aufwachen; (auf)wecken
(to) **wear** [eə]	**wore**	**worn**	tragen, anhaben
(to) **win**	**won** [ʌ]	**won** [ʌ]	gewinnen
(to) **write**	**wrote**	**written**	schreiben

Bildquellen

AA Photolibrary, Basingstoke (S. 26 unten; S. 75 unten rechts); Action Press, Hamburg (S. 29); Action Sport, Hamburg (S. 22); AKG, Berlin (S. 110/111/112 Hintergrund); AP, Frankfurt (S. 55); Anna Baker, York (S. 7 Mitte); Barnaby's Picture Library, London (S. 38 oben rechts; S. 41 Bild 5; S. 44 oben, S. 54); Bavaria Bildagentur, Gauting (S. 48 Bild 1, 2; S. 52 oben rechts; S. 103 oben rechts; S. 105 oben); John Birdsall, Nottingham (S. 53 unten; S. 62; S. 63; S. 72); Bosch Pressebild, München (S. 35 oben links); Viking ship by H. Oakes-Jones (20th C) Private Collection/Bridgeman Art Library, London/New York (S. 111 Mitte); The British Museum, London (S. 106 oben rechts); Brian Brown Photography, Dover (S. 74; S. 76; S. 89); J. Allan Cash Photolibrary, London (S. 26 Mitte; S. 61 Hintergrund; S. 101 oben rechts); Commission for Racial Equality, London (S. 64 oben); Crown Copyright, Historic Royal Palaces (S. 49 Bild 4; S. 106 Mitte links); Cartoons: Text © 1994 Terry Deary, Illustrations © 1994 Martin Brown, first published by Scholastic Ltd., London (S. 77; S. 110 oben, unten); David Dore, Guildford (S. 94); East Sussex Press, Crowborough (S. 48/49); The Edinburgh Photographic Library, Edinburgh (S. 38 links; S. 104/105); English Heritage, London (S. 73 Bild 5, Bild 6; S. 85; S. 110 Mitte; S. 112 oben links, Mitte rechts); e.t. archive, London (S. 112 unten links); Gareth Evans, Berlin (S. 115); Angelika Fischer, Berlin (S. 8/9; S. 17; S. 21; S. 34/35; S. 88; S. 90); Michael Ann Mullen/ Format Photographers, London (S. 100 rechts); Fotex, Hamburg (S. 65, Mitte, rechts); John Fryer, Manchester (S. 98, 99); HarperCollins Publishers, London (S. 70; S. 71); Tim Hetherington, London (S. 52 unten links); IFA-Bilderteam, Frankfurt (S. 38 oben); Image Bank, Berlin (S. 35 oben rechts, unten rechts; S. 41 Bild 2, 6); Peter Arkell/ Impact Photos, London (S. 52 unten rechts); Geray Sweeney/Impact Photos (S. 100 links); Ute Klaphake, London (S. 9 oben rechts); London Aquarium, London (S. 106 unten links; S. 107 unten); London Dungeon, London (S. 49 Bild 5); London Regional Transport, London (S. 8 unten links; S. 50); Mike Macfarlane, Stanford in the Vale (S. 36 Mitte); Madame Tussaud's, London (S. 51 unten); Mauritius-Halin, Mittenwald (S. 109 oben); MOMI, London (S. 48 Bild 3; S. 51 oben); Museum of London, London (S. 73 Bild 7; S. 75 Mitte rechts); Museum of London Archaeology Service © MoL, London (S. 73 Hintergrund, Bild 1); Museum of Welsh Life, St. Fagan's, Cardiff (S. 101 oben links); By Courtesy of the National Portrait Gallery, London (S. 111 unten links); The Natural History Museum, London (S. 106 Mitte); PPW-Fotoagentur Max Kohr, Berlin (S. 109 unten); Henrik Pohl, Berlin (S. 104/105 Shortbread); Private Eye, London (S. 80 oben); Punch Ltd, London (S. 93); Redferns, London (S. 65 links; S. 102); Science & Society Picture Library, London (S. 41 Bild 4; S. 44 unten; S. 45; S. 129 oben); Alasdair Smith, Aberdeen (S. 6 oben); Tim Smith, Bradford Festival (S. 61 links, Mitte, rechts; S. 64 unten); Sony, Köln-Ossendorf (S. 35 unten links); The Spectator, London (S. 81); Sportsphoto Agency, Scarborough (S. 103 Mitte); Bridgeman/Bildarchiv Steffens, Mainz (S. 73 Bild 4); Claus Hansmann/Bildarchiv Steffens (S. 73 Bild 2); Pieter Jos von Limbergen/Bildarchiv Steffens (S. 80 unten); Helmuth Loose/Bildarchiv Steffens (S. 73 Bild 3); Still Moving Picture Company, Edinburgh (S. 38 unten rechts; S. 41 Bild 3; S. 103 unten; S. 104 oben; S. 105 unten rechts); Anita Corbin/The Sunday Times, London (S. 37); Clay Perry/The Sunday Times (S. 36 unten; S. 41 Bild 1); Techniquest, Cardiff (S. 30 oben rechts); The Tower of London Virtual Tour (S. 106 unten rechts; S. 107 oben); Ullstein Bilderdienst, Berlin (S. 129 unten); Wales Tourist Board, Cardiff (S. 27; S. 30 oben links, unten links, unten rechts); Welsh Language Board, Cardiff (S. 101 unten); White Cliffs Experience, Dover (S. 79); York Archaeological Trust, York (S. 112 unten rechts)

Umschlag: Mauritius, Berlin (Tower Bridge); Bavaria, Gauting (Bus)

Text- und Liedquellen

S. 21: *You've got a friend* by Carole King. © 1971 by Colgmens–EMI Music Inc. USA. D/A/CH/Osteuropäische Länder: EMI Music Publishing Germany GmbH, Hamburg; *I miss you* by Björk Gudmundsdottir and Howard Simon Bernstein. © by Sony Music Entertainment Ltd. Sony/ ATV Music Publishing (Germany GmbH), Frankfurt; S. 29: *We are the champions* by Freddie Mercury © by Queen Music Ltd. D/A/CH/Osteuropäische Länder: EMI Music Publishing Germany GmbH, Hamburg; S. 44/45: *Dr Joe's Antiseptic* based on 'Two Great Discoveries' from *Storyline Scotland* by Bernard MacLaverty, © Oliver & Boyd, Edinburgh 1985; S. 54: *Maybe it's because I'm a Londoner* by Hubert Gregg © 1947 by Francis, Day & Hunter Ltd. London. Für D/A/CH/osteuropäische Länder: EMI Music Publishing GmbH; S. 55: *The Prince's school friend* from *Newsweek*, 15 December 1997 © 1997 Newsweek, Inc. All rights reserved. Reprinted by permission; S. 71: adapted from: *Anita and Me* by Meera Syal. © 1996 Meera Syal. Reproduced by permission of the author c/o Rogers, Coleridge & White Ltd., 20 Powis Mews, London W11 1JN; S. 77: *Girls had it harder* & *Roman Maths* adapted from: *The Rotten Romans* by Terry Deary/Martin Brown, Scholastic Children's Books, London; S. 89: *We don't need another hero* by Graham Lyle and Terry Britten.© by Myaxe Music Ltd./Good Single Ltd. D/CH/GUS/Osteuropäische Länder: Neue Welt Musikverlag. München/Musikverlag Rondor GmbH, Hamburg; S. 95: *Across the Roman Wall* by Theresa Bredlin, © A&C Black, Huntingdon, Cambridgeshire; S. 108: *Out of the mouths of babes* by Kathryn Clarke, © The Telegraph plc, London; S. 109: *Guns in the ghetto* © EMI Virgin Music Inc. Für D/A/CH/Osteuropäische Länder: EMI Virgin Music Publishing Germany GmbH, Hamburg.